LAW AND RELIGION IN A SECULAR AGE

LAW AND RELIGION

IN A SECULAR AGE

Rafael Domingo

The Catholic University of America Press
Washington, D.C.

Copyright © 2023

The Catholic University of America Press

All rights reserved

The paper used in this publication meets the minimum requirements of American National Standards for Information Science—Permanence of Paper for Printed Library Materials, ANSI Z39.48-1992.

∞

Library of Congress Cataloging-in-Publication Data

Names: Domingo, Rafael, 1963– author.
Title: Law and religion in a secular age / Rafael Domingo.
Description: Washington : The Catholic University of America Press, 2023. | Includes bibliographical references and index.
Identifiers: LCCN 2023042602 (print) | LCCN 2023042603 (ebook) | ISBN 9780813237299 (cloth) | ISBN 9780813237305 (ebook)
Subjects: LCSH: Religion and law. | Religion and law—Philosophy. | Canon law. | Religion and state. | Christianity and law. | Christian lawyers. | Ecclesiastical law. | International law. | Natural law.
Classification: LCC K3280 . D73 2023 (print) | LCC K3280 (ebook) | DDC 344/.096—dc23/eng/20231002
LC record available at https://lccn.loc.gov/2023042602
LC ebook record available at https://lccn.loc.gov/2023042603

*To my sisters Mariajosé, Conchita, and Marta,
a source of love, inspiration, and joy*

CONTENTS

Preface and Acknowledgments
— ix —

Introduction
— xi —

PART I
A MULTIDIMENSIONAL PERSPECTIVE ON LAW

1. Why Does Spirituality Matter for Law?
— 3 —

2. Body, Soul, and Spirit of the Law
— 34 —

3. Recovering God for Secular Legal Systems
— 56 —

4. Why Does Religion Require Special Legal Protection?
— 73 —

5. The Right to Religious Freedom: Extension or Erosion?
— 96 —

6. Law and Morality: One Hundred Years of Solitude
— 116 —

7. The Individual in International Law
— 138 —

8. Toward a Global Canon Law Centered on the Human Person
— 158 —

PART II
A BIOGRAPHICAL PERSPECTIVE ON LAW

9. Alberico Gentili and the Secularization of the Law of Nations
— 177 —

10. Robert Schuman and the Process of European Integration
— 193 —

11. Óscar Romero, a Martyr for Social Justice
— 211 —

12. John Paul II's Contribution to Law
— 228 —

13. Álvaro d'Ors as a Christian Jurist and Legal Scholar
— 248 —

14. John Witte, Jr., on Christianity and Law
— 264 —

Conclusion
— 285 —

Bibliography
— 291 —

Index
— 319 —

PREFACE AND ACKNOWLEDGMENTS

This book distills a portion of my scholarship during my recent years at the Emory Law and Religion Center and the University of Navarra Institute of Culture and Society. The volume seeks to restore the connection between spirituality and justice, religion and law, theology and jurisprudence, and natural law and positive law by building a new bridge suitable for pluralistic societies in the secular age. It aims to be a valuable antidote against the dominant legal positivism that has cornered public morality, the defiant secularism that has marginalized religion, and any other legal doctrine that diminishes the spiritual dimension of law and justice.

I remind readers of the vital role of religion in shaping the conceptual framework of Western legal systems, underscore the spirit of Christianity that inspired legal institutions, principles, and values, and recall the contributions of specific Christian jurists as central figures for the development of justice in society. I argue that the era of globalization of new technologies either must become deeply spiritual and solidary, or it will become immensely destructive.

Most of the essays published in this volume first appeared in top-ranked law journals or in book series by Cambridge University Press, Oxford University Press, Routledge, and University of Navarra Press. The reader can find the original publication reference in the opening footnote of each chapter. I thank these prestigious publishers for permission to use previously published material.

The volume owes much to my mentor, colleague, and friend John Witte, Jr., the Robert W. Woodruff Professor of Law, McDonald Distinguished Professor of Religion, and faculty director of the Emory Law and Religion Center.[1] He has permanently stimulated my critical thought and research interest. I have benefited from extensive and profound conversations with

---

1 See chapter 14 in this volume.

my friend Gonzalo Rodríguez-Fraile Díaz and with my center colleagues Abdullahi Ahmed An-Naim, Michael Broyle, Timothy P. Jackson, Michael J. Perry, and Johan D. van der Vyver. I thank Giovanni Minnucci, especially, for coauthoring chapter 9 on secularizing the law of nations and giving permission to use it here.

I am deeply grateful to my friend and colleague Gary S. Hauk, senior editor of the Center for the Study of Law and Religion, for editing this volume. With brilliant mastery, he has known how to cover the linguistic limitations of someone who writes in a nonnative language. My warm thanks to my friend and photographer Jerry Drisaldi for allowing the use of one of his beautiful photographs to cover the volume. The photo captures the idea that any organized and autonomous structure (such as a legal system) can benefit from the light from the outside (in our case, the light of religion). Autonomy does not mean independence and does not imply rejecting the existence of other relevant dimensions of reality.

I am also grateful to the Funciva Foundation (Madrid) for the generous support to develop this project and to John B. Martino, executive editor of the Catholic University of America Press, for his interest in publishing this book and his close attention during its preparation and production.

I dedicate this volume to my three sisters, Mariajosé, Conchita, and Marta. They have always been a source of inspiration and gratitude for me and an expression of abundant generosity and contagious joy.

Atlanta, March 19, 2023

INTRODUCTION

Secularization is a process of differentiating political from religious institutions in mature societies, and it is inspired by, among others things, the evangelical teaching "Render to Caesar the things that are Caesar's, and to God, the things that are God's" (Matt 22:21). The church-state structural dualism embodied in secularization is deeply beneficial for both religion and politics, since it protects religious communities from political domination and guards political communities against religious control. In many countries, however, secularization has been historically related to a progressive decline in the practice of religion and its increasing privatization. That connection, however, is not a necessary one.[1] For instance, the birth and development of the United States as a young nation were accompanied by a religious revival labeled the Great Awakening.[2]

Different from secularization is *secularism*, the ideological and exclusionary doctrine that promotes a process of secularization based on the marginalization or even exclusion of religion, religious institutions, and religious considerations from the public sphere. Secularism has challenged the value and validity of religion in modern liberal societies and triggered a new international debate about the place of individual and collective religious rights and liberties, as well as the limits of secular law in governing fundamental matters of conscience, belief, education, and charity.

This volume contributes to this debate by offering universally valid arguments in favor of the value of religion, spirituality, and natural law in secular societies and illustrating the fruitful interactions and lasting synergies between

---

1   See José Casanova, "The Secular, Secularizations, Secularism," in *Rethinking Secularism*, ed. Craig Calhoun, Mark Juergensmeyer, and Jonathan Van Antwerpen (Oxford: Oxford University Press, 2011), 54–74, esp. at 56.

2   See John Witte, Jr., Joel A. Nichols, and Richard W. Garnett, *Religion and the American Constitutional Experiment*, 5th ed. (Oxford: Oxford University Press, 2022), 35–58.

Christianity and law. *Law and Religion in a Secular Age* extends and deepens the argument I made in an earlier book, *God and the Secular Legal System*, published in 2016 through Cambridge University Press. That book was a ringing defense of the theistic conception of secular legal systems and an uncompromising attack on agnostic and atheist conceptions. This volume further shows that religion is fundamental to the rights that secularism purports to defend but cannot fully justify.

One of the crucial questions in the international debate about religious rights and liberties is whether long-established approaches to religious freedom can still be privileged in secular democratic societies. Based on claims of neutrality, objectivity, and equal liberty, some scholars claim that religious freedom should be recast as freedom of conscience or included within the framework of a general *right of ethical independence*.[3] I argue that considering religion only as a phenomenon of immanence and suggesting the foreclosure of the legal protection of transcendence constitutes an unjustified reductionism and a form of imposition of a secular religion, an *irreligious religion*.

A second key question in the debate concerns the distinction between spirituality and religion, which some secularists have used to corner the institutional dimension of religion and promote the idea of an ambiguous spirituality that does not require any legal protection. I argue instead that this relevant distinction between spirituality and religion at no time undermines the critical value of religion and cannot reduce religion to a mere organized structure or transform spirituality into amorphous spiritualism. Moreover, religions very often have shaped different spiritual traditions because spirituality, to some degree, requires embodiment in culture, history, faith, and communities, just as communication needs to be embedded in a language system.

A third key question in the debate is the role of natural law in the era of secularization. Many positivist scholars have rejected natural law out of hand. They assert, among other things, that the concept of natural law creates more problems than it solves. It is controversial in character because no fundamental human nature is present across all societies and cultures, while human reason itself is too corrupt to be trusted. In contrast, I argue that God, creation, nature, reason, and morality are inseparably connected. The created universe testifies to God's laws and communicates moral knowledge. The natural and the supernatural are not merely juxtaposed dimensions but

---

3 See chapter 5 in this volume.

two interconnected dimensions of a multidimensional reality that includes legal, political, moral, and spiritual dimensions. Each dimension of reality is autonomous in its own sphere of application and integrated into a deeper dimension—the legal in the political, the political in the moral, and the moral in the spiritual.

This volume consists of two parts totaling fourteen chapters. All of them, in one way or another, address these three questions I've raised about the relationship between law, politics, morality, religion, and spirituality. In the first part (chapters 1 through 8), I argue for a multidimensional view of reality that includes legal, political, moral, and spiritual dimensions of human nature and society. Each of these dimensions of life needs to recognize the existence, influence, and function of the others, which act as a filter or check on the excesses of each other. This multidimensionality of reality clarifies why no legal theory can fully account for law from the legal dimension alone, just as no moral theory makes perfect sense of morality from the moral dimension—and, for that matter, why nothing in physics can fully interpret the physical dimension of reality. The premises of a political community cannot be fully explained by the political dimension alone because the fundamental conditions and qualities of justice, freedom, and dignity touch all the dimensions of reality in which the human person acts, including the moral and the spiritual, not just the political.

Building on this multidimensional theory of reality, chapter 1 explores the core differences and the essential interconnections between law and spirituality and some of the legal implications of these connections. After arguing that spirituality is conceptually autonomous from religion and morality, I focus on the spiritual triad of *love, communion, and gift* as profoundly interconnected with the legal triad of *justice, agreement, and right*, and I clarify why individual and collective intentions and cultural values are the main channels of interaction between law and spirituality. I further explain how spiritualizing legal systems (among other methods) can promote greater justice, more substantial agreements, and more robust protections of rights. Properly pursued, the spiritualization of law promotes the *dematerialization* of the legal system, encourages the limitation of domination, inspires the reduction of coercion, stimulates communion and consensus in society, and increases respect for the law and legal systems. Spiritualization demands a recognition of the higher dimension of the law and, therefore, helps societies rethink, reorient, renew, reform, and reimagine law and legal systems.

Spiritualization of law is possible because law has a (sometimes latent) spiritual dimension. There is a *spirit of law*, as the tradition has long taught, just as there is a *body* of law and a *heart* or *soul* of the law. To demonstrate this, I analyze in chapter 2 the classic body-soul-spirit metaphor in the legal realm. Since legal systems are a product of human creation, they sometimes reflect the body-soul-spirit image of the human being. Based on this metaphor, I argue for respect for the law as a whole; the use of the spirit of foreign law by national legal systems; the living character of the constitutional body; the emergence of a global law founded on solidarity and not on the self-interest of nation-states; the intrinsic link between law and love; and the reasonable interaction between human law and suprarational (or divine) law.

While the first two chapters speak of law from the spiritual dimension, the third and fourth chapters speak of God and religion from the perspective of the legal dimension. Chapter 3 brings a legal perspective to the relationship between God and the secular legal systems of Western liberal democracies. It provides a normative argument for the compatibility of God and secular legal reasoning. In our age, when believing in God is no longer socially self-evident, and the right to religious freedom protects all kinds of theistic and nontheistic religious beliefs, creeds, and first philosophies, it seems contrary to religious neutrality for secular legal systems to single out God for removal.

This chapter also argues that although God and religion are inextricably intertwined, they affect the legal system differently because they are ontologically different. As many legal systems attempt to do, God cannot be reduced to a mere component of theistic religion. A proper understanding of secularization might call for keeping God outside the legal system, but not for driving God out of the public sphere of democratic societies. Secular legal systems are not atheist legal systems. Secular legal systems are legal systems without religion but not without God. A healthy secularization implies some degree of minimal recognition of God as a metalegal concept, and the specific degree of recognition of God appropriate for any given political community depends on its cultural and communitarian identity. It should be subject to the rules of democratic procedures and majorities.

Religion understood from a legal perspective is the topic of chapter 4. In it, I argue that religious questions should be settled outside the secular legal system—within the interior conscience of each human being and the internal religious laws of each religious community. Without such deference to religion, the secular legal system would not be genuinely secular. In a secular legal system devoted to protecting *justice, agreement, and rights,* religion demands special protection both as a private right and as a public good and social value, as it constitutes an extrinsic constitutional and cultural limit on the law. For a secular legal system, rational by character, protecting religion ultimately means protecting human beings' individual and collective pursuit of the suprarational, beyond the legal system. That is the challenge.

Protecting suprarationality has three significant legal consequences: (a) suprarational acts in the strictest sense should never be required as legal acts; (b) legal systems should not use suprarational arguments in legal discourse; and (c) secular legal systems should not regulate suprarationality or the essentials of the religious community. The protection of religion demands the dualistic structure that distinguishes the political community from the religious community and the legal treatment of religion as a right: the *right to religion*.

Chapter 5, on religious freedom, elaborates on this last point. Here I argue for religious freedom as a first-class right, and I criticize the views of some distinguished scholars who have rejected traditional legal norms that provided special protection for religion, focusing primarily on Ronald Dworkin's and Brian Leiter's views and arguments, which have been highly influential in American legal and political thought. I conclude that Dworkin's approach to religion belittles the idea of God and that conviction about the existence of God and the holding of profound ethical and moral convictions are not so independent, as Dworkin argues. Leiter's approach, on the other hand, belittles the idea of religion, which cannot be reduced to a matter of commands and consolation. Religion is more than a matter of conscience and a personal decision about ultimate concerns and questions. Religion cannot be reduced to moral conscience, let alone ethical independence on foundational issues. An increasingly globalized and pluralistic society demands a more comprehensive approach that fully protects all religions and creeds.

Chapter 6 is descriptive, and it was written for teaching purposes. It provides a sweeping overview of the long-running debate on the relationship between law and morality, starting with the 1934 publication of Hans Kelsen's *Pure Theory of Law* and continuing to present thinkers like Robert Alexy and John Finnis. This chapter analyzes the noteworthy arguments of English positivists H. L. A. Hart and Joseph Raz, Ronald Dworkin's harsh critique of positivism, critical contributions to the debate by John Rawls and Jürgen Habermas, and advances in natural law theory put forward by Jacques Maritain, Michel Villey, John Finnis, and Javier Hervada.

I further argue that the debate between law and morality demands restoring dialogue between legal theorists and theologians, given their overlap. Concepts like law, justice, marriage, sacrament, oath, obedience, authority, power, tradition, redemption, punishment, intercession, mercy, and confession have a legal and theological dimension owing to the shared sources used for elaborating them. Sometimes, it is even difficult to determine historically whether a concept originated in the legal sphere or the theological one.

Chapters 7 and 8 focus on the centrality of human persons in international law and canon law, which are universal and not national in scope. Chapter 7 deals with the individual in international law from the perspective of sacred natural law, combining reason and revelation in the elaboration and justification of legal arguments. God, creation, nature, reason, and morality are inseparably connected. The created universe testifies to God's laws and communicates moral knowledge. Natural law is known through inclination, intuition, reason, spiritual knowledge, and religious sources. The natural and the transcendent are not merely juxtaposed dimensions but two interconnected dimensions of a unique multidimensional reality that includes legal, political, moral, and spiritual dimensions.

Sacred natural law is oriented to the individual because every person has been created in the image of God. Consequently, sacred natural law supports the priority of the person in the international legal realm. As sacred natural law theories are not mandatory but optional, respect individual moral conscience, and acknowledge the obligatory force of positive law, they are valid for developing a universal (not compulsory) international metalegal framework that illuminates positive law. I call this framework *transcendent global law*. The development of a transcendent global law should use the best contributions and arguments of the sacred natural law traditions and overcome some futile discussions about the *nature* of natural law. Transcendent global law might transform an often self-interest-oriented international community of nation-states into a value-oriented global human community of image-of-God bearers. In this process, not only jurists but also philosophers and, especially, theologians condemned to silence have something to say.

Chapter 8 analyzes the similarities between public international law and Catholic canon law in the legal treatment of the human person. Catholic canon law and public international law are deeply interconnected through a common legal tradition, and the legal technique employed by both systems has often been close. As canon law and public international law are nonstate, that is, nonterritorial and, therefore, global systems, they had to be precise and careful when setting their jurisdictional limits and the scope of their rules. I argue that this fact has produced an overly technical and reductionist legal concept of personhood that has prevented the proper development of canon law and international law. Just as international law today has corrected course and is gradually becoming a global law increasingly focused on the human person and not only on nation-states, so, too, Catholic canon law, to fulfill its evangelizing purpose, should focus less on the baptized Christian and instead prioritize the centrality of every human person, created in the image of God and called to regeneration in the baptismal waters.

The second part of this volume (chapters 9 through 14) focuses on some influential Christians who have practically influenced Western law and legal theory along the healthy multidimensional lines I have argued for in part 1. If we accept that law is a partial expression of the culture of a particular society and that legal traditions reflect prevailing communal notions about ethical values that should be converted into law, it is difficult to overrate the significance of specific Christian individuals for the development of Western legal culture. Behind many legal and social achievements, such as the integration of Europe after World War II and the fall of communism after the Cold War, one finds Christian values and ideals as they were interpreted at a particular time. And behind those ideals, one often finds particular Christian figures who, perhaps unintentionally, left an indelible mark on our legal culture.[4] The biographical approach has great potential in legal science because it shows the complexity, ambiguity, and even the accidental nature of forms and reforms of secular legal systems. Lying behind rules and legal documents are facts and, beyond them, people.

I begin the gallery of some selected Christian jurists with Alberico Gentili in chapter 9, written in collaboration with my colleague Giovanni Minnucci. A prominent early modern Italian Protestant legal theorist and practicing lawyer, Alberico Gentili (1552–1608) designed a solid framework for the law of nations based on three pillars: the Greco-Roman idea of natural law, the Justinian compilation of Roman law, and the then-novel Bodinian notion of sovereignty. Gentili freed the law of nations from excessive scholastic influences and theological importations, avoiding metaphysical developments

---

4   See chapter 14, "The Biographical Perspective: The Idea of the Christian Jurist," in this volume.

and overly subtle dialectics. Providing some new arguments, he removed religion as a valid reason for conflict and war, advocated for the legitimacy of non-Christian regimes, especially the Ottomans, and tried to fix the tenuous lines of separation between jurisprudence and theology and between the internal forum and external forum of canon law. His world-famous saying, "Keep silence, theologians, in matters which concern others!" (*silete theologi in munere alieno*) commands the theologian not to be involved in other people's business and was claimed centuries later by legal scholars to argue in favor of legal secularism, beyond the limits Gentili himself intended.

The following chapters examine the lives of three Christian twentieth-century giants and their lives and contributions to law and justice. Chapter 10 explores the indispensable role played by Robert Schuman (1886–1963) in the processes of European integration and his potential contribution to the idea of global law. Schuman believed in an organized and united Europe based on the leadership of Germany and France, acting as two powerful lungs under equal rights with other nations. The heart of Europe should be Christian in character, however, because Christianity is, according to Schuman, the trustworthy inspirational source for forgiveness and love. He embodied and anticipated the values Europe should develop politically: diversity, solidarity, forgiveness, kindness, and generosity. In this sense, Robert Schuman was the first citizen and founding father of the European Union. In all of his political ideas and actions, he was guided and determined by his religious attitude. Out of his Christian outlook, he understood politics as a service to humanity, oriented to the common good and in harmony among individuals and peoples. Since both the European and global communities are incomplete and complementary, some analogies based on Schuman's approach to Europe can be established in developing a theory of global law.

Chapter 11 introduces the central figure of the Salvadoran archbishop Óscar Romero (1917–1980), a martyr for social justice canonized by Pope Francis on October 14, 2018. Romero advocated for the nonviolent defense of justice inspired by love, forgiveness, and social participation following the gospel and the social teachings of the Roman Catholic Church. He defended human rights and social justice in El Salvador, a country wounded by political, military, and paramilitary crime. He understood that the denunciation of brutal governmental atrocities was not a political issue but a requirement to establish the kingdom of God on earth. The preferential option for the poor was at the heart of his pastoral mission and action. As repression became firmly fixed in El Salvador, Romero was more resolute in denouncing the government's hostile attitude and demanding the urgent need for nonviolent social change. His moral judgment on the Salvadoran situation was clear and forceful: the desirable church-state cooperation in developing the common good in society must never collaborate with crime and repression. Only the truth liberates.

Chapter 12 examines John Paul II's contribution to the law as a statesman, world leader, and universal pastor of the Roman Catholic Church. His approach to the law was shaped by the stark realities of having suffered firsthand the injustice of two totalitarian regimes and the cruelties of the Second World War. An ardent defender of human rights, especially the rights to life and religious liberty, John Paul II (1920–2005) saw the concepts of human dignity and human solidarity as the two great levers for advancing the development of legal systems. This chapter also explores John Paul II's invaluable role in updating and reforming the canon law of the Catholic Church. He had a distinct role in promulgating the Code of Canon Law of 1983, the Code of Canons of the Eastern Churches of 1990, and the apostolic constitution *Pastor Bonus* of 1988 (in force until June 2022) on reforming the Roman Curia. John Paul II deserves the title of a Christian jurist for these and other significant legal contributions.

In the last two chapters, I explore the main contributions of two great Christian scholars who have shaped my academic life: my Spanish mentor, Álvaro d'Ors (1915–2004), with whom I worked for twenty years at the University of Navarra, and my American mentor, John Witte, Jr., with whom I have been working at Emory University for the past ten years.

Chapter 13 analyzes Álvaro d'Ors as a Christian jurist, a great Spanish polymath of the twentieth century, and a central figure in the development of the University of Navarra in northern Spain. Best known for his work on Roman law, he made significant contributions to political theology, political philosophy, legal theory, and legal history. Álvaro d'Ors was a scholar of antiquity and an original legal and political thinker devoted to university life. He especially advocated for: (a) recovering the Roman distinction between moral authority (*auctoritas*) and constituted power (*potestas*); (b) the primacy of moral legitimacy over legality; and (c) building an international community of peoples based on individual and social preferences rather than on sovereign territorial states. Most of his writings remain unknown in the English-speaking world.

The last chapter, 14, analyzes the contribution of John Witte, Jr., to the study of the relationship between Christianity and law as an autonomous branch within the broad field that studies the relationship between law and religion. First, I present Witte as a Christian jurist educated in Reformed Protestantism and influenced by Abraham Kuyper and Harold J. Berman, among others. Second, I describe and evaluate the interdisciplinary, interdenominational, and international project on Christianity and law headed by Witte, to which more than five hundred scholars (jurists, theologians, philosophers, historians, and sociologists) are contributing. Many of the essays published in this volume result from my collaboration with Witte on this international project.

I end the volume by summarizing some of the conclusions I have reached. Among these are the profound connectivity between law and spirituality, the need to restore the dialogue between theology and jurisprudence, the foundational significance of the idea of God, the deep legal value of the image-of-God metaphor, the value of suprarationality as the ultimate justification for legally protecting religion, the need to consider the right to religious freedom as a first-class right, the centrality of the person in all legal systems (including canon law), and the relevance of the role of Christian jurists in our pluralistic society for the development of legal systems.

PART I

A Multidimensional Perspective on Law

CHAPTER 1

WHY DOES SPIRITUALITY MATTER FOR LAW?

Introduction: Spirituality, Religion, and Morality

IN RECENT YEARS, SCHOLARS and scientists in different disciplines (sociology, medicine, business, and psychology, among others) have paid special attention to spirituality as a potential interconnecting factor of human and social development. They have argued that spirituality matters in informing decisions, guiding human activities, and promoting social cohesion and individual health.[1] However, academic focus on spirituality is rare in the

---

*   The original version of this essay appears in Rafael Domingo, "Why Spirituality Matters for Law: An Explanation," *Oxford Journal of Law and Religion* 8, no. 2 (2019): 326–34.

1   See, for instance, Luk Bouckaert and Laszlo Zsolnai, eds., *The Palgrave Handbook of Spirituality and Business* (London: Palgrave Macmillan, 2011); Mark Cobb, Christina M. Puchalski, and Bruce Rumbold, *Oxford Textbook of Spirituality in Healthcare* (Oxford: Oxford University Press, 2012); Lisa J. Miller, ed., *The Oxford Handbook of Psychology and Spirituality* (Oxford: Oxford University Press, 2012); Michael J. Balboni and Tracy A. Balboni, *Hostility to Hospitality: Spirituality and Professional Socialization within Medicine* (Oxford: Oxford University Press, 2018); Laszlo Zsolnai and Bernardette Flanagan, *The Routledge International Handbook of Spirituality in Society and the Professions* (London: Routledge, 2019); Marta Domingo-Osle and Rafael Domingo, "Nursing and Spirituality: A Discussion Paper on Intertwining Metaparadigms," *Journal of Nursing*

study of law and legal science.² This explanatory and normative essay intends to fill this gap by exploring the spiritual aspect of the law, the connection between law and spirituality, and some potential implications of this connection in legal systems and the evolution of law.

In this chapter, I refer to law only as human law—that is, as a social, rational, and coercive order that regulates and institutionalizes human interactions in accordance with justice. Human law is broader than mere positive law since human law also includes customary law, tradition, and moral principles used to decide hard cases. As a rational human creation, however, human law does not include the centuries-old compelling idea of divine or eternal law.³ Since divine law and its connection with human law presuppose the spiritualization of the law, I prefer not to use the expression divine law in this article. The deep connection between divine law and human law, spiritual in nature, should be methodologically preceded by an explanation of the connection between human law and spirituality, and that is exactly the purpose of this paper.⁴

I understand spirituality as an ontological and transcendent order that links and unites God, the divine, with humanity and the universe under love. My approach to spirituality is theistic, but it does not reject other attempts to develop spirituality without God.⁵ In some sense, my approach to spirituality is close to Raimon Panikkar's intuition of the *cosmotheandric experience*,⁶ which

---

Management 28, no. 6 (2020): 1268–74; and Rafael Domingo and Gonzalo Rodriguez-Fraile, *Spiritualizing Humanity* (Miami: self-published, 2021).

2   See Robert F. Blomquist, "Law and Spirituality: Some First Thoughts of an Emerging Relation," *UMKC Law Review* 71 (2003): 583–622; Harry J. Gensler, *Ethics and Religion* (Cambridge: Cambridge University Press, 2016), 112–32 (on natural law and spirituality); and Dániel Deák, "Spirituality and Law," in Zsolnai and Flanagan, *The Routledge International Handbook of Spirituality in Society and the Professions*, 280–88.

3   On this idea, see Rémi Brague, *The Law of God: The Philosophical History of an Idea*, trans. Lydia G. Cochrane (Chicago: University of Chicago Press, 2007). See also Rafael Domingo, *God and the Secular Legal System* (Cambridge: Cambridge University Press, 2016).

4   In some sense, divine law is spiritual law, that is, an unchangeable law of love that deeply governs the whole of reality.

5   See, for instance, Sam Harris, *Waking Up: A Guide to Spirituality without Religion* (New York: Simon and Schuster, 2014).

6   See Raimon Panikkar, *The Cosmotheandric Experience: Emerging Religious Consciousness* (New York: Orbis Books, 1993).

offers a completely integrated vision of all reality, and to the idea of spirituality used by Pope Francis in his encyclical letter *Laudato si'*.[7]

This chapter rests on the intuition (not the premise) that reality, although differentiated, is one. Therefore, all dimensions of reality and all epistemological approaches to reality (scientific investigation, logical reason, and contemplative intuition) are linked. The unity of reality has been accepted with different nuances by many spiritual traditions, philosophers, and mystics over centuries, and it has never been denied (and sometimes has been supported) by science.[8] Some scientists themselves are trying to illuminate a unitary epistemology from different scientific disciplines, an attempt called "consilience" by E. O. Wilson.[9] For centuries, philosophers from Plotinus[10] to Wittgenstein[11] have also reflected on the interconnectivity among objects, things, and thoughts.

In Hinduism, all things are thought of as having received their being and life from true reality, that is, from the inner spiritual eternal principle Atman-Brahman: the individual primary energy or soul (Atman) is the cosmic soul or ultimate divine reality (Brahman). In Buddhism, the image of Indra's net describes and symbolizes the interconnectedness of the universe and its interdependent origination. In Taoism, the Tao, both transcendent and completely immanent, is the life source of and cosmic force upon all reality.

---

7   Francis, Encyclical Letter *Laudato si'* (May 24, 2015), 63, 73, 75, 105, 111, and 240, among others.

8   The new context that physics offers us, in a certain way, makes possible a better understanding of spirituality. For instance, superstring theory of quantum gravity holds that the four fundamental forces of nature (gravity, electromagnetism, and strong and weak nuclear forces), as well as all matter, constitute different expressions of a single essence. For an overview, see Voler Schomerus, *A Primer on String Theory* (Cambridge: Cambridge University Press, 2017).

9   Edward Osborne Wilson, *Consilience: The Unity of Knowledge* (New York: Vintage, 1999).

10   In the third century, Plotinus, founder of Neoplatonism, pointed out: "The One is the first existence. But the Intelligence, the Ideas, and Being are not the first." See Plotinus, "The Good or the One," §2 in *The Essential Plotinus*, trans. Elmer O'Brien (Indianapolis, Ind.: Hackett Publishing Company, 1964), 75.

11   See Ludwig Wittgenstein, *Tractatus Logicus Philosophicus*, trans. C. K. Ogden (Mineola, N.Y.: Dover Publications, 1999), 2.0121, p. 30: "Just as we cannot think of spatial objects at all apart from space, or temporal objects apart from time, so we cannot think of any object apart from the possibility of its connection with other things."

In the Abrahamic religions, God, the Absolute One, is the sole creator, giver of life, and sustainer of the universe, that is, the reality that upholds and supports all reality. The essential distinction between a transcendent God and creatures does not necessarily exclude the unity of reality. The Shema praises God as being one (*echad*),[12] implying that God is one in the heavens and the earth and therefore permeates all material existence. In the First Letter to the Corinthians,[13] the Apostle Paul explains the culmination of the creation by saying that God is "all in all." Some centuries later, the Christian Neoplatonist Pseudo-Dionysius, influenced by Plotinus, affirmed, "nothing in the world lacks its share of the One. Just as every number participates in unity—for we refer to one couple, one dozen, one-half, one-third, one-tenth—so everything, and every part of everything, participates in the One."[14] In Islam, the Andalusian medieval mystic and scholar Ibn al-Arabi and his school supported the doctrine of the unity of being (Wahdat al-Wujūd). According to Ibn al-Arabi, God and creation are ultimately one, since all that was created preexisted in God's knowledge and will return to it. God alone is the all-embracing and eternal reality.[15]

Historically, the indispensable split between law and religion in democratic societies, which constitutes by itself a clear expression of the spiritualization of the law, paradoxically led to the separation of spirituality and law, encouraging a view that spirituality belonged inalienably to the sphere of religion. While intimately connected to religion, however, spirituality is broader; it has a life of its own.[16] Furthermore, spirituality precedes religion, as morality precedes law. Spirituality is an essential aspect of religion but cannot occupy the whole space of religion. Moreover, spirituality exists outside religion (e.g., in individual openness to transcendence), and many aspects of religion lie outside the realm of spirituality (e.g., positive canon

12   See Deuteronomy 6:4.

13   1 Corinthians 15:28. See also Romans 14:8: "For if we live, we live to the Lord, and if we die, we die to the Lord. So then, whether we live or whether we die, we are the Lord's" and 1 John 4:16: "God is love, and he who abides in love abides in God, and God abides in him." All biblical quotations are from the New American Standard Bible.

14   Pseudo-Dionysius, "The Divine Names," in Pseudo-Dionysius, *The Complete Works*, trans. Col Luibheid and Paul Rorem (Mahwah, N.J.: Paulist Press, 1987), 977C, p. 128.

15   An English translation of his book, *The Seals of Wisdom* (Fusus al-Hikam), is available at http://www.sufi.ir/books/download/english/ibn-arabi-en/fusus-al-hikam-en.pdf.

16   On this distinction, see Roger Haight, *Spiritual and Religious: Explorations for Seekers* (New York: Orbis Books, 2016), esp. 1–15.

law). Thus, spirituality can be considered an autonomous and fertile source of legal inspiration, in which not just meaning and reason but consciousness and purpose, good will and unity play an important role.

This separation between spirituality and religion at no time aims to undermine the important value of religions and divine revelation, or to reduce religion to an institution, or to promote a sort of individualistic spiritualism. Any suggested antithesis between religion and spirituality is misleading and inaccurate.[17] The very idea of the Spirit of God is both spiritual and religious at its heart, and it will play an important role in our reflections. Further, religions very often have shaped different spiritual traditions because spirituality in some degree requires embodiment in culture, history, faith, and communities, just as communication needs to be embedded in a language system.[18] Although spirituality is universal, expressions of spirituality are cultural.

Spirituality is also conceptually different from but intrinsically connected to morality. Roughly speaking, morality provides a system or code of principles, values, and rules according to which intentions, behaviors, and actions are judged to be good or bad. While morality refers to the good, spirituality refers to oneness and unity, as we will see. Goodness expresses something different from oneness, but where there is some degree of goodness, there is some degree of unity, and vice versa. Medieval philosophers explained that goodness and oneness, as transcendentals, were even interchangeable.[19] As we will see in section 7, the unity of value is a manifestation of the unity of goodness, and the unity of goodness as such is spiritual in character. This unity of goodness not only explains why the common good prevails over private good but also why a solid (spiritual) link exists between private and common goods.

Due to my background in Western Christian spirituality and the fact that the science of law has been formed mainly in the West,[20] I will refer above all

---

17 On the origin of the modern sense of spirituality, see Rady Roldan-Figueroa, "Spiritualité, Spirituality, and Espiritualidad: A Lexicographical Approach to the Conceptual History of the Modern Notion of Spirituality," *Church History and Religious Culture* 101, no. 4 (2021): 496–525.

18 Nonverbal communication (for example, body language) is also a system of language. In the same vein, see Evelyn Underhill, *Mysticism: A Study in the Nature and Development of Spiritual Consciousness* (Mineola, N.Y.: Dover Publications, 2002), x.

19 For an overview, see Wouter Goris and Jan Aertsen, "Medieval Theories of Transcendentals," in *The Stanford Encyclopedia of Philosophy*, ed. Edward N. Zalta, Winter 2016, https://plato.stanford.edu/archives/win2016/entries/transcendentals-medieval.

20 On this topic, see Harold J. Berman, *Law and Revolution I: The Formation of the Western Legal Tradition* (Cambridge, Mass.: Harvard University Press, 1983); Rafael

to the Western spiritual tradition and Western law. This does not mean any disparagement of other spiritual or legal traditions nor an expression of ethnocentrism but rather the opposite: a high respect for the variety of traditions and a strong desire that many scholars participate in the exciting project of establishing a bridge between law and spirituality from different perspectives.

Approaching Law and Spirituality: Some Similarities

Law and spirituality can be broadly understood as practical arts, speculative sciences, and traditions. Both also reflect an experience and an attitude in human persons. Spirituality and law are systems in the sense that both are constituted by a set of interdependent principles, interacting procedures, and connected ritual elements forming a specific complex whole. As systems, law and spirituality demand that all new elements from outside should be received into the system in accordance with its own language.[21]

Both law and spirituality constitute arts in the classical sense of experience-based practice (Greek *techne* or Latin *ars*).[22] As arts, both involve practical understanding and classification (rules, definitions, divisions) of universal things, not only pure accumulation of individual experiences. If the Roman jurist Juventius Celsus famously defined the law as the "art of goodness and fairness" (*ars boni et aequi*),[23] we might say, by imitation of his definition, that "spirituality is the art of oneness and love" (*ars unitatis et amoris*). But law and

---

Domingo, *Ex Roma ius* (Cizur Menor: Thomson Reuters Aranzadi, 2005); and John Witte, Jr., *The Blessings of Liberty: Human Rights and Religious Freedom in the Western Legal Tradition* (Cambridge: Cambridge University Press, 2021).

21 On the language of law and its connection with the mystical element, see Harold J. Berman, *Law and Language: Effective Symbols of Community*, ed. John Witte, Jr. (Cambridge: Cambridge University Press, 2013), 83. See also Harold J. Berman, *Faith and Order: The Reconciliation of Law and Religion* (Grand Rapids, Mich.: Eerdmans, 1993), 4–6.

22 For an overview of the very often ambiguous distinction between *episteme* and *techne* (sometimes interchangeable), see Richard Parry, "*Episteme* and *Techne*," in Zalta, *The Stanford Encyclopedia of Philosophy*, Fall 2014, https://plato.stanford.edu/archives/fall2014/entries/episteme-techne.

23 See Celsus and Ulpian, *The Digest of Justinian*, 1.1.1 pr., ed. Alan Watson, vol. 1 (Philadelphia: University of Pennsylvania Press, 1985). See Pietro Cerami, "La concezione celsina del ius," *Annali del Seminario Giuridico dell'Università di Palermo* 38 (1985): 5–249. See also Claudia Moatti, *The Birth of Critical Thinking in Republican Rome* (Cambridge: Cambridge University Press, 2015), 235–42.

spirituality are also creative intuition and speculative knowledge seeking for first principles and causes. In this broader and classical sense of science as knowledge or understanding (Greek *episteme* or Latin *scientia*), not in the narrower sense of modern empirical sciences, law and spirituality constitute ultimately a science: the science of law, traditionally called *jurisprudentia*,[24] and the science of spirituality, traditionally called, in the Western culture, pneumatology (referring to knowledge of the Holy Spirit), spiritual theology, or just spirituality.

As science, both law and spirituality have their respective sources, methods of interpretation, procedures, and specific language. Spiritual language, particularly the more experiential mystical language, is highly symbolic, often metaphorical. The reason for this is that the science of spirituality by definition cannot grasp the spirit, because the science of spirituality is mental and the spirit is metamental. The language of law, although more rational, is also open to symbols and metaphors to explain the deepest realities of the legal system.[25] As science, law and spirituality can be manipulated and corrupted. As there is evil law (e.g., slavery law, Nazi law), so there is also evil spirituality (e.g., occultism and magical arts). Behind these spurious realities lie more arrogance and domination than love and justice.

Law and spirituality embody different legal and spiritual traditions, respectively.[26] No legal or spiritual accumulated wisdom of the past—that is, no tradition—is handed over to the next generation merely on the basis of pure reason. Culture is repeatedly renewed and refreshed. Traditions are instrumental in joining spirituality and law with culture. Since all traditions contain some elements that are universal, therefore, some degree of inclusiveness and not just mere juxtaposition among traditions is possible and laudable.

Finally, we can say that law and spirituality can reflect a legal and spiritual attitude, respectively. There is a settled way of thinking or feeling about justice and spirituality that is reflected in a person's or a collective's behavior, and both

---

24   Inspired by Greek thought, Ulpian defined *jurisprudentia* as "the knowledge of things divine and human, of the just and unjust"; see Celsus and Ulpian, *Digest of Justinian*, 1.1.10.2.

25   See chapter 2 in this volume. See also John Witte, Jr., "Law, Religion, and Metaphor," in John Witte, Jr., *Faith Freedom, and Family: New Essays in Law and Religion*, ed. Norman Doe and Gary S. Hauk (Tübingen: Mohr Siebeck, 2022), 37–55. For the role of metaphor in the creation of meaning, see Paul Ricoeur, *The Rule of Metaphor: The Creation of Meaning in Language*, trans. Robert Czerny (London: Routledge, 1977).

26   On the idea of legal tradition, see H. Patrick Glenn, "A Concept of Legal Tradition," *Queen's Law Journal* 34 (2008): 427–45.

attitudes are well connected. The legal attitude provides a sense of social justice and responsibility, which leads to respect and protects the rights of others and the basic laws of a political community. The spiritual attitude leads to the liberation of the self and promotes a sense of fellowship with human beings, of harmony with the universe, and, ultimately, of union with the divine.

Holonic Dimensionality of the Legal vs. Holistic Metadimensionality of the Spiritual

The most crucial difference between the legal and the spiritual is that the legal is dimensional and holonic, while the spiritual is metadimensional and holistic. Since legal systems rule human behavior, and human behavior takes place in some region of space during some interval of time, legal systems usually have both a spatial and a temporal dimension and a sphere of validity.[27] What is valid in the United States is not necessarily valid in Europe or Australia, and what was valid in the past (e.g., slavery in the Code of Hammurabi or the Law of the Twelve Tables) is not necessarily valid today. Furthermore, since legal systems regulate human behavior in accordance to justice, there are many aspects of human behavior that are not under the legal domain (e.g., friendship, sport or culinary preferences, ultimate concerns, and religious beliefs). Finally, some rules of a legal system apply only to some kind of people (e.g., truck drivers, immigrants, pregnant women, retirees, minors, married people). In some sense, we can say that the law operates under four dimensions (temporal, spatial, material, and personal), just as in relativistic physics, in which three dimensions of space and one of time have been the traditional accepted norm: the four-dimensional space-time continuum. Just as the four dimensions do not completely explain physical reality, however, neither do the four legal dimensions completely explain legal reality.

Although autonomous, the legal dimension is also part of other superior dimensions and in this sense is holonic. The word *holon* was coined by Arthur Koestler.[28] *Holon* refers to something that is at the same time a whole and a part. In reality, the first general sense of the concept had been understood

---

27   See Hans Kelsen, *General Theory of Law and State*, trans. Andres Wedberg (Cambridge, Mass.: Harvard University Press, 1945), 42–44.

28   The word *holon* was coined by Arthur Koestler, *The Ghost in the Machine* (London: Hutchinson, 1967), 45ff. The idea has been extensively developed by Ken Wilber, *Sex, Ecology, Spirituality: The Spirit of Evolution*, 2nd ed. (Boston: Shambhala, 2000).

many centuries before, expressed in the well-known phrase "the whole is greater than the sum of its parts." But Koestler's term adds something more. Each emerging holon integrates what precedes it and, at the same time, transcends it. In the same way, a cell incorporates and transcends its component molecules, the molecules incorporate and transcend the atoms, and atoms include and transcend their particles. There is an antireductionist hierarchy of dimensions of reality in which each dimension is true in itself but subsumed in a higher one: the physical in the chemical, the chemical in the biological, the biological in the social, and so on up to the spiritual.

The legal dimension is autonomous (that is, a whole) but interdependent (that is, a part). It is autonomous because the law has its own language, rules, principles, penalties, and actors. At the same time, however, law is very dependent on other dimensions—for instance, the moral dimension—because the interpretation of law must use moral principles.[29] To be holonic implies that internal conflicts and oppositions of one dimension must be resolved in a superior dimension and ultimately in the holistic spiritual realm, which provides unity to the whole.

Unlike the legal dimension, the spiritual is metadimensional and holistic. The spiritual order overcomes and transcends the spatial and temporal sphere of validity. This is possible, even from a scientific point of view, because space is not necessarily the fundamental level of reality; therefore, not all phenomena accurately happen and fit within space.[30] Moreover, unlike what happens with legal systems, spirituality cannot be reduced to a determined number of persons or limited by the subject matter. With different nuances, degrees, and intensities, spirituality embraces all aspects of human life, and life in general. The ultimate reason for this is that God, who is Spirit[31] and the Absolute One,[32] is immeasurable and therefore irreducible to any dimension. The spiritual order is metadimensional because the Spirit of God is metadimensional. God is everywhere and cannot be confined to any point in space

---

29 See Ronald Dworkin, *Justice for Hedgehogs* (Cambridge, Mass.: Harvard University Press, 2011), 405–7.

30 Brian Greene, *The Fabric of the Cosmos: Space, Time, and the Texture of Reality*, 2nd. ed. (New York: W. W. Norton, 2011).

31 See John 4:24.

32 There is no contradiction between Absolute One and Absolute Other. As a transcendent Being, God is the Absolute Other; as an immanent Being, God is the Absolute One.

or moment in time.[33] God permeates and surfaces everything through divine power, presence, and essence. God exists "uncircumscribed in all things," says Bonaventure.[34] Moreover, all things are one with God without being themselves God. As Pseudo-Dyonisius pointed out, "The One cause of all things is not one of the many things in the world, but actually precedes oneness and multiplicity and indeed defines oneness and multiplicity."[35]

Spirituality, therefore, offers a holistic appreciation of the reality in which everyone and everything is harmoniously linked with everyone and everything else. "Each thing is in each thing," Nicholas of Cusa famously said,[36] since each thing reflects in some degree the oneness of the Spirit of God. "God is so one," Nicholas insists; God "is actually all that is possible."[37] Oneness is primary in God's knowledge and by extension in spiritual knowledge, just as otherness features in the conceptual domain, and therefore in the legal domain. The spiritual, thus, cannot be holonic because the condition of being a part of a larger reality fails. Inside the spiritual world are autonomous realities (God, human souls, angels), but the spiritual as such is not part of another reality. It is holistic rather than holonic.

The Spiritual Triad: Love, Communion, and Gift

In the Christian tradition, to deal with spirituality means to speak of the Holy Spirit, and to speak of love, communion, and gift. The Holy Spirit is the eternal mutual love between the Father and the Son.[38] For this reason, although God is love and the source of all love,[39] the Holy Spirit is especially called love[40] in some texts of the Holy Scripture.[41] The singularity of the Holy

---

33   See Psalm 139:7–12.

34   Bonaventure, *The Journey of the Mind to God*, in *The Works of Bonaventure*, trans. Jose de Vinck (Mansfield Centre, Conn.: Martino Publishing, 2016), 15.

35   Pseudo-Dionysius, "The Divine Names," 977C, p. 128.

36   Nicholas of Cusa, "On Learned Ignorance," in Nicholas of Cusa, *Selected Spiritual Writings*, trans. H. Lawrence Bond (Mahwah, N.J.: Paulist Press, 1997), sect. 117, 140.

37   Nicholas of Cusa, "On Learned Ignorance," sect. 14, 93.

38   See Saint Augustine, *The Trinity (De Trinitate)*, 15.17.27, trans. Edmund Hill (Hyde Park, N.Y.: New City Press, 1991).

39   See 1 John 4:16.

40   Augustine, *De Trinitate*, 15.17.29, in fine.

41   See Romans 5:5 and 1 John 4:7–16. For an interpretation of the texts, see Augustine, *De Trinitate*, 15.17.31.

Spirit is precisely that of being in communion, being in unity.[42] The Holy Spirit is an "unutterable communion of Father and Son," says Augustine of Hippo,[43] because it is neither of the Father alone, nor of the Son alone, but of both.

Gift is also a fundamental designation of the Holy Spirit.[44] If the characteristic of the Son is being born (*natus*), the characteristic of the Holy Spirit is being given (*datus*). The Holy Spirit is a gift of both the Father and the Son. This being given, however, at no point suggests a relation of subordination among the divine persons but establishes one of harmony (*concordia*). As Augustine explains, the Holy Spirit "is given as a gift of God in such way that He himself also gives himself as being God."[45] The second feature of the divine gift is that it is free. The Holy Spirit is freely given, and "whoever is united to the Lord becomes one spirit with him."[46] Using the words of Yves Congar, we can say that "the Spirit is the principle of our return to God,"[47] and spirituality the path to do it.

If the Spirit of God is love, communion, and gift, becoming spiritual for a Christian means essentiality living in love, in communion, and as a gift, or in other words, living in communion of love with God and others by considering ourselves as a gift from God to others. As a result, love of neighbor will become no longer a commandment imposed, so to speak, from without but rather a consequence deriving from spirituality that becomes active through communion, love, and gift.[48]

---

42   In the same vein, see Joseph Ratzinger, "The Holy Spirit as *Communio*: Concerning the Relationship of Pneumatology and Spirituality in Augustine," *Communio: International Catholic Review* 25 (1998): 324–37.

43   Augustine, *De Trinitate*, 5.11.12: "So the Holy Spirit is a kind of inexpressible communion or fellowship of Father and Son, and perhaps he is given this name just because the same name can be applied to the Father and the Son. He is properly called what they are called in common, seeing that both Father and Son are holy and both Father and Son are Spirit."

44   1 Corinthians 12:13; John 7:37. The central text, according to Augustine, is Jesus' conversation with the Samaritan woman, John 4:7–14. See Augustine, *De Trinitate* 15.19.33 and 34.

45   Augustine, *De Trinitate*, 15.19.36.

46   1 Corinthians 6:17.

47   Yves Congar, *I Believe in the Holy Spirit*, trans. David Smith (New York: Crossroad, 1997 reprint 2000), 88.

48   Similarly, Benedict XVI, Encyclical Letter *Deus caritas est* (December 25, 2005), 31, This and other papal documents are available at w2.vatican.va.

Love, communion, and self-giving are also the Eucharist, as Christ's loving presence in the community of the faithful: "the world which came forth from the hands of God the Creator," said John Paul II, "now returns to him redeemed by Christ."[49] Christian revelation of the mysteries of the Trinity and the Eucharist transcends all human explanations and is not accessible to natural reason. It demands faith. However, the general idea of becoming spiritual by living in a communion of love for the divine, for humanity, and for the universe in an attitude of self-giving is not only a Christian idea but a metarational intuition that can be accepted by any spiritual individual without having to believe in the mystery of the Trinity or even the existence of God. In this sense, the rational dimension is built upon a metarational intuitive ground and not inversely.

Communion represents an essential element of universal spirituality because it overcomes the apparent opposition between multiplicity and unity. To be in communion is to communicate with one another and to become part of each other. In full communion, nobody is any longer alone or separate from others.[50] Love is the transformative power that leads human beings to communion with God and others by an act of self-giving. Love of God and love of neighbor are interwoven, even inseparable, because ultimately love is divine. It comes from God, and it unites us to God and makes us one, overcoming all divisions.[51] Because love is divine, it is free. There is no spurious individual interest behind pure love, and it cannot serve as a way of achieving other goals. The genuine act of love, which is always an act of self-giving, has to be a free act. The world of spirituality is the world of full inner freedom. Freedom is not only a political and secular idea but also, first and foremost, a spiritual reality.

The Legal Triad: Justice, Agreement, and Right

While love, communion, and gift are the pillars of spirituality, justice, agreement, and right are the three pillars of law. Justice is often identified with law because achieving justice is the primary goal of the law and legal systems. It

---

49 John Paul II, Encyclical Letter *Ecclesia de Eucharistia* (April 17, 2003), 8.

50 In the Christian faith, that happens especially in the sacrament of the Eucharist, in which the recipients are assimilated into Christ, and being in communion with him, they communicate with one another. On the idea of *communio*, see Pope Benedict XVI, "Eucharist, Communion, and Solidarity," in *The Essential Pope Benedict XVI*, ed. John F. Thornton and Susan B. Varenne (New York: Harper Collins, 2007), 69–84.

51 Benedict XVI, *Deus caritas est*, 18.

is both an aspiration and an intrinsic aspect of all legal systems. As Augustine once said, a political community that is not governed according to justice would be just a bunch of thieves.[52] To legitimize any legal system, the law must be just; it must be created and applied under justice. Traditionally understood as giving to each his or her own,[53] the fundamental idea of justice is a matter of great disagreement. It depends on the values accepted by a political community as fundamental and on the community's own historical experience. For this reason, as John Rawls pointed out, "a well-ordered society is a society effectively regulated by a public conception of justice."[54] This public conception of justice is a culturally evolving phenomenon and constitutes the engine of any concrete social order.

Law in democratic societies is built up through general and particular agreements. In fact, legal systems and law consist of a multitude of contracts, pacts, treaties, transactions, protocols, compromises, deals, settlements, and many other agreements, both national and supranational. The legal system itself is a product and a development of a fundamental agreement (constitution) within the political community that establishes a system for elaborating enforceable general agreements (legislation), enforcing agreements (executive power), and resolving conflicts about those agreements (judiciary). Relevant doctrines, such as that of majority rule, social contract, or overlapping consensus, among many others, serve to integrate and consolidate political communities based on the idea of agreement. Agreements lead to social integration and coordinated action through the recognition and protection of individual and collective rights. This explains why Hans Kelsen considered the principle *pacta sunt servanda* (agreements must be kept) as the starting point or basic rule of international law.[55]

In a context of deep disagreement, which is a proper characteristic of a pluralistic society, it is crucial that the law respect and recognize every person as such.[56] The basic expression of respect for and recognition of others consists in respecting and recognizing their rights, the third element

---

52   Augustine, *De civitate Dei*, 4.4, http://www.thelatinlibrary.com/augustine/civ4.shtml: *"Remota itaque iustitia quid sunt regna nisi magna latrocinia?"*

53   Celsus and Ulpian, *Digest of Justinian*, 1.1.10 pr.

54   John Rawls, *Justice as Fairness: A Restatement*, ed. Erin Kelly (Cambridge, Mass.: Harvard University Press, 2001), 31.

55   Hans Kelsen, *Principles of International Law* (Clark, N.J.: The Lawbook Exchange, 2009), 316.

56   Robert Spaemann, *Persons: The Difference between Someone and Something*, trans. Oliver O'Donovan (Oxford: Oxford University Press, 2007), 188.

of the legal triad. Rights are individual or collective interests legally enforceable through coercive institutions.[57] To protect rights (and public order), physical coercion becomes an intrinsic aspect of law, though absent from other dimensions of reality. By practicing their civil and political legal rights, individuals develop themselves as human persons, participating in the law-creating process, and ultimately collaborating to consolidate the political community. A legal system without rights is like an oasis without water.

Deep Connectivity between the Legal Triad and the Spiritual Triad

The essential metadimensional aspect of spirituality supports the idea that although law is indeed a matter of justice, agreement, and rights, it is also, at least aspirationally, a matter of love, communion, and self-giving.[58] Let me explain.

In addition to justice, human beings need love. And justice is not the opposite to love. There is no real tension or conflict between true justice and true love. In fact, love presupposes justice. There is no love without justice, nor is it possible to achieve the plenitude of justice without love. "Love that perpetrates injustice is malformed love," affirms Nicholas Wolterstorff.[59] Law provides the necessary platform for justice to flourish, and justice provides the unique platform for love to flourish. On the other hand, love ennobles justice and strengthens legal systems. Justice is indeed "the first virtue of social institutions, as truth is of systems of thought,"[60] but only if it

---

57   See Hans Kelsen, *General Theory of Law and State*, trans. Andres Wedberg (Cambridge, Mass.: Harvard University Press, 1945), 79–80. Kelsen says that identifying right with interest protected is incorrect because one can have a legal right without knowing it, and in such a case, "there cannot exist any interest" (80). However, I think it is possible to have an interest without knowing it; for example, a baby has the interest to learn how to speak without knowing it.

58   Bibliography on the essential relation between law and love abounds. See, among others, Berman, *Faith and Order*, 313–18; Nicholas Wolterstorff, *Justice in Love* (Grand Rapids, Mich.: Eerdmans, 2015); Benedict XVI, *Deus caritas est*, 26–29; Timothy P. Jackson, *Political Agape: Christian Love and Liberal Democracy* (Grand Rapids, Mich.: Eerdmans, 2015); and Robert F. Cochran, Jr., ed., *Agape, Justice, and Law: How Might Christian Love Shape Law?* (Cambridge: Cambridge University Press, 2017).

59   Wolterstorff, *Justice in Love*, xvii: "Love that perpetrates injustice is malformed love."

60   John Rawls, *A Theory of Justice* (Cambridge, Mass.: Harvard University Press, 1971), 3. On p. 586, he refers to "the primacy of justice."

is referred to as loving justice. Love will always be necessary to not reduce the human person to merely a "legal person" or even a "legal object." "Whoever wants to eliminate love is preparing to eliminate humanity as such," Pope Benedict XVI points out.[61] The rule of law demands a rule of love. Any legal system that ignores love is preparing to remove the true law.

Many legal systems accept the idea of forgiveness as an expression of love that is compatible with justice. It implies renouncing the right to administer justice oneself and reestablishes the order as a whole by acquitting the offender and thereby placing him or her in a spiritually higher dimension of justice.[62] In the area of private law, this is the case, for instance, of condonation or remission of debt, which implies that the creditor pardons a debt by treating the debtor as if the debt never existed.

The second elements of the triads, communion and agreement, are also related. Making an agreement always requires some degree of communion: the meeting or communion of the minds of contracting parties. People who are spiritually developed can reach an agreement more easily than nonspiritual contracting parties. There are at least two reasons for this. First, people with spiritual skills (that is, looking for a union) understand the interest of other parties more readily than nonspiritual contracting parties. Second, people with spiritual skills are more able than nonspiritual others to effortlessly renounce self-interest to protect a common interest. On the other hand, agreements reached by spiritual people are more stable and deeper than agreements reached by nonspiritual self-interest-based people. A marriage rooted in a deeply spiritual mutual union between spouses has more possibilities of durability than a marriage based on strictly selfish interests (e.g., pleasure, companionship, and entertainment).

The connection between the third elements of the triads, right and self-giving, can be explained by analogy with the relation between self-love and love for others. Self-interest and the rights of the self can conflict with the interests and rights of others. Love, however—even self-love[63]—is never in

---

61 In the same vein, see Benedict XVI, *Deus caritas est*, 28.

62 In the same vein, see Romano Guardini, *The Lord*, trans. Elynor Castendyk (Washington, D.C.: Regnery, 1996), 351.

63 On self-love as the basis for loving others, see Thomas Aquinas, *Commentary on the Sentences*, bk. 3, dist. 29, q. 1, art. 3, ad 3: *"quod amicabilia quae sunt ad alterum, venerunt ex amicabilibus quae sunt ad seipsum, non ex causa finali, sed sicut ex eo quod est primus in via generationis"* ["The friendliness one has toward another comes from the friendliness

conflict with the other's interest and rights, because love is not conflictive by definition. Since self-giving is an act of love, self-giving cannot conflict with self-love, self-interest, or another's interest, personal rights, and rights. Spirituality shows that protected interest or rights should be used not only for one's own good but also for the good of others, that is, in accordance with the common good and as an expression of solidarity.

Rights are common to all human beings, irrespective of individualistic interests. For this reason, human beings are able to understand interests as common and to practice rights in solidarity. Conflicts of protected interests or rights are inevitable in any society, but they are easy to resolve when human beings live in a self-giving attitude, looking for the common good more than for the strictly individual good. Self-giving is the greatest expression of spiritual love, and it involves the "surrender of one's I"[64] without diminishing personal dignity and individual freedom. Self-giving emerges from the fact that human beings can share human nature and spirituality, enabling a human being to experience his or her life as completely united with the lives of others. When one exercises his or her rights in a self-giving attitude, rights become transformed from enforceable protected interests into "enforceable protected services,"[65] and society strengthens its ties of union.

Intentions and Values:
Two Channels of Interaction between
Law and Spirituality

The two main bridges of practical interaction between the spiritual and the legal realms are intentions (individual or collective) and values (cultural intentions). There are other channels of interaction, such as customs, traditions, procedures, and ceremonies, but in the end, intentions and values are the most important ones.

---

one has toward oneself, not as if from a final cause, but rather as from that which is prior in the process of generation"].

64   Karol Wojtyla, *Love and Responsibility*, trans. H. T. Willetts (San Francisco: Ignatius Press, 1981), 96–100.

65   On the idea of right as service, see Álvaro d'Ors, *Nueva introducción al estudio del derecho* (Madrid: Civitas, 1999), §62; Rafael Domingo, "Álvaro d'Ors," in *Great Christian Jurists in Spanish History*, ed. Rafael Domingo and Javier Martínez-Torrón (Cambridge: Cambridge University Press, 2018), 344–60, at 356.

The spiritual intention of any human action or attitude is its more profound and ultimate purpose. Spiritual intention arises from the deepest part of the human being, the heart,[66] and it affects and embraces all dimensions. It is metarational and, therefore, not mental, although it is connected with the mind.[67] Spiritual intention determines the purity or simplicity of the heart, that is, the intensity of love, the level of communion with others, and the degree of self-giving in any human action. It can be present in all human actions, not only in strictly spiritual ones, due to its metadimensional nature, and it can be shared with other secondary mental intentions, aims, purposes or interests. For example, one can be united to God while teaching, painting, cooking, or driving a school bus. Teaching, painting, cooking, and driving are not strictly spiritual actions, but the spiritual element can inspire and be present in all these activities. The more purified the spiritual intention, the more harmonically united to God, the divine, and others. Spiritual intention is a source of freedom, joy, and peace for human beings. It grants freedom to choose always in union with God, the divine, and others, and therefore to share others' freedom, and when that happens, freedom is expanded, since it is not limited by one's own will and circumstances. Spiritual intention also grants the joy of experiencing communion and love. Finally, it grants peace, that is, full harmony between one's action, another's action, and divine plans.

Human beings can do things with more than one rational intention in mind. Mary can buy a new car because she needs to travel more often or wants to lend it to her daughter occasionally. But she may also want to spend the money she deposited in a savings account of a bank involved in corruption because she no longer wants to patronize it as a customer. Usually, legal systems are interested only in some particular intentions—those that have some legal relevance in the application of norms: for example, whether Peter intentionally pulled the trigger or not; whether Albert really intended to kill Marc when he stuck his dagger in Marc's leg; whether Anne intended to revoke or merely to supplement her will when she ordered new instructions; and so on.[68] However, what is critical for this argument is that the mental

66 On this topic, see Michael Welker, ed., *The Depth of the Human Person: A Multidisciplinary Approach* (Grand Rapids, Mich.: Eerdmans, 2014).

67 In this vein, it can be said that the Holy Spirit is God's heart. See Guardini, *The Lord*, 170.

68 On intention, see the still-important contribution of G. E. M. Anscombe, *Intention* (Cambridge, Mass.: Harvard University Press, 1957). For an overview in the

or rational intention recognized by law can be inspired, supported, or illuminated by the spiritual intention. For instance, the law can recognize the intention of making a gift for charity, humanitarian aid, or benefit. For the law, it is important to know that the donor does not impose some contractual requirements and that the funds are awarded irrevocably in order to qualify the legal act as a private gift and not as a grant. Behind an uninterested private gift for a good cause, however, there is generosity, which is an expression of communion with others as a result of a purified spiritual intention. It is true that a private gift could be motivated as well by vanity or self-aggrandizement, but that does not invalidate the argument: spirituality, wherever it exists, touches the law.

Values are the second channel of interaction between law and spirituality. They are cultural distillations of individual and collective intentions. The whole idea of value implies selectivity and evaluation of "intersubjective-shared preferences and goods," if I may use Habermas's definition.[69] Like intentions, values are teleological, and they are able to lead and illuminate the development of political communities in accordance with their destiny. Unlike norms and rules, values allow a greater or lesser intensity code. They operate gradually and not under the dynamic of dualism and binary validity.[70] Values enable human beings to make judgments in different dimensions. Political values allow human beings to make political decisions, moral values moral decisions, and legal values legal decisions. However, political, moral, legal, and other values depend on one another and support each other coherently. This so-called unity of value is an old-established philosophical idea, a consequence of reality being one, and that all dimensions are ultimately related.

The unity of value is more strongly manifested in the holistic spiritual realm than in any holonic dimension, because communion is more profound in the spiritual metadimension than in any fragmented dimension of reality. That is why there is no conflict of values in the spiritual metadimension, as there very often is in the political and legal dimensions. Justice, love, peace, wisdom, freedom, joy, and mercy do not conflict in spirituality as, for

---

area of criminal law, see Andrew Ashworth and Jeremy Horder, *Principles of Criminal Law*, 7th ed. (Oxford: Oxford University Press, 2013), 168–75.

69 Jürgen Habermas, *Between Facts and Norms: Contributions to a Discourse Theory of Law and Democracy*, trans. William Rehg (Cambridge, Mass.: MIT Press, 1998), 255.

70 Habermas, *Between Facts and Norms*.

instance, pluralism, solidarity, compassion, inclusion, diversity, trust, tolerance, responsibility, justice, freedom, equality, and participation, among other values, contrast and collide in the legal dimension.

Spirituality interacts with the law through values in two different ways: directly and indirectly. It can operate directly because spiritual values (for example, love and communion) can openly act in every dimension of reality due to the holistic character of the spiritual. It can operate indirectly by spiritualizing specific values of other dimensions. Pluralism, for instance, is not a spiritual value strictly speaking, because it demands a political community to operate. However, it can be spiritualized when love and communion illuminate it, and when it is used to develop unity in society and not fragmentation. Something similar occurs with other political and legal values, such as tolerance and diversity. Spiritual values (again, for instance, love and communion) are hierarchically superior to other values, not because they are "unequivocally prescribed by ecclesiastical dogmas," to quote Max Weber,[71] but because they provide unity to all the values by illuminating all of them in the various dimensions of reality. In this sense, unity prevails over the good and the right and acts as a link between morality and law.

Evolution of Law through Spiritualization: Some Historical Examples

Most legal developments imply some degree of spiritualization of the law. Legal systems evolve through spiritualization in many different ways, such as (a) promoting the dematerialization of the legal system; (b) encouraging the limitation of domination; (c) inspiring the reduction of coercion; (d) stimulating the primacy of human communion and love; (e) provoking a more vital interaction between human and nonhuman animals and the environment; and (f) increasing respect for the law and legal systems.

a. Dematerialization of the legal system. Legal systems dematerialize as long as nonmaterial elements prevail over material elements. Dematerialization occurs, for instance, when intention prevails over literal interpretation, when legal systems reduce unnecessary formalism, and when they stimulate agency and representation as well as the creation of legal entities and institutions. The less tangible the legal system, the more spiritual.

---

[71] Max Weber, *Methodology of Social Sciences*, trans. Edward A. Shils and Henry A. Finch (New Brunswick, N.J.: Transaction Publishers, 2011), 19.

Let me provide some examples from history. In 93 BCE, Quintus Mucius Scaevola confronted his former colleague Lucius Licinius Crassus in the famous causa Curiana.[72] It was a trial before the centumviral court on the validity of a will written by a certain Coponius. Scaevola defended the strict literal interpretation of the wording of the will against the opinion of Crassus, who insisted that the will should be interpreted according to the testator's intention based on the ordinary use of the language and on equity. Crassus persuaded the court in favor of his client Manius Curius. This prevalence of intention over literal interpretation was expanded to the realm of contracts. For instance, Papinian affirms, "it was decided that intention rather than actual words must be taken into consideration in agreements between contracting parties."[73] The medieval jurist Azo of Bologna, among others, generalized the rule in his famous *Brocardica aurea*,[74] and now many legal systems use this rule.[75]

An excellent example of the reduction of unnecessary formalism is the establishment of consensual contracts in the first century BCE. Consensual contracts were concluded by formless consent. No transfer of property or symbolic act was required. Hence, such contracts could be formed between parties at a distance (*inter absentes*), that is, by letter or messenger,[76] unlike oral obligations, for instance. Consensual contracts were of great commercial and economic importance and constituted one of the most significant accomplishments of jurisprudence in the Roman Republic. Another example of reducing formalism comes from the French Civil Code, of which Articles 1.138

---

72   Cicero, *On the Orator*, 1.180–81, ed. E. W. Sutton and H. Rackham (Cambridge, Mass.: Harvard University Press, 1948). See also Rafael Domingo, *Roman Law: An Introduction* (London: Routledge, 2018), 65.

73   Papinian, *Digest of Justinian*, 50.16.219: *"in conventionibus contrahentium voluntatem potius quam verba spectari placuit."*

74   Azo of Bologna, *Brocardica aurea D. Azonis Bononiensis antiquorum iuris consultorum facile principis. In quibus omnes fere iuris antinomiae conciliantur, atque concordantes leges suis locis collocantur* (Naples, 1568; reprint, Turin: Ex officina Erasmiana, 1967), rubric 39 fol. 100. On this topic, see Rafael Domingo et al., eds., *Principios de Derecho Global*, 2nd ed. (Cizur Menor: Thomson Reuters Aranzadi, 2006), §425.

75   See, for instance, art. 1156 of the French Civil Code, art. 1362 of the Italian Civil Code, § 914 of the Austrian Civil Code, §133 of the German Civil Code, and art. 1281 § 2 of the Spanish Civil Code.

76   Gaius, *Institutes*, 3.136, ed. W. M. Gordon and O. Robinson (London: Duckworth, 1988).

and 1.153 accept, under some circumstances and conditions, the transfer of ownership based only on mutual consent of the parties without the need of delivery (*traditio*). Examples abound.

In the Middle Ages, civil lawyers and canonists applied by analogy the idea of person to corporations (*persona ficta et repraesentata*) with the aim of expanding the legal capacity of entities, universities, companies, and institutions in general.[77] Centuries later, the seventeenth-century philosopher Thomas Hobbes explained the principle of representation by appealing to unity (that is, in some sense to spirituality): "a multitude of men are made one person, when they are by one man or one person represented; so that it be done with the consent of everyone of that multitude in particular."[78] Nowadays, the development of so-called intellectual property, which protects the creation of a large variety of intellectual goods, is a new example of the spiritualization of law. It is precisely the intangible and indivisible nature of intellectual property law—covering copyrights, patents, trademarks, publicity rights, trade secrets, and moral rights—that conflicts with the traditional understanding of property law, which is based on the concept of land and tangible things.

The paradigm of legal dematerialization is the unwritten British constitution. Unlike most modern democratic states, Britain has a constitution only in the abstract—in a spiritual sense, we can say, comprising a host of historically momentous laws and principles, including the famous Bill of Rights (1689), parliamentary conventions, statutory law, works of authority, customs, and common law. Parliamentary sovereignty is the bedrock of this unique uncodified constitution.[79]

b. Encouraging the limitation of domination. The greater the domination allowed or exercised by a legal system, the lower the degree of legal spiritualization. Domination is the opposite of free communion and, therefore,

---

[77] See Santiago Panizo Orallo, *Persona jurídica y ficción: Estudio de la obra de Sinibaldo de Fieschi* (Inocencio IV) (Pamplona: Eunsa, 1975); Italo Birocchi, "Persona giuridica nel diritto medievale e moderno," in *Digesto. Sezione Civile*, vol. 13 (Turin: UTET, 1995), 407–20; and Kathleen G. Cushing, "Sinibaldo Fieschi (Pope Innocent IV) (1180/90–1254)," in *Law and the Christian Tradition in Italy: The Legacy of the Great Jurists*, ed. Orazio Condorelli and Rafael Domingo (London: Routledge, 2021), 70–81.

[78] Thomas Hobbes, *Leviathan*, ed. J. C. A. Gaskin (Oxford: Oxford University Press, 1998), pt. 1, chap. 16, sec. 13, p. 109.

[79] See Albert Venn Dicey, *Introduction to the Study of the Law of the Constitution*, 8th ed. (Indianapolis, Ind.: Liberty Classics, 1982).

of spirituality. Domination is based on inequality, force, and subordination. Communion, however, is based on unity, love, and freedom. If legal systems are established primarily and above all to restrict private and public domination, then legal systems evolve when they gradually move from private or public domination to communion.

Roman law, for instance, developed high degrees of private domination. Domestic paternal power (*patria potestas*), which originally included the power to kill family members, was brutal, as was the power of masters over slaves (*dominica potestas*) and, in a lower level, marital power (*manus*).[80] The story of Roman and Western family law is the story of the restriction, and even dissolution, of these dominative, cruel, and rude powers.

In the realm of constitutional law, a paradigm of liberation of public domination and high degree of spiritualization was the Declaration of Independence (1776), especially its famous second paragraph: "We hold these truths to be self-evident, that all men are created equal, that they are endowed by their Creator with certain unalienable Rights, that among these are Life, Liberty and the pursuit of Happiness." The declaration contrasts with the horrendous situation of slavery in the Thirteen Colonies and the fact that the drafter of the declaration himself, Thomas Jefferson, was the holder of so many slaves.[81] These facts, however, do not diminish the spiritual value of the declaration. They show us, however, that the process of spiritualization of law is not homogeneous.

In the law of nations, the concept of just war is a good example of restricting domination. Augustine of Hippo developed the theory of just war to limit the declaration and use of war as an instrument of domination. Thomas Aquinas completed the doctrine in the Middle Ages. Still, Hugo Grotius, in his work *The Law of War and Peace* (1625), articulated a systematic theory of just war founded on rationality and developed a legal framework for determining the justice of war. In the twentieth century, the codification of the 1949 Geneva Conventions strongly limited domination and suffering caused in war (*ius in bello*) by addressing the treatment of sick and wounded combatants, prisoners of war, and protection for civilians and noncombatants in times of military conflict.[82]

    80   See Domingo, *Roman Law*, 130.
    81   See Paul Finkelman, *Slavery and the Founders: Race and Liberty in the Age of Jefferson*, 3rd ed. (London: Routledge, 2014).
    82   For a history of international law, see Bardo Fassbender and Anne Peters,

c. *Inspiring the reduction of coercion.* Law is not just a matter of coercion. Law often facilitates, supports, exemplifies, encourages, and teaches without coercion. But law, as a legal system, requires coercion. Coercion is a necessary condition for the existence of the legal system. Since coercion restricts freedom, however, spirituality inspires the reduction of coercion to the necessary minimum. Examples in history also abound. For instance, an important conquest of spiritualization was the elimination of torture from legal systems, including canon law. Judicial torture disappeared in England about 1640. It was abolished in Germany in 1776 but not in France until 1789. The famous book by Marchese de Beccaria, *Dei delitti e delle pene* (1764), was instrumental in the abolition of torture across Europe. After the 9/11 terrorist attacks, a part of the U.S. population defended the morality and legality of torturing terrorists during interrogation, while some scholars rejected such a practice with solid arguments.[83] To share arguments opposing torture, however, a political community should have achieved a certain level of spiritualization. Otherwise, the elimination of torture seems to be considered unrealistic and utopian, and unfortunately, it still happens in our time in many parts of the world.

The death penalty abolition is also an excellent example of spiritual development. For centuries, the death penalty, following a fair trial, was accepted as appropriate under some circumstances by civil and religious authorities worldwide as an extreme means to protect the common good. Important countries like the United States, China, India, Japan, and most Islamic states retain capital punishment, even on moral grounds. Due to a process of cultural spiritualization, however, millions of people now consider the death penalty a violation of the right to life and opposed to the dignity and the communion of human beings. In the European Union, for instance, Article 2 of the Charter of Fundamental Rights prohibits the use of capital punishment. Recently, Pope Francis rejected the death penalty under all circumstances and approved a new draft of section 2267 of the Catechism of the Catholic Church, which affirms: "the death penalty is inadmissible because it is an attack on the inviolability and dignity of the

---

eds., *The Oxford Handbook of the History of International Law* (Oxford: Oxford University Press, 2014); Ignacio de la Rasilla, *International Law and History: Modern Interfaces* (Cambridge: Cambridge University Press, 2021).

[83] On this topic, see Jeremy Waldron, *Torture, Terror, and Trade-Offs: Philosophy for the White House* (Oxford: Oxford University Press, 2010).

person."[84] This is a clear example of how spiritual development purifies moral doctrines and rationales.

The abolition of any kind of coercion to practice or not practice religion is another spiritual conquest of Western culture. Since Western political communities were based on the assumptions that heresy was a crime, and that sharing religion was an important element of stability of the political community, religious freedom did not emerge until the modern era. The Protestant Reformation advocated for it after decades of bloody and bitter wars of religion.[85] In our day, however, although religious persecution still exists, religious freedom is universally accepted as one of the basic human rights and recognized as such by international treaties and instruments and national constitutions.[86] Finally, we can mention the nonviolent resistance and reconciliation movements of the twentieth century as spiritually grounded. The role played by Gandhi in India, Martin Luther King, Jr., in the United States, and Nelson Mandela in South Africa shows us in a practical way the profound relation between spirituality and law in the fulfillment of social goals such as peace and justice, and how the use of physical force is not always the best way to resolve social or political conflicts.

d. Stimulating the primacy of communion and love. Spirituality stimulates communion between and among peoples beyond the contingent plurality of institutions, groups, conflicts, and rights. The birth of the European Union is a good example of this kind of spiritual stimulation. The first and crucial steps of the long European integration process after the Second World War were possible, at least to some notable degree, thanks to the spiritual stature of the so-called European founding fathers: Konrad Adenauer, Robert Schuman, Jean Monnet, Alcide De Gasperi, and Joseph Bech, among others. They built a new Europe from the blood and ashes of the battlefields based on the values of reconciliation and communion and overcoming any

---

84   See the statement and the reasons at https://press.vatican.va/content/salastampa/en/bollettino/pubblico/2018/08/02/180802a.html.

85   See John Witte, Jr., *The Reformation of Rights: Law, Religion, and Human Rights in Early Modern Calvinism* (Cambridge: Cambridge University Press, 2007).

86   For an overview, see Anat Scolnicov, *The Right to Religious Freedom in International Law: Between Group Rights and Individual Rights* (London: Routledge, 2011); Linde Lindkvist, *Religious Freedom and the Universal Declaration of Human Rights* (Cambridge: Cambridge University Press, 2017).

domination, revenge, and retaliation.[87] On a global scale, the establishment and development of the United Nations as an intergovernmental organization to maintain international peace and security, develop friendly relations among nations, and achieve international cooperation is another example of the primacy of communing of nations and, therefore, of cultural spiritualization. Although its initiatives are often frustrated, the contribution of the United Nations to human cooperation has been remarkable.[88]

e. Provoking a more vital interaction between humans, animals, and the environment. Humanity is only a part of a boundless evolving universe. Spirituality thus inspires communion not only with other human beings but also with all living beings and the environment. Animals matter for spirituality, and animals matter for the law now more than ever. A new legal field has recently emerged to protect animals against cruelty and suffering and to develop a communicative interaction between humans and animals. Animal law is a body of laws, regulations, and agreements that govern human interaction with domestic animals (in agriculture, research, and entertainment) and wildlife.[89] Spirituality helps human beings to overcome the traditional hierarchical approach to animals and see them as beings with feelings, emotions, and worth, not just as property for human exploitation.

The protection of the environment also plays an important role in the relation between law and spirituality.[90] The so-called Earth Charter (2000),[91] as a civil society declaration endorsed by hundreds of international institutions, constitutes a valid framework for building a just, sustainable, and peaceful world in the twenty-first century. Widely grounded on spiritual values, the charter acknowledges the deep interconnections between protection of ecosystems, eradication of human poverty, social justice, and world peace.[92]

---

[87] See Desmond Dinan, *Origins and Evolution of the European Union*, 2nd ed. (Oxford: Oxford University Press, 2014).

[88] Thomas G. Weiss and Sam Daws, eds., *The Oxford Handbook of the United Nations* (Oxford: Oxford University Press, 2009).

[89] For an overview, see Thomas G. Kelch, *Globalization and Animal Law* (Alphen aan den Rijn: Kluwer, 2011); Kathy Hessler et al., *Animal Law: New Perspectives on Teaching Traditional Law* (Durham, N.C.: Carolina Academic Press, 2017).

[90] See Benedict XVI, *The Garden of God: Toward a Human Ecology*, ed. Maria Milvia Morciano (Washington, D.C.: The Catholic University of America Press, 2014).

[91] Document available at http://earthcharter.org/discover/the-earth-charter.

[92] Steven C. Rockefeller, "Global Interdependence, the Earth Charter, and

In business law, the new development of so-called corporate social responsibility (CSR) shows us how consumers consider not only the quality of services and goods when choosing a specific brand but also the social and environmental impacts of its operations and its implications in social issues. "People and planet" matter for customers, even when they are dealing with small things. This interconnected approach is spiritual at its heart.

f. Increasing respect for the law and the legal systems. Spirituality helps develop respect for legal systems as necessary tools for the development of human beings. Respect is the necessary starting point of true communion. Otherwise, the resulting union will be dominative but not communicative or spiritual. Moreover, one must respect the union's rules on its different levels, including the legal one. When human beings see the legal system and the legal dimension as a part of an instrument for a higher spiritual unity, it is easy for them to respect the legal systems more than when they consider the legal dimension a mere product of temporary human convention and agreement. The deeper the reason for respect, the more easily people offer respect.

Some New Challenges:
New Technologies and Globalization

Revolutionary changes in communication technologies and globalization have linked human beings in unimaginable ways in the past few decades, substantially improving the capacity of human interaction, reducing the relevance of geographical space and distance, overcoming national boundaries, and ultimately uniting humankind as a great community.[93] Information, services, goods, capital, labor, and research flow readily between nations. New technologies are dematerializing, decentralizing, and democratizing the world beyond political communities, and globalization allows a broader framework for action based on interdependence. However, a dark side exists. New

---

Christian Faith," in *Earth Habitat: Eco-Injustice and the Church's Response*, ed. Dieter T. Hessel and Larry Rasmussen (Minneapolis, Minn.: Fortress Press, 2001), 101–21; the entry "Earth Charter," in *Encyclopedia of Religion and Nature*, ed. Bron Taylor (Oxford: Oxford University Press, 2010), online.

    93   On this topic, see Richard Baldwin, *The Great Convergence: Information Technology and the New Globalization* (Cambridge, Mass.: Harvard University Press, 2016); Stephen D. King, *Grave New World: The End of Globalization, the Return of History* (New Haven, Conn.: Yale University Press, 2017).

technologies and globalization can operate not just as a unifying factor but also as a fragmenting force, exacerbating world disparities, dividing more and more the distribution of wealth, and generating great conflicts among political societies, global spaces, and cultures.

Now, as never before, global economic forces and political powers are able to dominate national and local communities and subordinate human beings and institutions. The risk is real, as antiglobalization movements rightly proclaim. New technologies and globalization can be used both as instruments of communion and as instruments of domination, depending on the individual and collective spiritual intentions of global players and the international community's values. Economic globalization, for instance, created new jobs in many countries, brought new goods to consumers of other regions, and accelerated world trade, but it also was instrumental in labor exploitation, including child labor, human trafficking, and a barbarous market for the body organs of poor people in medical transplants.

Because of the risk of domination inherent in new technologies and globalization, humanity should move to the highest degree of spiritualization. This level of spiritualization implies the deepest understanding of other cultures and peoples in order to live in harmony with them and a firm resolution to live in solidarity with others, avoiding harm to any human being, protecting nonhuman living beings, and taking care of the environment.

Levels of Legal Spiritualization

The explanation of the connection between law and spirituality from a theoretical perspective is insufficient. The use of the scientific method is required to verify that link and the evolution of law through spiritualization. Although this paper is explanatory rather than scientific, let me finish by providing a roadmap for potential scientific research using the following table.

Following the steps of the nineteenth- and twentieth-century evolutionary theorists,[94] I envisage all political communities as evolving along a typical track from barbarian societies to spiritual communities. Spiritual evolution is a process of spiritual understanding or level of consciousness and is

---

94 See, for instance, Lewis H. Morgan, *Ancient Society or Researches in the Lines of Human Progress from Savagery through Barbarism to Civilization* (New York: Henry Holt, 1878); Ken Wilber, *Sex, Ecology, Spirituality: The Spirit of Evolution*, 2nd ed. (Boston: Shambhala, 2000).

Table 1

	no legal system	no personal interest	community of love (not of law)	no conflicts	no rights	oneness (no equality)	no coercion	no money
Level 5 Spirituality								
Level 4 Solidary law	a highly developed and connected legal system	prevalence of common interest and solidarity	Global law for the human community	no war as a legal tool: arbitration	rights as enforceable services	inclusiveness and full respect of minorities; very low level of criminality	use of selected weapons by the police and the military	digital money and decentralized monetary systems
Level 3 Equality law	a coherent and independent legal system	balance between self-interest and common interest	international law based on equality among nation states	humanitarian law and just war allowed by an independent entity	development of individual civil, political, and collective rights	equality under law; voting and democracy; agreement	restrictions on both the manufacture and the use of weapons	monetary system based on a patron
Level 2 Egoic law	rule of law	prevalence of self-interest over common interest; development of private law	law of nations based on subordination	just war	individual rights	society based on privileges; restricting capacity of voting	restrictions on the general use of weapons	money used by its intrinsic value
Level 1 Barbarism	no legal system	complete domination and subordination	use of force with other communities	war	no rights	no equality	free use of weapons	no money: barter

oriented to love and communion, which is the highest expression of human development and happiness. I establish five levels, and the first is prelegal. It reflects the state of uncivilized people based on indiscriminate domination by force. No individual rights or equality among people are recognized. Money does not exist, only barter. Level five, at the top, is postlegal. It reflects the state of the full communion of love, and it is not achievable in the material world. At this level, there is no ego, no personal interest, no conflict, no rights, and no coercion. It is the reign of love, communion, peace, and happiness. The I and the We are very much the same since all intentions are shared. Legal systems are not necessary. The structure most in conformity with level five would be a very united, loving family or a spiritual community, integrated by members of the highest level of spirituality (for example, Gandhi, Mother Teresa, and Maximilian Kolbe).

Levels one and five coincide because they have no legal system, rights, equality, or money. Level one has no equality because of subordination; level five, however, lacks equality because of full union. Level one does not meet the basic requirements of society to establish a legal system, which remains only an aspiration. Level five, however, transcends the idea of a legal system, which would be superfluous. Level one has a barter system rather than money because of a lack of economic development. Level five, on the contrary, has no money because everything is accessible by definition in a spiritual community.

Levels two (egoic law), three (equal law), and four (solidary law) require legal systems. The legal system in level two is still not unified and coherent, but it does contain the basic ideas of the rule of law, jurisdiction and adjudication, some individual rights, and public institutions. There is no separation of powers or bill of rights. The political community is firmly structured in social classes based on prestige, power, and wealth. Relations with other peoples are ordered by an emerging law of nations based on just war and political and military subordination. Coins are guaranteed by their intrinsic value, that is, by the trade value of the metal (for example, gold or silver) used in their production. Ancient Roman law would be an excellent example of level two.

Level three demands a coherent and unified legal system and a fully independent judiciary. Democracy, participation, and equality are socially accepted. The government protects individual, political, and social rights. International law, the law of a community of equal sovereign national states, is integrated into the national legal system or is at least recognized as enforceable by international agreements. In level three, the achieved degree of solidarity allows the creation of supranational, transnational, and international institutions. Humanitarian law has been developed, but war still exists. The monetary system is involved in the process of dematerialization. It moves from gold-exchange standards to an international financial system based on pure fiat money regulated by central banking systems. Most of the democratic countries in our day are at this level of development. Legal systems such as those in Afghanistan, Cuba, Yemen, and Venezuela are between levels two and three, sharing aspects of both of them.

Level four (solidary law) is achieved after developing a highly sophisticated and interconnected legal system based on human solidarity and full recognition of human dignity. Common (including global) interests prevail over the particular interest of individuals or states, making possible the establishment of a global human community under law. All conflicts (including international conflicts) are resolved by arbitration, mediation, or judiciary systems, never by a formal declaration of war. Levels of economic and political corruption are very low, as is the threat of crime. Individual rights are conceived as enforceable services. Minorities are well protected. Communities are very much decentralized, as is the monetary system, which is no longer under central banks' control. All assets are dematerialized. In level four, the use of weapons is allowed only to avoid conflict with countries with lower levels of spiritual understanding. Level four demands a high degree of spiritual development in society that only a tiny percentage of humanity has achieved. Some countries are moving to this level at a higher speed than others, but no country in the world now lives according to all the standards of level four. It remains an aspiration.

These five levels of spiritualization, with the required accommodation, can be applied not only to legal systems but also to legal actors, legal subjects, and legal institutions. The pattern is similar: the evolution from coercive domination to free communion as an expression of spiritualization. When the intention of the legal actor (say, a lawyer or a judge) is egoic or dominative, the legal actor is at level two. A legal actor who tries to balance individual interests with common interests is at level three. However, if the deep intention of the legal actor is only to serve society, and the common interest prevails over their own interest, this legal actor would be in level four. Legal actors at level four are always social leaders, since people recognize their high degree of communion with others. At the institutional level, it is different: a parliament in which politicians search only for consensus to provide a good service to society (level four), a parliament in which politicians balance the common good with partisan interest (level three), and a parliament in which each politician is looking for his or her particular interests without taking into consideration any collective interest (low level three). The parliament cannot be established in level two because of a lack of elemental communion and understanding.

Conclusion

Establishing a just and fair legal system for a political community at the local, national, or supranational level is the ultimate achievement of law. Using coercion, among other tools, legal systems assure the inner cohesion required for the proper development of political communities. Spirituality, however, cannot be left out of that task. It affects the law by its holistic metadimensionality, which provides unity to moral, political, and legal values. Although functionally autonomous, legal systems are not independent of the spiritual element. As I have shown, the spiritual triad of *love, communion, and gift* is deeply interconnected with the legal triad of *justice, agreement, and right*. Individual and collective intentions and cultural values operate as a bridge between legality and spirituality. Legal systems evolve through spiritualization, among other ways, promoting the dematerialization of the legal system, encouraging the limitation of domination, inspiring the reduction of coercion, stimulating communion and consensus in society, and increasing respect for the law and the legal systems.

The legal implications of the interactions between law and spirituality should be explored in depth by twenty-first-century legal scholars. This exploration will serve as a vehicle to free the law and legal systems from the clutches of legal positivism and reductionism, and we can then envision the end of the era of rationalism.

CHAPTER 2

BODY, SOUL, AND SPIRIT OF THE LAW

IN THIS CHAPTER, I ADVOCATE a revival of applying the body-soul-spirit metaphor to legal science. The soundness of this metaphor, of course, cannot be justified by an appeal to empirical science because it is spiritual in character and, therefore, metascientific, though not in any way contrary to science.[1] Although the metaphor is not subject to the logical constraints that other methods demand (for example, geometry),[2] it is still valuable and appropriate because it is a source of inspiration and illumination. Deploying the body-soul-spirit metaphor, I try to recover the law's tridimensional structure and build a bridge between law and spirituality and between and among worldwide legal systems. Law is more than a system of rules, regulations, procedures, and institutions.

---

* The original version of this essay appears in Rafael Domingo, "Body, Soul, and Spirit of the Law: Towards a Holistic Legal Paradigm," *Oxford Journal of Law and Religion* 7, no. 2 (2018): 230–49.

1 For a reconciliation between spirituality and science, see, among others, Bruce Rosenblum and Fred Kuttner, *Quantum Enigma: Physics Encounters Consciousness*, 2nd ed. (New York: Oxford University Press, 2011).

2 See Paul Ricoeur, *The Rule of Metaphor: The Creation of Meaning in Language*, trans. Robert Czerny (London: Routledge, 2003), 11.

It is "a world in which we live,"[3] and this world has a spiritual dimension that should not be a stranger to the law.

In offering this body-soul-spirit metaphor, I propose a paradigm that overcomes both legal monism and dualism, and with them legal reductionism and isolation. First, I justify using the metaphor in the legal realm. I then defend the body-soul-spirit metaphor as an appropriate one for legal systems. Finally, I address some legal implications of applying this metaphor to current legal issues.

Law and Metaphor

Metaphors have been at the heart of Western legal culture since its foundation.[4] In both the civil and common-law traditions, it is easy to find a great variety of figurative expressions in legal discourse and judicial decisions. The age-long "sources of law" metaphor traces back at least to Cicero[5] and Livy.[6] The "legal remedy as path" metaphor was used by Emperor Justinian to temper rigid procedural formalism, offering a more flexible and general way of applying legal remedies and doing justice.[7]

---

3   See Robert Cover, "Nomos and Narrative," in *Narrative, Violence, and the Law: The Essays of Robert Cover*, ed. Martha Minow, Michael Ryan, and Austin Sarat (Ann Arbor: University of Michigan Press, 1992), 96. In a very similar way, Ronald Dworkin begins his famous book *Law's Empire* (Oxford: Hart Publishing, 1986; reprint, 2006), vii: "We live in and by the law. It makes us what we are."

4   See, among others, Bernard J. Hibbitts, "Making Sense of Metaphors: Visuality, Aurality, and the Reconfiguration of American Legal Discourse," *Cardozo Law Review* 16 (1994–1995): 229–356; Steven L. Winter, *A Clearing in the Forest: Law, Life, and Mind* (Chicago: University of Chicago Press, 2001); Francesco Galgano, *Le insidie del linguaggio giuridico: Saggio sulle metafore nel diritto* (Bologna: Il Mulino, 2010); Claudio Sarra, *Lo scudo di Dionisio. Contributo allo studio della metafora giuridica* (Milan: Franco Angeli Edizioni, 2010); David Gurnham, "Law's Metaphor: Introduction," *Journal of Law and Society* 43 (2016): 1–7; John Witte, Jr., "The Metaphorical Bridge between Law and Religion," *Pepperdine Law Review* 47, no. 2 (2020): 435–62; and John Witte, Jr., "Law, Religion, and Metaphor," in John Witte, Jr., *Faith Freedom, and Family: New Essays in Law and Religion*, ed. Norman Doe and Gary S. Hauk (Tübingen: Mohr Siebeck, 2022), 37–55.

5   Cicero, *De legibus* [On the Laws], 1.5.16 and 1.6.20.

6   Livy, *Ab Urbe condita* [*The History of Rome*], 3.34.6.

7   On the history of this metaphor, see Francesco Sitzia, "L'azione nelle Novelle di Giustiniano," *Bullettino dell'Istituto di Diritto Romano* 37–38 (1995–96): 171–98,

In the common-law tradition, metaphors abound. They were famously used by two of its most important judges and legal authors, Edward Coke and William Blackstone. In his renowned *Institutes*, Coke considered knowledge of the law to be "like a deepe well, out of which each man draweth according to the strength of his understanding."[8] On the other hand, Blackstone developed a detailed architectural metaphor comparing the whole common law with "a regular edifice," which over the years "was altered and mangled by various contradictory Statutes."[9] The English philosopher Thomas Hobbes employed the "state as artificial person" metaphor to explain his theory of action and the artificial character of political power.[10]

Some years later, the German polymath and philosopher Gottfried Wilhelm Leibniz compared the work of ancient Roman jurists to that of geometers and mathematicians and established the "law as geometry" metaphor. Leibniz argued that, as reason put into practice, the law should be subject to deductive processes, like geometry (*geometria juridica*).[11] In specific ways, this brilliant metaphor shaped the process of European codification. As a reaction against the codification movement, the German Historical School, led by Friedrich Carl von Savigny, coined the "spirit of the people" (*Volksgeist*) metaphor, arguing that each national community has its character, consciousness, or "national soul," which leaves its mark upon all its legal institutions and laws.[12]

---

at 173–90; Riccardo Fercia, "'Aliud petere' e la metafora dell'ὁδοί," *Rivista di Diritto Romano* 4 (2004): 1–16, http://www.ledonline.it/rivistadirittoromano/allegati/dirittoromano04fercia.pdf.

    8   Edward Coke, *The First Part of the Institutes of the Laws of England; or A Commentary Upon Littleton*, ed. Francis Hargrave and Charles Butler (Dublin: Brooke, Clarke and Sons, 1809), vol. 1, bk. 2, chap. 2, sect. 96, at fol. 71a.

    9   See letter from William Blackstone to Seymour Richmond, January 28, 1745/46, letter 4, quoted by Wilfrid Prest, "Blackstone as Architect: Constructing the Commentaries," *Yale Journal of Law and Humanities* 15 (2003): 103–33, at 104.

    10   Thomas Hobbes, introduction, in *Leviathan*, ed. J. C. A. Gaskin (Oxford: Oxford University Press, 1996), sect. 1, pt. 1, chap. 16, 7 and 106–10.

    11   See Gottfried Wilhelm Leibniz, *The New Method of Learning and Teaching Jurisprudence*, trans. Carmelo Massimo de Iuliis (Clark, N.J.: Talbot Lawbook Exchange, 2017), 113. For more on this metaphor, see Michael H. Hoeflich, "Law and Geometry: Legal Science from Leibniz to Langdell," *American Journal of Legal History* 30, no. 2 (1986): 95–121.

    12   On the expression *Volksgeist*, see Franz Wieacker, *A History of Private Law in Europe*, trans. Tony Weir (Oxford: Clarendon Press, 1995), 279–341.

American legal discourse has also long favored metaphors.[13] From the birth of the new nation, American political and legal thinkers have used metaphors to illuminate legal topics.[14] Due to the limited human capacity to create entirely new formulations, some founding fathers drew on familiar metaphors to describe a unique constitutional experience. James Wilson, a major force in drafting the U.S. Constitution and later an associate justice of the Supreme Court, was a master of figurative rhetoric and the generation of novel formulations to explain American federalism.[15] Wilson was fully aware of the moral significance of language, the power of imagination, and the epistemological value of metaphor in political and legal discourse. He rightly said, "in the philosophy of mind, it is impossible to avoid metaphorical expressions. Our first familiar notions are suggested by material objects, and we cannot speak intelligibly of those that are immaterial, without continual allusions to matter and the qualities of matter."[16]

Echoing the language of Roger Williams,[17] Thomas Jefferson used the "wall of separation" metaphor[18] to explain how church-state relations should

---

13 See, among others, Hibbitts, "Making Sense of Metaphors"; Winter, *A Clearing in the Forest*.

14 See, among others, I. Bernard Cohen, *Science and the Founding Fathers* (New York: W. W. Norton, 1995), esp. 36–59.

15 See Stephen A. Conrad, "Metaphor and Imagination in James Wilson's Theory of Federal Union," *Law and Social Inquiry* 13 (1988): 1–70.

16 James Wilson, *The Works of James Wilson*, ed. Robert Green McCloskey (Cambridge, Mass.: Harvard University Press, 1967), 101.

17 See Roger Williams, "Mr. Cotton's Letter Lately Printed" (1644), in *On Religious Liberty: Selections from the Works of Roger Williams*, ed. James Calvin Davis (Cambridge, Mass.: The Belknap Press of Harvard University Press, 2008), 70: "hedge or wall of separation between the Garden of the Church and the wilderness of the world."

18 A copy of the Danbury letter is available at https://www.loc.gov/loc/lcib/9806/danpre.html. In 1878, in *Reynolds v. United States*, 98 U.S. 145 (1878), the U.S. Supreme Court unanimously gave its imprimatur to the expression by declaring that the Constitution had established a wall of separation between the church and the state. Seventy years later, in *Everson v. Board of Education*, 330 U.S. 1 (1947), the Supreme Court confirmed the constitutional doctrine of the wall of separation. For a historical overview about the separation of church and state in the United States, see Philip Hamburger, *Separation of Church and State* (Cambridge, Mass.: Harvard University Press, 2002). For a deep critique, see T. Jeremy Gunn, "The Separation of Church and State versus Religion in Public Square: The Contested History of the Establishment Clause," in *No Establishment of Religion: America's Original Contribution to Religious Liberty*, ed. T. Jeremy Gunn and John Witte, Jr. (Oxford: Oxford University Press, 2012), 15–44.

be structured in the young republic. In a famous letter to the Danbury Baptist Association, written on January 1, 1802, he wrote, "I contemplate with sovereign reverence that act of the whole American people which declared that their legislature should 'make no law respecting an establishment of religion, or prohibiting the free exercise thereof,' thus building a wall of separation between Church & State." Jefferson also affirmed that the U.S. Constitution was "a good canvas, on which some strokes only want retouching,"[19] and that principles of the Bill of Rights "form the *bright constellation* which has gone before us and guided our steps through an age of revolution and reformation."[20] The metaphor of "freedom of speech as the great bulwark of liberty,"[21] or of states as "laboratories,"[22] and "rights as footprints,"[23] of the "seamless web" or "fixed star,"[24] or "magic mirror,"[25] are prominent examples of figurative language in American constitutional discourse.

European legal positivist scholars were more cautious than American scholars in using metaphors, but even they ultimately relied on them a great deal. Rhetorically, but no less certain, the founder of positivism, Jeremy Bentham, pointed out at the beginning of his famous *Introduction to the Principles of Morals and Legislation*, "But enough of metaphor and declamation: it

---

19   Thomas Jefferson, letter to James Madison, July 31, 1788, http://teachingamericanhistory.org/library/document/letter-to-james-madison-15.

20   Thomas Jefferson, First Inaugural Address, March 4, 1801, http://avalon.law.yale.edu/19th_century/jefinau1.asp.

21   See the Constitution of Virginia (1776), sect. 12, http://www.nhinet.org/ccs/docs/va-1776.htm: "That the freedom of the press is one of the great bulwarks of liberty, and can never be restrained but by despotic governments."

22   The metaphor first appeared in 1932 in a dissenting opinion of Justice Louis Brandeis in *New State Ice Co. v. Liebmann*, 285 U.S. 262, 311 (1932): "that a single courageous state may, if its citizens choose, serve as a laboratory, and try novel social and economic experiments without risk to the rest of the country."

23   See Jeremy Perelman and Katharine G. Young, "Rights as Footprints: A New Metaphor for Contemporary Human Rights Practice," *Northwestern Journal of International Human Rights* 9 (2010–2011): 27–58.

24   To refer to longstanding constitutional principles. See *West Virginia State Board of Education v. Barnette*, 319 U.S. 624, 638 (1943).

25   This metaphor was used by Oliver Wendell Holmes, Jr., to explain how, in the law, we can see reflected the lives of all members of a society. See Oliver Wendell Holmes, Jr., "The Law," in *The Occasional Speeches of Oliver Wendell Holmes*, ed. Mark DeWolfe (Cambridge, Mass.: Harvard University Press, 1962), 21.

is not by such means that moral science is to be improved."[26] He specifically criticized the metaphor of the body politic: "The figurative expression of a body-politic has produced a great number of false and extravagant ideas."[27] Hans Kelsen, too, in his *Pure Theory of Law*, attempted to clear, purge, and free legal science of alien elements.[28] But even this purification could not eliminate the legal metaphor. Indeed, legal positivism established the most salient metaphor of the twentieth century: the "legal system as pyramid" metaphor.[29]

Recently, some in the debate on European private law have used metaphors to argue that the European Union does not need a European Civil Code strictly but instead only a "toolbox" of rules from European contract law for lawmakers to use. Without being bound to do so, the national legislature could freely decide to dig into the box of tools offered by the European Union.[30] European contract law would be soft law, not mandatory.

Some Classic Applications of the Body-Soul-Spirit Metaphor to the Law

Metaphorical approaches based on the body-soul-spirit triad have often been used in the legal realm. The metaphor of the body, for example, was mainly employed in the Middle Ages by medieval glossators to refer to the *corpus iuris* (body of laws) compiled by the order of Emperor Justinian in the sixth century. Beginning in the sixteenth century, the metaphor was also used to denote the new body of canon law published by the Catholic Church in 1582 (*Corpus Iuris Canonici*).[31] To distinguish Justinian's compilation from

---

26 See Jeremy Bentham, *An Introduction to the Principles of Morals and Legislation* [1789] (Amherst, N.Y.: Prometheus Books, 1988), chap. 1, para. 2, p. 2.

27 Jeremy Bentham, "Essay on Political Tactics," in *The Works of Jeremy Bentham*, vol. 2, ed. John Bowring (Edinburgh: William Tait, 1843), 306.

28 See Hans Kelsen, *Pure Theory of Law*, trans. Max Knight (Berkeley: University of California Press, 1967), 1.

29 Kelsen's pyramid is not properly his but comes from his most distinguished disciple, Adolf Julius Merkl (1890–1970), the great architect of the normative hierarchical structure. Kelsen himself always recognized Merkl. See Hans Kelsen, "Selbstdarstellung" (1927), now reedited in *Veröffentlichte Schriften 1905–1910 und Selbstzeugnisse*, vol. 1 of *Hans Kelsen, Werke*, ed. Matthias Jestaedt (Tübingen: Mohr Siebeck, 2007), 23.

30 See Martijn W. Hesselink, "A Toolbox for European Judges," *European Law Journal* 17 (2011): 441–69.

31 Emperor Justinian himself gave no collective title to his compilation. He

the compilation of canon law, jurists usually termed the former *Corpus Iuris Civilis*, a name first given by Dionysius Gothofredus (Denis Godefroy) in his 1583 edition of the laws.[32]

In the medieval and early modern periods, the body metaphor also helped explain the figure and position of the European monarchs: the mystic fiction of the king's two bodies.[33] The king was simultaneously understood as a person and an office, that is, as a human being and an embodiment of the community of the kingdom. Recently, Lior Barshack has recovered the two-bodies doctrine to capture the transcendent dimension of constituents' power (which he identifies with sovereignty).[34]

In the domain of American legal philosophy, Lon Fuller's *Anatomy of Law* uses the body as a metaphor for characterizing "legal pathologies."[35] Like biological anatomy, the legal science, too, is concerned with the bodily structure of humans, animals, and other living organisms.

Many seminal contributions to Western legal culture also speak of the "spirit" of the law, not just as a metaphor but also as a reality with politico-legal implications. Among other works, classic masterpieces like Montesquieu's *The Spirit of the Laws* (1748),[36] Rudolph von Ihering's *The Spirit of Roman Law* (1852–1865),[37] and Roscoe Pound's *The Spirit of the Common*

---

mentioned only once the expression *corpus iuris* in the generic sense of body of law (CJ 5.13.1pr: *omne corpus iuris*).

32 See O. F. Robinson, T. D. Fergus, and W. M. Gordon, *European Legal History*, 3rd ed. (Oxford: Oxford University Press, 2000), 179.

33 See the classic book by Ernst Kantorovicz, *The King's Two Bodies: A Study in Mediaeval Political Theology* (Princeton, N.J.: Princeton University Press, 1957). On the absurdity of the "metaphaphisiological nonsense" of the king's two bodies doctrine, see Frederick Maitland, "The Corporation Sole," *Law Quarterly Review* 16 (1900): 335–54.

34 See Lior Barshack, "Constituent Power as Body: Outline of a Constitutional Theology," *University of Toronto Law Journal* 56 (2006): 185–222. According to Barshack, the collective sovereign body can operate both as a *communal body* (the collective body in the moment of its enactment by the group) or as a corporate body (absent body residing outside the group). Both notions—the communal body and the corporate body—refer to the group's imaginary collective body but take into consideration the different positions (and intensities) that the collective body occupies in relation to the group itself.

35 Lon L. Fuller, *Anatomy of the Law* (New York: Frederick A. Praeger, 1968).

36 Montesquieu, *The Spirit of the Laws*, trans. Thomas Nugent (New York: D. Appleton, 1900).

37 Rudolph von Ihering, *Geist des römischen Rechts auf den verschiedenen Stufen seiner Entwicklung*, 2 vols. (Leipzig: Breitkopf und Härtel, 1866). There is no English translation.

Law (1921)[38] argue from different perspectives that a spirit illuminating the whole legal body has animated diverse forms of government, constitutions, and legal systems. This spirit keeps legal bodies and political systems vital and dynamic. Moreover, it enables interactions between citizens in a globalized society with a vast diversity of legal systems.

The idea of the spirit of the law is also profoundly present in Eastern traditions and cultures. Here, the law is a wellspring for transcending personal consciousness and achieving the good.[39] The very essence of dharma, the hallmark of Hindu law, is immaterial; it is a concrete, preexistent archetype of behavior waiting to be fully realized. Dharma is the spirit of law insofar as it is a concept incarnated in rules, norms, or concrete behaviors, which become part of the body of law.

In our time, it has been the achievement of Alan Watson to lead as a general editor a series of books for the University of Georgia Press titled *The Spirit of Laws*, which covers different fields of the law. Monographs on the spirit of Roman law, Islamic law, classical canon law, Japanese law, traditional Chinese law, and biblical law have been written by distinguished scholars such as David J. Bederman, Calum Carmichael, John Owen Haley, R. H. Helmholz, Geoffrey MacCormack, Bernard G. Weiss, and Watson himself. These authors aim to illuminate the nature of legal systems throughout the world. They are concerned less with rules and regulations than with the law's fundamental principles, values, and attitudes toward the sources of law.

The Body-Soul-Spirit Metaphor in Saint Paul's Letters and Saint Edith Stein's Writings

I am using the biblical body-soul-spirit anthropological triad[40] in the light of the Christian tradition, mainly as it appears in the letters of Paul of Tarsus[41]

---

38   Roscoe Pound, *The Spirit of Common Law* (Boston: Marshall Jones, 1921).

39   See Donald R. Davis, Jr., *The Spirit of Hindu Law* (New York: Cambridge University Press, 2013), 1.

40   For an overview of biblical anthropology, see Joel B. Green, *Body, Soul, and Human Life: The Nature of Humanity in the Bible* (Grand Rapids, Mich.: Baker Academic, 2008).

41   On this Pauline anthropology, based on Hebraic and Hellenistic concepts, see, among others, Martin Meiser, "Some Facets of Pauline Anthropology—How Would a Greco-Roman Reader Understand It?" in *Anthropology in the New Testament and Its Ancient Context*, ed. Michael Labahn and Outi Lehtipuu (Leuven: Peeters, 2010), 55–85; George H. Van Kooten, "The Anthropological Trichotomy of Spirit, Soul and

and the writings of German philosopher and mystic Edith Stein.[42] Just as Paul often uses legal ideas as a metaphorical explanation for deep theological questions (the concept of divine filiation, for example),[43] I use Paul's theological ideas to understand the depths of legal systems.[44] And Edith Stein's approach offers one of the most brilliant and fruitful anthropological elaborations of the twentieth century.

The body-soul-spirit triad assumes the holistic unity of the human being, which is both corporeal and spiritual. It is a self-diversity in harmony, a fully integrated ontological whole in which distinct physical, philological, and spiritual functions are joined together. The unity of the human and spiritual dimensions is so profound that it forms a single totality: an embodied human existence. The whole of this living human being, not just a part of it, was created in the image of God and oriented toward a divine purpose.[45]

Saint Paul does not perceive the body as simply a material entity but as a living organism[46] composed of many members in one whole.[47] According to Saint Paul, the body is instrumental for glorifying God: "or do you not know

---

Body in Philo of Alexandria and Paul of Tarsus," in Labahn and Lehtipuu, *Anthropology in the New Testament and Its Ancient Context*, 87–119; and Michael Welker, "Flesh-Body-Heart-Soul-Spirit: Paul's Anthropology as an Interdisciplinary Bridge-Theory," in *The Depth of the Human Person: A Multidisciplinary Approach*, ed. Michael Welker (Grand Rapids, Mich.: Eerdmans, 2014), 45–57. For an overview, see *Dictionary of Paul and His Letters*, ed. Gerald F. Hawthorne, Ralph P. Martin, and Daniel G. Reid (Downers Grove, Ill.: InterVarsity, 1992).

42   See Edith Stein, *Finite and Eternal Being*, trans. Kurt F. Reinhardt (Washington, D.C.: ICS Publications, 2002). See also *Edith Stein, Philosophy of Psychology and the Humanities*, vol. 7 of *The Collected Works of Edith Stein*, trans. Mary Catharine Baseheart and Marianne Sawicki (Washington, D.C.: ICS Publications, 2000). On the body-soul-spirit triad in the writings of Edith Stein, see Marian Maskulak, *Edith Stein and the Body-Soul-Spirit at the Center of Holistic Formation* (New York: Peter Lang, 2007).

43   See Romans 8:17: "and if children, then heirs, heirs of God and joint-heirs with Christ—if we suffer with him so that we may also be glorified with him." (This and other biblical quotations are from the New Revised Standard Version, Catholic Edition [NRSV-CE]).

44   For a justification, see my argument in Rafael Domingo, "Theology and Jurisprudence: A Good Partnership?" *Journal of Law and Religion* 32, no. 1 (2017): 79–85.

45   Genesis 1:27.

46   For an overview on the idea of body in Saint Paul, see John A. T. Robinson, *The Body: A Study in Pauline Theology* (London: SCM, 1952).

47   1 Corinthians 12:20.

that your body is a temple of the Holy Spirit within you, which you have from God, and that you are not your own? You were bought with a price; therefore, glorify God in your body."[48] The human body is distinct from a merely physical thing because it is be-souled:[49] the soul animates the body. The corporeal and the spiritual elements meet and intertwine in the soul: "If one member suffers, all suffer together with it; if one member is honored, all rejoice together with it."[50]

Human beings are equivalent neither to their bodies nor to their souls. The human body is the ontological cause of individuation in the physical realm. Likewise, the human soul distinguishes individual beings from each other in the spiritual realm. What distinguishes the human body from pure matter is that the soul spiritualizes it. The human soul, unlike other animal souls, is spiritual. Yet the corporeal dimension embraces the internal and the external, the visible and the invisible. What distinguishes the human soul from a pure spirit is its embodiment.

Using biblical terms and Greek philosophical terminology, Paul distinguishes the soul (*psyche*) from the spirit (*pneuma*). He closes his first letter to the Thessalonians with a hope that God will sanctify his people wholly and an appeal that their "whole spirit [*pneuma*], soul [*psyche*] and body [*soma*] be kept blameless at the coming of our Lord Jesus Christ."[51] Paul's distinction does not imply that the human being is divided into three parts (by definition, the person's spiritual dimension is absolutely simple and, therefore, indivisible and nonextended). The body-soul-spirit tripartition should not mean that the human soul is a third reality interposed between two other realities (body and spirit) that can subsist without the soul and independently of one another. Rather, as Edith Stein affirms, "it is in the medium of the souls that spirituality and bodily sentient being meet and intertwine."[52]

---

48 1 Corinthians 6:19–20. See also 2 Corinthians 4:10–11: "We always carry around in our body the death of Jesus, so that the life of Jesus may also be revealed in our body. For we who are alive are always being given over to death for Jesus' sake, so that his life may also be revealed in our mortal body."

49 See Stein, *Finite and Eternal Being*, 366–70, esp. 367.

50 1 Corinthians 12:26.

51 1 Thessalonians 5:23. See also 1 Corinthians 7:34, where Saint Paul speaks of being devoted to the Lord in body (*soma*) and spirit (*pneuma*): "how to be holy in body and spirit." He also exhorts the Corinthians to purify themselves "from every defilement of flesh [*sarx*] and spirit [*pneuma*]" (2 Corinthians 7:1).

52 Stein, *Finite and Eternal Being*, 371.

According to Stein, the spirit is the higher aspect of the soul, an aspect specific to the human soul.[53] The distinction between the "body-bound being" and the "God-centered-being" can be found in the very essence of the soul, which unfolds by informing the body (living soul) and by communicating with God (life-giving spirit).[54] As long as the soul draws from its own source, it is possible to discover the image of the Father in the human soul; the image of the Son, the eternal and Incarnate Word, in the body; and the image of the Holy Spirit in the spiritual life (i.e., participation in the personal life of God).[55]

Since the loving God is triune (the Father is the Lover; the Son, the Beloved; and the Holy Spirit, the Love between them), all human beings, made in the image of God,[56] are triune too.[57] This triune self allows human beings to transcend both monistic and dualistic compositions. They are more than a body or a spirit (monism) and more than an incarnated spirit (dualism). Rather, the human being is a transcendent being called to union with God and, in God, with other spiritual beings. The spiritual aspect of the soul makes this communion possible. Owing to this communicative spiritual dimension of the soul, human beings can unite with God as a transcendent I who is also a We.[58] Spiritual communion draws human beings out of themselves toward God and thus also toward unity with all human beings.[59]

---

[53] In the same vein, John of the Cross uses the terms "soul" and "spirit" to distinguish the sensitive and lower element of the soul from the summit of the soul (spirit), which is specifically the capacity of communicating with God: "For the soul beholds itself converted into the immense fire of love that emanates from that enkindled point at the heart of the spirit" (John of the Cross, *Living Flame of Love*, 2.1).

[54] Stein, *Finite and Eternal Being*, 461.

[55] Stein, *Finite and Eternal Being*, 463.

[56] Genesis 1:27: "So God created mankind in his own image, in the image of God he created them; male and female he created them."

[57] Stein, *Finite and Eternal Being*, 464.

[58] See 1 John 4:16: "God is love, and he who abides in love abides in God, and God abides in him."

[59] In the same vein, see Benedict XVI, Encyclical Letter *Deus caritas est* (December 25, 2015), 14.

The Legal System as a Body-Soul-Spirit Totality

Since legal systems are a necessary human creation,[60] it is plausible to think that they reflect the image of the human being in some ways. There are many similarities between legal systems' structures and the human person's composition. First, a broad observation: the human body and the legal system are complex. Just as the human body comprises many interacting systems (cardiovascular, digestive, endocrine, muscular, reproductive, and so on), so, too, legal systems are made up of many interacting orders (constitutional, criminal, contract, administrative, procedure, and so on). Systems, either bodily or legal, do not work in isolation. Each system helps maintain itself, other systems, and the entire body. The health and well-being of the person depend upon the perfect interaction of all the body's systems, just as the well-being of the political community requires the appropriate exchange of all legal institutions, orders, and procedures.

This analogy extends to a more foundational level: the cell is the basic structural, functional, and biological unit of all living organisms, and therefore of the human body; in the same way, the norm is the basic structural, operational, and legal unit of the legal body. Likewise, as the cell is composed of atoms and subatomic or elementary particles, legal norms also have their logical elements (condition and consequence).[61] Just as quantum physics gives us information about the wave function of position, momentum, and other physical properties of a particle, the laws also provide hypothetical information about applying a norm, attaching a generally specified, obligatory consequence to a generally specified condition. And just as quantum physics suggests that retrocausality may be possible under certain circumstances,[62] legal science suggests that legal norms are retroactive in some cases.[63]

---

60   See Charles Louis de Secondat in Montesquieu, *The Spirit of the Laws*, vol. 1, 1: "Laws, in their most general signification, are the necessary relations arising from the nature of things."

61   On the structure of the norm, see Hans Kelsen, *General Theory of Norms*, trans. Michael Hartney (Oxford: Clarendon Press, 1991).

62   For an overview on quantum physics, see, among others, Kenneth W. Ford and Diane Goldstein, *The Quantum World: Quantum Physics for Everyone* (Cambridge, Mass.: Harvard University Press, 2005).

63   As an example, retroactive application makes sense in the area of commercial law, "when the benefits to be gained by replacing obsolete or undesirable practices with sound ones outweigh the minimal market disruption that may result." See David Frisch,

Like the human body, which can maintain a stable internal environment despite changes in external conditions (homeostasis), the legal system can maintain an internal coherence despite changes in social situations. Furthermore, living beings and legal systems are organized to preserve themselves as wholes. So even though bodily cells are constantly replaced, and legal norms (or even constitutions) are often changing, there is always an overarching capacity or power to preserve the human body or the legal system (the latter typically through constituent power).

Human bodies animated by souls are always alive and changing. The same is true of a legal system animated by a political community. Likewise, human beings are subject to death, and legal systems can also die and disappear. But just as ancestors can play a crucial role in sustaining a living community, laws no longer in force (such as ancient Roman laws) can continue to shape society as an enduring source of moral authority (*auctoritas*) without being politically coercive (*potestas*).[64]

To raise the analogy to a higher level, the law's soul is imperishable, just as the soul of a human being is immortal. As human souls provide life, meaning, reason, consciousness, and power to the body, the legal soul provides life, meaning, and power to the law. The soul of the law gives stability to the political community as a permanent community (*persona aeterna*). A legal system without a political community is like a body without a soul: it is dead. For this reason, when the political community rejects the legal system, that is, when the body of the law is separated from its soul, the legal system dies. As the human soul is incarnated in a body, the legal soul is incarnated in a legal body. As memory is a key feature of the human soul, culture is essential for the legal soul. Just as the highest aspect of the soul is the spirit, the spirit of the law is the highest element of the legal system. As the human spirit links human beings to God, the spirit of the law links human law to divine law. The human spirit and the spirit of the law are alike sources of freedom, value, meaning, and consciousness. Finally, just as the human spirit has some activity outside the body,[65] the concept of the spirit of the law motivates the search for universal common principles outside a concrete political body.

"Rational Retroactivity in a Commercial Context," *Alabama Law Review* 58 (2007): 765–809, at 809.

64   On the Roman distinction between *auctoritas* and *potestas*, see chapter 13 in this volume. See also Álvaro d'Ors, *Derecho privado romano* (10th ed., Pamplona: Eunsa, 2004), sect. 8 and bibliography; Rafael Domingo, *Auctoritas* (Barcelona: Ariel, 1999).

65   See 2 Corinthians 12:1.

New Applications of the Body-Soul-Spirit Metaphor in the Legal Realm

Using the metaphor fleshed out above, I want to suggest some of its implications in different realms of the law.

A Living Constitution

The body-soul-spirit metaphor suggests that the legal system, particularly the constitution, should be considered a living organism, not merely a legal document. Constitutions are not "dead constitutions," as some originalist legal scholars[66] claim: "The Constitution that I interpret and apply"—Antonin Scalia vigorously affirmed—"is not living but dead, or as I prefer to call it, enduring. It means today not what current society, much less the court, thinks it ought to mean, but what it meant when it was adopted."[67] Paraphrasing (and contradicting) Scalia, I would argue the opposite: the Constitution we interpret and apply is not dead but living. It means today *not only* what it meant when the text's framers adopted it, but also what the people—the true soul of the Constitution—have thought that it means. The people's ongoing constitutional understanding and practice must matter.

When a constitution is in force, it is alive, and new meanings flow. Originalism makes sense only if it becomes a *living originalism*, as Jack M. Balkin[68] argues: an originalism free of contradictions between the text's original meaning and its meaning for the people today. Scalia's vision would be coherent only if it applied to a constitution no longer in force—thus, following our metaphor, one whose constitutional body—the *constitutional corpse*—had been separated from its soul. This would indeed be a dead constitution. A constitution is in force, however, only and precisely when

---

66 For an overview on originalism, see Steve G. Calabresi, ed., *Originalism: A Quarter Century of Debate* (Washington, D.C.: Regnery Publishing, 2007); John O. McGinnis and Michael B. Rappaport, *Originalism and the Good Constitution* (Cambridge, Mass.: Harvard University Press, 2013); Frank Cross, *The Failed Promise of Originalism* (Stanford, Calif.: Stanford University Press, 2013); and Patrick J. Charles, *Historicism, Originalism, and the Constitution: The Use and Abuse of the Past in American Jurisprudence* (Oxford: Oxford University Press, 2014).

67 Antonin Scalia, "God's Justice and Ours," *Law and Justice: Christian Law Review* 156 (2006): 3–10, at 3.

68 See Jack M. Balkin, *Living Originalism* (Cambridge, Mass.: The Belknap Press of Harvard University Press, 2011).

it is animated by a soul. And where there is a soul, there is life; where life, meaning; and where meaning, interpretation. The soul of a democratic legal system is the people of the political community, not the framers of the constitution, the judges, or the lawgivers. It is the people who animate the legal body. It is the people who experience the living body of laws. To interpret the constitution is precisely to experience the constitutional living body. Interpretation searches for a good harmony between the legal soul and the legal body. The body itself limits the interpreting soul. If, while interpreting, the soul does not consider the nature of the body (a failure we might describe as legal pragmatism), a mismatch between soul and body occurs, and the legal system falls ill.

Since both the soul (the people) and the body of laws are constantly in flux, the quest for harmony between them is a permanent task. What was required for harmony yesterday may not be what is needed today: body and soul interact rhythmically. For this reason, harmony cannot be found *exclusively* in the vision and writings of the framers of a constitution. The framers are (or were) the creators of the constitution, but they are not the soul of it, only a part of it, as members of the people, and, therefore they cannot be the text's exclusive interpreters. In its own legal body, the political community recognizes the mark of its founders. Still, the body does not belong to the founders, only to the political community as a whole.

As a body, the legal system should follow the dictates of its soul. As a genuine soul, only the people can shape their changing body of laws. In this sense, law is deeply political.[69] Only a balanced body-soul dynamic can ensure harmonious evolution in legal systems. The process by which American courts applied select provisions of the Bill of Rights to the states (the so-called incorporation doctrine) is a good example of harmonious body-soul interaction and evolution: the soul of the law animates the whole body of laws, not just parts of it. In originalism, the body prevails over the soul; in legal pragmatism, the soul forgets that it is embodied. In a reasonable theory of interpretation, the soul remains superior to the body but is nevertheless limited by the body. In other words, the spirit triumphs over the letter of the law but is also confined by it.[70]

---

69 In the same vein, see Ronald Dworkin, *A Matter of Principle* (Cambridge, Mass.: Harvard University Press, 2000), 146.

70 This idea is at the heart of the Western legal tradition. In 93 BCE, the famous Roman jurist Quintus Mucius Scevola confronted his former colleague Lucius

The Use of Foreign Law

In some recent cases, the U.S. Supreme Court's use of foreign law has triggered an interesting debate about whether foreign law should be considered in constitutional interpretation.[71] From the perspective of the body-soul-spirit metaphor, international law (or supranational law) is part of the body of laws of any country.[72] International legal commitments bind both internationally and domestically, so international law is as directly applicable as national law. Yet its legitimacy is entirely different from that of foreign law because foreign law is not part of the body of law of a country. Its use demands justification to not offend against democratic values or self-governance. So, should a government take foreign law into consideration? According to our metaphor, the answer is yes, but only provided that we distinguish the body of foreign law from the spirit of foreign law.

All legal systems can learn from other legal systems. A comparative perspective always has value. It provides good information for decision-making processes. A country's body of law may even genealogically depend on another country's body of law (e.g., the French Civil Code was the North Star for Latin American codification, as the German Civil Code was for the Japanese Civil Code). In this sense, foreign law is natural to a country's legal interpretation in its continued emulation of that law, yet this is the full extent of foreign law's applicability. The body of law of a foreign legal

---

Licinius Crassus, the greatest orator of his time, in the *causa Curiana* (Cicero, *De oratore* 1.180–81). Scevola defended the strict literal interpretation of the wording of a will (the body prevails over the soul) against the opinion of Crassus, who insisted that the will (body) should be interpreted according to the testator's intention (soul) based on the ordinary use of language (*sermo communis*) and on equity. Crassus persuaded the court in favor of his client Manius Curius. On the *causa Curiana*, see Reinhard Zimmermann, *The Law of Obligations: Roman Foundations of the Civilian Tradition* (Oxford: Oxford University Press, 1996), 625–35.

71   Bibliographies abound. For an overview of the different arguments, see Ganesh Sitaraman, "The Use and Abuse of Foreign Law in Constitutional Interpretation," *Harvard Journal of Law and Public Policy* 32 (2009): 653–93. See also Mark Tushnet, "When Is Knowing Less Better than Knowing More? Unpacking the Controversy over Supreme Court Reference to Non-US Law," *Minnesota Law Review* 90 (2006): 1275–1302; Jeremy Waldron, *"Partly Laws Common to All Mankind": Foreign Laws in American Courts* (New Haven, Conn.: Yale University Press, 2012).

72   See Harold Hongju Koh, "International Law as Part of Our Law," *American Journal of International Law* 43 (2004): 43–57.

system can be a source of inspiration in the lawmaking process of a country or even in its legal interpretation, but foreign law can never be directly applied in a national government. Serious methodological concerns would arise in that scenario because two different bodies, the body of foreign law and the body of national law, cannot occupy the same space. The Chilean Code is not the French Civil Code, and the Japanese Civil Code is not the German Civil Code. This shows that bodies of laws are inevitably limited by their own jurisdiction, and that foreign law is not essential to rational decision-making, even if it can exert more general influence.

Legal systems, however, can share the same spirit, because the heart of the law extends beyond jurisdictions. It is metajurisdictional, that is, law that is not of any particular jurisdiction.[73] Jurisdiction, like matter, limits the application of bodies of law but not the spirit of the law. To return to my earlier argument, if human beings bear the image of God,[74] and if everything they create reflects God's image by extension, then all legal systems must share some common spirit. In turn, some legal principles must be somehow common. And when the principles are to some extent common, so must the rules be somewhat similar. These common principles are suggested by some of the profound structural similarities we can easily find even among legal bodies that are not genealogically or culturally connected. Fundamental human rights, principles like the rule of law and equal protection of the law, and standard legal rules such as "agreements must be kept" and "no punishment without a trial," among others, seem universal. They share the same spirit.

Endorsing the Emerging Global Law

The body-soul-spirit metaphor helps explain the differences between the normative paradigm of modern international law and the emerging paradigm of global law.[75] Although both legal paradigms share some purposes (peace and security), their approaches are different. The paradigm of modern international law grounds legal obligation in the principles of nation-states' self-interest and mutual consent (a primary source of obligation in this

---

73 In this vein, see Waldron, "*Partly Laws Common to All Mankind*," 3.
74 Genesis 1:27.
75 See Rafael Domingo, *The New Global Law* (New York: Cambridge University Press, 2010).

sphere). The paradigm of global law, however, grounds legal obligation in the principles of solidarity among peoples and in necessity.[76] Following our metaphor, we can say that international law relies upon the body and soul of law without considering the law's communicative spirit. By contrast, global law operates on that spirit, moving gradually to the soul and body.

Let me explain this distinction further. The paradigm of international law is rooted in the view that each sovereign nation should serve its national self-interest; in short, the soul should exclusively take care of its own body. A country should sign or ratify a treaty with single-minded regard to its own advantage. Only when there is a common interest between and among sovereign nations—that is, only when two or more national self-interests coincide—does it make sense for countries to keep an agreement because it is beneficial for all the parties to the agreement. As an example, the United States has not ratified many critical international treaties: the Kyoto Protocol (1997), the Ottawa Treaty (1997), the Rome Statute of the International Criminal Court (1998), the Optional Protocol to the Convention against Torture (2002), the International Convention for the Protection of All Persons from Enforced Disappearance (2006), the Convention on the Rights of Persons with Disabilities (2007), and the Convention on Cluster Munitions (2008), among others.[77]

Global law, by contrast, is paradigmatically committed to solidarity. It focuses on the spirit of the law, which is communicative, solidary, in character. Unlike international law, global law recognizes a more radical spiritual communion among all human beings, transcending whatever self-interest sovereign states may have and opening doors to a genuinely solidary unity. Global solidarity offers a new horizon that undercuts the importance of national self-interest and moves beyond the national-international dichotomy. Sovereign states can live in solidarity as a matter of course, and this solidarity is in some sense metalegal, that is, it is not a commitment derived from the strict application of the international paradigm, which is partly why international law is gradually changing to the paradigm of global law and encouraging solidarity.

---

76   See Rafael Domingo, "The New Global Human Community," *Chicago Journal of International Law* 12, no. 2 (2012): 563–87.

77   For treaties in force in the United States, see the documentation provided by the U.S. Department of State, http://www.state.gov/s/l/treaty/tif/index.htm.

The Integrity of Law

In legal theory, the body-soul-spirit metaphor supports integrating values, principles, and moral rights, on one hand, with rules, policies, and legal rights on the other. In some sense, the metaphor favors Ronald Dworkin's doctrine of law as integrity[78] and his critique of legal positivism.[79] Principles, values, and moral rights are an expression of the soul of the legal system; rules, policies, and legal rights reflect the legal body. The spiritual and corporeal domains of a legal system are required for its coherence, and they are completely interrelated. They need each other because they must express a single vision of justice.[80] Yet they operate differently. In the corporeal realm, decision-making procedures often leave no room for debate (for example, when a rule establishes that the national parliament is composed of 150 members). In the spiritual realm of law, however, there are no procedures or rules. Hence, principles and values require more subtle justification than rules and procedures because they cannot be applied in an all-or-nothing way.

Legal interpretation tries to preserve the integrity[81] of the whole legal system by harmonizing the different principles and rules that operate in the legal realm. As part of the body of laws, the rules, legal rights, and policies can clash, like different objects trying to occupy the same space.[82] As an expression of the spirit of law, however, principles, values, and moral rights cannot conflict (the spirit does not occupy space), but they should cohere as well as possible with the features of the body of law.

---

78 See Dworkin, *Law's Empire*, in which he defends the prominent role of interpretation in judgments along with the view that judges interpret the law in terms of consistent moral principles, especially justice and fairness.

79 See Ronald Dworkin, *Taking Rights Seriously: New Impression with a Reply to Critics* (London: Duckworth, 2005); Dworkin, *A Matter of Principle*, 119–45. For an overview on Dworkin's approach to the law, see Stephen Guest, Ronald Dworkin, 3rd ed. (Stanford, Calif.: Stanford University Press, 2013); Wilfrid J. Waluchow and Stefan Sciaraffa, eds, *The Legacy of Ronald Dworkin* (Oxford: Oxford University Press, 2016).

80 Dworkin, *Law's Empire*, 134.

81 On the idea of integrity and its relation to law, see Dworkin, *Law's Empire*, 176–275.

82 Dworkin's approach is different. See Dworkin, *Taking Rights Seriously*, 22–28, 71–80, 90–100.

Following and corroborating Dworkin's terminology and approach, we can say that hard cases[83]—cases lacking a result clearly determined by relevant rules and procedures—are not irresolvable cases. They should be resolved not through any exercise of discretion, as legal positivists affirm, but through applying principles.[84] Lawyers, policymakers, and judges can always find principles to ground case outcomes, since principles are a matter of human discovery, not a human creation. Principles operate in the spiritual realm, and the spirit is overwhelming.

Supporting an Integrative Jurisprudence

In some sense, the body-soul-spirit metaphor supports the idea of an "integrative jurisprudence," if I may use the expression coined and developed by Harold Berman.[85] According to Berman, integrative jurisprudence combines the approaches and doctrines of three classical schools of jurisprudence: legal positivism, natural law, and the German Historical School.[86]

Following our body-soul-spirit metaphor, we can say that each school has isolated one of the metaphor's three components. Legal positivism considers the law as a set of norms and rules created by the nation-state. It focuses on the body of law, neglecting the law's soul and spirit. The German Historical School holds that the law is only a product of a country's national character. It focuses on the soul of each legal system, the national soul (*Volksgeist*), neglecting the body of law and the spirit (the communicative aspect of the soul). Natural law theory holds that legal norms approved by political authorities that contravene the most basic principles of justice are not law in essence. These theorists focus on the spirit of the law, neglecting the body of law and the national soul. These three classical schools, then, each make essential contributions to law and legal science, but they become reductionist when they accentuate one element of legal systems without integrating the others.

---

83 On hard cases, Dworkin, *Taking Rights Seriously*, 81–130.
84 Dworkin, *A Matter of Principle*.
85 Harold J. Berman, *Faith and Order: The Reconciliation of Law and Religion* (Grand Rapids, Mich.: Eerdmans, 1993; reprint, 2000), 289–310.
86 For an excellent overview of the three schools, see John Maurice Kelly, *A Short History of Western Legal Theory* (Oxford: Clarendon Press, 1999), 203–325.

Reconciliation between Rational and Suprarational Law

The body-soul-spirit metaphor supports reconciliation between rational (or human) law and suprarational (or divine) law.[87] Suprarational law is that law operating in the spiritual dimension of the human person. It is not properly a part of the body of law unless it is specifically recognized as such. Suprarational law is ontologically spiritual, different from rational law, but it is still genuine law insofar as it tries to achieve justice by applying a system of binding rules. Suprarational law is (believed to be) the discovery of the human spirit, not a human invention. All forms of revealed law (for instance Jewish law, Christian law, and Islamic law) are expressions of suprarational law. In addition, the very law of one's conscience (*lex conscientiae*)—considered not as a mere subjective wish or desire but as the perceptible presence in human beings of a transcendent, objective law (reflected in the innate sense of justice we have)—could be regarded as a source of private suprarational law.[88]

Suprarational law might influence legal systems by illumination, attraction, and other modalities of causality[89] or by moral authority (*auctoritas*), but not by coercive power (*potestas*). It operates within the secular legal system as a value, as a source of transcendent wisdom and knowledge. It is an expression of the priority of the spirit over the body and the communion of the human spirit with the Spirit of God. By transcending legality (the body of laws), suprarational law protects secular legal systems from the virus of legalism.[90]

Conclusion

Metaphors are a form of conceptualization and reasoning, and they have a proper place in the legal realm. They have been at the heart of Western legal culture since its foundation and allow us to understand partially what we

---

87 See the excellent approach to this concept by Rémi Brague, *The Law of God: The Philosophical History of an Idea*, trans. Lydia G. Cochrane (Chicago: University of Chicago Press, 2007), esp. 39–82.

88 See Rafael Domingo, *God and the Secular Legal System* (New York: Cambridge University Press, 2016), 122–65.

89 For further discussion of the relation between divine law and practice, see Brague, *The Law of God*, 264.

90 John Witte, Jr., introduction, in *Christianity and Human Rights*, ed. John Witte, Jr., and Frank S. Alexander (Cambridge: Cambridge University Press, 2010), 14. In a similar way, see Berman, *Faith and Order*, xi.

cannot understand totally. Thus, all integrative frameworks are metaphorical. Drawing upon Saint Paul's letters and Edith Stein's writings, I have offered the triad of body, soul, and spirit as instrumental to understanding the most profound internal and external connections of legal systems. Like the human being, the law is not only corporeal but also spiritual, and the spirit of the law is essentially communicative and solidary, like the Spirit of God.

Legal systems are a necessary human creation, and by extension, they reflect the intrinsic unity of the human being's body, soul, and spirit. With this metaphor, I have tried to challenge legal reductionism and, consequently, legal isolation, and have argued for respect for the law as a whole. Just as the soul must respect the body, the political community must respect its body of laws. In some cases, the metaphor also supports the use of foreign law by national legal systems, owing to the law's essential communicative spirit. The spirit of the law is metajurisdictional, unlike bodies of rules, and this reality, in turn, makes it possible to consider a partly universal common law. The metaphor also encourages us to see constitutions as living documents and the legal system as a living entity; to recognize the goodness of an emerging global law founded on solidarity and not the self-interest of nation-states; and to seek reconciliation between law—the primary instrument of justice in human societies—and love, and a reasonable interaction between human (rational) law and suprarational (divine) law. In short, the body-soul-spirit metaphor offers a powerful antidote to legal reductionism.

CHAPTER 3

RECOVERING GOD FOR SECULAR LEGAL SYSTEMS

IN THIS CHAPTER, I OFFER a theistically oriented conception of secular legal systems, arguing that secular legal reasoning should be open to God to protect believers and nonbelievers. Legal systems of Western democracies can acknowledge God without sacrificing liberal democratic principles because the recognition of God does not preclude the foundational autonomy of secular legal systems. The most profound connections between God and the secular legal system lie outside legal systems but inside the human person, who, paradoxically, is at the center of the secular legal system.

I refer to God as a unique and infinite Supreme Being, creator of the universe and source of morality. God is someone, not just something. This is the idea of God as understood by the Abrahamic religions, other forms of transcendent monotheism, and even some deism, and despite the increasing worldwide diversity of views toward God, this conception of God remains the most popular.[1] My argument is compatible with any other idea of God or gods, but because Western legal systems have been established and developed for centuries based on this idea of God, this is the conception that should be central to the discussion.

---

* The original version of this essay appears in Rafael Domingo, "The Metalegal God," *Ecclesiastical Law Journal* 16, no. 1 (2014): 147–67.

1 See John Micklethwait and Adrian Wooldridge, *God Is Back: How the Global Revival of Faith Is Changing the World* (New York: Penguin Books, 2009), esp. 12–19.

Should secular legal systems renounce any idea of God to preserve their hallmark secularity? My response is no. The compelling autonomy of legal sources from revelation and religious authorities does not mean that secular legal systems should therefore marginalize God altogether. Such autonomy does not make God an inadmissible or deficient legal discourse. Using the famous American expression, we can say God is on both sides of the "wall of separation." The wall of separation, after all, divides institutions and ideas, church and state, religion and law, but not human beings, let alone God. Human beings can be and should be on both sides of the wall because God is neither a member of the political community nor the religious community. God is outside both but illuminates both. God embraces and illuminates all kinds of human communities, not just religious communities.

Secular legal systems constitute a good framework for establishing a society in which believers and nonbelievers can live together, in peace, under equal conditions, and share rational-legal arguments—provided that these arguments are open to God. The American legal experience has pride of place in my argument because the topic of God's relation to the legal system has been discussed at great length in this country for many years.[2] Moreover, on this issue, the world seems to be moving decisively in the American direction rather than the European.[3] The expression "under God" in the Pledge of Allegiance and, in general, the features of America's "ceremonial deism" (prayers at presidential inaugurations, presidential addresses invoking the name of God, the invocation of God proper to judicial proceedings, the national motto "In God We Trust") have sparked an interesting academic debate about the invocation of the name of God, which has been a helpful debate for the development of the arguments in this chapter.[4]

---

2   For an overview, see John Witte, Jr., Joel A. Nichols, and Richard W. Garnett, *Religion and the American Constitutional Experiment*, 5th ed. (Oxford: Oxford University Press, 2022), 35–58. For a European approach to the topic, see Jan Schmidt, *Religion, Gott, Verfassung. Der Religions- und Gottesbezug in der Verfassung pluralistischer Gesellschaften* (Frankfurt: Peter Lang, 2010), esp. 72–94; Norman Doe, *Law and Religion in Europe: A Comparative Introduction* (Oxford: Oxford University Press, 2011); and Lorenzo Zucca, *A Secular Europe: Law and Religion in the European Constitutional Landscape* (Oxford: Oxford University Press, 2013).
3   In the same vein, see Micklethwait and Wooldridge, *God Is Back*, 25.
4   About the concept of ceremonial deism, see Steven B. Epstein, "Rethinking the Constitutionality of Ceremonial Deism," *Columbia Law Review* 96 (1996): 2083–174, esp. 2094–96. More recently, see Martha Nussbaum, *Liberty of Conscience: In Defense of*

William O. Douglas's famous statement that "we are a religious people whose institutions presuppose a Supreme Being"[5] can be updated, in my opinion, to read, "We are now a religious and nonreligious people whose institutions presuppose a Supreme Being," or at least "whose institutions are open to a Supreme Being." It would be a mistake, however, to say that we are a people whose institutions no longer presuppose a Supreme Being, let alone a people whose institutions should be closed to a Supreme Being. I agreed with Justice Antonin Scalia when he affirmed that the "governmental invocation of God is not an establishment."[6] The fact that the number of unbelievers is increasing does not justify changing our institutions to the point of deleting any trace of God, but it does suggest a more open interpretation of institutions so that the rights of both believers and nonbelievers can be equally protected by law.

Secular Legal Systems: "Without Religion but Not without God"

The legal distinction between God and religion should constitute a salient feature of secular legal systems. Although the idea of God remains at the heart of the idea of religion, both ideas differentially affect legal systems, just as they do other domains of human knowledge and understanding. God's existence does not evidentially depend on religion, and some religions do not evidentially depend on the existence of God. Moreover, there is no need in God's nature that is not satisfied by God himself. Therefore, God should not be related to the legal system through religion. Just as it makes sense to talk

---

America's Tradition of Religious Equality (New York: Basic Books, 2008), esp. 265–72. For the Continental Congress's practice of invoking the name of God, see Derek H. Davis "The Continental Congress and Emerging Ideas of Church-State Separation," in *No Establishment of Religion: America's Original Contribution to Religious Liberty*, ed. T. Jeremy Gunn and John Witte, Jr. (Oxford: Oxford University Press, 2012), 180–207, esp. 183–86.

    5   *Zorach v. Clauson*, 343 U.S. 36 (1952) at 313. In the same vein, see *Abington School District v. Schempp*, 374 U.S. 203, 213 (1963): "The fact that the Founding Fathers believed devoutly that there was a God and that the unalienable rights of man were rooted in Him is clearly evidenced in their writings, from the Mayflower Compact to the Constitution itself."

    6   Antonin Scalia, Dissenting, *McCreary County v. American Civil Liberties Union of Kentucky*, 545 U.S. 16 (2005).

about God without religion and religion without God, as in the sort of "religious atheism" that Ronald Dworkin defends in his posthumous book,[7] it also makes sense to talk about legal systems with or without religion and with or without God. A legal system with an established theistic religion is a system with God and with religion; one with an established nontheistic religion has religion but not God. A secular legal system (the sort addressed here) can be with God but without religion, or without religion and without God (in other words, an atheist legal system, to which my argument is opposed).

Religion and belief in God are very close in practice, but God and religion are ontologically different. Thus, a political community may recognize God without having or imposing uniformity of religion,[8] and legal systems should take into account this essential difference. God is the subject; religion, by contrast, is the object. God is a person (*persona*); religion is a thing (*res*). God is the Supreme Being and Creator. Religion, however, is (in general terms) a path to God or to resolving ultimate questions and concerns about human existence.[9] Using Émile Durkheim's famous definition in his seminal book *The Elementary Forms of Religious Life*, we can say that religion is "a unified system of beliefs and practices relative to sacred things ..., that unite its adherents in a single moral community called a church."[10] Belief in God is insufficient to capture the thousands of religious beliefs, creeds, and experiences worldwide. On the other hand, to have and practice a religion, in the broadest legal sense, is insufficient to capture the idea of God entirely. Indeed, many religions do not recognize God.

God embraces the whole reality of human persons in their individual, social, and transcendent dimensions; religion, however, does not. If God exists, all dimensions of human life should be ordered according to God: the legal, the social, the political, and the spiritual. However, not all dimensions of human life should be ordered according to religion. There are many

---

7   See Ronald Dworkin, *Religion without God* (Cambridge, Mass.: Harvard University Press, 2013). See also a critique of this book in chapter 5 of this volume.

8   In this vein, see Roger Williams, "The Bloody Tenant of Persecution for Cause of Conscience" (1644), in *On Religious Liberty: Selections from the Works of Roger Williams*, ed. James Calvin Davis (Cambridge, Mass.: The Belknap Press of Harvard University Press, 2008), 87.

9   For a legal concept of religion, see Kent Greenawalt, *Religion and the Constitution*, vol. 1, *Free Exercise and Fairness* (Princeton, N.J.: Princeton University Press, 2006), 124–56.

10   Émile Durkheim, *The Elementary Forms of Religious Life* (Oxford: Oxford University Press, 2001), 46.

aspects of human life and understanding that lie outside religion: religion is just one expression of human flourishing. It is a very comprehensive and demanding human expression, but it does not necessarily impact everything in life, as God does. Politics is not religion. Legal reasoning is not religious reason. However, neither politics nor legality escape God. This might seem like a paradox, but it is not. On one hand, secular legal systems should by definition be totally separate from religion, but not from God. On the other hand, secular legal systems, although separated from religion, should regulate religious issues (though they cannot, of course, "regulate" God).

The existence of God is independent of human belief and adherence. Thus, God's existence affects not just believers in God but also nonbelievers. Unlike the existence of God, religion is limited to affecting (directly) religious persons and communities. There is no religion without religious people. Religion may become extinct, at least theoretically, and many religions have, but the extinction of religion would not entail the death of God.

The legal confusion between God and religion ultimately leads either to political atheism or to religious fundamentalism. Indeed, the rejection of God in political life, as if God were a religious issue, leads to a kind of political atheism, which makes it hard to protect believers in God. On the other hand, the imposition of God in political life through religion leads to religious fundamentalism, that is, to a political framework unable to establish the dualistic structure required in all political communities to differentiate religion and politics.

Religion is constrained by the secular legal system, since it can be regulated within limits by the latter, but God is not under legal systems, since legal systems aim at protecting human persons, not God. If God is infinite and utterly self-sufficient, God needs no legal protection. Secular legal systems are not under religion since religion cannot regulate legal systems, but they are "under God" in the deepest sense, in that God supports and illuminates all human creations and hence all legal systems. If God is really God, nothing escapes him. Moreover, if the end of legal systems is the protection of the human person, individually and socially, and the human person is a creature, then legal systems cannot close the door to the Creator if they hope to fully protect the human person as a whole and not just as a subject of the legal system.

The legal recognition of God that I am talking about does not require either an act of faith—that is, a free and voluntary personal or communitarian response to God—or scientific evidence for the existence of God. A political community can recognize God as a cultural phenomenon with some legal implications, that is, as a metalegal concept, as we shall see, without imposing any act of faith. As Justice Scalia rightly said, referring to the American religious experience: "Historical practices thus demonstrate that there is a distance between the acknowledgment of a single Creator and the establishment of a religion."[11]

Recognizing God does not entail believing in God or proving God's existence. This might raise a question: How can a legal system recognize God without first proving God's existence? Legal systems, however, have the legal tools to do it. As is well known, legal systems use legal fictions, presumptions, and other legal constructions and tools to identify subjects and objects of legal protection. The key to recognition by a legal system is not scientific evidence of someone or something's physical existence but the legal system's ability to identify the entity in question. Thus, the legal systems of most countries can and do presume the *death* of missing persons and validate the purchase and sale of future things, the unborn heir, and the so-called *cautio damni infecti* to prevent potential damages. Legal systems require a minimum of information about the missing person, the thing to be sold, and so on, but not scientific evidence of existence. Since millions of people believe in God as a Supreme Being, and since God is unique, the legal system can identify God. Moreover, there is no scientific evidence that God does not exist, nor will there be, unless robust atheistic interpretations of the universe are (erroneously) imposed.[12] Robert Spitzer, in his book on new evidence for the existence of God, argues that humanity has never had such a rational foundation for faith as we now have.[13] He also argues that quantum theory

---

11 Antonin Scalia, Dissenting, *McCreary County v. American Civil Liberties Union of Kentucky*, 545 U.S.10 (2005).

12 In the same vein, see Benedict XVI, *Christianity and the Crisis of Cultures* (San Francisco: Ignatius Press, 2006), 85. See also John Polkinghorne, *Quantum Physics and Theology: An Unexpected Kinship* (New Haven, Conn.: Yale University Press, 2008).

13 Robert J. Spitzer, *New Proofs for the Existence of God: Contributions of Contemporary Physics and Philosophy* (Grand Rapids, Mich.: Eerdmans, 2010). On Pope Benedict's interest in this debate as a young Joseph Ratzinger, influenced by the German physicist and philosopher Aloys Wenzl, see Peter Seewald, *Benedict XVI: A Life*, vol. 1, *Youth in Nazi Germany to the Second Vatican Council 1927–1965*, trans. Linah Livingston (Oxford: Bloomsbury Continuum, 2020), 187–90.

has expanded ontological horizons by forcing us to confront nonlocality and information fields, which have yielded new evidence for nonmaterial but informational dimensions of physical reality.

Considering God as a Supreme Being distinct from religion allows us to address the issue of religious neutrality in a different way from how it is currently addressed.[14] Neutrality, in the sense of impartiality, calls for diversity, so a legal system can be neutral or impartial in religious issues because there are many religions. Still, it cannot be neutral or impartial toward God, at least about the personal God we are talking about, because God is unique. Neutrality requires, by definition, at least two positive elements. The dilemma of "to be or not be"—the alternative of affirming or denying—is insufficient for neutrality because it lacks diversity.[15] So a legal system can be neutral in religious issues just as between theistic and nontheistic religions because these are two different kinds of religions. Still, it cannot be neutral between the existence or nonexistence of God. Neutrality can equally treat believers and nonbelievers in God, but not God and God's absence.

For believers and nonbelievers in God to receive equal treatment under the law, a legal system should be open to God. Otherwise, it treats believers in God as nonbelievers, which would be discriminatory. To regard believers as if they were nonbelievers promotes uniformity but not genuinely equal treatment. (It would be like a legal system that, by not recognizing marriage, treated both married and single people as if they were single.) If a legal system defends freedom of religion, and some religions are theistic, the system should recognize God in some way. Otherwise, it treats theistic religions as nontheistic, which would mean unequal treatment. This is not religious neutrality.[16] Rather, it is just a sort of discrimination in favor of nontheistic religious people.

That the existence of God affects the entire life of believers and nonbelievers is not a reason to deny God in order to keep God from being imposed

14   See, more recently, Andrew Koppelman, *Defending American Religious Neutrality* (Cambridge, Mass.: Harvard University Press, 2013), 15–45.
15   For more about this argument, see Rafael Domingo, "A Right to Religious and Moral Freedom? A Response to Michael Perry," *International Journal of Constitutional Law* 12, no. 1 (2014): 226–47.
16   For a defense of the American specification of religious neutrality, see Koppelman, *Defending American Religious Neutrality*, esp. 15–44; Kathleen A. Brady, *The Distinctiveness of Religion in American Law: Rethinking Religion Clause Jurisprudence* (Cambridge: Cambridge University Press, 2015).

on nonbelievers. The God recognized by legal systems does not generate any legal obligations for believers and nonbelievers beyond the duty of respect and recognition. Admittedly, to forcibly assimilate nonbelievers into believers would impose a sort of uniformity, contrary to equal treatment. The legal recognition of God, however, in no way implicitly treats nonbelievers as believers, because the legal recognition of God does not require an act of faith by anyone. In no case is it an imposition—that would be against the very nature of the secular legal system.

Singling out God does not require the legal system to make any statement about the existence of God, let alone about supposed proofs for the existence of God—that is, converging and convincing arguments for the truth of God's existence. Legal recognition of God is not a scientific, philosophical, or theological recognition of God, and legal systems have neither the power nor the tools to produce that. It is not their business, but it is the business of a secular legal system to protect religious neutrality. Therefore, the best way, perhaps the only way, to protect theists and nontheists alike is to single out God as a metalegal concept, as I shall explain.

To put too much emphasis on religious neutrality can be unfair, especially if one compares two ontologically different realities, such as God and religion. Statements about God are not subject to a similar analysis as statements about religion, so the fact that there are theistic and nontheistic religions does not mean that God cannot be singled out by a legal system, let alone that the name of God appearing in state constitutions should have only a "historical significance" without representing "a present and substantial doctrinal statement."[17]

God as a Metalegal Concept

Metalegal concepts come from outside the legal dimension but operate in it. They support and illuminate legal systems because they link them with other dimensions of human knowledge and understanding. They are also sources of legal value. Contracts, presumptions, legal procedures, mortgages, and international treaties are legal concepts, that is, legal creations or tools of legal systems. They are, therefore, not metalegal concepts. An example of a metalegal concept is marriage. Indeed, the concept of marriage is not

---

17 See Kent Greenawalt, *Religion and the Constitution*, vol. 2, *Establishment and Fairness* (Princeton, N.J.: Princeton University Press, 2008), 65n27.

a legal creation. It is a social, anthropological, religious, and cultural concept that affects human beings, not just legal subjects. Marriage existed before the creation of legal systems. On the other hand, the legal implications of marriage are obvious, not just in family law but also in tax law, labor law, and even constitutional law and international law. Freedom, dignity, religion, and the human person are other examples of metalegal concepts. They are primarily not legal concepts, but they significantly shape the boundaries of legal systems and the legal dimension as such.

Some metalegal concepts (marriage, for instance) are so critical for legal systems that they require specific legal definitions, but those specific definitions should not necessarily coincide with their metalegal definitions; rather, they should translate into legal standards the essence of the meaning of metalegal concepts. Legal definitions should express the hallmark of the metalegal concept. It would be nonsense to talk about legal marriage as a concept contrary to the metalegal concept of marriage—for instance, to classify as a legal marriage the cohabitation of a person with her pet. Religion, dignity, and freedom are metalegal concepts that previously lacked specific legal definitions but now are sometimes so defined. They should be legally interpreted insofar as they are frequently used in legal documents, judicial decisions, etc.

When a legal system treats metalegal concepts as legal concepts, it harms communities' political, social, and religious development. That happens, for instance, when a legal system tries to use the metalegal concepts of health, religion, or dignity as if they were just legal concepts, that is, legal terms completely submitted to legal standards and rules and without a life or meaning outside the legal system.

God is a metalegal concept possessing the two features of a metalegal concept. First, God came before the creation of any human legal system. God is a religious concept, a metaphysical concept, a theological concept, and a cultural concept, but not a legal concept, let alone one fixed by the standards of a secular legal system. God's existence as a cultural phenomenon is prior to the invention of any legal concept.[18] If God is not a necessary condition for recognizing morality within legal systems, even where God is

---

18   This is very clear in the case of the United States, as underscored by the famous statement attributed to many politicians (Bismarck and De Gaulle, among others) and quoted by Justice Scalia, 545 U.S. 17 (2005): "God watches over little children, drunkards, and the United States of America."

considered the ultimate source of morality, then neither is God a necessary condition for the existence of a legal system. If God is not a necessary condition for the existence of legal systems and is not a legal subject submitted to the legal system, therefore, God is not a legal concept.

Second, recognizing God has some legal implications since it contributes to a better understanding of the more profound features of the human person, whose protection is the end of the legal system. The deeper the legal understanding of the person's idea, the better the quality of the person's legal protection. A poor and reductionist concept of a person impoverishes and limits the legal protection of human beings, while the recognition of God facilitates proper interactions between and among the various dimensions of the human being (individual, social, and transcendent) and avoids the temptation of converting political power into a kind of god. A political community without God eventually deifies its own legal system. Sadly, history provides good (and tragic) evidence of this.

The recognition of God is also helpful for strengthening the deepest foundations of Western legal systems. With God in the picture, it is easier to justify, understand, and interpret critical metalegal concepts like dignity, freedom, solidarity, and human rights, as well as the connections between legality, morality, religion, and politics.[19] It is also easier to defend the validity of certain rights as moral absolutes.[20] This recognition of God does not mean that all secular legal systems should be based by definition on the idea of God, but only that Western legal systems are better understood and more securely founded when they are open to God without rejecting the concept of God, that is, when they recognize God as a metalegal concept.

The Relevance of Recognizing God as a Metalegal Concept

As I have suggested, the reason why secular legal systems should recognize God is convenience, not necessity. The religious God exists outside the secular legal system, and God's existence is not required to justify the essential morality of that system. Since the metalegal God is not a precondition for

---

19   See my argument in chapter 7, pp. 146–55, in this volume.
20   In the same way, Jeremy Waldron, "The Image of God: Rights, Reason, and Order," in *Christianity and Human Rights: An Introduction*, ed. John Witte, Jr., and Frank S. Alexander (Cambridge: Cambridge University Press, 2010), 216–35, at 234.

the existence of political communities' legal systems, therefore, the metalegal God does not fit with Lockean political thought, in which God has axiomatic centrality.[21] In Locke, the idea of God is the starting point. The metalegal concept of God instead locates God as an ending point.

I believe there are at least two strongly connected reasons for legal systems to recognize God as a metalegal concept. First, if the end and ultimate justification of legal systems is to protect the person, and the recognition of God serves to strengthen the protection of the person as a whole, it is appropriate for legal systems to recognize God as a metalegal concept. Second, if the Western legal tradition is firmly founded on the idea of the existence of God, so that the recognition of God's existence strengthens the pillars of Western legal systems, it is helpful for legal systems to recognize God as a metalegal concept.

The first reason is that the end of legal systems is to protect the human person.[22] By protecting the human person as a legal subject of rights and duties, legal systems contribute to the protection of the person as a whole. But this contribution is operative only if legal systems are open to an idea of personhood broader than that of a mere legal subject of rights and duties who operates only in the legal dimension. Therefore, the protection legal systems should provide to the human person should be integral. It has to be focused on the legal, but it needs to consider the existence of the other dimensions of the person (aesthetic, moral, spiritual, etc.) because all the dimensions are connected and mutually influenced. Legal systems should admit that the legal concept of person is reductive by definition since it covers just a part of the person—the legal dimension. When legal systems close the door to other dimensions of the human person, they violate the "personal status"[23] of the person, that is, his or her human dignity, which is

---

21 See John Locke, *A Letter Concerning Toleration*, in *The Selected Political Writings of John Locke*, ed. Paul E. Sigmund (New York: W. W. Norton, 2005), 158: "The taking away of God, even in thoughts, dissolves all."

22 See Hermogenian, *Digesta. Corpus Iuris Civilis*, vol. 1, ed. Theodor Mommsen and Paul Krüger, 16th ed. (Berlin: Weidmann, 1954), 1.5.2: *"cum igitur hominum causa omne ius constitutum sit"* ("all law is constituted for the sake of men"). See also *Institutiones Iustinianus* 1.12.12.

23 For further explanation about the idea of dignity as status, see Jeremy Waldron, *Dignity, Rank, and Rights* (Oxford: Oxford University Press, 2012); Jeremy Waldron, "How Law Protects Dignity," *The Cambridge Law Journal* 71, no. 1 (2012): 200–22, esp. 201.

the integrative meeting point of all the other dimensions and capacities of the human being.

Legal systems should recognize that if the human person can act outside the legal system, it is because there is morality outside the legal system. If there is morality outside legal systems, the human person, not the legal system, should ultimately integrate moral sources to make correct moral decisions. It is not the political community but the human person, particularly the human conscience, that serves as the integrative center of ultimate moral decisions: those that come from the legal system and those that come from other sources of morality. If God is considered an ultimate source of morality, the recognition of God by legal systems facilitates the protection of the human person as an integrated unity. In other words, if the human person has moral life outside the legal system, the legal system cannot ignore this life, although it does not need to regulate it. Otherwise, it is difficult to serve the human person as the human person needs to be served.

I am not arguing that legal systems should depend on the often-capricious personal opinion of each person. Rather, I am arguing is that when conflict arises between elements outside and inside the legal system, it is the person, not the legal system, that should make the ultimate moral judgment, provided that she can provide a reasonable justification that can be assumed and evaluated by legal systems. The priority of the person for a legal system means the priority of conscience, the "most sacred of all properties," as James Madison famously said;[24] this means the priority of the particular over the universal, and of the person over the political community, though the political community, too, has its own rights.[25]

The second reason for legal systems to recognize God is very much intertwined with the first: the recognition of God strengthens the deepest pillars of legal systems, linking them with the moral, political, legal, and religious domains. The legal system might be considered the exclusive source of public morality if there is no God. If there is a God, the legal system can be considered an autonomous source of morality and justice, as the most binding part of all morality, but not exclusive and utterly independent of other domains

---

24 See James Madison, "Property," *National Gazette*, Mar. 29, 1792, http://press-pubs.uchicago.edu/founders/documents/v1ch16s23.html. See also Robert P. George, *Conscience and Its Enemies* (Wilmington, Del.: ISI Books, 2013), esp. 106–14.

25 See Joseph Ratzinger, *Introduction to Christianity* (San Francisco: Ignatius Press, 2000), 161.

of morality. Legal systems should not monopolize moral sources, and the idea of God prevents legal systems from doing so. On the other hand, to keep God outside the legal system prevents any instrumentalization of the name of God for political interests.

The metalegal concept of God strengthens human equality since all human beings are created in the image and likeness of God (Genesis 1:26–27).[26] This does not mean that secular legal systems should accept the doctrine of the image of God, let alone that legal documents should reference the creation of humanity in the image of God. It means only that the idea of God is a supportive argument for making equal dignity a pillar of secular legal systems and, even more, that this idea of the image of God makes it easier to defend certain rights as moral absolutes—for example, the right not to be tortured, as Jeremy Waldron rightly argues.[27] U.S. Supreme Court Justice John McLean, in his strong dissent in the case of *Dred Scott*, appealed to the doctrine of the image of God as an ultimate recourse for justice, arguing that "[a] slave is not a mere chattel. He bears the impress of his Maker."[28]

The metalegal God strengthens morality as such, and thus the idea of justice, as the "chief part, and incomparably the most sacred and binding part, of all morality,"[29] since God is the source of morality, and political communities cannot avoid having a morality. Morality is a constitutive element of the political community and, ultimately, the legal system, which can avoid acknowledging the religious God but not the moral God.

The metalegal God as the creator also strengthens solidarity and explains the "spirit of brotherhood" in which the Universal Declaration of Human Rights was created.[30] Indeed, although the declaration does not mention God,

---

26   I develop this idea in chapter 7 in this volume.

27   Jeremy Waldron, *Torture, Terror, and Trade-Offs: Philosophy for the White House* (Oxford: Oxford University Press, 2010), esp. 261–74.

28   *Dred Scott v. Sanford*, 60 U.S. 393 (1856) at 550.

29   See John Stuart Mill, *Utilitarianism* [1863], chap. 5, in John Stuart Mill, *On Liberty and Other Essays*, ed. John Gray (Oxford: Oxford University Press, 2008), 195.

30   See art. 1: "All human beings are born free and equal in dignity and rights. They are endowed with reason and conscience and should act towards one another in a spirit of brotherhood." For the importance of this expression as a foundation of human rights, see Michael J. Perry, *Human Rights in the Constitutional Law of the United States* (Cambridge: Cambridge University Press, 2013).

the metalegal concept of God informs the document; its spirit of brotherhood can be fully understood only based on common paternity, which is that of God, Creator, and Father.[31] The metalegal God helps define the meaning of human beings as bearers of human rights and responsibilities since the theory and law of human rights are not secular.[32]

The metalegal concept of God also helps us to understand the legal ideas of mercy, compassion, forgiveness, and equity since God, as creator, is benevolent and provident toward creation.[33] The metalegal God helps us as well to understand the relationship between law and religion and between church and state since God is a source of unity for these essentially differentiated communities. The metalegal God explains why law and religion share such concepts as obligation, mercy, fault, responsibility, duty, and marriage, as well as such values as justice and equity, mercy and rule, and discipline and love—concepts that protect legal systems against the virus of legalism.[34] We could mention the many connections between God and the pillars of Western legal systems, but that is not the primary purpose of this essay.

Religion, Not God, Is a Matter of Toleration

Toleration refers to a posture of acceptance toward practices, attitudes, or behaviors of which one disapproves but which one allows, defusing contention.[35] Only things (*res*) in the broadest sense, not persons, are the object of toleration.

---

31 In the same vein, see Francis, Encyclical Letter *Lumen fidei* (June 29, 2013), 54, http://www.vatican.va/holy_father/francesco/encyclicals/documents/papa-francesco_20130629_enciclica-lumen-fidei_en.html: "Modernity sought to build a universal brotherhood based on equality, yet we gradually came to realize that this brotherhood, lacking a reference to a common Father as its ultimate foundation, cannot endure. We need to return to the true basis of brotherhood."

32 In this vein, see John Witte, Jr., *God's Joust, God's Justice: Law and Religion in the Western Tradition* (Grand Rapids, Mich.: Eerdmans, 2006), esp. 31–48.

33 In this vein, see Timothy P. Jackson, *The Priority of Love: Christian Charity and Social Justice* (Princeton, N.J.: Princeton University Press, 2003), esp. 70–169.

34 John Witte, Jr., introduction, in Witte and Alexander, *Christianity and Human Rights*, 14. In a similar vein, see Harold J. Berman, *Faith and Order: The Reconciliation of Law and Religion* (Grand Rapids, Mich.: Eerdmans, 1993), xi.

35 For an expanded historical overview of the concept, see Rainer Forst, *Toleration in Conflict: Past and Present*, trans. Ciaran Cronin (Cambridge: Cambridge University Press, 2013), 1–446.

Persons tolerate things, but they do not tolerate other people. Persons should be tolerant, especially in our globalized world based on diversity, but people should not tolerate persons as such. People are objects of respect or recognition, and it is a consequence of this principle that people should tolerate certain attitudes and behaviors of which they disapprove. Personal dignity calls for respect and recognition of other people but not for toleration. A person as such never is objectionable and therefore is not a proper object of toleration. Therefore, we can object to a person's concrete attitude or behavior but not to the person as such. We might say that people recognize people but tolerate things. For example, people should respect or recognize immigrants, but tolerate excessive immigration (if they judge it to be so). Republicans and Democrats should respect each other but tolerate different political approaches and understandings of the good life. When we apply the concept of toleration to people, we insult them: "To tolerate means offending," says Goethe in his famous *Maximen und Reflexionen*.[36]

If, according to the metalegal concept of God, God is a Supreme Being—that is, a personal being—God should never be a matter of toleration by legal systems or by citizens, as if God were a thing (*res*) rather than an object of recognition and respect. To tolerate God means offending God, to paraphrase Goethe. So secular legal systems should recognize, not just tolerate, the metalegal God, for God is not something but someone. The new paradigm of religious freedom tries to reduce God to a thing, a tool of theistic religions, and thus an object of toleration. This is an erroneous way for legal systems to treat God.

Religion, on the other hand, can and should be tolerated by people.[37] Religion (or nonreligion) is a matter of toleration because it is a thing, a spiritual path, an attitude, and a behavior, not a person. Atheism is also a matter of toleration, not a matter of recognition, because the absence of God cannot be identified with God. Atheism is an attitude, a behavior that citizens

---

36   Johann Wolfgang von Goethe, *Maximen und Reflexionen*, in *Werke*, vol. 6, *Vermischte Schriften* (Frankfurt: Insel, 1981), 507: "Toleranz sollte nur eine vorübergehende Gesinnung sein: sie muss zur Anerkennung führen. Dulden heißt beleidige" ["Tolerance should only be a temporary attitude: it must lead to recognition. To tolerate means offending"].

37   For a different approach on religious toleration, see Brian Leiter, *Why Tolerate Religion?* (Princeton, N.J.: Princeton University Press, 2013). I offer a critique of Leiter's approach in chapter 5 in this volume.

of political communities should tolerate. We should respect and recognize theists and atheists as persons, but we should tolerate theism and atheism.[38]

What might seem to be a matter of toleration and not of recognition is the invocation of God in the public sphere as well as the use of the name of God in legal documents since these acts reflect an attitude toward God's position in legal systems. This attitude could generate a "normative substantive objection," as Rainer Forst puts it.[39] However, I think there is no justification for rejecting these practices. Recognition affects the totality; toleration affects just an attitude of a person. We can recognize Peter, therefore, but tolerate his drunkenness. Recognition implies invocation. The mention or invocation of a person affects the entire person as such, so it should not be a matter of toleration but of recognition. Invocation is external recognition. Thus, the possibility of being mentioned is the first consequence of recognition. Therefore, the recognition of the metalegal God entails public invocation of God. Otherwise, it is not an accurate recognition.

Conclusion

God should not be considered by Western secular legal systems as just a tool of theistic religion but rather as a metalegal concept. Acknowledging the metalegal concept of God helps protect the person as an integrated unity and not just as a legal subject. It also helps protect the moral boundaries of legal systems from outside. The metalegal God strengthens other metalegal ideas, such as dignity, solidarity, equality, and freedom, which are at the heart of all democratic legal systems.

The recognition of the metalegal God does not require either a personal or a communitarian act of faith, because the metalegal God is God without the religious dimension. The metalegal God does not demand legal protection or a specific legal status, because the legal system is for the sake of human beings, not God. The metalegal God is outside the legal system but illuminates it, since God's existence permits a deeper understanding of ultimate connections of legal systems with morality. The metalegal concept of God also preserves religious neutrality.

---

38   Against the toleration of atheism, see John Locke, *A Letter Concerning Toleration*, in Sigmund, *The Selected Political Writings of John Locke*, 158.
39   Forst, *Toleration in Conflict*, 18.

A secular society should be tolerant of both theistic and nontheistic beliefs, creeds, and first philosophies. The metalegal God, however, should be recognized, not just tolerated. God is someone, not something. Religious neutrality is not opposed to the metalegal God, since the metalegal God does not embrace the religious dimension of God. Using American legal terminology, then, we can say that God is outside the establishment clause of the First Amendment. The recognition of God as a metalegal concept, however, allows the use of God's name in legal documents and the invocation of God in the public sphere without violating religious neutrality. The metalegal concept of God allows us to establish and develop in peace a political community consisting of both believers and nonbelievers in God; to protect and defend the rights of all citizens. In sum, secular legal systems can have a place for God who exists outside the legal systems while illuminating them, and this is possible through legal recognition. God bless secular legal systems!

CHAPTER 4

WHY DOES RELIGION REQUIRE SPECIAL LEGAL PROTECTION?

Suprarationality as the Ultimate Justification for the Protection of Religion

IN A MULTIFACTOR CONSTITUTIONAL APPROACH to religion, there are many rationales for protecting it.[1] However, we can attempt to find the ultimate justification as a good starting point for analyzing other aspects of the relationship between religion and the secular legal system because that justification would provide a legal rationale to legitimize the secular legal

---

*   The original version of this essay appears in Rafael Domingo, "The Constitutional Justification of Religion," *Ecclesiastical Law Journal* 18 (2016): 14–35.

  1 In the same vein, see Kent Greenawalt, *Religion and the Constitution*, vol. 1, *Free Exercise and Fairness* (Princeton, N.J.: Princeton University Press, 2006), 137. For different rationales, see, among others, Andrew Koppelman, *Defending American Religious Neutrality* (Cambridge, Mass.: Harvard University Press, 2013), 120–65; Brian Leiter, *Why Tolerate Religion?* (Princeton, N.J.: Princeton University Press, 2013); Kathleen A. Brady, *The Distinctiveness of Religion in American Law: Rethinking Religious Clause Jurisprudence* (Cambridge: Cambridge University Press, 2015), 285–99; and John Witte, Jr., Joel A. Nichols, and Richard W. Garnett, *Religion and the American Constitutional Experiment*, 5th ed. (Oxford: Oxford University Press, 2022), 9–57.

system's protecting religion as such; all extensions of such protection (to phenomena sufficiently similar to easily recognizable examples of religion) are analogical. Without justification for that protection of religion (that is, without the focal case), there is no potential extension to related phenomena. Well-founded secular legal systems should be able to differentiate the boundaries of justification from the boundaries of extension; the analogical reasoning that this calls for is ubiquitous in law. In the case of religion, the extension of the same protection of religion to all types of secular beliefs and even to nonreligious beliefs is justified precisely by such analogical reasoning.

In this chapter, I argue that the ultimate justification for legally protecting religion is the need to protect suprarationality,[2] which can be understood in both a subjective and an objective sense. In a subjective sense, suprarationality refers to the capacity of each person to (a) freely overcome his or her own materiality, individually or collectively, in the search for the fundamental and most profound truths about the origin, meaning, and purpose of human life and the universe; and (b) freely follow and share these truths as he or she understands them.[3] In this subjective sense, suprarationality is an experiential capacity—to experience conversion, regeneration, and purification; develop spirituality; receive grace; gain assurance; develop cosmic consciousness; and so on. According to this subjective sense, suprarational understandings, beliefs, and commitments come together and can be manifested in a single act (e.g., of worship).

In an objective sense, suprarationality is the unseen order of everything beyond or above the range of a regular or merely rational human experience. The objective approach refers to suprarationality as a potential source of religious knowledge, transcendent justice, spiritual happiness, and love as a result of achieving harmony with that suprarational order through adjustment of our lives

---

2   In a similar vein, see Timothy Macklem, *Independence of Mind* (Oxford: Oxford University Press, 2006), 131–40. Macklem considers faith as a basis for freedom of religion. I prefer, however, the word suprarationality, since it expresses much better the intrinsic relation between religion and reason. On the relation between rationality and religious commitment, see Robert Audi, *Rationality and Religious Commitment* (Oxford: Clarendon Press, 2011), esp. 191–285.

3   On the human capacity of achieving transcendent truth, see Joseph Ratzinger, *Truth and Tolerance*, trans. Henry Taylor (San Francisco: Ignatius Press, 2003), 138–61. See also Raimon Pannikar, *Opera Omnia*, vol. 2, *Religion and Religions*, ed. Milena Carrara Pavan (Maryknoll, N.Y.: Orbis Book, 2015), 260: "rationality is not the only criterion for truth."

to conform with transcendence. Since objective suprarationality can be pursued by different people in concert, its pursuit can be organized and institutionalized; however, an objective suprarational dimension has private and public dimensions.

Religion is, by nature, both public and private. It deals with the whole spectrum of life and action on which the common good depends, but from a suprarational perspective. Because religion has a public dimension,[4] religious issues affect the heart of culture and society. It is precisely this public character of religion that makes suprarationality something that we might call translegal (that is, on the other side of, but connected with the law) rather than merely extralegal (unrelated to the law). Public and objective suprarationality *touches* the legal without being legal; suprarationality is thus a public external limit of the secular legal system. Suprarationality cannot be explained from the perspective of rationality; the higher cannot be explained by or derived from the lower. Although rationality and suprarationality are complementary,[5] not in competition, the line between them is easily blurred. Suprarationality does not imply the progressive obliteration of the rational but connotes its progressive expansion. The rational is not entirely separated from the suprarational, for the latter must cohere with the former; the divine reason is also a reason.[6] What distinguishes suprarationality is that it cannot be expressed according to the requirements of scientific or secular philosophic discourse. The language of suprarationality is fully understood only within the life of a religious community.

There are two converging approaches, therefore, to understanding the relationship between suprarationality and secular legal systems. First, secular legal systems are not suprarational, because their purposes, goals, and aims are not suprarational. And second, they *should not be* suprarational, because (legal) coercion is incompatible with suprarationality. In this sense, suprarationality constitutes an extrinsic constitutional limit of the secular legal system, and it has at least three crucial legal consequences: (a) suprarational acts in the strictest sense (pursuits of the suprarational) should never be

---

[4] On this public dimension, see, especially, Mary Ann Glendon, "Religious Freedom: A Second-Class Right?" *Emory Law Journal* 61 (2012): 971–90.

[5] On this complementarity, see John Paul II, Encyclical Letter *Fides et ratio* (September 14, 1998), 36–42.

[6] See Giambattista Vico, *New Science*, trans. David Marsh (New York: Penguin Books; reprint, 2013), 409: "Now, since God is pure reason, divine reason and authority are the same thing: and good theology places divine authority on a level with reason."

imposed by a secular legal system; (b) suprarational argumentation should not be used in legal discourse; and (c) the secular legal system cannot regulate religion or the essentials of any religious community. These three consequences are expressions of the natural incompatibility between legal coercion and suprarational freedom.

The Exclusion of Suprarational Acts from the Secular Legal System

For legal purposes, suprarational acts are those religious acts that, though legally protected, should be constitutionally excluded from secular legal systems in all circumstances (e.g., the obligation to make a profession of faith; to go to the synagogue, the church, or the mosque; or to take a religious oath). Excluding suprarational acts from secular legal systems is not an obstacle to their legal protection; their exclusion justifies their protection. Excluding suprarational acts from the secular legal system recognizes its lack of competence in suprarational matters.

Following classical analyses of moral acts, we can consider an act to be suprarational when both the subject matter and the primary purpose or intention of the act are strictly suprarational. The subject matter of an act is suprarational when suprarationality is the primary good toward which the action is directed. Acts of faith and worship constitute two paradigmatic suprarational subject matters of pivotal importance to most religious faiths; thus, they are crucial to a legal understanding of religion in both the national and the international realms.[7]

I understand an act of faith in the general sense as a free response of an individual to the suprarational. It involves an ascent of the intellect and will to a transcendent truth, specifically to God. It is probably the first religious experience, as it opens the door to suprarationality. I understand worship as offering praise and adoration to a Supreme Being, acting in reverence to other gods or transcendent beings, and participating in individual and collective religious rituals of both theistic and nontheistic religions. Worship is a consequence of faith.

---

[7] This is the reason why, in some European countries, some acts against worship and faith were criminalized (and in some cases still are). For an overview of the protection of worship and religious doctrine in Europe, see Norman Doe, *Law and Religion in Europe: A Comparative Introduction* (Oxford: Oxford University Press, 2011), 139–63.

Religious education, however, would not involve suprarational subject matter in this strictest sense, as a such educational practice is directed chiefly toward deepening understanding of religion and only indirectly toward suprarationality. Religious education involves suprarationality just insofar as and because suprarationality is a subject matter of education. Religious indoctrination, in the value-neutral sense of a process of imparting doctrine in an authoritative way (e.g., as in catechism), will be a suprarational act according to the subject matter since the act is mainly directed to suprarationality through education and not to education through suprarationality.

A similar point applies to proselytizing in the sense of an attempt to convert people to one's religion. It is a suprarational act because the object is deliberately directed toward suprarationality; therefore, it should be allowed in the public sphere as a manifestation of religion but excluded from political authorities. Any coercion or threat is wholly opposed to true proselytism; it transforms proselytism into a criminal offense;[8] however, promoting religion, in general, is not necessarily a suprarational subject matter, just as promoting marriage is not a marital act, but a political one that is beneficial to marriage.

By promoting religion, a legal system is not necessarily acting suprarational. For this reason, establishing religion is not correctly a suprarational act but both a religious and political activity in the broadest senses. Therefore, establishment, or at least some types of noncoercive establishments, could be appropriate to a secular legal system.[9] A different question is whether the establishment of a religion is the best framework to protect religious freedom. In my opinion, no establishment is the best way to fully protect religious freedom; indeed, it is the best way to protect religion. History has confirmed this statement many times.

In sum, the only suprarational acts that must be avoided in all circumstances by political authorities are those whose subject matter and main purpose are strictly suprarational, and where changed circumstances have not altered their (primary) purpose. When a legal system fails to exclude suprarational acts from political control in this strict sense, it abandons its secular character.

[8] For an overview of the regulation of proselytism, see John Witte, Jr., and Richard C. Martin, eds., *Sharing the Book: Religious Perspectives on the Rights and Wrongs of Proselytism* (Maryknoll, N.Y.: Orbis Books, 1999).
[9] In the same vein, see Human Rights Committee, General Comment 22, art. 18, para. 9 (Forty-eighth session, 1993). Compilation of General Comments and General Recommendations Adopted by Human Rights Treaty Bodies, U.N. Doc. HRI/GEN/1/Rev.1 at 35 (1994).

The Suprarational Argument as an Irrelevant Legal Argument

Suprarational arguments are those whose premises (typically propositions, statements, or sentences) in support of a claim (the conclusion) are beyond reason unaided by revelation. "Since God redeemed humankind, human beings should love each other" is an example of a suprarational conclusion drawn from a suprarational premise. "Homosexual acts should be legally banned because the Bible rejects them" is also based on a suprarational premise. Suprarational arguments are chiefly based on premises derived from pronouncements of religious authorities and books, traditional religious practices, or mystical or revelatory experiences.[10] Suprarational arguments should not be used in the legal discourse of democratic communities, however, because secular legal systems should operate always within the rational realm.[11] Reason is the only language that secular legal systems can understand; therefore, suprarational arguments should receive the same treatment as suprarational acts, that is, they should be placed outside the secular legal system. This exclusion is exactly what makes a legal system secular in the first place.

This hallmark of the secular legal system, however, does not necessarily put religion as a whole outside the domain of public reason, as John Rawls suggested,[12] nor does it expel religion from political deliberation. The realm of political deliberation is larger than the realm of strictly legal deliberation. And what is placed outside the legal system is only suprarational argumentation, which is only a part of any religion. This exclusion is because the suprarational argument is essentially unintelligible by secular legal systems. The suprarational argument should be outside the legal realm because it cannot correctly be imposed: suprarationality requires free adherence, so a coercive suprarationality is a contradiction in terms. Since legal systems are, by definition, coercive, they cannot use suprarational arguments. This is not

---

10   For a more detailed approach to the religious argument, see Andrew F. March, "Rethinking Religious Reason in Public Justification," *American Political Science Review* 107 (2013): 523–39.

11   In chapter 7 in this volume, I explain how and why a suprarational argument (the image of God) can illuminate a rational argument. On the relation between rational and suprarational argument, see Robert P. George, *In Defense of Natural Law*, rev. ed. (Oxford; Oxford University Press, 2001).

12   See John Rawls, *Political Liberalism*, expanded ed. (New York: Columbia University Press; reprint, 2005), 224–25.

a matter of discrimination by exclusion; it is a matter of the nature of the system and types of argumentations in question.

Secular legal systems should protect the suprarational, but they cannot deploy it. In this sense, I do not agree with Christopher Eberle when he argues that "each citizen should feel free to support coercive laws on the basis of her religious convictions—even on the basis of her religious convictions alone—so long as she conscientiously regards her religious convictions as providing a sufficient basis for those laws."[13] Behind this statement lies a category error—using legal coercion for suprarational reasons. Legal coercion can be used only for legal purposes and must be reduced to the realm of the legal. In order to legitimize the use of legal coercion to protect religious convictions, religious convictions must be supported by a legal rationale. There are, for instance, both religious and legal arguments for using legal coercion to avoid political corruption, but there is no legal argument for supporting some expressions of so-called blue laws in the United States (e.g., restricting or banning the sale of alcohol beverages on Sundays for religious reasons).[14]

But let us not mistake a part for a whole. Suprarational arguments cannot be converted into rational arguments by changing the premise, as the result would be a different argument; however, religious ideas and values, not suprarational arguments, can be used in political deliberations, and many of them can be converted into legal rationales for public policy. It is not possible to erect a barrier between culture, including religious culture, and public deliberation. Since religion operates in the public sphere, and religious communities are inescapably a part of the political community, religion cannot be ostracized.

As Michael McConnell has shown, Americans owe much to Calvinist and Baptist preaching in support of independence; Protestant ministers were the ideological commissars of the American Revolution, and the principal arguments for religious freedom and against establishments were religious in content.[15] Something similar is true of the birth of the European Union, in which the Christian idea of forgiveness after the Second World War played

---

13 Christopher J. Eberle, *Religious Conviction in Liberal Politics* (Cambridge: Cambridge University Press, 2002), 333.

14 For a historical overview of blue laws in the United States, see Alan Raucher, "Sunday Business and the Decline of Sunday Closing Laws," *Journal of Church and State* 36 (1994): 13–33.

15 Michael W. McConnell, "Secular Reason and the Misguided Attempt to Exclude Religious Argument from Democratic Deliberation," *Journal of Law, Philosophy and Culture* 1 (2007): 162–64.

a decisive role,[16] and of the U.S. civil rights movement, led by Martin Luther King, Jr., and other religious figures. Religious ideas, however, require a transformation to become legal, and this transformation is possible because the suprarational presupposes the rational. It is beyond the rational but not contrary to the rational. Behind the U.S. Constitution, the human rights movement, and the birth of the European Union stand many wonderful and beautiful religious ideas, ideals, and aspirations, but the final *legal* result (e.g., the U.S. Constitution, the Civil Rights Act of 1964, and the Treaty of Lisbon) does not include suprarational arguments. Each is secular by nature.

In other words, the secular can be founded on secular and religious bases. In the latter case, the secular will follow a transformation process (appropriate secularization). To fail to recognize this second source of genuine secularity is to forget the source of legality itself. The very idea of law was originally religious before being developed into a secular idea.[17] Moreover, there are sometimes deeper religious arguments for a particular policy than there are strictly secular arguments—as, for example, for abolishing the death penalty.[18] Religious arguments can and should be used in political deliberation to urge against abortion, the death penalty, and torture, but the final legal ban on abortion, the death penalty, or torture should be based on a secular argument: the respect and protection of every human life and dignity, for instance. This is the only type of argument that a legal system can recognize.

I basically agree with Robert Audi's formulation of what we might call a principle of secularity, meant to moderate legal appeals to religious reasons. Audi affirms: "Citizens in a democracy have a prima facie obligation not to advocate or support any law or public policy that restricts human conduct unless they have, and are willing to offer, the adequate secular reason for this advocacy or support."[19] Inspired by Audi's formulation, I would say that the secular legal system of democratic societies should not contain any law or

---

16   See chapter 10, on Robert Schuman, in this volume. See also Joseph Weiler, *Un'Europa cristiana. Un saggio esplorativo* (Milan: Rizzoli, 2003).

17   See Rémi Brague, *The Law of God: The Philosophical History of an Idea*, trans. Lydia G. Cochrane (Chicago: University of Chicago Press, 2007).

18   In this vein, on torture, see Jeremy Waldron, "Two-Way Translation: The Ethics of Engaging with Religious Contributions in Public Deliberation," *Mercer Law Review* 63 (2012): 845–68.

19   Robert Audi, *Democratic Authority and the Separation of Church and State* (Oxford: Oxford University Press, 2011), 65–66.

public policy restricting human conduct based exclusively on suprarational considerations. Unlike Audi's formulation, my formulation is legal and put in negative terms since I see the suprarational as an extrinsic constitutional limit of the secular.

Because it is formulated in positive terms, Audi's principle is more restrictive than my formulation. Audi incorporates a judgment about the adequacy of the secular reason. This element makes sense when dealing with the secular legal system from within, but not when dealing with the secular legal system from without. From a legal perspective, the most critical feature of Audi's principle of secular reason is that it is not exclusive; therefore, it is not antireligious. It does not put away religious reasons. Rather, it demands a secular rationale to supplement religious reasons, based on the idea that "freedom is the default position in a liberal democracy."[20]

My formulation does not imply that religion should be privatized in liberal democracies, let alone that citizens have the civil obligation to vote according to secular arguments. A Muslim can defend legalizing polygamy for religious reasons, but a law allowing polygamy should be based on a secular argument (e.g., sexual freedom and free private partnership).[21] On the other hand, a Catholic can defend banning polygamy for religious reasons, but a law banning polygamy should be based on a secular argument (e.g., sexual equality, tradition, education of children, etc.). In a referendum on polygamy, both parties can vote based on religious premises. However, a bill passed without a rational argument supporting it would go against the constitutional nature of the secular legal system.

In sum, suprarational argumentation cannot be the *exclusive* justification of legal deliberation. Legal deliberation demands a secular rationale. This fact does not take away religious argumentation from political deliberation, let alone reduce it to the private realm. The demand of rationality is simply an expression of the essence of the secular legal system, which should be open to transcendence but not be involved in suprarational issues. In order to be inside the legal system, the suprarational argument should be supported by a rational argument; otherwise, it cannot be legal.

---

20 Audi, *Democratic Authority and the Separation of Church and State*, 69.
21 On this topic, see John Witte, Jr., *The Western Case for Monogamy over Polygamy* (New York: Cambridge University Press, 2015).

Structural Dualism

Structural dualism means that the legal constitutional model of a political community must protect the transcendent or suprarational dimension of human beings by guaranteeing sufficient autonomy for religion and religious communities. Such dualism is a necessary, though not sufficient, condition for guaranteeing equal religious freedom for all citizens and preventing unfair religious interference with the political realm. Without dualism, a secular legal system cannot be appropriately developed, and no state can be reasonably classified as a liberal democracy. Dualism benefits religion and politics—it protects religious communities from political communities and political communities from religious communities.[22] Dualism is the most important consequence of the incompatibility between religious suprarationality and legal coercion.

At least four considerations support this dualistic structure of society, all of which are deeply related to and ultimately based on freedom. The first has already been explained: religion, in the strictest sense of suprarationality, is a constitutional limit of the legal system of a political community. (That is not true of other goods and values, such as art, knowledge, and sociability.) But religion, in the broadest sense, does have political dimensions. It can and should be manifested in the public sphere. There is no reason for restraint. Yet it also has a constitutive, nonpolitical dimension, insofar as it involves the suprarational, which should not be a matter of state coercion. This is not a stipulation about what I mean by "religion," but the formulation of an aspect of religion with important legal relevance.

We can make the same two points from the perspective of politics. It has a religious dimension, in that it embraces all types of communities, including religious. At the same time, politics has a constitutive, nonreligious dimension insofar as it is not religious in the strictest sense—that is, suprarational. In the suprarational realm, politics has no place. Politics and religion are two sides of the public sphere. At the center of the public sphere stands the person, not the political community, because the person is at the same time both a religious and a political being—a rational being open to suprarationality. But while politics and religion are not incompatible, some aspects of religion cannot mix with some aspects of politics—namely, suprarationality and legal coercion, respectively.

---

22 See John Rawls, "The Idea of Public Reason Revisited," in Rawls, *Political Liberalism*, esp. 476.

The second consideration is that the intrinsic unity of the person (that is, the integration of the person's individual, social, and transcendent dimensions), which is founded in basic human dignity, cannot be projected onto the community as a whole, for dignity is a status of the human person exclusively. When a political community, using (or abusing) its sovereign power, tries to claim this intrinsic three-dimensionality of the human person for itself, it becomes totalitarian. In some ways, the absolute nation-state, based on the idea of sole and exclusive sovereignty, is an attempt to substitute dignity for sovereignty as the state's character (appropriating for itself the centrality of the human person).[23] An analogous error occurs when a religious community becomes a political community without differentiating its religious structure from its political structure or its religious beliefs from its political action.

The third consideration is that the act of adherence to a faith or creed is, by nature, completely free and personal. Faith can be shared within a community of voluntary membership, as it is in the religious community, but not within a community of compulsory membership, as in the so-called complete political community. Every person must be a member of at least one political community to satisfy his or her basic needs and develop his or her personal capacities, but a compulsory political community cannot manage transcendence. Therefore, a dualistic structure is a democratic constitutional right that guarantees freedom of religion for the sake of the person's full development.

At the heart of religious freedom is the idea that the purpose of a political community is not to make an act of faith based on some religious truth, for citizens in this case would not have the required freedom to practice or not practice religion. Thus, political and religious communities have different purposes, even though both have been established for the sake of the human person. Political communities can share religious values, which do not require acts of faith, but they cannot share concrete religious beliefs as matters of law. The communion of faith demands the fullness of freedom without restrictions. This fullness of freedom can be achieved only in a religious community of voluntary membership, not in a political community of compulsory membership.

The fourth consideration in favor of a dualistic structure is the public nature of suprarational law.[24] The suprarational law of historical religions has a public nature derived from the communion of faith insofar as suprarational law

---

23   For more on this argument, see Rafael Domingo, *The New Global Law* (Cambridge: Cambridge University Press, 2010), 65–73, 131–36.

24   On the foundation of the idea of transcendent law, see Brague, *The Law of God*.

binds the religious community as a whole, not only each of its members. In some religions, such as Judaism and Islam, the public dimension of suprarational law is a presupposition of the existence of the very community—there is a community because there is suprarational law, not vice versa. Thus, the religious community is at the heart of the political community. For the religious community to avoid taking control of the political community and for suprarational law not to be confused with the law of the secular legal system, the secular legal system must recognize a religious communitarian structure that is ontologically different from the political structure and in which only transcendent law operates.[25]

From a political point of view, an essential consequence of the requirement of a dualistic structure is that a political community's legal system does not need any religious legitimation since a political community is not an extension of religion but an utterly autonomous community. Another necessary consequence is that the democratization of religious communities cannot be a demand of the political agenda of democratic governments. The political community cannot impose its constitutional model on the religious community because they are ontologically different. Each community has its own rules, institutions, and proper scope, regardless of which community was born first. Both community structures need each other, however, for the good of humanity.

Constitutional dualism warns against the existence of total community structures. In general, total community structures are those that do not make any substantive distinctions between transcendent law and positive law, or those that deny, at least implicitly, transcendent law. Religious and political communities become total communities by mutual absorption or mutual exclusion. A religious community becomes total when, based on the principle of self-determination, it also becomes an independent, or at least autonomous, political community and objects to the creation of a new dualistic structure that differentiates between the religious community and the new political community. A religious community also becomes total when it tries to impose its religious rules on areas that are outside its sphere of business or uses coercive political power to impose its criteria on religious issues. On the other hand, a political community becomes total when it tries to control religious communities or entirely exclude them from the public sphere. History, life's teacher, offers us many examples of total communities in both senses.

---

25 For further explanation, see Rafael Domingo, "A New Global Paradigm for Religious Freedom," *Journal of Church and State* 56 (2014): 427–53.

The first claim of constitutional dualism is that both communitarian structures, the political and the religious, should recognize each other, since they operate in the same territory, and a greater or lesser proportion of the political community is also part of the religious community structure. Without at least an explicit act of recognition, there can be no dualistic structure, only a monistic one, which is, by definition, totalitarian.

These two communitarian structures, the political and the religious, should be ontologically autonomous yet politically interdependent, as all members of religious communities must be members of a political community, but not vice versa. Additionally, religious communities operate inside and across the territories of a political community, so the distinction between political communities and religious communities is a matter of each community's different goals and aims. If a political community fails to recognize the value of religion, it will never fully recognize a religious community as an intrinsic piece of the dualistic structure.

The Election of the Dualistic Model as a Constitutional Decision

The status that the legal system gives religious communities and the degree of interdependence of these communitarian structures determine the dualistic constitutional model of a political community. Dualistic structures can adopt various systems according to history, culture, political experience, and religious diversity.[26] The options can be classified into four basic categories: (a) unilateral state primacy over religion (e.g., French laïcité); (b) state neutrality (e.g., U.S. no establishment); (c) mutual cooperation in common purposes (e.g., German collaborationism); and (d) state singling out and adoption of a religion as the state religion (e.g., England's church establishment). There is a fifth category, the integration of the political community into the religious community as an extension of it (theocracy), but this model is incompatible with the secular legal system. Therefore, I do not address it here.

The models can be specified so many ways that systems belonging to the same group can differ quite widely. French laïcité is different from Mexican or Turkish laïcité. German collaborationism is different from Spanish, Italian, or Brazilian constitutional models. Among established churches, England's

---

[26] See, in this vein, W. Cole Durham, Jr., "Patterns of Religion State Relations," in *Religion and Human Rights: An Introduction*, ed. John Witte, Jr., and M. Christian Green (Oxford: Oxford University Press, 2012), 360–78.

constitutional model is different from that of Greece (where the national religion is Greek Orthodox), Denmark (with a strong, established Lutheran church), or Malta (where the state religion is Catholicism). The model of the United States is, in some ways, unique because of its originality and the singular judicial interpretation of the First Amendment.[27] All four constitutional frameworks can be under constitutional dualism. There are, however, some restrictions that more directly affect the extreme models (e.g., laïcité, at least in the French sense)[28] and church establishments.

Laïcité is different from neutrality. Neutrality might involve avoiding any official expression of religiosity in the public sphere in order to protect freedom of religion, freedom from religion, and social pluralism, but laïcité, specifically French laïcité, is based on state sovereignty, whereas American neutrality, for example, is bilateral, with mutual noninterference between religion and politics. Historically, French laïcité was a constitutional political reaction against the dominance of Catholicism; American neutrality, on the other hand, was a political decision about managing Christian religious diversity. French laïcité is a consequence of strictly applying the principle of state sovereignty to religious issues,[29] whereas American neutrality is a consequence of strictly applying the principles of justice and equality to religious issues.[30]

Thus, under French law, strong state interference with religion is compatible with the principle of laïcité since there is no formal state recognition of institutional religious autonomy. Additionally, as Michel Troper points out, "the power of the state over religion in France is not just a consequence of

27   For an overview of the different models of church-state separation in Western countries, see James Q. Whitman, "Separating Church and State: The Atlantic Divide," *Historical Reflections* 34, no. 3 (2008): 86–104. For theocratic governance, see Ran Hirschl, *Constitutional Theocracy* (Cambridge, Mass.: Harvard University Press, 2010). For a European overview, see Doe, *Law and Religion in Europe*. For a general view of the U.S. model, see Witte, Nichols, and Garnett, *Religion and the American Constitutional Experiment*.

28   For a general view of laïcité, see Guy Haarscher, *La Laïcité*, 5th ed. (Paris: PUF, 2011), including the bibliography at 124–26; Émile Poulat, *Notre Laïcité Publique* (Paris: Berg International, 2003); and T. Jeremy Gunn, "Religion and Law in France: Secularism, Separation, and State Intervention," *Drake Law Review* 57 (2008–2009): 949–84.

29   In this vein, see Michel Troper, "Sovereignty and Laïcité," *Cardozo Law Review* 30, no. 6 (2009): 2561–574.

30   On specific American neutrality, see Koppelman, *Defending American Religious Neutrality*, esp. 15–45.

a preexisting doctrine of sovereignty; it is also constitutive of sovereignty, in the sense that the doctrine of sovereign State has been conceived from the beginning as an instrument of a religious policy."[31] If the state is sovereign, no subject matter can escape its power, not even religion. Thus, if the French state abstains from regulating religion, it is because it decides not to exercise any sovereign power over religion; however, it could do so if it pleased, based on its sovereignty. This justifies the state having ownership of religious buildings and the prohibition of wearing religious symbols or subsidizing religious schools. Laïcité defends dualism but submits the religious community to the unique sovereignty of the political community. Therefore, a robust and unhealthy form of laïcité could violate individuals' free exercise of religion.

Having a church establishment can fit with the principle of dualism, but again only with some restrictions. First, the church and state should be perfectly differentiated. An established church cannot and should not be a "department of the state." Church establishment should not imply or impose on citizens an act of faith or use a concrete religious argument in legal deliberation. Religious establishments should never support recognizing a religion as a true religion, since a political community is not competent in suprarational matters. Religious establishment should imply exclusively an official recognition of the social values of a concrete religion, which is precisely what justifies a specific legal position for a concrete religious community inside a political community. In my opinion, this is the only way to justify establishing a religion in a democratic society. In practice, church establishment often endangers both individual freedom and equality. Even if it is formal, it promotes a political entanglement with religion, which may lead to a lack of impartiality in treating religion as a social phenomenon and often in how it treats individual citizens, especially secular citizens. Experiences of this abound.

The other two constitutional models of dualism—state neutrality (U.S. no establishment) and collaborationism (the German model)—fit entirely with the dual system. State neutrality is based on the opposing principle of abstention as the best way to promote and guarantee the proper development of religious phenomena in public life. The model of collaborationism is based on the positive principle of cooperation, searching for collaboration between political and religious communities to achieve common goals. Both models have advantages and disadvantages. U.S. neutrality promotes equal treatment of religion and protects the required autonomy of religious

31 Troper, "Sovereignty and Laïcité," 2564.

communities, but it risks degenerating into a strict separationist model, nearer to laïcité, which defends a secular establishment in which individual religious freedom is restricted. The advantages of the model of religious collaborationism are its openness to religion and the fact that religion is regarded as a public good with a clear space in public life. There are, however, two disadvantages of the collaborationist model: (a) the model can easily fall into an excessive and undesirable entanglement between religion and politics, and (b) it can come to involve religious preference and thus unequal treatment of communities and citizens. The German system of a church tax, which covers approximately 80 percent of the entire church budget, is probably a case of excessive entanglement between religious and political communities.

The precise scope of the protection of religion depends on the nature and framework of the constitutional model. Extensions of protection are justified by reasons of equality (which favor treating sufficiently analogous phenomena similarly), not by the precise argument that justifies the protection of religion. A secular legal system is not equipped to weigh the rational coherence of theological doctrine; that is not its business. However, the secular political community should favor religion because, without religion, there is no secularity, just as without sheep, there is no shepherd.

I prefer the American model of neutrality;[32] however, the political community has the exclusive power and right to freely decide the constitutional model of its relationship to the religious communitarian structure. The religious communities should not share this decision because it is a political decision in the strictest sense and should be based on cultural, historical, and moral grounds. According to their constitutional model, political communities can allow or ban concrete religious education in public schools and religious symbols and ceremonies in public institutions. Political communities can be more or less open to the celebration of religious holidays and the intensity of the presence of religious values in the legal system. They can defend religious equality or, on the contrary, can even promote the concrete values of a specific religion as a state religion. Political communities can consider religion one of their most important sources of values or as mere matters of individual and social freedom that require legal protection. All political communities, however, should recognize religious communities, even those that defend ideas and views contrary to their own legal system, provided that the religious communities operate in accordance with the legal

---

32 In the same sense, see Koppelman, *Defending American Religious Neutrality*, 1–14.

system. This variety of regulation on religious matters, according to the dualistic constitutional model adopted by the political community, protects global pluralism and personal freedom while assuring the minimum of religious freedom demanded by human dignity.

Autonomy and Independence of Religious Communities

An important legal consequence of constitutional dualism is that religious communities (that is, organized religions in the form of churches, congregations, or religious societies) should be both autonomous and independent, whatever their legal position may be in the secular legal system.[33] Religious communities are autonomous in the secular sphere and independent in the strictly religious sphere (that is, in relation to religious acts in the narrowest sense).[34] The subject matter determines the differences between the regime of autonomy and the regime of independence. This distinction between autonomy and independence allows us to establish a normative framework to define the limits of competencies and capacities of religious communities in internal affairs.

Autonomy is relational and thus relative and externally limited; independence, however, is sovereign and, therefore, absolute. Religious communities are autonomous, in the relational meaning of the term, insofar as they operate inside the territory of a political community and are submitted to the secular legal system of the political community. If political communities are different from religious communities, and religious communities operate within the territories of the political community, political communities must have the power and duty to regulate some religious matters insofar as they affect constitutional essentials and the rights of other citizens. There is no religious matter, aside from religious acts, that cannot be regulated by the political community in order to achieve its own legitimate ends and purposes. Religion as a social

---

33 For an overview of church autonomy in Europe and the United States, see Gerhard Robbers, ed., *Church Autonomy: A Comparative Survey* (Frankfurt am Main: Peter Lang, 2001).

34 In *Hasan and Chaush v. Bulgaria* (2002), App No 30985/96, 34 EHRR 55, 10 BHRC 646, IHRL 3186 (ECHR 2000), October 26, 2000, the Grand Chamber of the European Court of Human Rights forcefully upheld the autonomy of religious communities. However, the decision does not make any specific distinction between autonomy and independence, which in my opinion is critical to a proper understanding of the topic.

phenomenon, which affects the people of a political community, is also a political issue, because all matters that touch the people are political by definition.

Secular legal systems can provide legal, administrative, or executive autonomy to religious communities; however, a political government has something to say about religious groups as social groups that operate inside a state. Because religious communities are autonomous in the secular domain, legal systems can demand that religious groups structure themselves according to some legal framework to enjoy the recognition and potential benefits of the relevant legal status.[35] A political community may legitimately intervene in the affairs of a religious community based on some limitations prescribed by the legal system. The domain of this potential interference and, therefore, the domain of potential autonomy extend to all acts that are not strictly religious, and that can be submitted to the ordinary law of the legal system. This domain of autonomy depends on the constitutional model of each country; thus, the proper degree of autonomy is a relative matter.

On the other hand, religious communities are independent in the spiritual domain, as legal systems cannot make religious acts or use suprarational arguments. This domain of independence is constitutive of the religious community. Without structural independence, the right to religious freedom cannot be fully protected either individually or collectively. Based on the principle of independence, political governments should not interfere with the internal structure of governance (hierarchical vs. congregational), formation, and decision-making processes of faith-based institutions when they affect strictly religious matters. This is not a matter of mere autonomy; it is a matter of independence. Therefore, political communities should recognize the existence of some type of transcendent law of religious communities that is beyond the secular legal system and control of the state power. These include systems of Christian law (especially canon law), Islamic law (sharia), Jewish law (halacha), and other systems of religious law. This recognition of suprarational law does not demand the formal recognition of it, though many states do recognize it; it just demands political abstention from interference.

For instance, based on the principle of independence, no legal power in the world can oblige the Catholic Church to ordain women as priests, even

---

[35] For an overview of the legal position of religious organizations in Europe, see Doe, *Law and Religion in Europe*, 88–113. For an overview of the legal position of religious organizations in the United States, see Witte, Nichols, and Garnett, *Religion and the American Constitutional Experiment*, 241–362.

if a constitutional nondiscrimination law is applied in the country in which Catholic religious communities (that is, dioceses) operate. Since the Catholic argument for the no ordination of women is based on suprarational law,[36] it is beyond the domain of secular legal systems' antidiscrimination laws; it constitutes a limit of the legal. This limit should be respected, even where the religious organization lacks recognition as a legal person under the legal system in question. The reason is that this transcendent (suprarational) law is a religious matter par excellence.

Based on such a principle of independence, the U.S. Supreme Court, in a unanimous 2012 decision,[37] held that the government could not intervene in the decisions of religious schools regarding the employment of ministers. The ruling, written by Chief Justice John Roberts, concluded that both clauses of the First Amendment, the Free Exercise Clause, and the Establishment Clause, "bar the government from interfering with the decision of a religious group to fire one of its ministers." In this case, since the hiring (and later firing) of the teacher was considered by the religious community to be a response to a call from God, it could be considered a religious act (subject matter and intention were strictly religious); therefore, the government had no right to interfere. The decision to fire was a matter of independence. Analogously, European religious law accepts, as a general principle, that political communities must not interfere in the appointment of ministers of religion or in their status within religious communities.[38]

The Right to Religion

One of the most important consequences of secularization is that religion is recognized by secular legal systems as a *right to something* (e.g., the right to education, the right to marriage, or the right to work) and no longer simply

---

36 See also the Apostolic Letter *Ordinatio Sacerdotalis*, issued by Pope John Paul II on May 22, 1994, https://www.vatican.va/content/john-paul-ii/en/apost_letters/1994/documents/hf_jp-ii_apl_19940522_ordinatio-sacerdotalis.html. See also Can. 1379 § 3 of 1983 Code of Canon Law (revised on June 1, 2021, by Pope Francis): "Both a person who attempts to confer a sacred order on a woman, and the woman who attempts to receive the sacred order, incur a *latae sententiae* excommunication reserved to the Apostolic See; a cleric, moreover, may be punished by dismissal from the clerical state."

37 See *Hosanna-Tabor Evangelical Lutheran Church and School v. Equal Employment Opportunity Commission*, 565 U.S. 171 (2012).

38 See abundant legislation in Doe, *Law and Religion in Europe*, 127–29.

as a constitutional liberty (e.g., freedom of thought, freedom of conscience, or freedom of speech). As a result of secularity, secular legal systems should protect an individual and collective *right to religion,* not only a *right to freedom of religion.*[39] Religious freedom is a necessary condition for the existence of this basic human right to religion, but it is not a sufficient condition. The point of the right to religion is to protect not only freedom in the religious field, which is instrumental here, but all religions in both the individual and communitarian dimensions. Without recognizing religion as a specific right, a secular legal system cannot fully protect the consequences of its own secularity. Without recognizing a right to religion, it is easy to reduce freedom of religion into a subcategory of freedom of conscience and to convert religion into a private matter.[40]

Recognizing freedom of religion was the first step that opened the door to the existence of secular legal systems in modernity. Recognizing a right to religion is a new step for consolidating the secular legal systems in the age of secularization. This recognition allows for the suprarational argument and suprarational acts to be placed completely beyond legal discourse and coercion while secular legal systems continue protecting religion. The right to religion prevents the government from meddling in religious matters. It also prevents governments from instrumentalizing religion, by recognizing the existence of autonomous religious communities.

The right to religion includes the right to hold and change religions and beliefs, which is an absolute right, and the right to practice or manifest religion and belief, which is a relative or qualified right. The right to change religions includes the right to apostasy, just as the right to practice religion includes the right to spread the faith and the negative right not to declare one's religious belief. The practice of religion implies the prohibition of any type of direct and indirect discrimination (with the necessary exception of defending the religious identity of an organization), incitement to discriminate, religious harassment, and victimization. In U.S. terminology, the right to religion also includes the traditional articulations of the nation's founders, such as freedom of exercise or practice, religious equality before the law, freedom from

39   On these constitutional structures of the rights, see Robert Alexy, *A Theory of Constitutional Rights*, trans. Julian Rivers (Oxford: Oxford University Press, 2002), 120–62.

40   For further argumentation, see Rafael Domingo, "A Right to Religious and Moral Freedom? A Response to Michael Perry," *International Journal of Constitutional Law* 12, no. 1 (2014): 226–47.

religious discrimination, and freedom from religion or from coercion in religious matters.[41] It does not, however, include freedom of conscience.

Freedom of conscience, though closely related, should remain distinct from the right to religion in secular legal systems, so that all moral decisions of conscience may be protected, whether or not they are based on a religious or nonreligious moral rationale.[42] In other words, the secularization of conscience imposed by the secular legal system demands the separation between freedom of conscience and the right to religion, but does not reduce religion to a matter of freedom of conscience. Without freedom of conscience, the right to religion cannot exist, but the right to religion should be distinguished from the right to conscience, as the right to free speech and expression should be separated from the right to freedom of thought.

A legal system usually recognizes a new right when a public good cannot be protected directly by the ordinary political process of legislation, since the right demands a legitimacy and normative autonomy higher than the legitimacy that can be provided by ordinary legislation. The degree of legitimacy and normative autonomy demanded by religion in secular legal systems of the twenty-first century is stronger than the degree of legitimacy and normative autonomy afforded by early secular legal systems, in which the dualistic structure of religious and political communities did not belong to their constitutional essentials and religiosity was taken for granted. In other words, to legitimately regulate the lives of the common believer and nonbeliever citizens through positive law *in a secular fashion* and to separate church and state legally, a secular legal system should protect religion as a right.

Unlike freedom of religion, the right to religion can be understood as a three-point relationship. The first element is the beneficiary of the right (every person and religious community); the second is the addressee of the right (the political community and each of its members); and the third element is the content or subject matter of the right (religion). The content of a right to something is always an act of an addressee,[43] in this case, the political community and each of its members (e.g., to provide the required permission to build a church or to open a religious school in the city). The

---

41   Witte, Nichols, and Garnett, *Religion and the American Constitutional Experiment*, 41–70.

42   For further argumentation, see Rafael Domingo, "Restoring Freedom of Conscience," *Journal of Law and Religion* 30, no. 2 (2015): 176–93; Rafael Domingo, *God and the Secular Legal System* (Cambridge: Cambridge University Press, 2016), 113–17.

43   See Alexy, *A Theory of Constitutional Rights*, 121.

right to religion often embraces the structure of a *right to* noninterference by the addressee when there is a general prohibition against a particular act (e.g., no interference with the practice of male circumcision by a Jewish family when there is a general prohibition to practice circumcision outside hospitals; or no interference with peyote use as a Native American religious ritual when there is a general prohibition against the use of hallucinogenic drugs). This right to religion is not absolute and should be limited by public order, morals, and other rights. The limits of the right to religion depend on the constitutional model adopted by different secular legal systems.

As a constitutional freedom, the old framework of freedom of religion required an absence of command or prohibition, but not necessarily an act by the addressee. (A similar structure is found in freedom of conscience, where no addressee of the right must act in order to satisfy the right of the rightholder.) By converting freedom of religion into a right to religion, this right can prevail over general prohibitions of certain forms of conduct, opening the door to the religious exception as a generally applicable exception to laws to protect religion. The most relevant distinction between the right to religion and the right to freedom of religion is that the right to religion incorporates the religious exception as a constitutive element. The religious exception is best understood in the context of a right to religion. It is an affirmative legal defense that protects a citizen's right to religion against unjustified interference by political authorities or other citizens in religious issues, even when the interfering law is religiously neutral. If a citizen or a religious community can prove that the subject matter of a legal act is subjectively or objectively religious in the strictest sense, he or she can benefit from religious exceptions against political authorities or other citizens.

What I have tried to justify here is not any particular religious exception in any particular country, but the appropriateness and even necessity of the religious exception in general in order to protect the right to religion. The limits between restraint and religious exception should be established according to the constitutional model of the community in question. However, every constitutional model should take into consideration that the existence of the religious exception has intrinsic legal justification, so that the bare neutrality of a law duly passed by the legislative branch is not sufficient justification for denying a religious exception outright. On the contrary, in most cases, neutral legislation is the trigger for a religious exception. Neutrality of the law legitimizes the statute, but it does not weaken the legitimacy of the religious exception. The exception loses its legitimacy when there are reasons of public order or public morality for limiting the religious exception.

Conclusion

Suprarationality is a sufficient condition for the existence of religion and the ultimate justification for its legal protection, because suprarationality constitutes an extrinsic limit of the legal, just as the land is an extrinsic limit of the seas. However, the protection of religion cannot be reduced to the protection of suprarationality. By analogical extension, protection of religion should be applied to protect other types of beliefs and even nonreligion. To treat believers and nonbelievers equally, however, does not require treating religion the same as nonreligion; that would be a contradiction in terms. Rather, suprarational acts and arguments should be viewed as falling outside of legal reasoning. Since suprarational acts demand complete individual and collective freedom, a dualistic structure in which they are beyond the reach of coercion should be established in all democratic societies in order to protect religions and freedom of religion.

Secular legal systems should protect religion as a *right to,* not just as a constitutional liberty. This is a consequence of the secularity of secular legal systems. The right to religion implies a beneficiary and an addressee who must act to satisfy the former's interest. This right thus implies both the free practice of religion by citizens and the toleration of religion by secular legal systems. The specific tool to protect the right to religion is the religious exception. By granting the religious exception to neutral laws, the secular legal order acknowledges the existence of another dimension of the human being and the priority of human dignity over political sovereignty.

CHAPTER 5

THE RIGHT TO RELIGIOUS FREEDOM

Extension or Erosion?

AS A CENTRAL PHENOMENON OF our age, secularization has challenged one of the inner pillars of political communities and legal systems, namely, the place and role of religion in society.[1] As a result, an international debate about the rights and liberties of religion, belief, and conscience has emerged in the twenty-first century.[2] The critical question is whether traditional approaches to religious freedom, though widespread, can be sustained in an era of secularization. Based on straightforward claims of neutrality, objectivity, and equal liberty, some leading scholars—among them Ronald Dworkin[3] and

---

* The original version of this essay appeared in Tom Angier, Iain T. Benson, and Mark D. Retter, eds., *The Cambridge Handbook on Natural Law and Human Rights* (Cambridge: Cambridge University Press, 2022), 418–31.

1   See Charles Taylor, *A Secular Age* (Cambridge, Mass.: Harvard University Press, 2007). See also Iain T. Benson, "Considering Secularism," in *Recognizing Religion in a Secular Society*, ed. Douglas Farrow (Montreal: McGill-Queens, 2004), 83–88, which shows how religious citizens must be included in our understanding of the secular.

2   On the secularization debate, see Pippa Norris and Ronald Inglehart, *Sacred and Secular: Religion and Politics Worldwide*, 2nd ed. (Cambridge: Cambridge University Press, 2012), 3–32.

3   Ronald Dworkin, *Religion without God* (Cambridge, Mass.: Harvard University Press, 2013).

Brian Leiter[4]—argue from different methods and perspectives that the right to religious freedom ought not be privileged in secular democratic societies. Instead, they claim, religious freedom should be recast as freedom of conscience or should be included within the framework of a general right of ethical independence. In this light, it is not surprising that a champion of religious freedom like Mary Ann Glendon should affirm: "Religious freedom is in serious danger of becoming a second-class right—in the sense that it can all too easily be trampled by other rights, claims, and interests."[5]

The idea of religious freedom is an ancient teaching of the Western tradition.[6] The expression *libertas religionis* (freedom of religion) was coined by Tertullian of Carthage in 197 CE.[7] Some years later, in his letter to Scapula, Proconsul of Africa, who had begun persecuting Christians, Tertullian famously said: "However, it is a human right and a natural power [*humani iuris et naturalis potestatis est*] for everyone to worship what he or she thinks is good; religion brings neither harm nor benefit to the other. It is not even a matter of religion to compel religion, since it has to be adopted by free will and not by force; for even sacrifices are only required of a willing disposition."[8]

This original idea of freedom of religion was developed over subsequent centuries by thinkers such as Duns Scotus, Marsilius of Padua, Jean Gerson,

---

4   Brian Leiter, *Why Tolerate Religion?* (Princeton, N.J.: Princeton University Press, 2013).

5   Mary Ann Glendon, "Is Religious Freedom an Orphan Right?" in *The Changing Nature of Religious Rights Under International Law*, ed. Malcolm Evans et al. (Oxford: Oxford University Press, 2015), 1–8, at 1. See also Mary Ann Glendon, "Religious Freedom: A Second-Class Right?" *Emory Law Journal* 61 (2012): 971–90; "Making the Case for Religious Freedom in Secular Societies," *Journal of Law and Religion* 33, no. 3 (2018): 329–39.

6   See Robert Louis Wilken, *Liberty in the Things of God: The Christian Origins of Religious Freedom* (New Haven, Conn.: Yale University Press, 2019). See also John Witte, Jr., *The Blessings of Liberty: Human Rights and Religious Freedom in the Western Legal Tradition* (Cambridge: Cambridge University Press, 2021), 1–13, 76–104.

7   Tertullian of Carthage, *Apologeticum* 24:6, http://www.thelatinlibrary.com/tertullian/tertullian.apol.shtml.

8   Tertullian of Carthage, *Ad Scapulam*, chap. 2, https://www.tertullian.org/latin/ad_scapulam.htm: "*Tamen humani iuris et naturalis potestatis est unicuique quod putauerit colere; nec alii obest aut prodest alterius religio. Sed nec religionis est cogere religionem, quae sponte suscipi debeat, non ui, cum et hostiae ab animo libenti expostulentur*" (my own translation).

Francisco de Vitoria, and Bartolomé de Las Casas, among others.[9] But it was during the Protestant Reformation[10] and, later, the Enlightenment, that religious freedom shifted into a true "right to religious freedom" to protect "mutual toleration of Christians in their different professions of religion."[11] Religious freedom was thus the political freedom required to accomplish the duty of rendering to God what human beings as creatures owed to God according to justice or, in the words of James Madison—the father of religious freedom in the United States—"the duty which we owe our Creator and the manner of discharging it."[12] The purpose of religious communities was understood to be "the public worship of God, and by means thereof the acquisition of eternal life."[13] The idea of God was central to the understanding of religious freedom as a right deserving of special treatment and different from the rights to freedom of speech, press, association, and more. As America's early advocate of religious freedom, Roger Williams, put it, "God requires not uniformity of religion to be enacted and enforced in any civil state."[14] Freedom of conscience was the legal tool to protect the free exercise of religion. The original end of freedom of conscience was not to protect conscience against potential political immorality but to protect the free choice of one's own religious path.

For centuries, then, the right to religious freedom was progressively extended in Western countries to guarantee equal protection and nondiscrimination and to prevent the religious or cultural majority from using the power of the state to impose its beliefs on others. By the second half of the twentieth century, international human rights instruments had firmly

9   John Witte, Jr., "The Right of Freedom of Religion: An Historical Perspective from the West," in *Routledge Handbook on Freedom of Religion and Belief*, ed. Silvio Ferrari et al. (London: Routledge, 2020), 9–24; Witte, *The Blessings of Liberty*.

10   See also John Witte, Jr., *The Reformation of Rights: Law, Religion, and Human Rights in Early Modern Calvinism* (Cambridge: Cambridge University Press, 2007).

11   John Locke, *A Letter Concerning Toleration*, in *The Selected Political Writings of John Locke*, ed. Paul E. Sigmund (New York: W. W. Norton, 2005), 126.

12   See James Madison, "Memorial and Remonstrance against Religious Assessments" (1785), no. 1, https://founders.archives.gov/documents/Madison/01-08-02-0163.

13   Locke, *A Letter Concerning Toleration*, 134.

14   Roger Williams, "The Bloudy Tenent of Persecution for Cause of Conscience" (1644), in *On Religious Liberty: Selections from the Works of Roger Williams*, ed. James Calvin Davis (Cambridge, Mass.: Harvard University Press, 2008), 87.

enshrined the right to religious freedom as protection not only for theistic and nontheistic religions but also for nonreligious communities and creeds and even the so-called freedom from religion.[15] Scholars and jurists widely discussed concrete aspects of that expansion of rights in relation to the great variety of constitutional models for relating religion and the state (e.g., state neutrality, church-state cooperation, religious establishment, *laïcité*, and more), but they paid less attention to the fact that religious freedom as such requires special legal protection.

Religious freedom was considered a first-class right, or the first right, since it protects the most profound beliefs of each individual and the transcendent dimension of human life, which essentially informs and undergirds the dignity of every human being. Indeed, seeing transcendence as unnecessary to the legal concept of religion, in order to extend the rights of religious freedom to other kinds of convictions and beliefs, does not eradicate transcendence (and especially God) from the idea of religion, let alone eliminate the right to religious freedom from the universal catalog of human rights.

The protection of transcendent and institutionalized religions has some implications that the protection of private faiths, beliefs, or first philosophies does not have. To consider religion only as a phenomenon of immanence and to suggest the foreclosure of the legal protection of transcendence constitutes an unjustified reductionism, a form of the imposition of a secular religion. It is precisely transcendence that gives pride of place to the right of religious freedom. We can best understand the lack of X by first understanding X itself. It is easier to understand nontranscendence by first grasping transcendence than to do the reverse. Thus, it is reasonable that the starting point of a comprehensive legal paradigm for religious believers and nonbelievers should be religiously oriented instead of nonreligiously oriented. Otherwise, it is easy to fall into an oppressive legal reductionism.

---

15   See, for instance, Organization for Security and Co-operation in Europe, *Guidelines for Review to Legislation Pertaining to Religion or Belief*, adopted by the Venice Commission at its 59th Plenary Session, Venice, June 18–19, 2004, Title II, Section A, no. 3, http://www.osce.org/odihr/13993. The expression "freedom from religion" is better understood as the "freedom from religious coercion," and it should not cover, as some argue, freedom from even the incidental dimensions of religious practice in the public sphere (guaranteed in Article 18 of the International Covenant on Civil and Political Rights [ICCPR]).

Although many distinguished authors react against traditional conceptions of religious freedom and the special protection of religion as such by legal systems,[16] in this essay, I analyze only the approaches of Brian Leiter and Ronald Dworkin. I chose to focus on their work because they intend their arguments to apply universally (not just to the U.S. legal system), and their relevance in the international debate has been enormous.

In formulating his argument, Leiter goes further and, in some ways, more profoundly than Dworkin does, but, in general, Dworkin's elaboration is sharper than Leiter's, as we shall see shortly. But these two thinkers complement each other. Dworkin undervalues the idea of God by considering the divine existence an untested scientific hypothesis (an alleged fact) and, therefore, epistemologically irrelevant. Leiter undervalues religion in his efforts to understand what is distinctive about it. Both agree that the defense of freedom of conscience, which Dworkin calls ethical independence, also legally and fully protects religion.

Why Protecting Religion Is Morally and Legally Defensible

In his provocative book *Why Tolerate Religion* (2013),[17] Leiter asserts that Western democracies are wrong to single out religious freedom for special legal protection. According to Leiter, singling out religion is indefensible because there is no compelling moral principle or legal basis for such special protection. If matters of religious conscience deserve toleration, Leiter argues, it is because they involve matters of conscience, not religion per se.

---

16   See, for instance, Christopher L. Eisgruber and Lawrence G. Sager, *Religious Freedom and the Constitution* (Cambridge, Mass.: Harvard University Press, 2010); Micah Schwartzman, "What If Religion Is Not Special?" *University of Chicago Law Review* 79, no. 4 (2012): 1351–427; Richard Schragger and Micah Schwartzman, "Against Religious Institutionalism," *Virginia Law Review* 99, no. 5 (2013): 917–85; and Lawrence G. Sager, "In the Name of God: Structural Injustice and Religious Faith," *Saint Louis University Law Journal* 60, no. 4 (2016): 585–600. For a critique, see John Witte, Jr., Joel A. Nichols, and Richard W. Garnett, *Religion and the American Constitutional Experiment*, 5th ed. (Oxford: Oxford University Press, 2022), 343–60.

17   Leiter, *Why Tolerate Religion?* For a profound critique of the book, see Michael W. McConnell, "Why Protect Religious Freedom?" *Yale Law Journal* 123 (2013): 772–810, at 810: "Leiter wants to return to the earlier regime, but with secularism rather than Anglicanism in charge."

For this reason, exemptions from neutral laws of general applicability should be available to all conscientious objectors as long as the exemptions do not shift burdens onto others. If a nonviolent Sikh boy is permitted to wear his ceremonial dagger (*kirpan*) to a middle-school classroom, why should a nonreligious Texan boy be expelled for packing a knife? This is the question Leiter tried to resolve in examining a real Canadian case in which the court allowed a Sikh boy to wear the kirpan.[18] Leiter concludes that there is no justification for legal systems to accord special treatment and toleration to religious obligations and not to other obligations of conscience and that "both boys should be out of luck: that there should not be exemptions to general laws with neutral purposes unless those exemptions do not shift burdens or risks onto others."[19]

As Leiter argues—and I agree—a secular legal system might find good reasons to ban both the Sikh and the Texan behaviors if needed to protect public order.[20] A legal system could also find some reasons (more complicated, indeed) to allow both. Or the law might find good reasons to tolerate the Sikh's behavior and not the Texan's, as the Canadian court did. I do not think, however, that a secular legal system could marshal good reasons for accommodating the Texan's behavior without tolerating the Sikh's. That is a clear sign that the scope of the religious exemption is broader than the scope of the nonreligious exemption and that religious behavior demands a different regulation in legal orders. Religious toleration implies moral accommodation, just as religion implies conscience, but religion cannot properly be reduced to a matter of conscience, as it is much broader than that.

If Leiter cannot find a compelling argument to protect freedom of religion and conscience, it is because of his untenably negative conception of religion.

18 Leiter, *Why Tolerate Religion?* 5–6, 64–66, 161n4. The example is based on the Canadian case *Multani v. Commission scolaire Marguerite-Bourgeoys* [2006] 1 S.C.R. 256, 2006 SCC 6. In its judicial decision, the Supreme Court of Canada struck down an order of a Quebec school authority that had prohibited a thirteen-year-old Sikh child from wearing a kirpan to school as a violation of freedom of religion under section 2(a) of the Canadian Charter of Rights and Freedoms. This order could not be saved under section 1 of the charter. The ceremonial dagger could be sewn into the garment to render it less of a danger to students; failure to make this concession meant that the blanket restriction was not a "minimal impairment" as demanded by the section 1 analysis. I thank Iain Benson for this clarification.
19 Leiter, *Why Tolerate Religion?* 4.
20 Leiter, *Why Tolerate Religion?* 4: "I argue that both boys should be out of luck."

His attitude becomes evident in the first line of the preface when he mentions that his interest in religious toleration arose when he witnessed "the pernicious influence of reactionary Christians on both politics and public education."[21] Leiter reduces the idea of religion to three specific features: "categoricity of its commands" (how believers experience religious commands), "insulation from reason and evidence" (a claim about religious doctrine), and "existential consolation."[22] But these three categories by no means embrace the full richness of religion, let alone the Abrahamic religions specifically.

A multifactorial constitutional approach to religion need not provide a single justification for protecting religion but can offer many rationales.[23] But the ultimate justification for legally protecting religion lies in the need to protect the transcendent dimension of the human being, which a community of religious believers can share.

Transcendence marks a limit to the proper domain of any secular legal system. The legal system, after all, operates within the realm of the rational, and transcendence is suprarational. Legal systems should respect individual and collective freedom to ensure people's adequate access to and pursuit of transcendence. Thus, the right to religious freedom establishes a constitutional limit on governments by protecting the suprarational capacity of the human person against political monopolization. On the other hand, the right to religious freedom also protects *governments* against improper religious interference by religious citizens and authorities. The right to religious freedom prevents governments from instrumentalizing religion and effectively turning into religious authorities themselves.

Religious freedom is different from freedom of conscience. Conscience is a sort of protective shell around people's privacy: it safeguards them from potential abusive intrusions by the law and constitutes a private limit of the legal system, while religion constitutes a public limit. Since legal systems cannot help but have a public morality, as expressed in the moral decisions

21 Leiter, *Why Tolerate Religion?* ix.
22 Leiter, *Why Tolerate Religion?* 37–53.
23 See chapter 4 in this volume. In the same vein, see Kent Greenawalt, *Religion and the Constitution*, vol. 1, *Free Exercise and Fairness* (Princeton, N.J.: Princeton University Press, 2006), 137. For different rationales, see, among others: Witte, Nichols, and Garnett, *Religion and the American Constitutional Experiment*, 24–40; Andrew Koppelman, *Defending American Religious Neutrality* (Cambridge, Mass.: Harvard University Press, 2013), 120–65; Kathleen A. Brady, *The Distinctiveness of Religion in American Law* (Cambridge: Cambridge University Press, 2015), 285–99.

they inevitably make to coordinate and regulate public life, the free practice of private morality in the public realm cannot be absolutely protected as a political right. Providing such a right would be self-defeating from the legal system's point of view.

In other words, religion must be kept outside the secular legal system[24] but, at the same time, protected by it. Conversely, morality cannot be entirely outside the legal system since the secular legal system should be nonreligious but never nonmoral. This tension explains why the practice of one's morality can be allowed only to the extent that it does not contravene the public morality enforced by the legal system. This also explains why the scope of the right to religion is different from—and in this respect wider than—the scope of the right to freedom of conscience.[25]

From a normative legal perspective, the right to religious freedom demands toleration (the Sikh boy). From a legal perspective, toleration means accepting the consequences of others' having and exercising rights. Toleration is, then, the flipside of a right. It is the minimum respect required by a legal system for others' rights protected by the same system. One must tolerate others' rights because the secular legal system must guarantee protection from—it must itself *not* tolerate—the infringement of rights. Thus, if there is a right to religious freedom, everybody must tolerate religious exercise. One can fiercely oppose the American individual's right to bear arms, but all American citizens and residents must tolerate the exercise of that right so long as the U.S. legal system recognizes it. Likewise, one can furiously oppose religious manifestations on the ground that religion poisons and divides political society, but one must tolerate religion as a citizen of a political community ruled by a secular legal system where religion is a matter of right.

Freedom of conscience, by contrast, demands accommodation (the Texan boy). The appropriate form for protecting individual moral conscience

---

24   Obviously, cannibalism or female genital mutilation could and should validly be constrained by law despite being claimed as religious practices.

25   I develop this argument in Rafael Domingo, "Restoring Freedom of Conscience," *Journal of Law and Religion* 30, no. 2 (2015): 176–93. Against this idea, and in favor of a right to religious and moral freedom, see Michael J. Perry, *Human Rights in the Constitutional Law of the United States* (New York: Cambridge University Press, 2013), 112. See also Rafael Domingo, "A Right to Religious and Moral Freedom? A Response to Michael Perry," *International Journal of Constitutional Law* 12, no. 1 (2016): 226–47; Michael J. Perry, "A Right to Religious and Moral Freedom? A Reply to Rafael Domingo," *International Journal of Constitutional Law* 12, no. 1 (2014): 248–55.

in the public realm is not toleration but accommodation, for there is no constitutional right to practice one's private morality in the public realm as there is to practice religion. The legal relationship between religion and politics is essentially different from the relationship between private and public morality since morality is prelegal and religion is translegal.[26]

Accommodation is not a matter of rights in the strictest sense; it is a matter of good reason, respect, prudence, or wisdom in applying the law based on justice, solidarity, diversity, and, ultimately, dignity. Accommodating individual moral conscience is a way of practicing solidarity in political communities based on human dignity. Legal systems promote social cohesion and integrity by accommodating individual moral conscience, turning individual claims into the shared objective of peaceful coexistence. This allows each person to participate in the needs and potentialities of other citizens and makes the community more integrated through respect for difference. Integration and solidarity, in this sense, are at the heart of the practice of legal accommodation in secular legal systems.

A relevant problem created by reducing religious freedom to freedom of conscience is that freedom of conscience does not require a dualistic constitutional model of church-state relations, as religious freedom does.[27] Brian Leiter is very conscious of the importance of dualism and even argues that religious establishment is compatible with principled toleration.[28] However, once Leiter reduces religious freedom to conscience, religious establishment or nonestablishment becomes just a pure constitutional formalism: "a tolerant state could, in principle, be either a religious or an antireligious one."[29]

No constitutional model of a political community can adequately protect the transcendent dimension of human beings without creating an effective dualistic structure of political and religious authorities that guarantees sufficient autonomy for institutionalized religion and religious communities. Such dualism is also necessary, though not sufficient, to guarantee equal religious freedom for all citizens and prevent unfair religious interference within the political realm.

Without the dualistic structure of religion and state—of course, not understood as watertight compartments—a secular legal system cannot be

---

26   I develop this argument in Rafael Domingo, *God and the Secular Legal System* (Cambridge: Cambridge University Press, 2016), 73–166.

27   See more about this argument in Rafael Domingo, "A New Global Paradigm for Religious Freedom," *Journal of Church and State* 56, no. 3 (2014): 427–53.

28   Leiter, *Why Tolerate Religion?* 129.

29   Leiter, *Why Tolerate Religion?* 4.

properly developed, and no state can be reasonably classified as a liberal democracy. Such dualism benefits both religion and politics—it protects religious communities from political communities and political communities from religious communities.[30] Dualism is the most important consequence of the incompatibility between religious transcendence and legal coercion. The de facto eradication of the dualistic model brought about by radical secular liberalism would be the beginning of the end of political liberty because it's a sort of camouflaged political totalitarianism.

Returning to the example provided by Leiter at the beginning of his book, we can end this section by saying that the case of the Sikh boy wearing a dagger in middle school falls into the domain of the right to religious freedom and, therefore, into the realm of religious exception and toleration. Only a regulation that promotes public order tightly enough to survive strict scrutiny can limit the right of the Sikh to wear a dagger. The example of the Texan boy belongs to the domain of conscience and, therefore, of accommodation but not to the realm of *religious exemptions*, for there is no recognized right for him to invoke except an unimaginable right to bear arms in schools. The Texan boy has no real right to wear a dagger as the Sikh boy does. The Texan's behavior could be accommodated, where political prudence would allow, and the Sikh's right could be limited to avoid harm. But the Texan and the Sikh boys, though equal under the law, pose two different questions and demand two different answers.

Religious Atheism or Religious Freedom?

In *Religion without God* (2013), Dworkin tried to recover the concept of religion as a value to integrate it with his theory of the unity of value.[31] According to Dworkin, religion is an "interpretative concept"[32] in that people use the word without understanding its meaning. Therefore, religion belongs

---

30   See John Rawls, "The Idea of Public Reason Revisited," in *Political Liberalism*, expanded ed. (New York: Columbia University Press, 2005), especially 476.

31   See the book review symposium: "Ronald Dworkin's Religion without God and the Challenges of Theistic Epistemology," *Journal of Law and Religion* 29 (2014): 510–47. For an expanded version of my critique, see Rafael Domingo, "Religion for Hedgehogs? A Critique against the Dworkinian Approach to Religious Freedom," *Oxford Journal of Law and Religion* 2, no. 2 (2013): 371–92; Rafael Domingo, "The Dworkinian Religion of Value," *Journal of Law and Religion* 29, no. 3 (2014): 526–34; and Domingo, *God and the Secular Legal System*, 56–60.

32   Dworkin, *Religion without God*, 7.

to the domain of values and arguments, not facts and explanations. God, by contrast, is a matter of fact that requires scientific explanation. As Dworkin puts it, somewhat ironically, the existence of a personal God "is a very exotic kind of scientific fact. But it is still a scientific fact."[33] Thus, religion and God could and should be isolated from each other, given the impossibility of supporting "a value judgment—an ethical or moral or aesthetic claim—just by establishing some scientific fact."[34] This is what Dworkin calls "Hume's principle," which supports the independence of morality, with its standards of justification, as a knowledge domain.[35] This principle, Dworkin thinks, is based on "the conceptual truth that nothing but another value judgment can support a judgment of value."[36] For Dworkin, this statement is like a mathematical truth. Both "mathematics and value are immune from questions about their birth or causal provenance."[37]

For Dworkin, "religion is deeper than God."[38] Because the existence of God is an (alleged) scientific fact and, therefore, not a source of value, believing in God demands a background value judgment that highlights the relevance and consequences of the untested (alleged) fact of God's existence. Thus, belief in God is independent of the existence of God. Believing in God is just a potential consequence of a more profound worldview, which is religion. Furthermore, religion, precisely as an interpretative concept, can provide value by itself. Therefore, the reality of religion as a value is independent of the existence of God as a fact: "the value part [of religion] does not depend—cannot depend—on any god's existence or history."[39]

Inspired by Albert Einstein's religious ideals[40] and by Thomas Nagel's approach to religious temperament,[41] Dworkin argues for the existence of a

---

33   Dworkin, *Religion without God*, 27.
34   Dworkin, *Religion without God*, 26–27.
35   Dworkin, *Religion without God*, 26. See also Ronald Dworkin, *Justice for Hedgehogs* (Cambridge, Mass.: Harvard University Press, 2011), 17, 222.
36   Dworkin, *Religion without God*, 90.
37   Dworkin, *Religion without God*, 90.
38   Dworkin, *Religion without God*, 1.
39   Dworkin, *Religion without God*, 9.
40   See, for instance, Albert Einstein, *The World as I See It*, trans. Alan Harris (New York: Philosophical Library, 1949); Albert Einstein, *Einstein on Cosmic Religion and Other Opinions and Aphorisms* (Mineola, N.Y.: Dover Publication, 2012).
41   Thomas Nagel, *Secular Philosophy and the Religious Temperament* (Oxford: Oxford University Press, 2010).

religious attitude that holds that human life and wonder at the beauty of the universe have objective intrinsic value. The religious attitude or impulse is the human being's capacity to discover value in everything. This *religion of value* is entirely independent of scientific explanation, that is, of facts, and therefore also independent of the existence of any god or gods.

For Dworkin, the possibility of the existence of God does not make any difference to the objective truth of atheistic religious values: "the distinction between theism and atheism is therefore itself indistinct."[42] This beauty of all objective inherent value plays a parallel role in God's role as an uncaused cause in the Abrahamic religions. According to Dworkin, this religious attitude could be shared by both theists and atheists, and thus could ground a broader right to religious freedom, protecting both theistic and atheistic convictions: "What divides godly and godless religion—the science of godly religion—is not as important as the faith that unites them," concludes Dworkin.[43]

I agree with Dworkin that both theists and atheists share a religious attitude and that atheism is not a good argument for nonreligiosity. A religious instinct is innate in human beings since all human beings ask themselves at some point about the ultimate meaning of their lives. But I disagree that the divorce between God and religion is an epistemic norm. Instead, a shared epistemology for both theists and atheists is possible if God is not only a matter of fact but also a matter of value and, therefore, relevant to morality and religion. Moreover, religions, or at least the Abrahamic religions, are not just a matter of value but also a matter of fact, since they hold that God creates human beings (fact) and for God (value). Thus, the distinction between fact and value breaks down when we are dealing with a personal living supreme being who is love and, therefore, never ceases to draw human beings to the divine self. A living and loving God surpasses this distinction of rational human knowledge between explanation and argumentation. On the other hand, any cosmological account posits a relationship between *techne* and *telos* perceptible by human reason, and this human reason, like human nature, is universal and emerges from the idea of an ordered cosmos.

According to the Abrahamic religions, the revelation of God is primarily an event, a fact. The divine plan of revelation is simultaneously realized by deeds and words that are intrinsically bound up with each other. They cannot be separated as Dworkin would like. No, the conventional theistic religions

---

42   Dworkin, *Religion without God*, 31.
43   Dworkin, *Religion without God*, 29.

do not consist of two separable and independent parts, "a scientific part and a value part."[44] They form an indivisible unity that cannot be analyzed separately without falling into oversimplification, which is exactly what happens when Dworkin reduces the existence of a personal God to the scientific fact of there being an entity that "cannot of his own will create right answers to moral questions or instill the universe with a glory it would not otherwise have."[45] Religious events are value-facts. For Christians, for instance, the resurrection of Jesus is a historical event that nevertheless transcends history, opening the door to a new dimension of human existence, to a new space of life with value of its own. Moreover, for Christians, Jesus is Truth: a fact and an objective value. To subject the truth claims of Christ to a fact/value analysis distracts from the nature of the truth claims themselves.[46]

Continuing with Dworkin's terminology, we can also affirm that God is both the supreme fact (supreme being in the Western tradition) and the supreme value (supreme good and supreme beauty in the Western tradition), because as creator, God gives the real meaning, the ultimate value, to the goodness and beauty of human life and the universe. Likewise, revelation is both a religious fact and a religious value. In some ways, revelation provides us automatically with the "background value judgment" that allows us to make a correct, though partial, judgment about God. This statement is consistent with the idea that God does not need to figure in an acceptable explanation of morality and religion, and that revelation is not the only source of knowledge, even of God's knowledge. Some explanation of objective value can be provided without adverting to God's existence, but that does not necessarily mean that no further explanation is required or available, or that the existence of God cannot be the ultimate explanation of morality, religion, and objective value. Similarly, a reasonable explanation of objective value can be provided without adverting to divine revelation as a constitutive part of the Abrahamic religions, but that does not mean that morality, religion, and objective value cannot be explained further or ultimately by divine revelation.

According to the Abrahamic religions, only God—God's existence and action (God-living fact)—can fully answer questions about the good and the beautiful (God-value), because God, as supreme good and ultimate beauty, is

44 Dworkin, *Religion without God*, 23.
45 Dworkin, *Religion without God*, 26.
46 For a deep critique of the language of value, see Iain T. Benson, *Civic Virtues and the Politics of Full-Drift Ahead* (Sydney: Center for Independent Studies, 2017).

the foundational, the ultimate, and even the exclusive source and condition of morality and religion. However, the existence of such a living and loving God does not affect believers alone. It radically affects all human beings, both believers and nonbelievers. Therefore, exclusivity does not mean that nonbelievers remain outside morality or religion, because morality and religion are reasonable, and the human being is rational. Religion and morality presuppose reason. Thus, reason as such—not in a narrow, positivistic sense open only to strictly scientific explanation, but in the broadest sense—can be considered a source of morality and religion to the extent that it is a creation of God. Reason is the meeting point between believers and nonbelievers. For believers, human reason is a gleam of the divine reason; for believers and nonbelievers, it is the most potent human capacity to find the good and the beautiful, that is, objective, value. If the starting point is reason and not objective value, we do not need to separate scientific reason from religious reason. They can be united.

The existence of creative reason is not a miraculous idea but a metascientific one that recognizes the validity and benefits of the scientific method, the autonomy (but not total independence) of morality, and the intrinsic limitations of both.[47] Just as scientific reason is not the whole of reason, neither is creative reason. The latter is a foundational form of reasoning, but not the only possible form. Through creative reason, one can find reasonable ways of approaching God by contemplating the order and beauty of the cosmos and the human person's reality as a free creature open to objective truth and beauty and longing for happiness. These converging arguments are not based on a scientific explanation but on human experience and on causality, though they are rejected by Dworkinian epistemology. Dworkin, following Nagel, asserts that divine creation does not provide a better explanation of human life than random mutation, but the scientific explanation is not the only source of knowledge. Thus, an expanded reason that integrates scientific explanation, sapiential understanding, and human experience (e.g., of love, faith, and hope) is, in my opinion, more conducive to the idea of divine creation than to the idea of simple random mutation.

Dworkin excludes any transcendent source of divine reality from his epistemology, however vague: "religious atheism does not believe in a god and so

---

47 On creative reason, see Pope Benedict XVI's Regensburg lecture, "Faith, Reason and the University: Memories and Reflections," University of Regensburg, September 12, 2006.

rejects the science of conventional religions and the godly commitments."[48] The Dworkinian approach to religion closes the door to any consideration of a revealed belief or transcendent knowledge as an epistemological axiom, reducing potential religious knowledge to a matter of personal conviction with limited epistemological relevance. He argues that "if we declare our faith in some special religious form of perception, however, we have no way of integrating our belief in the faculty that delivers that perception with any more general account of how that faculty functions."[49] However, Dworkin's epistemological paradigm impedes the development of such an account by closing the door to any transcendent religious epistemology. That is why he argued that "the science of a godless religion may provide, in a different way, all that the science of godly religions can actually propose."[50]

The god or gods that Dworkin discusses are caricatures of the Abrahamic God and thus are genuinely unbelievable gods for adherents of the Abrahamic religions. That is why he lowers religion to the status of a religious attitude toward human life, forgetting the superabundant light that revelation provides to human beings. The Abrahamic God, in turn, is unthinkable according to Dworkin's epistemological framework because it rejects any external and metaethical inspection of morality, religion, and truth. Taking religion seriously, and not as a mere attitude, demands a truly integrated epistemology—not in the Dworkinian sense but in the sense of integrating faith and reason, religion and knowledge, metaphysics and epistemology, theology and history, and data and interpretation: that is, all modes of human understanding (including imperfect ones, like analogical reasoning). In sum, epistemology should be open to the possibility of a transcendent reality without any limitation besides reasonableness. Otherwise, it cannot support a holistic normative paradigm for both religion and religious freedom.

Dworkin affirms that "the religious attitude rests finally on faith."[51] However, the faith he demands for religion is simply the conviction that mathematics demands: the mere conviction that all the systems work, that the system of value judgments generates objective value. Faith is the "irresistible conviction in our experience of value."[52] Faith for Dworkin, then, is just a

48 Dworkin, *Religion without God*, 24.
49 Dworkin, *Justice for Hedgehogs*, 84.
50 Dworkin, *Religion without God*, 151–52.
51 Dworkin, *Religion without God*, 18.
52 Dworkin, *Religion without God*, 21.

matter of convinced knowing, not as it's defined in the Abrahamic religions: an adequate response to the invitation of God to live in God's own company. Abraham was a man of faith because he submitted freely to the word of God, and a response to God is both a fact and a value. It is a response that transcends history and generates value by itself. Religious faith and nonreligious faith are different, however, because the field of knowledge and experience of one (religion) is more significant than that of the other (atheism).

For that reason, believing in God (conventional religion) can contribute to living well (ethics) and to treating others well (morality). For religious believers, believing in God is a necessary but not sufficient condition for living well. Believing in God and living well have different meanings, but they are related. The more a person's belief in or obedience to God contributes to living well and treating others well, the better that person's belief is in political terms. It therefore makes sense to speak of *believing* well. As a source of value, the human person can integrate ethical, political, moral, and religious beliefs to recognize and transmit truths that cut across all of these dimensions of life. In this sense, the Dworkinian idea of the unity of value is constructive. What is needed, however, is a holistic unity of value beliefs that considers transcendent truths and virtues and values, as opposed to the more reductive Dworkinian conception.

Human cognition forms an organic whole, but this organic whole is not complete without incorporating the human person's transcendent religious experience. That requires recovering the sapiential dimension of human knowledge, which is critical to search for ultimate meaning. Dworkin's epistemology has to acknowledge the human being's capacity to transcend factual and empirical data to contemplate foundational reality in the search for truth through analogical reasoning. To avoid the fragmentation of knowledge, an adequately integrated moral epistemology must be based not only on the unity of value but also, and mainly, on the unity of the human person as such, in his or her physical and transcendent dimensions.

Dworkin's approach to religion (especially to religious atheism) demands only a very narrow protection of religious freedom. If religion is just a matter of convictions, without divine commitments and a duty of ritual worship, the right to religious freedom could be protected simply as a matter of what Dworkin calls "ethical independence." In other words, there is no reason to treat religious freedom as a special right. Dworkin affirms: "The problem we encountered in defining freedom of religion flows from trying to retain that right as a special right while also decoupling religion from a god. We should consider, instead, abandoning the idea of a special right to religious freedom with its high hurdle of protection and, therefore, its compelling need for strict limits and careful definitions."[53]

In Which Religious Communities Will Emerge Ethical Independence Instead of Religious Freedom?

The concept of ethical independence is the key to understanding Dworkin's arguments.[54] According to the Dworkinian principle of ethical independence, government must not rely on any justification that directly, indirectly, or covertly supposes any ethical conviction about what is better or worse for a good life. Thus, ethical independence "stops government from restricting freedom only for certain reasons and not for others."[55] Ethical independence means absolute personal sovereignty in foundational matters, such that a person should never accept any judgment in place of his or her own. Insofar as religion is a foundational matter, no government may constrain religion for any reason except when necessary to protect the life, security, or liberty of others (especially to enforce nondiscrimination). Moreover, in no case may a political community dictate ethical convictions to its citizens.

The political community may force us to live under collective decisions only if it does so without imposing ethical convictions. Therefore, there is no place for any religious "ethical paternalism" that favors one faith over others. Thus, according to Dworkin, ethical independence requires individuals to refrain from imposing ethical convictions by treating a particular religion as *sui generis* or treating religion as such as special. Consequently, a "priority of non-discriminatory collective government over private religious exercise seems inevitable and right."[56] According to the norm of ethical independence, religious exemptions from neutral laws have no justification. In this light, Dworkin probably would have resolved Leiter's proposed case of the Sikh boy by affirming the prohibition of his attending the ceremonial school day with the dagger.

By applying the principle of ethical independence, Dworkin reduces freedom of religion to freedom of conscience and freedom of conscience to

---

53 Dworkin, *Religion without God*, 132.
54 Dworkin, *Religion without God*, 130–32.
55 Dworkin, *Religion without God*, 131.
56 Dworkin, *Religion without God*, 137.

"freedom of personal choice." Because freedom of religion is just a matter of convictions, Dworkin would provide the same treatment to both moral and religious convictions. It is, therefore, understandable that he would reject religious exemptions to provide equal protection to citizens.

My argument, however, is different: the application of religious exemptions is a consequence of equal protection and a demand for the right to religious freedom that is irreducible to freedom of conscience. Freedom of religion protects religion; freedom of conscience, by contrast, protects individual moral conscience. Without freedom of conscience, there is no freedom of religion, but freedom of religion embraces some areas (e.g., education, public manifestation of faith, worship) that do not fall directly into the realm of freedom of conscience.

Religious freedom is based on the idea that political communities are structurally nonreligious communities, but at the same time, religious communities should be established within political communities. Their nonreligious structural character justifies the existence of a political right to religious freedom that protects citizens and religious communities against any political intrusion in religious matters, even based on potentially neutral legislation.[57] The specific and unique legal tool for protecting religious freedom as an affirmative defense against neutral laws is the religious exemption, which the judiciary should recognize.

Freedom of conscience protects a minimal area of moral freedom that under no circumstances may be violated. Where the frontier between private life and political authority should be drawn is "a matter of argument, indeed of haggling," we can say with Isaiah Berlin.[58] The principle of accommodation suggests that in many areas, there is no one size that fits all public morality, and there is a need for a modus vivendi beyond the standards of public morality. The scope of freedom of conscience should be narrower than religious freedom since political communities retain the freedom to

---

[57] An internationally famous American case defending "neutral legislation" is the peyote case (Employment Division, Department of Human Resources of Oregon, 494 U.S. 872 [1990]), in which Justice Antonin Scalia (1936–2016), writing for the majority, observed that "We have never held that an individual's religious beliefs excuse him from compliance with an otherwise valid law prohibiting conduct that government is free to regulate" (at 878–79).

[58] Isaiah Berlin, "Two Concepts of Liberty," in *Four Essays on Liberty* (Oxford: Oxford University Press, 1969), 125.

develop their own public morality under the common good but not their own public religion. Because of our mutual interdependence, the exercise of freedom by some citizens always comes at the expense of restricting the freedom of others.

Freedom of conscience should be supported not by a norm of ethical independence, but by *ethical autonomy*, a substantially different concept that emphasizes the indispensable relationship between human freedom and moral order in all dimensions of the human person—individual, social, and transcendent. According to ethical autonomy, it is possible to harmonize legality, morality, religion, and freedom. For ethical autonomy, the essence (and the end) of moral freedom is the pursuit of the good, in accordance with which people can shape their own choices. As Joseph Raz rightly emphasizes: "Autonomy is valuable only if exercised in pursuit of the good."[59]

Conclusion:
Taking Religious Freedom and Freedom of Conscience Seriously

The right of religious freedom operates in the three dimensions of the human person. It operates in the individual dimension (along with freedom of conscience) by protecting the human person in his or her personal search for God, the divine, and the truth against any constraint by political authorities. In the social dimension, the right to religious freedom allows individuals to live their faith in a community and protects political communities against religious and secularist fundamentalisms as rejections of legitimate pluralism. Finally, in the transcendent dimension, the right to religious freedom operates by protecting religion as a basic good and opening the door to transcendent truths. Because freedom of religion is the inclusive patrimony of both religious believers and nonbelievers, it fully protects from religion those who choose to have nothing to do with religion and protects the religious from those who wish to use constructions of "the secular" or "secularism" that unduly restrict religious people and their communities from appropriate public involvements.

Dworkin's and Leiter's new approaches protect the individual dimension, but they banish the other two dimensions, the social and the transcendent. This is why they completely undervalue the public dimension of religion.

---

59 Joseph Raz, *The Morality of Freedom* (Oxford: Clarendon Press 1986), 381.

Dworkin's approach to religion belittles the idea of God, yet conviction about the existence of God and the holding of profound ethical and moral convictions are not so independent, as Dworkin argues.[60] Leiter's approach belittles the idea of religion, which cannot be reduced to a matter of commands, a lack of evidence, and consolation.

Religion is more than a matter of conscience or a personal decision about ultimate concerns and questions. Thus, it cannot be reduced to moral conscience, let alone to ethical independence in foundational matters. An increasingly globalized and pluralistic society demands a more comprehensive approach that fully protects all religions and creeds. The proper protection of religion, therefore, demands a specific right of religious freedom even beyond freedom of conscience.

Religious freedom is still a first-class right, although some secularist legal scholars have sought to diminish, if not demolish, one of the pillars of Western legal culture. By denaturing religious freedom, Dworkin and Leiter denature dignity; by denaturing dignity, they denature democracy. I would say in favorable terms: upgrading religious freedom means upgrading dignity and democracy. A worthy democracy demands the first-level right to religious freedom.

---

60 Dworkin, *Religion without God*, 146.

CHAPTER 6

LAW AND MORALITY
One Hundred Years of Solitude

THE DEBATE ABOUT THE (EVER-COMPLEX) relationship between morality and law has been intense, polemical, and illuminating in the past one hundred years. It has been argued against the backdrop of, first, the Second World War and the Nazi Holocaust; then the birth of the United Nations, the Universal Declaration of Human Rights, the Cold War, and the fall of the Berlin Wall; and, most recently, globalization and new technologies that have universalized the conversation and made English the official language of the debate.

This debate has featured well-known intellectuals of the magnitude of (in alphabetical order) Robert Alexy, John Finnis, Jürgen Habermas, Herbert L. A. Hart, Hans Kelsen, Jacques Maritain, Gustav Radbruch, John Rawls, Joseph Raz, Robert Spaemann, Charles Taylor, Michel Villey, and even Pope Benedict XVI, who dedicated a discourse on this subject in Germany's Federal Parliament on the occasion of his 2011 apostolic journey to Germany. Among other things, Benedict affirmed the following: "A positivist

---

* This is an English revised version of my Spanish-language paper "El derecho y la moral: Cien años de soledad," *Scripta Theologica* 52, no. 3 (2020): 763–92. This introductory overview of many of the main themes of contemporary jurisprudence was written for teaching purposes and is not to be considered a contribution to research.

conception of nature as purely functional, as the natural sciences consider it to be, is incapable of producing any bridge to ethics and law, but once again yields only functional answers."[1]

As a jurist, I approach this debate from the perspective of the law, which has had a huge philosophical influence due to its reliance on arguments and doctrines propounded by great thinkers like Aristotle, Thomas Aquinas, Thomas Hobbes, John Locke, Immanuel Kant, Jeremy Bentham, John Austin, and Max Weber, as well as contemporary philosophers like Niklas Luhmann, Jürgen Habermas, Robert Spaemann, and Alasdair MacIntyre, among many others. Despite the importance of Thomas Aquinas's writings to natural law theorists, theology has not played a relevant role.

The legal debate has not strictly confronted positivist (the dominant) and natural law perspectives, though neither has been missing. The strongest critiques of legal positivism have come not only from the ranks of the natural law theorists (Maritain, Villey, Finnis) but also, and mostly, from nonpositivist and non-naturalist intellectuals like Ronald Dworkin. The critiques from within positivism (e.g., that of Hart against Bentham, Austin, and Kelsen, or from Raz and his teachers Kelsen and Hart) have been so certain that they have influenced the very meaning of positivism. The natural law doctrines are also divided, especially among Protestant Christians who have incorporated Christian revelation into the debate (VanDrunen) and those, especially Catholics, who have resigned themselves to rationalist arguments (Villey, Hervada, Finnis, George).

The positivist thinkers have been progressively internally divided in their conceptions of the relationship between law and morality and have lost interest in natural law theory, possibly because, in the rigors of the debate, it has become pretty clear that it is impossible to separate morality and law in the way the most radical positivists have done in the past, and the way legalists continue to do today. The elaboration and application of these norms, just as in the resolution of concrete issues, need to constantly refer to moral principles, either implicitly or explicitly.

John Gardner (1965–2019), a professor at Oxford until his death, qualified the strict positivist separation between law and morality as a half-myth, and he is right.[2] It should not surprise the reader that, on occasion, it is

---

[1] Benedict XVI, "Speech to the German Parliament," Berlin, September 22, 2011.

[2] John Gardner, "Legal Positivism: 5½ Myths," *The American Journal of Jurisprudence* 46, no. 1 (2001): 199–227, reprinted in John Gardner, *Law as a Leap of Faith: Essays on Law in General* (Oxford: Oxford University Press, 2012), 19–53.

those very same positivists who defend positions that have for centuries been considered natural law doctrines, while natural law theorists often harbor positivist perspectives. At its core, then, the strict categorization of positivist and natural law intellectuals, although valid at first glance, is fallacious. Thomas Aquinas, the most significant natural law advocate of all time, was a great defender of the positivity of human law.[3] H. L. A. Hart, the greatest Anglo-Saxon positivist, acknowledged a minimal content of natural law.[4] On occasion, positivists are attacked for not giving sufficient consideration to morality, which is not always true. On other occasions, natural law theorists are attacked for having forgotten legal positivism, which is seldom true.

Kelsen's Positivism and His German Critics: From Radbruch to Alexy

Our debate began in 1934, when the Czech-born Austrian jurist Hans Kelsen (1881–1973) while serving as a professor in Geneva, published in Vienna his "pure" theory of law—in German, *Reine Rechtslehre*. A second edition, greatly enlarging his influential theory, was published in 1960, when Kelsen was a professor at the University of California, Berkeley. The English translation was not available until 1967.[5]

Influenced by neo-Kantianism, from which he took the idea of "validity," as well as by the positivism of Bentham and Austin, Kelsen proposed to develop a theory of law serviceable in any time or territory to elevate the legal discipline to the category of an independent normative science with its own method and object. The law must be methodologically purified from moral, economic, sociological, or political contaminants, he argued.

This purist methodology demanded, among other things, a strict separation between law and morality, following the most classical positivist model

---

3   Thomas Aquinas, *Summa Theologiae*, II–II, q. 57, a. 1. See John Finnis, *Aquinas: Moral Political, and Legal Theory* (Oxford: Oxford University Press, 1998), 269.

4   H. L. A. Hart, *The Concept of Law*, 3rd ed. (Oxford: Oxford University Press, 2012), 193–99.

5   Hans Kelsen, *Reine Rechtslehre. Einleitung in die rechtswissenschaftliche Problematik* (Leipzig: F. Deuticke, 1934; 2nd ed., 1960). The second edition was translated into English by Max Knight: Hans Kelsen, *Pure Theory of Law* (Berkeley: University of California Press, 1967). In the second edition, Kelsen expounded on more sociological and voluntaristic positions so that the influence of North American law can be seen.

but also defining the line of separation between facts and the law (here, Kelsen deviates from classical positivism). Just as the law, unlike fact, is occupied with what ought to be (*sollen*) and not what is (*sein*), his legal theory must have been essentially normativist; that is to say, it served to determine the criteria to corroborate the validity and coherence of the norms.

The legal order—which Kelsen identifies as the state—is conceived as an aggregate of coercive norms of similar character organized hierarchically according to a pyramid structure. At the foundation, one finds the *Grundnorm*, or basic norm of a hypothetical nature, which validates all rules. In this way, the binding nature of legal norms does not require an external force from the legal order, whether God or the personification of nature, the state, or the nation.

For Kelsen, the legal order, at its core, has only procedural qualities of validity; it is more of an instrument than an end. For this reason, the norms can support any content, since the content is not strictly legal. One might say that, according to Kelsen, the law studies how to make bottles (norms), not their contents (wine, beer, or water), which are later introduced to them through morality, economics, psychology, and politics. To make a pure theory of law, separating the moral element (the contents) from the legal element (the container) is essential. Just like the so-called natural morality, what is understood as justice in every time and country would be much more a part of the container than the normative content, which has more to do with ideology than with the law. This content, as such, has no interest in a pure theory of law, which is fundamentally formalist and normativist. A valid legal norm (bottle) will not stop being legal because of the immorality of its content (poison); thus, law and morality constitute independent normative systems.

In summary, Kelsen discards all ethical and political value judgments to strictly center himself in the frame of legal positivism. As a consequence, Kelsen criticizes natural law doctrines as antiscientific.[6]

The German philosopher of law and politics Gustav Radbruch (1878–1949) reacted vigorously against Kelsen's theory. Radbruch defended the view that Nazi law was mere coercive force, not law in a proper sense because it lacked moral substance and was radically unjust. In Radbruch's view, the law encapsulates ethical values and ideals of justice, and the fundamental

---

6   Hans Kelsen, *What Is Justice? Justice, Law, and Politics in the Mirror of Science* (Clark, N.J.: The Lawbook Exchange, 2013), 228, 285ff.

principles of human morality form part of the very concept of law. No promulgation of positive law, even if it fits the formal criteria of validity of legal order, can be considered legally valid if it is unbearably unjust and contravenes the basic principles of morality.[7] This is Radbruch's well-known formula, still in use today in service of German constitutional jurisprudence.

A contemporary of Radbruch, Leo Strauss (1899–1973), was a German professor who immigrated to the United States and finished an exceptional career at the University of Chicago. In his book *Natural Right and History* (1953),[8] Strauss, from non-Thomistic positions, tried to revive the Greco-Latin tradition, criticized the lack of consistency in positivism, and reclaimed for legal-political theory the need to approach questions of ontology and the history of metaphysics.

Inspired by the ideas of Radbruch, Arthur Kaufmann (1923–2001), a professor in Munich, held that justice belongs to the very essence of law. For this reason, the "unjust law" constitutes a contradiction of terms. The mere approval and promulgation of a law (*Gesetz*) cannot become the ultimate foundation for establishing a just law (*Recht*).[9]

Following Radbruch, Robert Alexy (b. 1945), professor emeritus at the University of Kiel, has offered a sharp critique of Kelsen's positivism and has formulated a nonpositivist theory of law. Alexy has propounded three theses to articulate the relationship of law and morality: 1) all legal order contains principles (the incorporative thesis); 2) the law must be related to a common morality (the moral thesis); and 3) the law must be related to a just morality (the correctness thesis). Just as the law coerces the behavior of individuals and provides them with a decisive reason for action, the correction that the law affirms also has to be moral.[10]

---

7   Gustav Radbruch, "Gesetzliches Unrecht und übergesetzliches Recht" (1946), in Gustav Radbruch, *Gesamtausgabe*, vol. 3, ed. Arthur Kaufmann (Heidelberg: C. E. Müller, 1990), 83–89. Kelsen and Radbruch share a common neo-Kantian paradigm. Any deep analysis of their relationship would need to consider Radbruch's prewar legal philosophy and the development of his views during the Second World War.

8   Leo Strauss, *Natural Right and History* (Chicago: University of Chicago Press, 1953; 2nd ed., 1971).

9   On Kaufmann, see Ulfrid Neumann, "Arthur Kaufmann (1923–2001)," in *Juristas universales*, ed. Rafael Domingo, vol. 4 (Madrid: Marcial Pons, 2004), 692–98. For an overview, please see Arthur Kaufmann, *Rechtsphilosophie* (Munich: Beck Verlag, 1994; 2nd ed., 1997).

10   See, above all, Robert Alexy, *The Argument from Injustice: A Reply to Legal*

Hart, Architect of
Anglo-Saxon Legal Positivism

Oxford professor Herbert L. A. Hart (1907–1992) has been acclaimed as the most significant English legal philosopher since Jeremy Bentham. A writer of exquisite style and a man of great intelligence, Hart accepted part of Kelsen's "pure" theory, critically refined it, perfected it, and adapted it to the scope of Anglo-American law.[11] Despite having lived more than thirty years in the United States, Kelsen never gained the influence in that country that he had in Europe, Latin America, and Japan.[12]

As for the debate over the relationship between morality and law, Hart's original position is similar to that of Kelsen (strict conceptual separation between law and morality), but there are many critical nuanced distinctions, as both Kelsen and Hart evolved intellectually on this matter.

In April 1957, Hart delivered a lecture at Harvard University titled "Positivism and the Separation of Law and Morality."[13] In it, Hart positioned himself in favor of the separationist thesis that had been defended in the United States, with somewhat picturesque tints, by Harvard professor and Supreme Court Justice Oliver Wendell Holmes, Jr. (1841–1935). Even today, Holmes is considered one of the most-cited jurists in Anglo-American law.[14]

Positivism, trans. Stanley Paulson and Bonnie Litschewski Paulson (Oxford: Oxford University Press, 2002). The original text was published in 1992: Robert Alexy, *Begriff und Geltung des Rechts* (Freiburg im Breisgau: Verlag Karl Alber, 1992).

11   See the famous debate between Hart and Kelsen, in November 1961 in California, found in H. L. A. Hart, "Kelsen Visited," *Essays in Jurisprudence and Philosophy* (Oxford: Oxford University Press, 1983), 86–308. Another of Hart's criticisms of Kelsen is found in Hart, "Kelsen's Doctrine of the Unity of Law," *Essays in Jurisprudence and Philosophy*, 309–42.

12   Kelsen, a lover of precision, wrote his "pure" theory of law in German until it was completed in 1960. Underlying this decision was a semantic reason: the word *law* in English has a much more extensive meaning than *Gesetz* in German or *lex* in Latin or *ley* in Spanish, just as the word *right* in English has a more limited meaning than *Recht* in German or *ius* in Latin or *derecho* in Spanish. In the field of legal theory, every translation is, in some way, a betrayal.

13   H. L. A. Hart, "Positivism and the Separation of Law and Morals," *Harvard Law Review* 71 (1958): 593–629, reproduced in Hart, *Essays in Jurisprudence and Philosophy*, 49–87.

14   See Holmes's famous lecture, "The Path of Law," *Harvard Law Review* 10 (1897): 457–78.

A few months after Hart's lecture, the *Harvard Law Review* published, along with a note from Hart, a thorough criticism by Harvard professor Lon Fuller (1902–1978),[15] initiating what has come to be known as the Hart-Fuller debate, one of the most important for North American jurisprudence in the last century.[16] Hart advocated the absence of a necessary connection (though never denied the contingency) between morality and the law, while Fuller held that legal orders have their own internal morality, of a fundamental procedural character.

Three years later, in 1961, after meticulous preparation, Hart published his masterpiece, *The Concept of Law*, where he presented his vision of law from a positivist perspective, refining Bentham's, Austin's, and Kelsen's thoughts. His focus is the object of analytical jurisprudence and that of what he calls a descriptive sociology, which perceives the birth of law as arising from a set type of social facts that establish validity criteria.[17]

Hart affirmed that legal order as such is a system of rules. These can be primary or secondary. Primary rules impose obligations and requirements, while secondary rules enable the creation of new primary rules or the modification or dissolution of existing ones. The rule of recognition is a secondary rule that all others depend on. It is the ultimate referential rule, valid because it has been socially accepted. The similarity to Kelsen is evident. With this construction, morality does not affect in any way the validity of the law; in other words, conformity with other standards of morality is not a necessary condition for the existence of legal order.

Hart discusses his separationist approach to law and morality in *The Concept of Law*. In chapter 9, he says, "Here we shall take Legal Positivism to mean the simple contention that it is in no sense a necessary truth that laws reproduce or satisfy certain demands of morality, though in fact they have often done so."[18]

For Hart, undoubtedly, there are quite a few connections between morality and law—one connection being their social purpose—but moral principles are not necessarily a source of law, although they could become so

15   Lon L. Fuller, "Positivism and Fidelity to Law: A Reply to Professor Hart," *Harvard Law Review* 71 (1958): 630–72.
16   On this debate and its real policy implications, see Peter Cane, ed., *The Hart-Fuller Debate in the Twenty-First Century* (Oxford: Hart Publishing, 2010).
17   H. L. A. Hart, *The Concept of Law*, 3rd ed. (Oxford: Oxford University Press, 2012).
18   Hart, *The Concept of Law*, 185–86.

if they were formally clothed as a norm. But the reverse is also true: morally unjust provisions can be legally valid if they are normatively enforced. Hart comes to accept a "minimum content of natural law" to ensure the purpose of survival in the various modes of association of human beings.[19]

Lon Fuller again criticized Hart's position, and in 1964, he published his famous book *The Morality of Law*, revised in 1969 to include responses to his critics, Hart among them.[20] Inspired by Gustav Radbruch, Fuller forcefully rejected the positivist perspective and affirmed that the validity of law requires moral control. Moral requirements are contained in eight formal principles of legality that he calls "the internal morality of law," and constitute a kind of test of morality. According to Fuller, a legal system can be considered as such only if the law is: (a) general, (b) public, (c) prospective, (d) intelligible, (e) coherent or noncontradictory, (f) practicable, (g) stable, and (h) congruent. Hart defended Fuller's critics, alleging that what Fuller called morality could not be considered as such.[21]

Dworkin's Critique of Positivism Turns the Debate Around

Ronald Dworkin (1931–2013), Hart's successor on the Oxford faculty, per his express desire, and subsequently professor at New York University (NYU) and University College London, offered the first overwhelming criticism of Hart's positivism in an article titled "The Model of Rules," published in the law journal of the University of Chicago.[22] With this article, Dworkin initiated a dynamic debate between both philosophies of law that had as significant an impact in the Anglo-Saxon world as in the scope of continental law.[23] In Dworkin's well-known work *Taking Rights*

---

19 Hart, *The Concept of Law*, 193–99.

20 Lon L. Fuller, "Reply to Critics," in *The Morality of Law* (New Haven, Conn.: Yale University Press, 1964; 2nd ed., 1969), 198–244.

21 Hart's criticism of Fuller's book *The Morality of Law* can also be seen in Hart's review of the book in *Harvard Law Review* 78 (1964–65): 1281–95, reproduced in Hart, *Essays in Jurisprudence and Philosophy*, 343–64.

22 Ronald Dworkin, "The Model of Rules," *University of Chicago Law Review* 35 (1967–1968): 14–46, reproduced in Ronald Dworkin, *Taking Rights Seriously* (Cambridge, Mass.: Harvard University Press, 1977), 14–45.

23 On this debate, see Scott Shapiro, "The Hart-Dworkin Debate: Law, Morality, and the Guidance of Conduct," *Legal Theory* 6 (2000): 127–70.

Seriously (1977),[24] which reproduces, among others, Hart's review of *The Model of Rules*, Dworkin affirms that the positivists do not offer an adequate explanation of the law or what happens in practice when judges and courts apply it. Dworkin does not limit himself, however, to criticizing Hart's theory; he also offers an alternative from the perspective of the rights and principles that he continued to develop in later works, such as *A Matter of Principle* (1985), *Law's Empire* (1986—his best-known book), and his final analytical volume, *Justice for Hedgehogs* (2011).[25]

According to Dworkin, Hart, in his theory of rules, forgets those principles that are necessary to resolve certain cases that Dworkin categorizes as difficult (*hard cases*), which undoubtedly have a moral component. With numerous examples from North American jurisprudence, Dworkin refers to important cases resolved by courts that affect the U.S. Constitution and those in which the courts have considered discernible moral principles in the process of deliberation and decision. For Dworkin, there does not exist a neutral moral process of validating legal norms because the law itself is a complex lattice of principles, legal rules, and morals.

Dworkin criticized and rejected any positivist pyramidal structure of law, whether it was founded in the power of a sovereign, as Austin argued, in the fundamental norms argued by Kelsen, or in Hart's rule of recognition. For Dworkin, all law is based not on formal rules but on moral principles, such that law and morality cannot be considered totally independent systems. If there are valid judicial standards, it is because they are morally valid. For Dworkin, the law is a branch of a grand morality tree.[26]

Legality is determined not only by social practice or from social facts but also by morality. According to Dworkin, this relationship between morality and law is precisely what permits courts to resolve legal conflict when they encounter a legal loophole. Therefore, it is necessary to appeal not to pure discretion, as positivists contend, but to principles that

---

24 See the appendix to Dworkin, *Taking Rights Seriously*, which contains "A Reply to Critics," 291–368.

25 Ronald Dworkin, *A Matter of Principle* (Cambridge, Mass.: Harvard University Press, 1985); Ronald Dworkin, *Law's Empire* (Cambridge, Mass.: Belknap Press of Harvard University Press, 1986); and Ronald Dworkin, *Justice for Hedgehogs* (Cambridge, Mass.: Belknap Press of Harvard University Press, 2011). In chapter 19 of *Justice for Hedgehogs*, Dworkin offers his ultimate analysis of the relations between law and morality.

26 Dworkin, *Justice for Hedgehogs*, 171, 400–414.

undoubtedly have a moral component. As Dworkin himself explains: "law includes not only the specific rules enacted in accordance with the community's accepted practices but also the principles that provide the best moral justification for those enacted rules."[27]

Dworkin joined in Fuller's criticism of Hart and recognized, with the natural law theorists, that every legal tradition contains principles of justice that are essential ingredients in the law. For Dworkin, therefore, the moral dimension of law was substantive, and the principles of justice and equity, with inexorable moral content, were precisely the way weight was given to the law.

In his moral and political theory of law, the *principles of equal concern and respect* had critical moral implications.[28] Equal concern means that every citizen merits the same consideration and interest from public powers. Equal respect signifies that public powers must respect individual dignity and permit everyone to decide for themselves what it means to live a good life. Based on this principle, Dworkin affirms the existence of a *right to moral independence* that limits the reach of public powers in matters that he calls *foundational ethical matters*,[29] intending to protect the responsibility of people to find value in their own lives.[30]

According to Dworkin, governments cannot dictate any ethical convictions of "what is good" to citizens in foundational matters; instead, they must respect equally any form or style of living. According to Dworkin, this right justifies, for example, public power abstaining from penalizing pornography,[31] abortion, or euthanasia, despite the damage that even Dworkin acknowledges these practices cause to the public interest.[32] These fundamental principles demand a space for individual liberty that is more protected than the essence

---

27   Dworkin, *Justice for Hedgehogs*, 402.
28   Dworkin, *Taking Rights Seriously*, 180–83, 272–78.
29   Dworkin, *Justice for Hedgehogs*, 368. It seems that Dworkin does not consider that this decision is, in itself, a moral imposition of the government on the citizens consistent with artificially separating private morality from public.
30   Ronald Dworkin, *Is Democracy Possible Here? Principles for a New Political Debate* (Princeton, N.J.: Princeton University Press, 2006), 66.
31   See Ronald Dworkin, "Do We Have a Right to Pornography?" in Dworkin, *A Matter of Principle*, 335–72.
32   Ronald, Dworkin, *Life's Dominion: An Argument about Abortion, Euthanasia, and Individual Freedom* (New York: Vintage, 1994).

of other rights. At the same time, the principle of equal attention and respect excludes laws concerning public morality, considering them unjust for citizens who do not share those same moral ideologies.

According to Dworkin, this *right to moral independence* protects all intimate personal matters (e.g., reproduction, marriage, sexual orientation, sex changes, assisted suicide), as well as religious liberty, ethical beliefs, politics, and morals.[33] The list of foundational ethical matters protected by this right, according to Dworkin, is open to additions[34] in the event that new questions that affect convictions that define the personality are identified, through which one creates value in one's life.[35] The public powers can limit this right only when necessary to protect life, security, or the liberty of others.[36]

In 1994, on the publication of the second edition of his *The Concept of Law*, Hart's editors, Penelope Bulloch and Joseph Raz, included a posthumous writing by Hart responding to criticisms by Dworkin and other authors, some of which Hart accepts.[37] In this writing, Hart speaks of *soft positivism*, which has been called inclusive, and which admits that Hart's latest criteria of legal validity explicitly incorporate principles of justice or substantive moral values.[38] The progenitors of this *soft positivism*—including, among others, Jules Coleman, Matthew Kramer, and Will Waluchow—affirm that moral considerations could become an integral part of the law if the sources themselves implicitly or explicitly considered them.[39]

In light of this positivism, a more exclusive positivism has risen, led (unabashedly) by Joseph Raz (1939–2022), Hart's disciple, a professor at Columbia University and King's College London and teacher of a host of

---

33   Dworkin, *Justice for Hedgehogs*, 368–69.
34   Dworkin, *Justice for Hedgehogs*, 369.
35   For a criticism of this right, see Rafael Domingo, *God and the Secular Legal System* (Cambridge: Cambridge University Press, 2016), 146–48.
36   Dworkin, *Justice for Hedgehogs*, 369.
37   Hart, *The Concept of Law*, 238–334.
38   Hart, *The Concept of Law*, 247: "In some systems of law, as in the United States, the ultimate criteria of legal validity might explicitly incorporate besides pedigree, principles of justice or substantive moral values, and these may form the content of legal constitutional restraints."
39   For an overview, see W. J. Waluchow, *Inclusive Legal Positivism* (Oxford: Oxford University Press, 1994).

excellent legal philosophers. Raz is credited with one of the best criticisms of Hart, Kelsen, and Dworkin. Raz argues that the existence and content of law depend exclusively on social sources. With that, he would settle precisely law's claim of authority, which would be left depleted if there were no exclusive reason behind it. In this sense, Raz is positioned between Hart, who denies any pretention of morality in the authority of law, and Dworkin, who defends the morality of law in everything except mere barbarism.

Raz's exclusive positivism is made compatible with the argument for a liberalism known as perfectionist, which respects the principles of classical political liberalism but, against Dworkin's ideals, abandons the necessity of neutrality from public powers against the diverse conceptions of good.[40]

John Rawls and His Public Reasoning Filter

At this point in the debate, it is necessary to introduce, if only briefly, John Rawls (1921–2002), considered by many the most influential American liberal political philosopher of the twentieth century. In his work *A Theory of Justice*, published in 1971,[41] this Harvard professor and former student of Hart at Oxford articulates a political and liberal theory of justice as an alternative to utilitarianism, based on Kantian principles like impartiality, universalization, and respect for people. He elaborated and completed his theory in *Political Liberalism* (1993), *The Law of Peoples* (1999), and *Justice as Fairness: A Restatement* (2001).[42] This theory has had great influence on legal arguments about public morality and the practice of law in Western democracies, as well as in the lives of their citizens.

Beginning with what he terms an "original position," in which rational individuals deliberate and elect the most adequate (that is to say, the most just) institutions to distribute burdens and benefits, Rawls approaches the political problem of justice practically, not theoretically or epistemologically, but with

---

40 See Joseph Raz, *The Morality of Freedom* (Oxford: Clarendon Press, 1986); Joseph Raz, *Ethics in Public Domain: Essays in the Morality of Law and Politics* (Oxford: Oxford University Press, 1994).

41 John Rawls, *A Theory of Justice*, rev. ed. (Cambridge, Mass.: The Belknap Press of Harvard University Press, 1999).

42 John Rawls, *Political Liberalism* (New York: Columbia University Press, 1993; 2nd ed., 2005); John Rawls, *The Law of Peoples* (Cambridge, Mass.: Harvard University Press, 1999; 2nd ed., 2001); and John Rawls, *Justice as Fairness: A Restatement*, ed. Erin Kelly (Cambridge, Mass.: Harvard University Press, 2001).

the pretense of formulating the best public criterion of justice. For this, he approaches the moral question through public prudential orders concerning justice that rational citizens agree to share by overlapping consensus on the basic principles of justice and fundamentals of the constitution.

Rawls proposes a platform of political values accepted by rational citizens in which the concept of law has priority over the concept of good.[43] This prioritization of law permits all citizens to maintain their own *comprehensive doctrines* concerning the moral concept of good but limits the kinds of moral considerations that count publicly as legitimate reasons in political deliberations within the frame of accepted principles of justice.

In their deliberations and decisions, citizens must reconcile their particular preconceptions of the good with shared and accepted principles of justice. To reconcile these, Rawls develops the concept of *public reason*,[44] which acts as a sort of argumentative filter in public debate and endeavors to reconcile the private life of the citizenry with the standards of political justice. For Rawls, it is a requirement of public reasoning that citizens must justify their political decisions by relying only on publicly available values and standards. Therefore, for example, it would not be an argument in line with political reasoning to affirm that euthanasia should not be permitted because of a Christian mandate prohibiting murder; on the other hand, a Christian could argue that euthanasia undermines the dignity of all people (not only Christians) and detracts from the value of human life.

Rawls's public reasoning considerably limits the reasons for promulgating public moral laws of any sort since one can easily argue that comprehensive doctrines are being employed, as has happened de facto in the abortion debate. Public reasoning drastically reduces the jurisprudence of any field of law that directly or indirectly affects public morality. On the other hand, public reasoning cuts through natural law positions that can easily be branded as comprehensive doctrines. Concretely, in *Political Liberalism*, Rawls criticizes those *rationalist believers* who think their beliefs are open to reason and can be established in line with it.[45]

---

[43] Rawls, *A Theory of Justice*, 28: "In justice as fairness the concept of right is prior to that of the good."

[44] The best exploration of this idea is found in Rawls, *The Law of Peoples: With "The Idea of Public Reason Revisited,"* 2nd ed.

[45] Rawls, *Political Liberalism*, 152–53.

Rawls's suggestive approaches dominate the space of political (and legal) philosophy and have generated their own debate. His sharpest critic came from his own home, Harvard, with the publication of the book *Liberalism and the Limits of Justice* (1981) by Michael Sandel.[46] A little later, Scottish philosopher Alasdair MacIntyre joined in the criticism with his book *After Virtue* (1984),[47] as did Charles Taylor[48] and Michael Walzer,[49] among others. Rawls himself, and supporters of liberalism like Ronald Dworkin, Jürgen Habermas, and Will Kymlicka, joined in this great debate, which certainly merits a separate article, since it transcends the legal sphere.[50]

Habermas and His Equivocal Distinction between Ethics and Morals

Claims similar to those of John Rawls regarding the formulation of a liberal theory acceptable by citizens with any comprehensive vision of reality were made by philosopher Jürgen Habermas (b. 1929),[51] professor emeritus of the University of Frankfort am Main and one of the most influential thinkers of our day. Like Rawls, Habermas studied, from the perspective of philosophy, procedural theories that satisfied the need to substantiate positive law in democratic societies. As opposed to Rawls, however, Habermas did this from the institutionalization of procedures of distinct rational discourses.[52]

Habermas's fundamental work for understanding his multidisciplinary approach to law is *Facticity and Validity* (in German: *Faktizität und*

---

[46] Michael Sandel, *Liberalism and the Limits of Justice* (Cambridge: Cambridge University Press, 1981).

[47] Alasdair MacIntyre, *After Virtue: A Study in Moral Theory* (Notre Dame, Ind.: University of Notre Dame Press, 1984).

[48] Charles Taylor, *Sources of the Self: The Making of the Modern Identity* (Cambridge, Mass.: Harvard University Press, 1989).

[49] Michael Walzer, *Spheres of Justice; A Defense of Pluralism and Equality* (Oxford: Basil Blackwell, 1983); Michael Walzer, *Interpretation and Social Criticism* (Cambridge, Mass.: Harvard University Press, 1987).

[50] On this debate, see Stephen Mullhall and Adam Switt, *Liberals and Communitarians*, 2nd ed. (Malden, Mass.: Blackwell Publishing, 2007).

[51] For an overview, see Amy Allen and Eduardo Mendieta, eds., *The Cambridge Habermas Lexicon* (Cambridge: Cambridge University Press, 2019).

[52] For the parallels, see Todd Hedrick, *Rawls and Habermas: Reason, Pluralism, and the Claims of Political Philosophy* (Stanford, Calif.: Stanford University Press, 2010).

Geltung), published in 1992.[53] A few years earlier, in 1986, he referred explicitly to the relationship between morality and law in the Tanner Lectures at Harvard.[54]

Habermas asserts that the principal tension in law is found between facticity and validity. Facticity implies that the law is a coercive, positivist system whose sanctions impose obedience even for those who do not share in the normativity of the legal system. Validity implies legitimacy, that is, the quality of the law as morally dignified, respected, and obeyed, which is a necessary condition for the validity of the law.[55] And it is precisely here that the law is connected to morality, as all legitimate law carries an implicitly complementary, not hierarchical, relationship with morality.[56]

Although discursive principles govern both morality and the law, the context of discourse differs between them. The moral discourse is universal and deals only with universalizable interests, while the law is inserted in a specific state and social framework determined by the political community. This difference explains why legal norms are not only translated moral interests but also ethical and pragmatic. This distinction between moral and ethical is the key to understanding Habermas.

Moral discourse differs from ethical discourse, as the latter is not universal but refers to individual or community values. "Ethics" has to do with what we consider ourselves to be or what we think is the best for us based on what we want to become. "Morals," on the other hand, refers to the demand to respect and protect what corresponds with the interests of everyone.[57] In the legal sphere, moral discourse, being universal and shared, demands strict tests of generalization, implying that all citizens must accept its consequences (e.g., basic procedural principles like not convicting without sufficient proof); this is not so with ethics, which requires only a process

---

53   Jürgen Habermas, *Faktizität und Geltung. Beiträge zur Diskurstheorie des Rechts und des demokratischen Rechtsstaats* (Frankfurt am Main: Suhrkamp, 1992); in English, Jürgen Habermas, *Between Facts and Norms: Contributions to a Discourse Theory of Law and Democracy*, trans. William Rehg (Cambridge, Mass.: MIT Press, 1996), especially 104–17.

54   Jürgen Habermas, *Law and Morality*, The Tanner Lectures on Human Values, delivered at Harvard University, October 1–2, 1986, https://tannerlectures.utah.edu/_documents/a-to-z/h/habermas88.pdf.

55   Habermas, *Between Facts and Norms*, 47–48.

56   Habermas, *Between Facts and Norms*, 106.

57   Jürgen Habermas, *Justification and Application*, trans. Ciaran Cronin (Cambridge, Mass.: MIT Press 1996), 1–17.

of collective self-comprehension, of compromise, tolerance, and strategic action, which overcomes individualism.[58]

The problem lies in determining which subjects correspond to each discourse. For example, Habermas affirms that questions about abortion or euthanasia are ethical, not moral, since their evaluation pertains to community religious ethics, which should not be accepted universally; therefore, what is demanded is tolerance,[59] which is the price every citizen must pay to live in a democratic community based on equality and formed for citizens with distinct ethical convictions.

The lack of solid distinction between ethics and morality has been criticized for being contrary to the principle of moral unity and the unity of the human person as an individual and social being. Sound criticisms along these lines have been advanced by various thinkers, including John Finnis and Robert P. George.[60]

The Resurgence of Natural Law

The natural law movement, though it has grown in recent decades, continues to be a minority in legal sciences.[61] With different nuances, natural law theorists have continued to defend the view that all legal order must aspire to justice, that this ideal has an inextricable moral component, that all law demands a rational standard and obligatory moral conduct, and that morality precedes the law and is independent of the will of human beings and the sovereignty of peoples.

Natural law theorists have affirmed with new arguments that the law does not always decide whether something is just or unjust, but rather many times only recognizes it, since there are certain rational principles of justice

---

58   Similarities in the line of thinking between Dworkin and Rawls are obvious.

59   Jürgen Habermas, "Reply to Symposium Participants," *Cardozo Law Review* 17 (1996): 1477–557, especially 1489–90.

60   John Finnis, "Natural Law and the Ethics of Discourse," *Ratio Iuris* 12 (1999): 354–73.

61   For an overview, see Cristóbal Orrego, "Iusnaturalismo contemporáneo," in Jorge Luis Zabra Zamora and Álvaro Núñez Vaquero, eds., *Enciclopedia de teoría y filosofía del derecho* I (Mexico City: Instituto de Investigaciones Jurídicas, 2015), 37–59. For an overview of naturalism, see Fernando Simón, "Natural Law Theories and Constitutionalism," in *Max Planck Encyclopedia of Comparative Constitutional Law* (Oxford: Oxford University Press, 2018), online edition.

prior to the law (among them obedience to the law) that are universal, and that all legal systems must respect. Many natural law theorists, inspired by Thomas Aquinas, argued that positive law derives in some sense from the natural law, either by direct derivation (the prohibition against murder) or through what are called *determinations*,[62] that is, the codifications or specifications made by the legislator through free decision-making but not devoid of moral content (e.g., traffic regulations).

The natural law theory has argued that there exists a moral obligation to obey the law. Moreover, following Augustine and Thomas Aquinas, natural law theory has affirmed that positivist law contrary to natural rights is not law (*lex inusta non est lex*) but, rather, is the appearance of law or the corruption of law (*legis corruptio*).[63] The specific explanation of this famous maxim has varied from author to author (e.g., Finnis and Hervada differ). In every case, however, this rule does not imply an impairment of positive law but rather upholds its dignity, by giving it an ethical foundation as a requirement for legitimacy. The maxim has been applied, with as much frequency as with little foundation, by some positivists as a throwing weapon against natural law theorists.

In the flowering of naturalism in the last hundred years, two French thinkers, among others, have been key: Jacques Maritain (1882–1973) and Michel Villey (1914–1988). Maritain, a convert to Catholicism in 1906 and a continuer of the Aristotelian-Thomist tradition, had a particular prominence in Europe (including the Vatican) and in the United States, where he spent many years teaching at American universities, especially at Princeton. A personal friend of Pope Paul VI, Maritain made a great effort to marry the best philosophy of Aquinas with democratic ideals and human rights, establishing a clear connection between natural law and human rights.

Maritain believed that ethical norms were rooted in human nature. Inspired by Aquinas,[64] Maritain affirmed that the natural law is known principally not through philosophical arguments and demonstrations but through inborn knowledge. It is an operation of the preconscious intellect, which, because of natural inclination, permits a genuine understanding of reality.[65]

---

62   See Aquinas, *Summa Theologiae*, I–II, q. 95, a. 2.
63   Saint Augustine, *De libero arbitrio*, I,5,11; Aquinas, *Summa Theologiae*, I–II, q. 95, a. 2.
64   Aquinas, *Summa Theologiae*, II–II, q. 45, a. 2.
65   Jacques Maritain, *Natural Law: Reflections on Theory and Practice*, ed. William Sweet (South Bend, Ind.: St. Augustine's Press, 2001), 23.

The intellect, to make its judgments, consults the subject's internal inclinations.[66] This type of understanding is the foundation of an understanding of God, of artistic activity, but also of morality, in so far as it provides the first principles of morality as well as an understanding of one's own subjectivity. These moral principles are universal and must inform any positivist legislation as well as any application of the law. Otherwise, the human being is not respected. Maritain argues that human rights have their roots in natural law.[67]

Michel Villey is considered the main philosopher of postwar French law. Firmly anchored in the sources of Roman law and the Thomist tradition (though not in scholasticism), and with a profound knowledge of the history of legal thought, Villey set out to develop a theory of an objectively just law, protected and applied by judicial institutions.

The goal of law is to maintain a social order and resolve conflict in a just and objective way concerning tangible or intangible goods in which humans are interested. Villey differentiates the internal dimensions, proper to morality, from the external, proper to law. The idea of justice is presented in both dimensions; it is intrinsic to the idea of law so that the law is not reducible to the mere will of the legislator.

According to Villey, the law is a Roman invention based on the nature of things. Law is an art of the good and the just (*ars boni et aequi*),[68] where the good and justice intertwine until they meld. For Villey, the objective meaning of law gave way to subjective rights after Ockham, particularly after Hobbes, whose break with the Aristotelian "science of the just" has dominated modernity, including contemporary jurisprudence. The objective version of law has been lost with the emphasis of human rights, which are the maximum expression of the subjectivity of law.[69]

Many of Villey's ideas penetrated the depths of two Spanish professors at the University of Navarra: a Romanist, Álvaro d'Ors (1915–2004),[70] and a canonist and philosopher of law, Javier Hervada (1934–2020). Álvaro d'Ors developed a theory of natural law as a limit of positivist law, based

---

66 Jacques Maritain, *Man and State* (Washington, D.C.: The Catholic University of America Press, 1984), 91.
67 Maritain, *Man and State*, 95–107.
68 Celsus, in Ulpian, *Libro primo institutionum*, Digesta 1.1.1pr. in *Corpus Iuris Civilis*, vol. 1, ed. Theodor Mommsen and Paul Krüger, 16th ed. (Berlin: Weidmann, 1954).
69 Michel Villey, *La formation de la pensée juridique moderne*, 2nd ed. (París: PUF, 2003).
70 See chapter 13 in this volume.

on the premise that natural law is the application of "common sense" to the right.[71] Hervada elaborated a robust theory of rights like "the just" based on the Thomist formulations and the historic investigations of Villey. Hervada placed value on the centralization of norms to hand them over to just decision. For Hervada, norms are valued in the degree to which they are instruments for deciding law—that is, justice in the concrete case.[72]

The division between Catholic and Protestant thinkers concerning natural law continues to the present day but cannot be exaggerated. The works of Protestant theologian David VanDrunen, in particular, have promoted the biblical study of the concept of natural law, inherent in creation but also in the covenant of God with his people.[73] Reading VanDrunen, one can see the great continuity of the natural law tradition and the proximity between Protestant and Catholic thought in many respects. Recently, moreover, as a consequence of religious dialogue, certain theories of natural rights have been argued by Jewish and Muslim thinkers.[74]

The Grisez-Finnis School

In the Anglo-American sphere, the school of new natural legal theory has shone with its own light, led by the French-American philosopher Germain Grisez (1929–2018), the Benedictine Abbot Joseph M. Boyle (1941–2018), and the Australian legal philosopher John Finnis (b. 1940).[75] Outstanding among the members of this school is Robert P. George (b. 1955), a disciple of Finnis

---

71   Álvaro d'Ors, *Derecho y sentido común* (Madrid: Thomson Civitas, 1995), reviewed by Rafael Domingo, "Álvaro d'Ors. Derecho y sentido común: Siete lecciones de Derecho natural como límite del Derecho positivo," *Persona y Derecho* 35 (1996): 293–98.

72   Javier Hervada, *Introducción crítica al derecho natural* (Pamplona: Ediciones Universidad de Navarra, 1981; 11th ed., 2011); Javier Hervada, *Lecciones propedéuticas de filosofía del derecho* (Pamplona: Ediciones Universidad de Navarra, 1992). For my critique, see Rafael Domingo, "*Ius, ius suum, res iusta:* Una crítica a la *Introducción crítica* de Hervada," *Persona y Derecho* 86 (2022): 249–66.

73   David VanDrunen, *Divine Covenants and Moral Order: A Biblical Theology of Natural Law* (Grand Rapids, Mich.: Eerdmans, 2014), 255.

74   Anver M. Emon, Matthew Levering, and David Novak, eds., *Natural Law: A Jewish, Christian, and Islamic Trialogue* (Oxford: Oxford University Press, 2014).

75   For an overview and critique of this school, see Nigel Biggar, ed., *The Revival of Natural Law: Philosophical, Theological, and Ethical Responses to the Finnis-Grisez School* (London: Routledge, 2016); Russell Hittinger, *A Critique of the New Natural Law Theory* (Notre Dame, Ind.: University of Notre Dame Press, 1989).

and professor at Princeton University who has played an important role in defending natural law doctrines in public forums, especially for Americans.[76]

This school holds that there exists a shared human nature, and that the first principles of practical reason, which constitute the most basic precepts of natural law, are evident in and of themselves, and are thus indemonstrable.[77] The school has crafted its own interpretation of Thomas Aquinas (distinctly different from a certain scholasticism, which to them was erroneous), and tries to identify basic human goods, such as understanding, religion, or friendship, that have an inherent value for human flourishing. These goods constitute, in their own right, ultimate reasons for human action and do not derive from more fundamental principles or values. As such, they constitute a much higher starting point than Kelsen's alleged hypothetical base norm. These basic or intrinsic goods are accessed through practical reason acting on one's own experiences.

Of the founders of the school, John Finnis has played the larger role in the debate on law and morality. A disciple of Hart and professor at Oxford and Notre Dame, Finnis has been recognized by Anglo-Saxon positivist jurists as an important interlocutor in the debate.[78] Finnis has made solid arguments against the positions of Hart, Rawls, Dworkin, and Raz, among others.[79] He recently initiated, with Robert Alexy, perhaps the most interesting contemporary debate on the subject.[80]

In 1980, Finnis published his masterpiece, *Natural Law and Natural Rights*,[81] in which he develops his theory that human goods can be secured

---

[76] See Robert P. George, ed., *Natural Law Theory: Contemporary Essays* (Oxford: Clarendon Press 1992); Robert P. George, *In Defense of Natural Law* (Oxford: Oxford University Press, 1999); and Robert P. George, *Entre el derecho y la moral*, trans. Pedro José Izquierdo (Cizur: Thomson Aranzadi, 2009).

[77] In this vein, see Aquinas, *Summa Theologiae*, I–II, q. 94, a. 2.

[78] On Finnis, see Robert P. George, "The Achievement of Finnis," in *Reason, Morality, and Law*, ed. John Kewon and Robert P. George (Oxford: Oxford University Press, 2013), 1–9.

[79] George, "The Achievement of Finnis," 1–9.

[80] See Robert Alexy, "Some Reflections on the Ideal Dimension of Law and on the Legal Philosophy of John Finnis," *American Journal of Jurisprudence* 58, no. 2 (2013): 97–110, and the reply: John Finnis, "Law as Fact and as Reason for Action: A Response to Robert Alexy on Law's Ideal Dimension," *American Journal of Jurisprudence* 59, no.1 (2014): 85–109.

[81] John Finnis, *Natural Law and Natural Rights* (Oxford: Oxford University Press, 1980; 2nd ed., 2011).

only through legal institutions, which alone can satisfy certain requirements of practical reasonableness. Based in the Aristotelian-Thomist tradition, and strongly influenced by the ideas of Grisez, Finnis offers an elaborate explanation of natural law after having debated for years with his teacher, Hart, and his colleagues Ronald Dworkin, Joseph Raz, Jeremy Waldron, and John Gardner. It was, in fact, Hart himself who invited Finnis to write a book on natural law and natural rights for the Clarendon Law Series of Oxford University Press. Forty years after the publication of this work, *Natural Law and Natural Rights* continues to be an important reference for the analysis of the basic ideas upon which naturalism is based. These ideas include, among others: justice and its requirements, the common political good; rights and their identification; the rational bases for respect of and obedience to the law and political authority; and the nature and social function of law.

Finnis's book is complemented by another on Thomas Aquinas: *Aquinas: Moral, Political, and Legal Theory* (1998).[82] This meticulous investigation has put Aquinas back at the center of the debate over legality and morality. It is interesting to confirm that, with almost eight more centuries of history on the shoulders of humanity since the age of Aquinas, the current era of globalization and new technology keeps us asking ourselves the same old questions and going back again and again to the same sources.

Conclusion

The holistic structure of reality and the gradation of knowledge permit us to understand that the lower dimensions of reality are more basic but are less relevant than the upper, which provide us with more qualified information. The hydration of the human body, for example, is more basic but less relevant than education. A person without water dehydrates; a person without education may survive, but education serves a purpose greater than hydration. Thus, it is more relevant. Without education, there is no development.

This distinction between the basic and the relevant illuminates the relations between law and morality. The law is more basic but less relevant than morality. The law, like water, is a necessary condition for community, but not a sufficient condition. Morality, however, is more relevant than law, and

---

[82] John Finnis, *Aquinas: Moral, Political, and Legal Theory* (Oxford: Oxford University Press, 1998).

thus fulfills a higher purpose. Therefore, the law among morally perfect people can be reduced to an organizing minimum.

The positivists (Kelsen and Hart) focused on what is basic (the validity of the norm), methodologically disconnecting it from what is relevant (morality, justice, and the common good). However, natural law theorists (Maritain, Villey, Finnis) studied what is relevant and integrated it into what is basic, thus achieving a superior harmony and capturing more deeply the sense of the basic. In disconnecting conceptually and methodologically the basic from the relevant (law from morality), the positivists fragmented the unity of reality and of the very person who the law, in theory, must protect. The positivists have not realized that the basic and the relevant, though autonomous, are interdependent, not independent.

Rawls wanted to found a democratic society on what is basic (the original position), leaving each human being to judge what they consider relevant (their comprehensive doctrine). Rawls's error lies precisely in his not realizing that one can better identify what is basic from the perspective of what is relevant.

Dworkin's error is in identifying as basic what is not: the right to ethical independence. This false identification leads to an intransigent defense of individualism, even at the cost of real objective damage to society (the famous rights to pornography, abortion, or euthanasia). In separating ethics from morality, Habermas tries to divide what is relevant, granting ethics the category of something basic. Alexy is the thinker about the basic who is most served by the relevant, and Finnis is the thinker about the relevant who most considers the basic.

I conclude by paraphrasing a hidden comment in the famous novel *One Hundred Years of Solitude* by Gabriel García Márquez: "Colonel Aureliano Buendía hardly understood that the secret of a good law is nothing more than an honest pact with morals."[83] At your orders, my colonel!

---

[83] Gabriel García Márquez, *One Hundred Years of Solitude* (New York: Vintage Español, 1967), 242–43. The original phrase, in English translation, is: "Colonel Aureliano Buendia could understand only that the secret of good old age is simply an honorable pact with solitude."

CHAPTER 7

THE INDIVIDUAL IN INTERNATIONAL LAW
A Natural Law Perspective

RECENT YEARS HAVE BROUGHT A renaissance of studies in natural law, including the study of so-called sacred natural law.[1] Unlike rational natural law theories, sacred natural law theories are rooted in theological and scriptural accounts of created reality. They combine reason and revelation in their elaboration and justification of legal arguments.[2]

---

* This essay will be published as Rafael Domingo, "The Individual in International Law from the Contemporary Sacred Natural Law Perspective," in *The Individual in International Law: History and Theory*, ed. Anne Peters and Tom Sparks (Oxford: Oxford University Press, 2024), chap. 9 (forthcoming).

1 For an overview, see Stephen J. Grabill, *Rediscovering the Natural Law in Reformed Theological Ethics* (Grand Rapids, Mich.: Eerdmans, 2006); David VanDrunen, *Divine Covenants and Moral Order: A Biblical Theology of Natural Law* (Grand Rapids, Mich.: Eerdmans, 2014), 1–36; Anver M. Emon, Matthew Levering, and David Novak, eds., *Natural Law: A Jewish, Christian, and Islamic Trialogue* (Oxford: Oxford University Press, 2014); and Norman Doe, ed., *Christianity and Natural Law: An Introduction* (Cambridge: Cambridge University Press, 2017).

2 For an overview on the distinction, see Richard Tuck, "The 'Modern' Theory of Natural Law," in *The Languages of Political Theory in Early-Modern Europe*, ed.

For sacred natural law theories, God, creation, nature, reason, and morality are inseparable. The created universe testifies to God's laws and communicates moral knowledge. For some sacred natural law theories, natural law is known naturally (through inclination, intuition, and reason)[3] and supernaturally (through spiritual knowledge and religious sources that illuminate and complete natural knowledge). According to these theories, the natural and the supernatural are not merely juxtaposed dimensions but rather two interconnected dimensions of a unique multidimensional reality that includes legal, political, moral, and spiritual dimensions. Each dimension of reality is autonomous in its own sphere of application and integrated into a deeper dimension—the legal in the political, the political in the moral, and the moral in the spiritual dimensions.[4]

To achieve the most significant degree of harmony in reality and to understand and protect the human person as a multidimensional individual being, each dimension needs to recognize the existence, influence, and function of the other dimensions, which in some sense act as a filter or check on the excesses of the others.[5] For instance, an unjust law (such as a Nazi law or a slave code) might be valid in the legal and the political dimensions of reality but immoral under the higher moral dimension. Some natural law scholars, following Saint Augustine and Saint Thomas Aquinas,[6] would say that an unjust law is not a true law (*lex iusta non est lex*) but a corruption of law; others would affirm that it is true positive law but contrary to morality or justice. Regardless of the specific categorization, what is crucial is the substantial difference between a law promulgated in accordance with the standards of the moral dimension and one promulgated in contradiction of those moral standards.

Anthony Pagden (New York: Cambridge University Press, 1987), 99–119; VanDrunen, *Divine Covenants and Moral Order*, 1–36; and Doe, *Christianity and Natural Law*, esp. xiii–xvii and 1–16.

    3 See Jacques Maritain, *Man and the State* (Washington, D.C.: The Catholic University of America Press, 1998), 91.

    4 See Rafael Domingo, "Why Spirituality Matters for Law: An Explanation," *Oxford Journal of Law and Religion* 8, no. 2 (2019): 326–34.

    5 See chapter 1 in this volume.

    6 See Saint Augustine, *De libero arbitrio*, ed. and trans. Francs E. Touscher (Philadelphia: Peter Reilly, 1937), 1.5.11; Thomas Aquinas, *Summa Theologiae* I-II, q. 96, a. 4, c, online edition, ed. Enrique Alarcón, *Corpus Thomisticum, S. Thomae de Aquino Opera Omnia* (Pamplona: University of Navarra, 2000).

This multidimensionality of reality clarifies why no legal theory can fully account for law from the legal dimension alone, just as no moral theory makes perfect sense of morality from the moral dimension—and for that matter, nothing in physics can fully interpret the physical dimension of reality. In this sense, the so-called Böckenförde dictum is illustrative and certainly true: "The liberal, secularized state is sustained by conditions it cannot itself guarantee."[7] The premises of a secular liberal state cannot be fully explained by the political dimension alone, because the fundamental conditions and qualities of justice, freedom, and dignity touch all the dimensions of reality in which the human person acts (the political, the moral, the spiritual), not just the political one.

While natural law theories of various sorts have long been a central teaching of Christian theology, ethics, anthropology, and jurisprudence, natural law has been more marginal in Judaism and Islam.[8] Recently, however, as a result of a fertile interreligious dialogue, some theories of natural law increasingly are being developed in Jewish and Muslim traditions.[9] However, it would be problematic to talk about a Jewish natural law tradition or an Islamic natural law tradition in the same way that we talk about the Christian natural law tradition. Many Jewish scholars think that the idea of natural law is alien to the sources and character of Judaism.[10] Something similar can be said more strongly about Islamic legal scholars, who consider the law of revelation to be sufficient.[11]

Among Christian traditions, sacred natural law theories have been more developed and discussed in Protestantism and Roman Catholicism than in Orthodox Christianity, which makes no distinction between sacred

---

[7] Ernst-Wolfgang Böckenförde, "The Rise of the State as a Process of Secularization" [1967], in *Ernst-Wolfgang Böckenförde: Religion, Law, and Democracy: Selected Writings*, ed. Mirjam Künkler and Tine Stein, trans. Thomas Dunlap (Oxford: Oxford University Press, 2020), 2:167. For a commentary on this dictum, see Tine Stein, "The Böckenförde Dictum—On the Topicality of a Liberal Formula," *Oxford Journal of Law and Religion* 7, no. 1 (2018): 97–108.

[8] Norman Doe, "Natural Law in the Interfaith Context: The Abrahamic Religions," in Doe, *Christianity and Natural Law*, 184.

[9] See David Novak, *Covenantal Rights: A Study in Jewish Political Theory* (Princeton, N.J.: Princeton University Press, 2000); David Novak, *Natural Law in Judaism* (Cambridge: Cambridge University Press, 2008); Anver M. Emon, *Islamic Natural Law Theories* (Oxford: Oxford University Press, 2010); and Emon, Levering, and Novak, *Natural Law: A Jewish, Christian, and Islamic Trialogue*.

[10] On this topic, see Abraham Joshua Heschel, *Heavenly Torah as Refracted through the Generations* (New York: Continuum, 2006).

[11] For an overview, see Emon, *Islamic Natural Law Theories*.

and rational natural law.[12] Contemporary natural law approaches have been provided by, among others, such Christian thinkers as (alphabetically) Ernst-Wolfgang Böckenförde, Norman Doe, John Finnis, Robert P. George, Mary Ann Glendon, Javier Hervada, Russell Hittinger, Matthew Levering, C. S. Lewis, Jacques Maritain, Martin Rhonheimer, Robert Spaemann, David VanDrunen, and Michel Villey.[13] The role that each author gives to sacred natural law is different, and many times they use opposing arguments (e.g., Hittinger vs. Finnis[14]), but all the authors agree on the relevance of the transcendent dimension for the development of legal order.

Sacred Natural Law as a Metalegal Concept

Sacred natural law theories are more comprehensive and integrated than rational natural law theories. They offer a bigger picture of the foundations of normativity based on the creative purpose, providence, and wisdom of God, maker of the universe and universal lawgiver. They investigate and integrate abundant sources to discern the content and meaning of sacred natural law—nature and creation, experience and intuition, practical reason and divine revelation—in order to protect the person as a whole.

Sixteenth-century Italian jurist Alberico Gentili was among the first Western jurists to recognize and argue clearly for the role of sacred natural law in the development of a secular law of nations and rational law of nature.[15] While some medieval scholars had anticipated some of his insights, Gentili was distinct in arguing for a concept of a secular law of nations that did not question either the supremacy of the laws of God over human law, or the understanding of natural law as divine law, or, as a result, the supremacy of natural law over civil law. Gentili's theory of legal secularization was a theistic theory of secularization, one firmly based on Christian principles and ideals and their role in the legal sphere, including the sphere of the law of nations, the *ius gentium*.

12   Stanley S. Harakas, "Eastern Orthodox Perspectives on Natural Law," *The American Journal of Jurisprudence* 24, no.1 (1979): 86–113.
13   See chapter 6 in this volume and John Witte, Jr., "Natural Law in Europe and America (1600–)," in *The Encyclopedia of the Bible and Its Reception*, ed. Hans-Josef Klauck et al. (Berlin: DeGruyter, 2022).
14   Russell Hittinger, *A Critique of the New Natural Law Theory* (Notre Dame, Ind.: University of Notre Dame Press, 1988).
15   See chapter 9 in this volume.

Nonetheless, Gentili insisted that the legal and spiritual dimensions remain separate, even if they are connected. His influential dictum *Silete theologi in munere alieno* (Be silent, theologians, about things that are foreign to you!)[16] underscored the necessary autonomy of the disciplines of law and theology as well as his belief that questions related to the law of nations and, therefore, to natural law should be dealt with and resolved by legal scholars. Jurists, not theologians, are the faithful and final interpreters of the law, he insisted, even if they draw widely on sacred sources. Gentili's dictum has been claimed centuries later by scholars of European public law to argue for the complete secularization of the law and the absolute divorce of law and theology. This later modern view, however, goes far beyond the limits Gentili himself intended.[17]

A generation after Gentili, the Dutch jurist Hugo Grotius argued similarly for the place of biblical and other expressions of sacred natural law within the secular legal sphere. His famous legal works on the law of nations, war and peace, maritime law, and international law thus drew heavily on the Bible and Christian teachings, and he wrote commentaries on the Bible as well as a famous tract on *The Truth of the Christian Religion,* which bled into his legal work.[18] Nonetheless, he insisted that the legal sphere must be autonomous and that the law of nature and nations could and should exist and operate fully "even if there were no God."[19] As Janne E. Nijman has pointed out, however, "Grotius' famous *etiamsi daremus* experiment never meant to disconnect humanity and human nature from the work of God in this world. Rather, Grotius depends on the relationship between God and human beings for his theory of the *Ius naturae et gentium.*"[20]

---

16   Gentili, *De iure belli libri tres*, trans. John C. Rolfe (New York: Oceana Publications, 1964), 1.12.92, p. 57. On this topic, see Giovanni Minnucci, *Silete theologi in munere alieno. Alberico Gentili tra diritto, teologia e religione* (Milan: Monduzzi Edizione, 2016).

17   See Carl Schmitt, *The Nomos of the Earth in the International Law of the Ius Publicum Europeaum*, trans. G. L. Ulmen (New York: Tellos Press, 2006), 126.

18   Hugo Grotius, *The Truth of the Christian Religion*, ed. Maria Rosa Antognazza (Indianapolis, Ind.: Liberty Fund, 2012).

19   Hugo Grotius, *De Iure Belli ac Pacis Libri Tres*, ed. James Scott, trans. Francis Kelsey (Oxford: Clarendon Press, 1925), Prolegomena, para. 11, p. 13: *"etiamsi daremus … non esse Deum."*

20   Janne E Nijman, "Grotius' *Imago Dei* Anthropology: Grounding *Ius Naturae et Gentium*," in *International Law and Religion: Historical and Contemporary Perspectives*, ed. Martii Koskenniemi, Mónica García-Salmones Rovira, and Paolo Amorosa (Oxford: Oxford University Press, 2017), 87–110, at 106.

Like these two early modern legal giants, I believe in maintaining a sacred natural law alongside a rational natural law. I do not see any opposition between a theistic approach to law that includes appreciation for sacred sources of law and a positive secular international legal order based on treaties, conventions, and declarations. So long as the theistic framework is optional and noncoercive, the starting point of any legal framework for believers and nonbelievers today should be theistically oriented.[21] Such an orientation of the law prevents the legal system from being reduced to a mere legal set of conventional rules. If that were to happen, law would not protect human persons in their multidimensional integrity, would not have built-in safeguards against tyrannical abuse, and would not foster a solidary collaboration between believers and nonbelievers in the search for justice and peace in our globalized world.

Beyond providing a theistic orientation and a necessary check on law and rational-legal discourse, sacred natural law theories emphasize the robust connectivity between theology (including natural theology) and jurisprudence. Historically in the West, jurisprudence was firmly rooted in and shaped by theology.[22] In my opinion, theology should continue to buttress the pillars of secular law, including international law, from the outside by supporting the dignity and freedom of individuals, developing a culture of human rights, and blocking the assumption of a divine role by international legal authorities and institutions: if God exists, no human power has the right to become a god.[23]

How is it possible to protect the necessary autonomy of international law and other legal systems when nonlegal sources are legitimated and when law is understood as interconnected with other different dimensions of reality, not least the spiritual? Sacred natural law can and should operate in the legal system as a *metalegal concept*, not a legal one.[24] Metalegal concepts illuminate

---

21   See Rafael Domingo, *God and the Secular Legal System* (Cambridge: Cambridge University Press, 2016), 167; Rafael Domingo, "The Metalegal God," *Ecclesiastical Law Journal* 16, no. 1 (2014): 147–67.

22   See Carl Schmitt's famous dictum that "all significant concepts of the modern theory of the state are secularized theological concepts," in *Political Theology: Four Chapters on the Concept of Sovereignty*, trans. George Schwab (Chicago: University of Chicago Press, 2005), 36.

23   See Rafael Domingo, "Theology and Jurisprudence: A Good Partnership?" *Journal of Law and Religion* 32, no. 1 (2017): 79–85.

24   On metalegal concepts, see chapter 3.

the legal concepts and arguments from outer, higher dimensions. They do not use the essential method of legal systems—coercion—nor do they generate specific legal doctrines of contract, agreement, or treaty. Instead, they involve higher principles like honor, promise, or covenant. They also do not require full acceptance by all citizens, because technically the metalegal is not "in force." Metalegal concepts are not part of the legal system in the strictest sense, but they are part of the legal order in the broadest sense, just as the type of soil and the landscape around a house are not strictly part of the house but are critical for its construction and its views.

Metalegal concepts are categories, values, and ideas beyond the legal dimension that still have legal significance in legal systems—in our case, international law. To have legal significance does not mean that a metalegal concept has a direct legal effect in the strictest sense[25] but instead can be seen more through illumination, support, guidance, or understanding. Indeed, a metalegal concept can enter into practice as a light that shines and guides, as a framework that attracts, or as an aid or support to advancement.[26] Metalegal concepts are sometimes recognized as rights or values (e.g., religious freedom). In these cases, metalegal concepts operate in the legal realm as both legal and metalegal concepts. This is not the case, however, for the concept of sacred natural law in the international law order, where sacred natural law is a mere metalegal concept.

Although not strictly legal, metalegal concepts do not obscure the essence of international law; on the contrary, they illuminate international law at its heart. They support international law by linking it with other human knowledge and understanding dimensions and are also sources of value in the realm of international law and international relations. An example: Whether norms are classified as peremptory (*ius cogens*) depends on Article 53 of the Vienna Convention more than on a direct decree of God,[27] but the reality of a divine providence adds value to the idea of *ius cogens*. Peremptory norms are connected to immutability, permanence, and perpetuation granted by divine providence.

---

25   On legal causation, see H. L. A. Hart and Tony Honoré, *Causation in the Law*, 2nd ed. (Oxford: Clarendon Press, 1985).

26   See, in the same vein but applied to divine law, Rémi Brague, *The Law of God: The Philosophical History of an Idea*, trans. Lydia G. Cochrane (Chicago: University of Chicago Press, 2007), 264.

27   Jeremy Waldron, "What Is Natural Law Like?" in *Reason, Morality, and Law: The Philosophy of John Finnis*, ed. John Keown and Robert P. George (Oxford: Oxford University Press, 2013), 72–89, at 88.

The birth of the European Union is an excellent example of this kind of illumination provided by metalegal concepts. The first and crucial steps of the long European integration process after the Second World War were possible, at least to some notable degree, because of the spiritual stature of the so-called European founding fathers: Konrad Adenauer, Robert Schuman, Jean Monnet, Alcide De Gasperi, and Joseph Bech, among others. They were able to build a new Europe from the blood and ashes of the battlefields through reconciliation, forgiveness, and communion (three metalegal concepts) and by overcoming any domination, revenge, and retaliation.[28]

The Image of God as the Ultimate Ground for the Protection of the Person in International Law

The image-of-God doctrine—the idea that God created humanity in the divine image—provides some spiritual, moral, and anthropological standards that have important implications for international law and legal science in general, especially for illuminating the ideas of human dignity and equality. Centuries ago, Grotius founded his anthropological approach to the law of nations in this *imago Dei* doctrine.[29]

As is well known, the book of Genesis stresses the relevant position of human beings in the world by saying that humankind was created in the *image and likeness of God*.[30] Biblical scholars of every tradition have discussed the meaning of this expression for centuries, developing many different and even controversial approaches.[31] In recent Protestant and Catholic theology,[32] following, among others, Saint Augustine[33] and Saint Thomas

28 See Desmond Dinan, *Origins and Evolution of the European Union*, 2nd ed. (Oxford: Oxford University Press, 2014).
29 Nijman, "Grotius' *Imago Dei* Anthropology."
30 Genesis 1:26–28; 5:1–3; and 9:6.
31 The impact of original sin in the image-of-God bearers, for instance, is interpreted in many different ways in many Christian denominations. See VanDrunen, *Divine Covenants and Moral Order*; Doe, *Christianity and Natural Law*; and Gabrielle Thomas, *The Image of God in the Theology of Gregory of Nazianzus* (Cambridge: Cambridge University Press, 2019).
32 Edith Stein, *Finite and Eternal Being*, trans. Kurt F. Reinhardt (Washington, D.C.: ICS Publications, 2002).
33 Augustine of Hippo, *The Trinity (De Trinitate)*, 2nd ed., ed. John E. Rotelle, trans. Edmund Hill (Hyde Park, N.Y.: New City Press, 2012), 9–10.

Aquinas,[34] one finds the most robust affirmation that the notion of humanity made in the image of God validates the relevant place of each person in the universal order and inside the political community. Each person is substantially a mirror of God, reflecting their personal relationship with God. In other words, the relationship or representation and resemblance to God are constitutive of—that is, inseparable from—the human being.

This image of God is fundamentally personal, not only in the sense that each human being, male or female (Gen 1:27), is made in the image of God but also in the sense that the image is of an incarnated divine person, Jesus Christ, and ultimately the image of a personal triune and loving God. The plural pronoun used in the Genesis narrative ("Let us make humankind in our image after our likeness") emphasizes this Trinitarian context.[35]

In the following sections, I analyze how the *imago Dei* doctrine sheds light on, among other concepts, the legal notions of human dignity, individual freedom and responsibility, solidarity, pluralism, diversity, and even the emerging idea of global law.

Human Dignity:
The Status of the Image-of-God Bearers

Dignity is a polyhedric concept with many nuances and implications.[36] It is the human being's most radical and inherent quality and one of the constitutive ideas of the entire international human rights body. It is more than a right, essential good, value, or principle.[37] It is the transcendental ground, the

---

34 Thomas Aquinas, *Corpus Thomisticum. S. Thomae de Aquino Opera Omnia*, ed. Enrique Alarcón (Pamplona: Universitatis Studiorum Navarrensis 2000), I, q. 93, http://www.corpusthomisticum.org/iopera.html.

35 Thomas A. Smail, "In the Image of the Triune God," *International Journal of Systematic Theology* 5, no. 1 (2003): 22–32; James Hanvey, "Dignity, Person, and Imago Trinitatis," in *Understanding Human Dignity*, ed. Christopher McCrudden (Oxford: Oxford University Press, 2013), 209–28.

36 On dignity, see Robert Spaemann, *Love and the Dignity of Human Life: On Nature and Natural Law* (Grand Rapids, Mich.: Eerdmans, 2011); McCrudden, *Understanding Human Dignity*; Jeremy Waldron, *Dignity, Rank, and Rights* (Oxford: Oxford University Press, 2015); Michael Rosen, *Dignity: Its History and Meaning* (Cambridge, Mass.: Harvard University Press, 2018); and Martin Schlag, "Christianity and the Principle of Dignity," in Domingo and Witte, *Christianity and Global Law*, 214–30.

37 On human dignity and international law, see Paolo Carozza, "Human

fundamental premise for human equality, human freedom, and human rights and duties. As the Universal Declaration of Human Rights preamble states, the "recognition of the inherent dignity and of the equal and inalienable rights of all members of the human family is the foundation of freedom, justice, and peace in the world."[38]

Sacred natural law provides a metalegal and objective validity to the general idea of dignity as the status of every human being made in the image of God.[39] Without a theistic approach, dignity can easily be reduced to a subjective substantial self, a pure capacity for rational autonomy, a mere self-respect as a necessary condition for living well and taking seriously moral responsibilities,[40] or a simple right to be recognized as a legal person. In the worst case, it can be transformed into a formal, vacuous concept without a specific function in the international realm because of its calculated ambiguity, and when the idea of human dignity weakens, the international system of human rights falters.

According to sacred natural law theories, the status conferred by dignity on human beings is neither temporary nor territorial. Rather, it is personal and constitutive of any human being, which makes human beings unique. The status provided by dignity implies—among other goods—respect, human freedom and responsibility, human equality, and human rights.

The image-of-God doctrine strengthens the respect of human beings because they are in a special relationship with God. They are not an accident in cosmic history; instead, they are a whole and an end. They are creatures made with some features of their Creator: they are active creatures who freely collaborate with their Creator in the development of the universe and the fulfillment of the Creator's plans. Human freedom is a marvelous expression of the divine image, because creation was essentially an act of loving divine freedom, not a necessary emanation from the divine. If human

---

Dignity," in *International Human Rights Law*, ed. Dina Shelton (Oxford: Oxford University Press, 2013), 345–60.

38   See Universal Declaration of Human Rights (1948), http://www.un.org/en/universal-declaration-human-rights.

39   On the connection between human dignity and image of God, see Bernd Oberdorfer, "Human Dignity and Image of God," *Scriptura* 204 (2010): 231–39; Hanvey, "Dignity, Person, and Imago Trinitatis"; and Janet Soskice, "Human Dignity and the Image of God," in McCrudden, *Understanding Human Dignity*, 229–43.

40   See, for instance, Ronald Dworkin, *Justice for Hedgehogs* (Cambridge, Mass.: The Belknap Press of Harvard University Press, 2011), 13–14.

creatures are free, it is because God the Creator is free and created humans in the divine image—that is, with the capacity for freedom, responsibility, and love.

Dignity is shared by all human beings, without exception, and it is a unique and equalizing status. Thus, human equality is also an expression of the fact that all human beings have been made in the same unique image of God, of one God living eternally in three equal persons: Father, Son, and Holy Spirit. Each divine person, though distinct from the others given their relationships, does not divide unity because there is no diversity of being among them. On the other hand, each divine person of the Trinity is equal to the Trinity itself. As Saint Augustine pointed out: "so total is the equality in this triad that not only is the Father not greater than the Son as far as divinity is concerned, but also Father and Son together are not greater than the Holy Spirit, nor is any single person of the three less than the Trinity itself."[41]

This profound understanding of the value of each human being as a bearer of the divine image produces natural deference for human rights, the primary manifestations in the legal dimension of this spiritual image.[42] Reflecting the image of God, human rights have an individual but also a communitarian scope. Self-giving enables human beings to experience their individual lives as wholly united with the lives of others. When one exercises rights in a self-giving (communitarian) attitude, rights transform from enforceable protected interests into "enforceable protected services,"[43] and society strengthens its ties to the union.[44]

---

41 Saint Augustine, *The Trinity (De Trinitate)*, 8.1, p. 241.

42 On the relation between Christianity and human rights, see John Witte, Jr., and Frank Alexander, eds., *Christianity and Human Rights* (Cambridge: Cambridge University Press, 2010). For a different approach, see Samuel Moyn, *Christian Human Rights* (Philadelphia: University of Pennsylvania Press, 2005); Samuel Moyn, "Christianity and Human Rights," in Domingo and Witte, *Christianity and Global Law*, 323–36.

43 On the idea of right as service, see Álvaro d'Ors, *Nueva introducción al estudio del derecho* (Madrid: Civitas, 1999), 62; chapter 13 in this volume on Álvaro d'Ors.

44 See chapter 1 in this volume.

Universal Moral Principles Shared by the Image-of-God Bearers

The image of God represented in the human being is a living image of a living God. It has the potential to inspire sound principles for judging when human affairs and actions might either preserve or harm the quality of the divine image in every human person. For this reason, according to most sacred natural law theories, human beings can know naturally some aspects of God's fundamental law, which is written in the human heart.

In his letter to the Romans, Saint Paul confirms this important doctrine when he affirms that the natural law written on human hearts allows human beings to know moral obligations naturally, even without knowing the Mosaic law: "Indeed, when Gentiles, who do not have the law, do by nature things required by the law, they are a law for themselves, even though they do not have the law."[45] Paul explains how Jews, under Mosaic law, and Gentiles, under a law manifested by nature, can share some basic universal moral standards. Many of these moral standards and conventional practices are, of course, contextual and depend on cultural traditions, but some natural law principles as such remain as a source of binding common principles among all human beings beyond the inevitable cultural differences.

This doctrine of a universal natural law written in human hearts has an extraordinary impact in international law because it recognizes the individual as a true original source of legal validity: *ex persona ius oritur* (the law comes from the individual). The doctrine also supports the idea that no legal system, including the international legal system, is self-contained, because some aspects of legal systems are ordered beyond the systems.

The moral natural law written in human hearts should lead the international law-making process to limit any potential arbitrariness of nation-state sovereignty. According to natural law, there is in the deepest dimensions of human existence a law that remains unchangeable, whose derogation by political authorities is not allowed by nature. It is a sort of natural *ius cogens*, which enlightens positive *ius cogens* and human governance. The rule of *pacta sunt servanda* (agreements must be kept), which is basic to both natural and positive law, is a good example of how natural law impinges on international law

---

[45] Romans 2:14–15.

at the fundamental level. Along with this respect for promises and contracts, sacred natural law demands, among other things, respect for the integrity of creation and its resources, as well as reparation of injustice.

Pluralism, Diversity, and the Image of God

To be bearers of the image of God serves to identify human beings as persons but not to make them uniform. The image of God is a source of pluralism and diversity since it is the image of a triune personal living God. The idea of person is essentially rooted in relationship and diversity; therefore, each person is different from every other. It is precisely this difference that allows us to affirm that, despite being God the Absolute One, a distinction of three divine persons is possible based on their relations of origin: the Father generates, the Son is begotten, and the Holy Spirit proceeds. Made in the triune image of God, each member of humanity is different and should be protected in that difference. This diversity enriches human society and supports pluralism as a political value. Pluralism is based on unity, because the former comes from the latter, not vice versa.[46] Pluralism is the way of living out unity in diversity in democratic political societies.

Sacred natural law theories support a unifying foundational pluralism instead of the individualistic pluralism of well-ordered societies.[47] Individuals do not determine their personal fulfillment and flourishing by stipulating a minimum hypothetical contract to live in society. Unity is neither contractual nor based on a conception of the self as independent from any conception of the good but rather is deeper than that: unity is the oneness of the image of God reflected in each human being within the political community. The image-of-God unity is precontractual, prepolitical, and prelegal. It transcends, precedes, and shapes any kind of organization of democratic societies.

Solidarity and the Image-of-God Doctrine

The word "solidarity," derived from the Latin *solidus* (solid), is as fresh as it is revolutionary, as rich as it is classical, and as strong as necessary. Although the word was first pronounced in French (*solidarité*) in the context of the French

---

46   In this sense, the motto of the United States—*E pluribus unum*—contradicts what I am defending.

47   John Rawls, *A Theory of Justice*, rev. ed. (Cambridge, Mass.: The Belknap Press of Harvard University Press, 1999), 397–405.

Revolution,[48] the idea of solidarity is as old as the Bible, Greek philosophy, and Roman law, the three great pillars of Western civilization.

The word "solidarity" is used technically in the most varied areas of private and public law, but beyond all technicalities and differences lies the central intuition that gave rise to solidarity in Roman law. Roman law uses "solidary" (*in solidum*) to describe joint and several liability—for example, when several debtors, several creditors, or several wrongdoers share entirely and at the same time in certain obligations stemming from a stipulation, a contract, or a private wrong (*delictum*).[49]

The Roman jurist Gaius, in his well-known *Institutes*, resorts eight times to the expression *in solidum*. For example, in *Institutes* 3.121, Gaius tells us that before the emperor Hadrian changed the law by means of an official letter (*epistula*), sureties were bound jointly and severally for the entire amount of the debts of the principal debtor, and the creditor was at liberty to collect the whole debt either from the debtor or from each of the sureties.[50] In another example, in *Institutes* 4.71, Gaius explains that when a father places his son or his slave in charge of a ship or other business, the liability is *in solidum*—that is, shared by the father and the son or slave.

Based on the same central idea of Roman law solidarity, the sacred natural law principle of solidarity states that each person, as a full image-of-God bearer, is *liable* for the protection of the whole image of God, not only in the person's individual self but also in every other human being, as well as in any community of human beings, including the global human community. Since God is a spirit, the image of God is not divisible, and therefore the liability to protect this image always extends to the whole (*in solidum*). Thus, just as there is no distinction between the individual divine image and the divine image of every member of the political community of human beings, so there is no substantial distinction between the individual ethos and the ethos of any political community—that is, between

---

48   See Marie-Claude Blais, *La solidarité. Histoire d'une idée* (Paris: Éditions Gallimard, 2007); Serge Audier, *La pensé solidariste* (Paris: Presses Universitaires de France, 2010). See also Kurt Bayertz, ed., *Solidarity* (Dordrecht: Kluwer, 1999); Hauke Brunkhorst, *Solidarity: From Civic Friendship to a Global Legal Community* (Cambridge, Mass.: MIT Press, 2005).

49   Lucio Parenti, *In solidum obligari. Contributo allo studio della solidarietà da atto lecito* (Naples: Edizioni Scientifiche Italiane, 2012).

50   Gaius, *The Institutes of Gaius*, ed. Francis De Zulueta (Oxford: Clarendon Press, 1953), 3.121.

the individual good and the common good of local, intermediate, and global communities.

As the image of God is only one, so the good is also one. In God, there are three persons but not three goods. The Father is the whole good, the Son is the whole good, and the Holy Spirit is the whole good. The good, like God, and therefore like the image of God, cannot be divided but only shared. Thus, the common good is part of the individual good, and vice versa. Any wall of separation between the common and the particular good is artificial. In contrast, individual interests can conflict with each other and with the local, the national, or the international interest. The reason for this difference is that interest is always individualistic and therefore fragmentary. Common interest is the sum of individual interests; it is the totality of particularities, but not the universality of the diversity. Common interest promotes cooperation, the process of working together for the same purpose, but not solidarity in the fullest sense. International law is based on international cooperation among sovereign states; global law, however, goes to the next step: the solidary unity of the global community.[51]

The image-of-God doctrine reveals the need to transform cooperation into solidarity: one cannot possess the image of God just for oneself. If human beings are united and there is an indivisible common good, anything that happens to another matters, especially if it affects dignity. Common good thus becomes a moral requirement. The image of God universalizes the idea of neighbor without reducing it to a simple abstraction, and asks for practical commitment.[52]

Subsidiarity and the Image-of-God Doctrine

Intimately tied to responsibility and freedom is the principle of subsidiarity, which tries to protect the person's priority, specifically the individual's inalienable freedom, against strong intervention by higher and more powerful social structures and groups.[53] Developed specifically

---

51   See Rafael Domingo, "Christianity, Solidarity, and Law," in *The Oxford Handbook of Christianity and Law*, ed. John Witte, Jr., and Rafael Domingo (Oxford: Oxford University Press, 2023), 832–39.

52   See Benedict XVI, Encyclical Letter *Deus caritas est* (December 25, 2005), 15.

53   On subsidiarity, see Paolo Carozza, "Subsidiarity as a Structural Principle of International Human Rights Law," *American Journal of International Law* 97 (2003): 38–79; Gerald L. Neuman, "Subsidiarity," in *International Human Rights Law*, ed. Dina

by Catholic social teaching,⁵⁴ the foundational idea of the principle of subsidiarity lies in the ontological priority of each human person (and each person's freedom), as an image-of-God bearer, to any kind of social grouping or community. Thus, the starting point of any well-structured legal system, including international law, should be the individual and not the political community.

Subsidiarity protects the necessary freedom to fulfill personal responsibilities and allows individuals the fulfillment of solidary obligations that cannot be delegated to higher structures. Cooperation, support, and help from more powerful groups are legitimized only when individual or lower groups are not able to accomplish their purpose on their own. In this sense, subsidiarity is a complementary principle of solidarity.⁵⁵ Subsidiarity constitutes the limit of a potentially fake solidarity transformed into paternalism or domination or social privatism.

Although always governing with the aim of protecting the individual, the European Union has used the principle of subsidiarity with a more technical and narrow meaning. It represents only a principle of administrative decentralization to regulate the exercise of the Union's nonexclusive powers. Article 5 (3) of the Treaty on European Union states that in areas which do not fall within the exclusive power of the European Union—that is, in areas shared by the European Union and the member states—"the Union shall act only if and in so far as the objectives of the proposed action cannot be sufficiently achieved by the Member States, either at the central or at regional and local level, but can rather, by reason of the scale or effects of the proposed action, be better achieved at Union level."⁵⁶

Shelton (Oxford: Oxford University Press, 2013), 360–78; James E. Fleming and Jacob T. Levy, eds., *Federalism and Subsidiarity* (New York: NYU Press, 2014); Maria Catherine Cahill, "Subsidiarity," in *Catholic Social Teaching: A Volume of Scholarly Essays*, ed. Gerard V. Bradley and E. Christian Brugger (Cambridge: Cambridge University Press, 2019), 414–32; and Thomas C. Kohler, "Christianity and the Principle of Subsidiarity," in Domingo and Witte, *Christianity and Global Law*, 303–20.

    54   See Pius XI, Encyclical Letter *Quadragesimo anno* (May 15, 1931), 80; John Paul II, Encyclical Letter *Centesimus annus* (May 1, 1991), 48; and Benedict XVI, Encyclical Letter *Caritas in veritate* (June 29, 2009), 57–58. For an overview, see Kohler, "Christianity and the Principle of Subsidiarity."

    55   See Francis, Encyclical Letter *Fratelli tutti* (October 3, 2020), 187.

    56   See consolidated version (2016) of the Treaty on European Union, https://eur-lex.europa.eu/collection/eu-law/treaties/treaties-force.html.

The Global Law Community of the Image-of-God Bearers

At the heart of sacred natural law, then, lies the idea that all human beings form a united natural community of image-of-God bearers, which grants metalegal legitimacy to the global human community and its specific law—the global law.

The global human community is first and foremost a community of human persons, not a society or federation of sovereign states.[57] Of course, the only way for persons to work together in a global context would be through different global institutions, supranational entities, nation-states, transnational corporations, NGOs, and other nonstate actors that integrate the global human community.[58] Working through these global actors, however, does not remove the person as a global citizen from the spotlight. The centrality of the person, and as a result humanity as such, is the key that opens the door to a new constitutionalism beyond the state, and the sacred natural law supports this movement from a spiritual dimension.

The global human community is universal because it includes every human being without exception, and it is unique. This is why the global human community cannot be structured as a unique sovereign world state or a mere federation of sovereign states. To exist, a sovereign state requires the existence of at least one other state susceptible to being excluded from its territorial jurisdiction. There is no sovereign state without other sovereign states.[59] The concept of the state, like that of sibling or friend, requires otherness: for any of these to exist, there must be at least two of its kind. One is not enough.

The most critical consequence of universality is that the global human community is nonvoluntary but necessary.[60] As such, it requires no

---

57 The argument is developed in Rafael Domingo, "The New Global Human Community," *Chicago Journal of International Law* 12, no. 2 (2012): 563–87; Rafael Domingo, "Global Law and the New Global Human Community," *Revista Brasileira di Direito* 13, no. 3 (2017): 27–39; and Rafael Domingo, "Derecho global y comunidad humana global," in *Las transformaciones del derecho en la globalización*, ed. Jorge Fabra Zamora (Mexico City: Universidad Autónoma de México, 2020), 45–58.

58 For more on these new actors, see Anne Peters et al., eds., *Non-State Actors as Standard Setters* (New York: Cambridge University Press, 2009), esp. 1–32 in the editors' introduction.

59 This argument was firmly defended by Hermann Heller, *Die Souveranität. Ein Beitrag zur Theorie des Staats-und Völkerrechts* (Berlin: Walter de Gruyter, 1927), 20–23.

60 For the legal consequences of compulsory membership in communities,

consent for membership, and indeed consent is not possible: no human being could ever leave this community and join another one, as no human being can give up the condition of being an image-of-God bearer. This compulsory membership has to be balanced by a high degree of citizen participation in the decision-making process and by reducing the goal of global law to a minimum: the protection of those specific human goods that necessarily have to be satisfied and protected globally (global public goods), such as global peace and security, global health, and conservation of the planet.

The Inherent Connection between International Law and Love

If God is love,[61] and, again, the human being is made in God's image, human beings were created to love and be loved. As a transformative power that leads human beings to communion with God and others, love is the fulfillment of any law,[62] including international law. Love of God and love of neighbor are interwoven, even inseparable, because, ultimately, love is divine. It comes from God, unites us to God, and makes us one, overcoming all divisions. Because love is divine, it is free.[63]

As an expression of love compatible with justice, international law accepts the idea of forgiveness (e.g., condonation or remission of sovereign debt). Forgiveness reestablishes the order as a whole by acquitting offenders, thereby placing them in a spiritually higher dimension of justice. Hannah Arendt refers to forgiveness as "the necessary corrective for the inevitable damages resulting from action."[64] Forgiveness establishes "redemption from the predicament of irreversibility"[65] and "serves to undo the deeds of the past, whose 'sins' hang like Damocles' sword over every new generation."[66]

---

see Tony Honoré, "Nécessité Oblige," in *Making Law Bind* (Oxford: Clarendon Press, 1987), 120–21.

61   1 John 4:16.

62   Romans 13:9–10.

63   On love, see the still interesting and fresh work by C. S. Lewis, *The Four Loves* (Fort Washington, Pa.: *Harvest Book* Company, 1971).

64   Hannah Arendt, *The Human Condition*, 2nd ed. (Chicago: University of Chicago Press, 1971), 238.

65   Arendt, *The Human Condition*, 236.

66   Arendt, *The Human Condition*, 237.

For this reason, as Martha Minow points out, "there is value in considering how and when law can usefully make space for forgiveness."[67]

The true development of international law should be understood in the light of love and forgiveness. Justice is not the opposite of love, and there is no real tension or conflict between true justice and true love. Moreover, love presupposes justice. There is no love without justice, nor is it possible to achieve the plenitude of justice without love. "Love that perpetrates injustice is malformed love," affirms Nicholas Wolterstorff.[68] Law provides the necessary platform for justice to flourish, and justice provides the unique platform for love to flourish. On the other hand, love ennobles justice and strengthens legal systems.

Justice is true "the first virtue of social institutions, as truth is of systems of thought,"[69] but only if it is referred to as loving justice. Love will always be necessary to not reduce the human person into a "legal person" or even a "legal object." Whoever tries to eliminate love and forgiveness is trying to eliminate the image of God in humanity. The rule of law demands a rule of love. For this reason, any international legal system that ignores love is preparing to remove the true law and to diminish the protection of the dignity of persons in their integrity.

Conclusion

Sacred natural law theories are strongly oriented to the individual because every person has been created in the image of God. Consequently, sacred natural law theories support the priority of the person in the international legal realm. As sacred natural law theories are not mandatory but optional, respect individual moral conscience, and acknowledge the obligatory force of positive law, they are valid for developing a universal (not compulsory) international metalegal framework that illuminates positive law.

More than a century ago, the German jurist Otto Gierke (1841–1921) rejected as mistaken all the attempts to reduce natural law to a bodily existence—that is, to a sort of "simulacrum." But he insisted that the "undying spirit" of natural law will never be extinguished: "If it is denied entry into the body of

---

67 Martha Minow, "Forgiveness, Law, and Justice," *California Law Review* 103 (2015): 1615–45, at 1645.

68 Nicholas Wolterstorff, *Justice in Love* (Grand Rapids, Mich.: Eerdmans, 2015), xvii.

69 Rawls, *A Theory of Justice*, 3. On p. 586, he refers to "the primacy of justice."

positive law," he concluded, "it flutters about the room like a ghost, and threatens to turn into a vampire which sucks the blood from the body of Law."[70]

The development of a *transcendent global law* should use the best contributions and arguments of the sacred natural law traditions and overcome some futile discussions about the *nature* of natural law. Transcendent global law might lead the transformation of a very often self-interest-oriented international community of nation-states into a value-oriented global human community of image-of-God bearers. In this process, not only the jurists but also the philosophers and the theologians condemned to silence have something to say. Using Gentili's Latin language, this essay ends by inviting the theologians to stop their long silence and open their mouths wide again to illuminate the secular law from outside: *Adaperite, theologi, ora vestra, et scientia vestra afferte iuri lucem!*[71]

---

70   Otto Gierke, *Natural Law and the Theory of Society* (1883), trans. Ernest Barker, vol. 1, 2nd ed. (Cambridge: Cambridge University Press, 1934), 226.
71   "Open your mouths, theologians, and enlighten the law with your science."

CHAPTER 8

TOWARD A GLOBAL CANON LAW CENTERED ON THE HUMAN PERSON

INTERNATIONAL LAW AND CANON LAW share obvious similarities in legal technique because they transcend state law as global legal systems.[1] In this essay, I refer to one of these similarities, namely, the way both systems treat the legal status of the human person. For some decades now, public international law, in its transition toward a common law of humanity or global law, has been changing the legal status of the human person.[2] Due

---

*   See the original version in Rafael Domingo, "Toward a Global Canon Law Centered on the Human Person," *Ius Canonicum* 62 (2022): 1–22.

1   See Rafael Domingo, *The New Global Law* (Cambridge: Cambridge University Press, 2010), 18.

2   See chapter 7 in this volume. For the most comprehensive study on this subject, see Anne Peters, *Beyond Human Rights: The Legal Status of Individuals in International Law* (Cambridge: Cambridge University Press, 2016). See also Christian Walter, "Subjects of International Law," in *Max Planck Encyclopedia of Public International Law* (Oxford: Oxford University Press, 2007), online; Simone Gorski, "Individuals in International Law," *Max Planck Encyclopedia of Public International Law*, online; Chiara Giorgetti, "Rethinking the Individual in International Law," *Lewis & Clark Law Review* 22 (2019): 1085–149; and James Crawford, *Brownlie's Principles of Public International Law* (Oxford: Oxford University Press, 2019), 105–90.

to the similarities between the systems of canon law and international law, the important implications of this change seem to invite a similar paradigm shift in the canonical legal sphere, so that these implications do not go unnoticed by canonists.

The essay is divided into four parts. The first part analyzes the status of the physical or natural human person in the international order. The second part deals with the concept of person in canon law. Part three compares the person's status in the international and canonical legal systems in terms of personality and shows their identical legal technique and the reasons for it. Finally, part four advocates a global canon law, that is to say, a law that makes central the human person created in the image of God[3] rather than the Christian regenerated by baptism, which is the basis of the whole Christian life.[4] Implementing this global canon law would in no way undervalue the spiritual power of the baptismal sacrament but, quite the contrary, would call for a paradigm shift in the canonical discipline.

The first part of the essay is written from an internationalist perspective, the second from a canonical perspective, the third from a comparative perspective, and the fourth from a more theological perspective. This is a multidisciplinary essay with all its methodological advantages and disadvantages.

The Status of the Individual in Modern International Law

Modern international law is generally known as the enlightened law of nations that emerged from the Peace of Westphalia (1648), which ended the Thirty Years' War (1618–1648) and the bloody European religious wars. Modern international law is primarily a law among sovereign, free, and equal states, which are regarded to be the only subjects of international law and the only entities with international legal personality. The human person, who until the seventeenth century had played a certain role in the so-called law of nations (*ius gentium*), was left out altogether from the new international order. A natural person's relationship to the international order existed through and thanks to the nation-state of which that person was a citizen. The human person was rightfully a citizen of a nation-state, but not of the international

---

3 Genesis 1:26–28; 5:1–3; and 9:6.
4 *Catechism of the Catholic Church*, 2nd ed. (Vatican City: Libreria Editrice Vaticana, 1997), no. 1213.

community, which did not recognize the individual as a subject of rights and duties in the international sphere.

This new international law born of Westphalia was masterfully elaborated and structured by the Swiss diplomat Emmer de Vattel (1714–1767) in his famous treatise *Les droit des gens; ou Principes de la loi naturelle appliqués à la conduite et aux affaires des nations et des souveraines* (1758).[5] This book represents in international law what the marriage manual of the Jesuit Tomás Sánchez represents in post-Tridentine canon law—a new formulation that updated earlier principles for a new age.[6]

Vattel's work formulated, ordered, and classified the rules of this new international society of states recognized as equal, free, and independent, and now ordered under a positive law of nations, whether voluntary, conventional, or customary, and informed by the application of natural law.[7] Once this interstate law had been stripped of any trace of natural law, Jeremy Bentham referred to it by coining the term "international law"[8] in 1789—the first-ever use of this expression, which today has replaced "the law of nations."

In Vattel's *Le droit des gens*, the famous Gaius-Justinian tripartition of persons-things-actions[9] that had shaped all Western civil law was replaced by

---

5   Emmer de Vattel, *Le droit des gens, ou Principes de la loi naturelle, appliqués à la conduite et aux affaires des nations et des souverains*, 3 vols. (Washington, D.C.: Carnegie Institution of Washington, 1916); vol. 3 contains an English translation edited by Charles G. Fenwick, with an introduction by Albert de Lapradelle, the French original of which can be found in vol. 1.

6   On Tomás Sánchez and his treatise, see Rafael Domingo, "Thomas Sanchez," in *Christianity and Family Law: An Introduction*, ed. John Witte, Jr., and Gary S. Hauk (Cambridge: Cambridge University Press, 2017), 245–58.

7   See Vattel, *Le droit des gens*, Preliminaires §7. On this law, see Rafael Domingo, "Gaius, Vattel, and the New Global Law Paradigm," European *Journal of International Law* 22, no. 3 (2011): 627–47.

8   Jeremy Bentham, *An Introduction to the Principles of Morals and Legislation*, 2nd ed., ed. James H. Burns and Herbert L. A. Hart (Oxford: Oxford University Press, 1996), chap. 17, no. 25, p. 296: "These may, on any given occasion, be considered either as members of the same state, or as members of different states: in the first case, the law may be referred to the head of internal, in the second case, to that of international jurisprudence." Bentham added a footnote: "The word international, it must be acknowledged, is a new one; though, it is hoped, sufficiently analogous and intelligible."

9   Gaius, *Institutiones* 1.8, in Rafael Domingo, ed., *Textos de Derecho Romano* (Pamplona: Aranzadi, 2000), sect. 2. The phrase has also been reproduced in Justinian's

the triad consisting of states, relations between states, and war.[10] Indeed, in the international sphere, the subject of law par excellence became the state, not the person; things were reduced to interstate rights and duties, and the way to resolve conflicts between states, once diplomacy had been exhausted, was war, not legal action.

Continuing the work of Vattel's master, Christian Wolff (1679–1754), Vattel's treatise was the real embodiment of the idea of international law as an autonomous, positive science, distinct, therefore, from national civil law and natural law. In order to explain the conception of the modern state as one among the society of states, Vattel focused on the figure of the Roman *paterfamilias*, in his relations with other *patres familias*, as full subjects of civil law. Basically, Vattel conceived each state as a sort of Roman family, subject to the absolute power of a *pater* (or monarch). Therefore, relations between sovereign states would be like relations between parents, always of a private nature. Hence, while it was public, international law often and ultimately used private legal concepts. States were inwardly public entities, yet operated privately (by means of treaties, agreements, or diplomacy) in their external relations.

August Wilhem Heffter (1796–1880) took quite a different tack than Vattel and Bentham. In his treatise on *ius gentium europaeum*, Heffter sought to bring back the model of the old Roman *ius gentium*, rejecting Vattel's reductionism as well as Bentham's new nomenclature of international law. For Heffter, this new enlightened statist paradigm, due to its clearly reductionist character, moved away from the classical paradigm by covering only one part of the law of nations, that of relations between states. The Roman law of nations was more than that, however, since it also included the rights common to all people (*allgemeine Menschenrechte*).[11] Moreover, even if, strictly speaking, international law did not acknowledge a human authority superior to that of independent sovereign states, nor a supreme supranational court other than the court of history, this international law had to seek, as nature demanded, the harmony of the community formed by the great family of

---

Digest 1.5.1, ed. Theodor Mommsen and Paul Krüger, *Digesta. Corpus Iuris Civilis*, vol. 1, 16th ed. (Berlin: Weidmann, 1954).

10 On this major legal change, see Domingo, *Gaius, Vattel, and the New Global Law Paradigm*, 627–47.

11 August Wilhelm Heffter, *Das europäische Völkerrecht der Gegenwart, auf den bisherigen Grundlagen*, 8th ed. (Berlin: H. W. Müller, 1888), §2, p. 4.

humankind. Heffter was a prophet unheeded in his time. In my opinion, however, his voice today resounds not only in internationalists' ears but also in canonists' ears.

This new interstate and sovereign paradigm of international law, which excluded the natural person from the order, was predominant throughout the drafting of the 1917 Canon Law Code of the Roman Catholic Church, and the absence of the person explains a lot. Thus, in 1912, the famous internationalist Lassa Oppenheim, in the second edition of his *International Law: A Treatise*, stated emphatically: "The importance of the fact that subjects of the Law of Nations are States exclusively is so great that I consider it necessary to emphasise it again and again throughout this work."[12] Indeed, in Oppenheim's opinion, the only subject of international law was the sovereign state, and the reason for this was obvious, the same as Vattel had argued a century and a half earlier: international law was a law between sovereign states and exclusive to them, so that states were the only subjects of international law. Any individual's action in relation to international law passed through the filter of national law. Individuals had no rights at the international level, nor could they litigate in international courts. Individuals were completely dependent on their state and were covered by its diplomatic protection. This position was upheld in 1928 by the Permanent Court of International Justice, the predecessor of the International Court of Justice, when it stated that "an international agreement, cannot, as such, create direct rights and obligations for private individuals."[13]

The paradigm created in Westphalia in 1648 collapsed, however, three centuries later, at the end of the Second World War, which exposed the serious inadequacies of the international order. The international community then began to gradually open its doors to certain actors of great vitality and prominence and has kept doing so to this day: indigenous peoples, national liberation movements, special independent agencies, NGOs, multinational companies, and transnational corporations all gained recognition in the international order, which granted them certain rights and duties within the international

---

12   Lassa Oppenheim, *International Law: A Treatise*, vol. 1, *Peace*, 2nd ed. (London: Longmans Green, 1912), 22, §13.

13   Jurisdiction of the Courts of Danzig (Pecuniary Claims of Danzig Railway Officials who have Passed into the Polish Service, against the Polish Railways Administration) [Advisory Opinion] 15 (March 3, 1928), http://www.worldcourts.com/pcij/eng/decisions/1928.03.03_danzig.htm.

community. The monopoly of states as exclusive members of the international community, traditionally and by exception joined by the Holy See, the Order of Malta, and, later, the Red Cross, among others, was thus broken.

Yet it was really the Universal Declaration of Human Rights (1948) that opened the door to the individual human person as the bearer and depositary of human rights in the international community. Indeed, Article 6 of the Declaration states that "everyone has the right to recognition everywhere as a person before the law."[14] The same tenor is repeated in Article 16 of the International Covenant on Civil and Political Rights (1966). Moreover, a very similar wording is found in Article 3 of the American Convention on Human Rights (1969), while a similar version in substance, but with a quite different wording, is found in Article 5 of the African Charter on Human and Peoples' Rights (1981).

Ever since the Universal Declaration of Human Rights, the human person has acquired real status in the international order. This gradual inclusion of the individual as a subject of rights and obligations, and therefore with legal personality, has been only partial and asymmetrical, the result of a progressive emancipation of the human person with respect to the state in some fields of international law, the broadest of which is undoubtedly the field of human rights. Individuals have increasingly more means of asserting their own rights at the international level, including the means to complain directly to the United Nations about violations of basic rights. The Council of Europe has played a decisive role in this regard, especially since 1998, when it allowed individuals direct access as petitioners to the European Court of Human Rights.[15]

But the individual's increased presence in international law covers other fields as well, for example, international humanitarian law protects persons not taking part in hostilities; international economic law grants rights to individuals as a result of bilateral investment treaties between states; and international procedural law allows a person to directly initiate proceedings

---

14   Available at https://www.un.org/en/universal-declaration-human-rights.

15   See Protocol No. 11 of May 11, 1994, in force since 1998, which allowed individuals direct access to the court, without any intermediation by another institution. Article 34 of the protocol: "The Court may receive applications from any person, nongovernmental organisation or group of individuals claiming to be the victim of a violation by one of the High Contracting Parties of the rights set forth in the Convention or the Protocols thereto. The High Contracting Parties undertake not to hinder in any way the effective exercise of this right," https://www.echr.coe.int/documents/convention_eng.pdf.

before international tribunals or to be sued directly. However, individuals are still a long way from becoming full subjects of international law in the same way as sovereign states. This is why the doctrine of our times tends to regard the natural person only partially as a subject of international law, using confusing terminology. There is no general provision that regulates in detail the proper status of individuals in international law.

International law often uses the words "legal capacity" and "legal personality" synonymously, to the point that they are interchangeable. In my opinion, however, personality cannot be partial and cannot be waived. You either have it or you do not, and if you have it, you have it forever. What is partial or limited is the capacity to act. Even making a concession that many authors would deem inconceivable, one might think that legal capacity could be renounced, insofar as it is granted and not merely recognized. Thus, Roman law recognized the personality of the family's children but not their legal capacity (though it did acknowledge their capacity to act, which was always limited).

In a nutshell, individuals today enjoy a more relevant, albeit still very moderate, status in international law. They possess certain rights and duties, which they can protect through purpose-designed international mechanisms and procedures, yet international law remains a law between states, though no longer exclusively between them.

The transition from the international law of a community of states to a global law of humanity, in which personal dignity prevails over state sovereignty, is the unfinished business of international legal science.[16] Ultimately, it is a question of placing the human person, not the state, at the center of supranational law, as in most domestic legal systems. International law between states must, of course, continue (a person cannot be a party to an international treaty), but this law must be only a small part of the much larger global law of humanity.

---

16 See, among others, William Twining, *Globalization and Legal Theory* (Cambridge: Cambridge University Press, 2000); Jelena Madunic and John J. Kirton, eds., *Global Law* (New York: Routledge, 2009); Rafael Domingo, *The New Global Law*; Ruti Teitel, *Humanity's Law* (Oxford: Oxford University Press, 2011); Neil Walker, *Intimations of Global Law* (Cambridge: Cambridge University Press, 2015); Giuliana Ziccardi Capaldo, *The Pillars of Global Law*, 2nd ed. (London: Routledge, 2016); Maciej Dybowski and Rafael García Pérez, eds., *Globalization of Law: The Role of Human Dignity* (Cizur Menor: Thomson, Reuters Aranzadi, 2018); and Rafael Domingo and John Witte, Jr., eds., *Christianity and Global Law* (London: Routledge, 2020).

The Human Person in Canon Law

The model of international law I have briefly described bears great similarities to the paradigm adopted by the 1917 and 1983 Roman Catholic codes of canon law (though not with the 1990 Code of Canons of the Eastern Churches). The main reason for these similarities is that, until a few decades ago, modern international law had been markedly Eurocentric, the product of European conflicts and established according to the standards and legal technique of the Western tradition, based on Roman and medieval canon law.[17] Only recently has international law opened up to the powerful influence of Anglo-American law and other rights, in which the word "person," from a legal point of view, does not enjoy so much technical relevance.

Canon 87 of the 1917 Code of Canon Law and Canon 96 of the 1983 Code recognized the canonical juridical personality of only the baptized. The start of Canon 87 of the 1917 Code, which opens the second book, on persons, is as sober as it is unequivocal in its expression: *"Baptismate homo constituitur in Ecclesia Christi persona"* ("By baptism a human being is constituted a person in the Church of Christ"). Canon 96 of the 1983 Code opens with similar wording: *"Baptismo homo Ecclesiae Christi incorporatur et in eadem constituitur persona"* ("By baptism a human being is incorporated into the Church of Christ and is constituted a person in it").

Both of these seem to be clear about and to share the same intention: to acknowledge only the canonical personality of Christians, because canon law is basically a law among and for Christians.[18] Until these codes, as Jean Gaudemet explains so well, canonists had preferred to use the phrase *membrum Ecclesiae* (member of the Church) instead of *persona*.[19] With this

---

17 On this connection between canon law and international law, see chapter 8 in this volume. See also Giulio Bartolini, ed., *A History of International Law in Italy* (Oxford: Oxford University Press, 2020).

18 For a brief yet excellent and comprehensive account of the controversy and the two opposing positions, see Javier Otaduy, "Persona física," in *Diccionario de Derecho Canónico* 6 (Cizur Menor: Universidad de Navarra, Aranzadi, 2012), 172–79, with bibliogaphy. See also Ruggero Maceratini, ed., *La persona nella Chiesa. Diritti e doveri dell'uomo e del fedele Atti del Convegno, Trento, 6–7 giugno 2002* (Padua: CEDAM, 2003); Javier Otaduy, "Quién es persona en Derecho canónico," *Fidelium Iura* 11 (2011): 65–87; and Luis Navarro, *Persone e soggetti nel diritto della Chiesa. Temi di diritto della persona*, 2nd ed. (Rome: Edusc, 2017).

19 On person in canon law, see Jean Gaudemet, "Persona," *Christianesimo*

change in 1917, the legislator, in Gaudemet's opinion, wanted to strengthen the Catholic Church as a perfect society on the model of the most important secular civil codes, the French Code of 1804 and the German Bürgerliches Gesetzbuch (BGB) of 1900.[20] Canon 96 of the Code of 1983, which actually copies Canon 5 of the proposed schema of the unfinished Fundamental Law (*Lex Fundamentalis*), followed the tradition of Canon 87 of 1917, in the light of two important documents of the Second Vatican Council: *Lumen Gentium* (no. 14) and *Unitatis redintegratio* (no. 3), both of which date from 1964. Neither document, however, uses the word "person" in the sense of Canon 96 of the Code of 1983.[21]

Canon 96 of the Code of 1983 (I omit the references to the Code of 1917) acknowledges that Christians who are not in full communion with the Church or legitimately sanctioned undoubtedly have a canonical personality, but it reduces their rights and duties. The Code has given catechumens their own legal status (Canons 206, 788, 851, 1°, 1170, 1183). The unbaptized are obviously recognized as having a natural personality and are granted a certain capacity to act, for example, when they are expressly permitted to administer baptism in case of necessity (Canon 861 § 2), to enter into canonical marriage with a Christian (Canon 1086), to be a witness in a canonical process (Canon 1549), to bring action in a canonical trial (Canon 1476), or to dispose of their goods in favor of the Catholic Church (Canon 1299 § 1). Furthermore, under canon law, a previous valid marriage between unbaptized persons can be dissolved by granting the Pauline privilege (Canons 1143–44).

By recognizing the canonical personality of only baptized persons, canon law does not violate Article 6 of the Universal Declaration of Human Rights, insofar as canon law legislation recognizes the personality of every human being, including the unborn,[22] which, unfortunately, is not the case in many national legal systems.

---

nell storia 9 (1988): 465–92, reproduced in J. Gaudemet, *La doctrine canonique médiévale* (London: Routledge, 1994), no. 14, with a bibliographical guide on the first page.

    20   Gaudemet, "Persona," 471.
    21   Gaudemet, "Persona," 472.
    22   Its condemnation of abortion with excommunication *latae sententiae* (new Canon 1397§2) is clear proof of canon law's concern for the protection of all human life.

Similarities between the International Paradigm and the Canonical Paradigm

The thesis I want to demonstrate in this section is that, in their respective legal paradigms, public international law and canon law use the same legal technique of clearly dissociating legal personality from natural or physical personality, thus solving similar problems in a similar way.

Unlike national legal systems, which start from the human person and then extend personhood to corporations, to nature,[23] and perhaps in the future to animals or robots,[24] the canonical and international legal systems were based on a very technical, fictitious concept of person, different from the human person as such, although the concept presupposed the actual person: in the case of canon law, the baptized human being, that is, the Christian; and in the case of international law, the sovereign group of human beings, that is, the state. This fictitious idea of personality, developed directly by canon and international law scholars, was the one that offered the most security and guarantees to both legal systems, because they could control the fictitious idea as a means of self-protection, with the only limits imposed by the fictitious idea itself. To use popular terminology, by employing this set of fictions, the canonical and international legal systems were playing with a homefield advantage. This control over personality allowed the them to impose their own rules of the game and to protect themselves against conflicts with national legal systems or excessive incursions by political powers. Indeed, a right between states and exclusive to them, such as international law, could not be claimed by any national law, any more than a right exclusive to Christians could be.

Understanding this need for protection that international and canon law both sought entails remembering that neither the international community

---

[23] Article 10, second paragraph, of the 2008 Constitution of the Republic of Ecuador states that "Nature shall be the subject of those rights that the Constitution recognizes for it." Article 71 states that "Nature, or Pacha Mama, where life is reproduced and occurs, has the right to integral respect for its existence and for the maintenance and regeneration of its life cycles, structure, functions and evolutionary processes." Article 72 recognizes that "Nature has the right to be restored." English version: https://pdba.georgetown.edu/Constitutions/Ecuador/english08.html; Spanish version: https://www.oas.org/juridico/pdfs/mesicic4_ecu_const.pdf.

[24] See Visa A. J. Kurki and Tomasz Pietrzykowski, eds., *Legal Personhood: Animals, Artificial Intelligence and the Unborn* (Cham: Springer, 2017).

nor the Catholic Church is limited to a territory, although nation-states and the Vatican City are. Moreover, as I have said, both the international and canonical legal systems presuppose the existence of national legal systems, which are coercively much stronger than these supranational systems. This coercive force of national laws has been particularly evident during the recent sexual abuse crisis within the Catholic Church.[25] Without the coercive collaboration of civil authorities, it would have been very difficult to get over the abuse crisis.

The final issue to note is that international and canon law each have strong ties with another science, without which they cannot be understood: international law with politics, canon law with theology. This means that both international law and canon law often have to use metalegal concepts to which jurists and internationalists tend to attribute a strong technical significance to avoid losing necessary scientific autonomy.

The fact that international law and canon law lack territoriality, are coercively weak, essentially complement national laws (e.g., canon law does not need to regulate traffic), and depend on metalegal principles means that both international law and canon law need to define the limits of their jurisdiction and the scope of their rules with great technical precision. Territorial matters are far easier to delimit than nonterritorial matters, just as noncomplementary matters are much easier to delimit than essentially complementary matters. To delimit and protect the orders, international and canon law opted for the principle of exclusion rather than inclusion. Anyone who was not an international or canonical person—a status determined by the system itself—was *ipso iure* excluded from the system.

Technical-Legal Parallels between the International and Canonical Legal Systems

This similarity of paradigm between the canonical and international legal systems is particularly evident in certain technical parallels, to which I refer below. The systems resemble each other in defining very clearly who is and who is not a person and how they are constituted, in order to then analyze

---

25 For an overall perspective, see Gabriele Kuby, *Abuse of Sexuality in the Catholic Church* (Menomonee Falls, Wisc.: Divine Providence Press, 2019).

the problematic cases that, on the basis of this definition, require special attention. Let us look at some examples of these parallels.

(a) Just as the international community is a community of states, and only they are subjects of international law, so, too, the Church is a community of the baptized, and only they have canonical personality. Just as international law, for centuries, recognized international personality for only one political subject, the state, so, too, canon law recognizes canonical personality for only one theological subject, the Christian. The status of states in international law, from this technical perspective, is very similar to the status of the baptized in canon law.

(b) Just as in international law, a political group acquires legal personality through its constitution as a state, so, too, in canon law, a human being is constituted as a canonical person through baptism. From this legal-technical perspective, baptism represents for canon law what the act of constituting a state is for international law.

(c) Just as international law grants a special status to certain nonstate institutions, such as the Holy See, the Red Cross, the Order of Malta, etc., so, too, canon law grants a special status to certain nonbaptized persons, such as catechumens.

(d) Just as states may or may not be recognized and may be sanctioned by the international community, though neither recognition nor sanction affects their status as international persons, so, too, in canon law, the baptized may or may not be in full communion with the Catholic Church, though neither communion nor possible sanctions affect their status as canonical persons.

(e) Just as international law, for centuries, recognized the juridical dimension of every human person, but did not recognize them as an international personality, so, too, canon law recognizes the juridical dimension of every human being, even if it does not recognize them as a canonical personality. Therefore, just as the acts of certain nonstate actors can become internationally relevant when the international legal system recognizes them, so, too, certain acts of nonbaptized persons can become canonically relevant when the canonical legal system so provides. However, recognition of these acts of will of the nonbaptized or of nonstate actors is always aimed at fulfilling the purposes of canon law or international law.

(f) Just as, in international law, every legal relationship is established for states, or between states, or in the interests of states or the international community, so, too, in canon law every legal relationship is established for baptism, or between the baptized, or in the interests of the baptized, in particular, or of the Church in general.

(g) Just as, after the Second World War, the physical person gradually gained relevance in international law, so, too, in canon law, after the Second World War and also gradually, a growing school of thought (Mario Petroncelli, Pedro Lombardía, Javier Hervada, Gaetano Lo Castro, Luis Navarro, and José María Vázquez García-Peñuela, among others[26]) began to openly and firmly advocate for the personality of every human being in the canonical order.

This use of the same technique explains why many canonical texts could be transferred to international law (and vice versa) by substituting the canonical word for the corresponding word in international law: "Church" for "international community"; "state" for "baptized"; "communion" for "recognition"; and "baptism" for "act of constitution as a state." Canon 96 is a good example: "By baptism (read: *act of being constituted as a state*), one (man) (read: *a political group*) is incorporated into the Church of Christ (read: *international community*) and is constituted a person in it, with the duties and rights which are proper to Christians (read: *states*), in keeping with their condition, insofar as they are in ecclesiastical communion (read: *are recognized*) and unless a legitimately issued sanction stands in the way."

Toward a Global Canon Law

Just as international law—in other words, the law of the community of states—is gradually turning into a global law—in other words, the law of humanity—in which the dignity of the person replaces the sovereignty of states at the heart of the order, so, too, canon law should gradually turn into

---

26 See, among others, Mario Petroncelli, "I soggetti dell'ordinamento canonico," *Il diritto ecclesiastico* 53 (1942): 276–82; Javier Hervada, *El ordenamiento canónico, I. Aspectos centrales de la construcción del concepto* (Pamplona: Universidad de Navarra, 1966), 140–55; Pedro Lombardía, "Contribución a la teoría de la persona física en el ordenamiento canónico," *Ius Canonicum* 57 (1989): 11–106; Gaetano Lo Castro, "La persona nella Chiesa e il suo diritto," in Maceratini, *La persona nella Chiesa*, 70–78; José María Vázquez García-Peñuela, "La persona ante el ordenamiento canónico. Algunas claves de interpretación del canon 96 desde el realismo jurídico," in Maceratini, *La persona nella Chiesa*, 121–39; and Navarro, *Persone e soggetti nel diritto della Chiesa*.

a global canon law by shifting the centrality hitherto occupied by the baptized person to the whole human person.

When recent popes and the Second Vatican Council have spoken of the person's centrality, they have referred not only to the baptized person but to every human person in particular.[27] Every human person, made in the image of God and redeemed by him, is ineffably but definitely bound to the Church founded by Christ, which is an instrument of universal redemption,[28] or, as Saint Paul VI called it, *"il disegno visibile dell'amore di Dio per l'umanità"* ("the visible plan of God's love for humanity").[29] Although it is only through baptism that a person is sacramentally incorporated into the Church, the Church as a sacrament nourishes all human beings regardless of their culture, religion, or beliefs. The catechism of the Catholic Church reminds us of this in precise words: "The Church's first purpose is to be the sacrament of the inner union of men with God. Because men's communion with one another is rooted in that union with God, the Church is also the sacrament of the unity of the human race."[30]

From its beginnings, canon law found in the salvation of souls (Canon 1752) its proper end, its supreme law. The exclusivist nature of the canonical personality, however, does not contribute with the required radicality to the achievement of this end, it does not maximize the *salus animarum*, and it does not facilitate it from a pastoral point of view, because it imposes a particular limitation, at least legally, on the essentially universal sacramentality of the Church. The universal divine plan of salvation establishes such a strong spiritual bond between the Church founded by Christ and every human

---

27 John XXIII, Encyclical Letter *Pacem in terris* (April 11, 1963). See also, among many other documents, Vatican Council II, Pastoral Constitution *Gaudium et spes* (December 7, 1965), no. 26; John Paul II, Encyclical Letter *Redemptor hominis* (March 4, 1979), 17; Benedict XVI, Encyclical Letter *Caritas in veritate* (June 29, 2009), 47; Pope Francis, "Address to the Participants in the Plenary Session of the Pontifical Council for Culture," November 18, 2017; Francis, Encyclical Letter *Fratelli tutti* (October 3, 2020), 8, 12, 13, 18, and passim.

28 Dogmatic Constitution *Lumen gentium* (November 21, 1964), no. 9, https://www.vatican.va/archive/hist_councils/ii_vatican_council/documents/vat-ii_const_19641121_lumen-gentium_en.html.

29 Paul VI, *Discorso al Sacro Collegio*, June 22, 1973, https://www.vatican.va/content/paul-vi/it/speeches/1973/june/documents/hf_p-vi_spe_19730622_sacro-collegio.htm.

30 *Catechism of the Catholic Church*, no. 775.

being, not only the baptized, that it requires, in my opinion, a clearer, firmer, and broader legal manifestation in terms of canonical personality and legal subjectivity to support it. In this respect, I think Carlos José Errázuriz is right when he describes canon law as *"la dimensione giuridica del disegno comunionale della salvezza"* ("the juridical dimension of the communal plan of salvation").[31]

Conclusion

Canon law and public international law are deeply interconnected through a common legal tradition, and the legal technique employed by both systems has often been similar. As both canon law and public international law are nonstate, that is, nonterritorial and therefore global, systems, they had to be very precise and careful when setting their jurisdictional limits and the scope of their rules. To do so, both resorted to the idea of the person in a very technical, delimiting, protective, but also, in a certain way, excluding and reductionist sense. This idea of *persona ficta* (a fictitious person created under law), created by the medieval canonists, was the one that offered the most security and guarantees, as it allowed the canonists the free use of the legal tool, limited only by the very idea of fiction, much broader in any case than limits imposed by reality.

Public international law continues to make progress in acknowledging the international personality of every human being, thus considering each person to be a full subject of rights and duties. Although giant strides have been made in canon law, especially in human rights, there is still a long way to go until a genuinely global canon law based on the centrality of all persons as created in the image of God is developed. This new law in no way undervalues baptism but emphasizes the most universal human condition: if every human being can be baptized, it is precisely because he or she is a repository of the *imago Dei*.

This transition from modern canon law to global canon law calls for the spiritualization of canon law,[32] a more significant legal harmony with the Church's intrinsic evangelizing mission. Legal techniques must never obscure spiritual realities. "Person" is a concept with a profound spiritual

---

31   Carlos José Errázuriz, "La persona nell'ordinamento canonico: Il rapporto tra persona e diritto nella Chiesa," *Ius Ecclesiae* 10 (1998): 3–36, at 23.

32   On the necessary spiritualization of law, see chapters 1 and 2 in this volume.

content and has a relevant legal dimension. The legal dimension, whether international or canonical, must be at the service of all the dimensions of the person: spiritual, moral, rational, social, emotional, and biological. The idea of person in the twenty-first century cannot be used as a legal tool, as it was in previous centuries. The same modernization required by public international law is required by canon law. In this necessary modernization, following the teaching of recent popes, there is only one place for the human person, for any human person, whether baptized or not: the center. Prioritizing the person also gives priority to the baptism that regenerates the person.

Part II

A Biographical Perspective on Law

CHAPTER 9

ALBERICO GENTILI AND THE SECULARIZATION OF THE LAW OF NATIONS

Introduction

A PROMINENT EARLY MODERN ITALIAN legal theorist and practicing lawyer, Alberico Gentili is regarded, along with Francisco de Vitoria and Hugo Grotius, as one of the founders of the science of the modern law of nations (*ius gentium*) and a major figure in the development of international relations. He designed a thorough and autonomous framework for the law of nations based on three pillars: the Greco-Roman idea of natural law, the Justinian compilation of Roman law, and the then-novel Bodinian notion of sovereignty as supreme, perpetual, and indivisible power.[1]

---

* This chapter is co-authored with Giovanni Minnucci. See the original version of this essay as Rafael Domingo and Giovanni Minnucci, "Alberico Gentili and the Secularization of the Law of Nations," in *Christianity and Global Law*, ed. Rafael Domingo and John Witte, Jr. (London: Routledge, 2020), 98–111.

1 See Jean Bodin, *On Sovereignty*, ed. Julian H. Franklin (Cambridge: Cambridge University Press, 1992). For the original version, see Jean Bodin, *Les six livres de la République* (Myriel: Le Plessis Trévise, 2017).

Gentili freed the law of nations from excessive scholastic influences and theological importations, avoiding metaphysical developments and overly subtle dialectics. He tried to build a system based on practice and experience. His legal construction is more inductive from events, episodes, customs, and facts, than deductive from unchanged premises. Providing some new arguments, he removed religion as a valid reason for conflict and war,[2] advocated for the legitimacy of non-Christian regimes, especially the Ottomans, and tried to fix the tenuous lines of separation between jurisprudence and theology and between the internal forum and external forum of canon law. Neither the pope nor the Roman Catholic Church has a place in Gentili's systematic account. His world-famous saying—*silete theologi in munere alieno!*[3]—commands the theologian not to be involved in other people's business and was claimed centuries later by the jurisprudence of European public law to argue in favor of the secularization of the law, beyond the limits Gentili himself intended.[4]

Gentili lived in turbulent times of recurring wars and strong religious conflicts, when European powers were expanding overseas and a new political theory of sovereignty and the nation-state was emerging. He was a transitional figure, able to partially combine the standards and methods of the old Italian school of civilians and the new style and categories of the humanists. He adjusted the medieval law of nations to the early modern idea of sovereignty by merging both traditional authorities and new developments.

A man of great erudition and passion for history, he admired and drew upon many influences: Greek and Roman philosophers, historians, and poets such as Xenophon, Aristotle, Cicero (whom he called "our friend"),[5] Virgil, and Seneca; the ancient Roman jurists Pomponius and Ulpian; theologians like Tertullian, Augustine, and many other church fathers; the Byzantine

---

2   Alberico Gentili, *De iure belli*, 1.9.64, in *Classics of International Law*, trans. John C. Rolfe, vol. 2 (New York: Oceana Publications, 1964), 41; hereafter *De iure belli*. In general, I follow the English translation but have made some adjustments when necessary. Gentili recognizes that "the learned" Francisco de Vitoria and Diego de Covarrubias also declare that religion is not a good reason for war (*De iure belli* 1.9.61).

3   See Gentili, *De iure belli*, 1.12.92: "Keep silence, theologians, in matters which concern others!"

4   Carl Schmitt, *The Nomos of the Earth in the International Law of the Ius Publicum Europeaum*, trans. G. L. Ulmen (Candor, N.Y.: Tellos Press, 2006), 126.

5   Gentili, *De iure belli*, 1.15.111.

emperor Justinian, promoter of the *Corpus iuris*; the late medieval Italian jurists Bartolus de Saxoferrato and Baldus de Ubaldis, as well as the Italian humanist Machiavelli; the German reformers Luther and Melanchthon; and, last, but not least, the French humanist Jean Bodin, whose masterpiece, *The Six Books of the Republic*, constitutes one of the main sources of Gentili's inspiration.

Gentili's reputation and significance declined shortly after his death, especially with the publication of Grotius's monumental work *On the Law of War and Peace* (*De iure belli ac pacis*, 1625), even though Grotius praised and borrowed much from him.[6] It was not until the end of the nineteenth century that the interest in and attraction for the work and thought of Gentili revived, thanks primarily to Sir Thomas Erskine Holland (1835–1926), who delivered his inaugural lecture at Oxford on Gentili (1874)[7] and provided a new scholarly edition of Gentili's main work on the law of war (1877). Since then, Gentili's legacy and academic interest in his life and thought have only grown.[8] However, there is still a long way to go until we fully understand his work and thought, for example, not all Gentili's works have yet been published.[9]

This chapter offers a short biographical narrative, including an explanation of Gentili's main works, then focuses on his idea of the law of nations and his approach to the secularization of that law.

---

6   Grotius, *De Iure Belli ac Pacis Libri Tres*, trans. Francis Kelsey (New York: Oceana Publications, 1964), Prolegomena §38: *"cuius diligentia sicut alios adiuvari posse scio, et me adiutum profiteor"* ("from his work I confess I have derived assistance, as I believe others will profit too"). The lecture caused an enormous patriotic impact on the young kingdom of Italy.

7   Thomas Erskine Holland, *An Inaugural Lecture on Albericus Gentilis Delivered at All Souls College, November 7, 1874* (London: Macmillan, 1874).

8   In our day, scholars like Benedict Kingsbury, Benjamin Straumann, Diego Panizza, Andreas Wagner, Ursula Vollerthun, Peter Schröder, Anthony Pagden, Giovanni Minnucci, Diego Quaglioni, and Alain Wijffels, to mention some of them, have produced impressive scholarship on Gentili.

9   Recently, Giovanni Minnucci edited Gentili's work *De Papatu Romano Antichristo*, manuscript D'Orville 607, Bodleian Library, University of Oxford (1580–1585 and 1591). See Alberico Gentili, *De Papatu Romano Antichristo*, ed. Giovanni Minnucci (Milan: Monduzzi Editoriale, 2018).

His Life and Works

Alberico Gentili was born into a well-established family in San Ginesio in the Papal States (now the province of Macerata) on January 14, 1552.[10] He was the eldest of seven children of the marriage between Matteo Gentili and Lucrezia Petrelli. Alberico received his early education, especially in Latin and Greek, from his father, a distinguished physician and a man of wide culture. In 1569, Alberico enrolled at the University of Perugia, where the memory of Cino da Pistoia, Bartolus, and Baldus—all of whom had taught there— dominated all legal education. At the Perugia law school, Gentili was trained entirely in the medieval style of disputation (*mos italicus*) and graduated in civil law on September 23, 1572, at the age of twenty. He was elected a judge with jurisdiction in civil and criminal cases in Ascoli, and in 1575, he became the municipal lawyer of his native San Ginesio. In that capacity, he revised the statutory laws of the town, a task that he completed in October 1577.

Due to his adherence to the Reformation, Gentili was forced to flee in 1579 with his father and brother Scipione.[11] The three first went to Ljubljana, now in Slovenia. From there, Alberico went to Germany (Tubingen and Heidelberg) and finally, in 1580, settled in London, where a small community of Italian religious reformers welcomed him. There Gentili was introduced to, among others, Robert Dudley, Earl of Leicester, a favorite and close friend of Queen Elizabeth I, and to her secretary of state, Sir Francis Walsingham. Under Dudley's mentorship, Gentili began teaching at Saint John's College in Oxford in 1581. In Oxford, Gentili became friends with the cosmological theorist Giordano Bruno, who was temporarily lecturing there (Bruno was later burned at the stake in Rome). Both met again in 1586 in Wittenberg, where Gentili most likely had gone to try to get a position in a German

---

10   For further biographical information, see Gesina H. J. van der Molen, *Alberico Gentili and the Development of International Law: His Life, Work and Times*, 2nd ed. (Leiden: A. W. Sijthoff, 1968); Angela de Benedictis, "Gentili, Alberico," in *Dizionario Biografico degli Italiani*, vol. 53 (Rome: Istituto della Enciclopedia Italiana, 2000), 245–51; Giovanni Minnucci, "Gentili, Alberico," in *Dizionario Biografico dei giuristi italiani*, ed. Italo Birocchi et al. (Bologna: Il Mulino, 2013), 967–69; and Giovanni Minnucci, "Alberico Gentili (1552–1608)," in *Law and the Christian Tradition in Italy. The Legacy of the Great Jurists*, ed. Orazio Condorelli and Rafael Domingo (London: Routledge, 2021), 281–96.

11   Scipione Gentili also became a famous jurist. During his lifetime, his fame in Europe surpassed that of Alberico. See Lucia Bianchin, "Gentili, Scipione," in Birocchi et al., *Dizionario Biografico dei giuristi italiani*, 1:969–70.

university. The reason for his interest in Germany was the opposition from some sectors of the Puritan party, led by the theologian John Rainolds (long his relentless and bitter adversary), to Gentili's proposed appointment as Regius Professor of Civil Law at Oxford. Gentili finally obtained this appointment on June 8, 1587, the eighth person (the first foreigner and still the only Italian) to hold the prestigious chair established in 1540. He was highly regarded by his colleagues and contemporaries.

In 1588 or 1589, Gentili married Esther De Peigny, a woman of French origin from a well-to-do family, and they raised five children. In 1600, Gentili became a member of Gray's Inn (the same Inn to which Francis Bacon belonged) and began forensic practice. In 1605, he retired from university teaching to devote himself to legal activity as an official attorney of the Spanish embassy in the Admiralty Court in London, with jurisdiction over maritime contracts, torts, injuries, and offenses. Gentili died in London on June 19, 1608, and was buried in the churchyard of St. Helen's Bishopsgate in London.

Gentili published more than thirty works in Latin[12] on a great variety of topics of law, theology, and politics, including the law of nations and international relations, conflicts between canon law and civil law, biblical exegesis, the limits of sovereign power, rebellion, conspiracy, and marriage. His contribution to the law of nations is basically contained in the following books: *De legationibus libri tres* (London, 1585); *De iure belli libri tres* (Hanau, 1598); and *Hispanicae Advocarionis libri duo*, which appeared posthumously (Hanau, Frankfurt, 1613). These three books have been translated into English,[13] as has *De armis Romanis libri duo* (Hanau, 1599).[14]

De legationibus contains a treatise on ambassadors and includes an introductory historical account on legations. Its origin was in a diplomatic incident

12 A complete list of Gentili's works is offered by I. W. F. Maclean, "Alberico Gentili: His Publishers and the Vagaries of the Book Trade between England and Germany," in I. W. F. Maclean, *Learning and the Market Place: Essays in the History of the Early Modern Book* (Leiden: Brill, 2009), 323–37.
13 Alberico Gentili, *De legationibus libri tres*, trans. Gordon J. Laing (New York: Oceana Publications, 1964); *De iure belli libri tres*, trans. John C. Rolfe (New York: Oceana Publications, 1964); and *Hispanicae Advocationis libri duo*, trans. Frank Frost Abbott (New York: Oceana Publications, 1968).
14 Alberico Gentili, *The Wars of Romans: A Critical Edition and Translation of De Armis Romanis* (1599), ed. Benedict Kingsbury and Benjamin Straumann, trans. David Lupher (Oxford: Oxford University Press, 2010).

in 1583, when the Spanish ambassador (and spy) Bernardo de Mendoza was accused of being implicated in a plot to dethrone Queen Elizabeth (an allegation later proven true). The English government invited two foreign lawyers, Gentili and his friend Jean Hotman, secretary to the Earl Leicester and professor at Oxford, to advise the government before the pronouncement of a final judgment. Both defended the criminal immunity of the ambassador, and as a result, Mendoza was expelled in 1584. In *De legationibus*, Gentili argued in favor of the critical role of ambassadors in the international realm, the principle of diplomatic inviolability, the justice of maintaining international relations with the Turks, and the right of embassies to remain undamaged and unaffected by religious differences. Gentili devoted the third book of the treatise to discussing the qualification and main virtues (fidelity, fortitude, temperance, and prudence) required of an ambassador, and he finished (chapter 22) with a model of "the perfect ambassador," inspired by the figure of the English poet, scholar, and soldier Sir Philip Sidney (1554–1586).[15] Gentili's theoretical position in the *De legationibus* on the differences between a law of religion (*ius religionis*) and a human law (*ius humanum*) was later confirmed in correspondence (1593–1594) with the Puritan theologian John Rainolds and in Gentili's subsequent works. From this conviction, he derived the necessity of circumscribing to their respective fields the functions of theologians and jurists—a distinction that ultimately led Gentili to propose the secularization of law.

By far, the most illustrious and influential of Gentili's works is *De iure belli* (Hanau, 1598). A monograph at the confluence of two related movements in the sixteenth century—the Protestant Reformation and the defense of absolute monarchy—*De iure belli* was nevertheless still influenced by medieval European *ius commune* scholasticism. Gentili emphasized controversial issues, providing arguments to support two contrasting positions. On one hand, this method did not allow for a solid systematic exposition of any given issue. On the other hand, it underlined the commentator's hermeneutic effort in his attempt to reconcile very divergent opinions. The outcome was a treatise in the typical sixteenth-century literary style, starting with a few basic items and evolving through a quite logical presentation. Gentili's approach to these issues was empirical, by case study, to establish a common, shared rule

---

15 See Gentili, *De legationibus* 3.22.231. On the *De legationibus*, see Mordechai Feingold, "What's in a Date? Alberico Gentili and the Genesis of *De legationibus libri tres*," *Notes & Queries* 64 (2017): 312–17.

(*regula*). Gentili often used *exempla*, stories that illustrate a general principle or moral lesson, often taken from historical events and current conflicts among the European powers. Sometimes, however, the accumulation of exempla concealed his argument.

In *De iure belli*, Gentili tried to establish an unambiguous, clear, and well-defined legal framework for the law of war. The work consists of three books. The first is especially devoted to the definition and causes of war, which Gentili defined as "a just and public contest of arms,"[16] waged, therefore, by sovereigns.[17] He emphasized that the origin of war had to be a "real and actual necessity" because it is inevitable that "the decision between sovereigns should be made by arms."[18] The reason for necessity is related to the fact that "there cannot be judicial processes between supreme sovereigns or free peoples unless they themselves consent, since they acknowledge no judge or superior."[19] The sovereign cannot have "an earthly judge, for one over whom another holds a superior position is not a sovereign."[20] Necessity for war arrived only after all peaceful means for settling a dispute (for example, arbitration) had been exhausted.

The second book is devoted to the so-called *ius in bello*, that is, the law that governs the conduct of warfare: "just as you ought to observe justice in beginning a war, so you should wage it and carry it on justly,"[21] Gentili affirmed. He defended the importance of the formal declaration of war: without it, no war is just. He disapproved of the murder of enemies and the killing of prisoners, since soldiers are defending the rights of their sovereigns. Children and women (except if the latter assumed the duties of men) should be spared, and no violence should be done to unarmed farmers.

The third book treats the law of peace, which Gentili considers as "the end of war for which all ought to strive."[22] The victor's behavior will depend on the significance of the injury that initiated the war and the need for establishing an enduring peace, but Gentili reiterated the importance of justice and fairness during military occupation, negotiation of treaties, and

16   Gentili, *De iure belli*, 1.2.17.
17   Gentili, *De iure belli*, 1.3.22.
18   Gentili, *De iure belli*, 1.3.23.
19   Gentili, *De iure belli*, 1.3.22.
20   Gentili, *De iure belli*, 1.3.23.
21   Gentili, *De iure belli*, 2.1.209.
22   Gentili, *De iure belli*, 3.1.470.

the imposition of terms and conditions. Cruel punishment is always unjust barbarism: "Punishments which any respect for nature would forbid should have no place here."[23]

Finally, *Hispanica Advocatio*, published by Gentili's younger brother, Scipio, is a collection of the most essential notes on cases in which Gentili engaged as the Spanish advocate in England against the Dutch and other foreigners, as well as some opinions in private law. In his notes, Gentili combined rules of Roman law with historical precedents, and he advocated for the doctrine of territorial sovereignty as the main principle supporting the mutual rights and duties between and among nations, whether engaged in war or neutral.

Other important works of Gentili include *De iuris interpretibus dialogi sex* (London, 1582); *Disputationum de nuptiis libri septem* (Hanau, 1601);[24] *De unione Angliae et Scotiae* (London, 1605); *Regales disputationes tres* (London, 1605); and *In titulum Digestorum de verborum significatione* (Hanau, 1614). In 1603, Gentili's works were included in the Roman Catholic *Index of Prohibited Books*.[25]

Gentili's style is clear, energetic, very direct, and elegant (though not as elegant as Erasmus's or Vitoria's). For instance, he opened his treatise on the law of war by saying that no serious book had been written on the topic so far;[26] he confessed to having no "patience with the modern commentators";[27] he dared to call Erasmus a "flighty dilettante";[28] he wanted to deal "only with the ignorant and not with the perverse as well";[29] and he warned theologians not to get involved in matters that did not concern them.[30] In his disputation on marriage, he expressed his desire to toss into a fire the books on canon law, and not only the *Liber Sextus*, as happened, in fact, in France: "Into the fire with the detestable books of the barbarians; and with the impious books of the Antichrist! Into the fire ... as the great Luther

23 Gentili, *De iure belli*, 3.2.482.
24 On the importance of this work to understanding Gentili's thought, see Giovanni Minnucci, *Silete theologi in munere alieno. Alberico Gentili tra diritto, teologia e religione* (Milan: Monduzzi Edizione, 2016), 190–96.
25 *Index librorum prohibitorum SS. Domini nostri Gregorii XVI Pontificis Maximi* (Rome: Monteregali, 1841), 196: "Gentilis, Albericus, Disputationum de nuptiis libri VII, Dec. 7 aug. 1603; - et caetera ejusdem opera omnia, dec. 7 aug. 1603."
26 Gentili, *De iure belli*, 1.1.1–2.
27 Gentili, *De iure belli*, 1.1.3.
28 Gentili, *De iure belli*, 1.5.46.
29 Gentili, *De iure belli*, 1.1.8.
30 Gentili, *De iure belli*, 1.12.92.

taught us to do!"[31] These diatribes, invectives, and denunciations, abundantly quoted by scholars, in no way represent Gentili's final opinion. The same Gentili who once asked for burning the books on canon law later accorded an important role to canonical sources.[32]

Approach to the Law of Nations

Gentili examines the law of nations as a peaceful *private* order between and among *public* sovereign states, based on natural law and governed by the principles and rules of Justinian Roman law. Departing from imperialist positions, which consider the law of nations to be an extension of civil law, Gentili tried to find in the law of nature the necessary autonomy required by the law of nations. Following Cicero,[33] Gaius,[34] Ulpian,[35] and Justinian,[36] and basing his

---

31 Gentili, *Disputationes de nuptiis libri septem* (Hanau: Apud Guilielmum Antonium, 1601), 112–13: "*Flammis, flammis libros spurcissimos barbarorum, non solum impiissimos Antichristi. Flammis omnes, flammis: ut Lutherus magnus facere docuit!*" On this topic, see Minnucci, *Silete theologi in munere alieno*, 196–202.

32 Alberico Gentili, *Disputationes tres:* I. *De libris Iuris Canonici* (Hanau: Apud Guilielmum Antonium, 1605). On this topic, see Giovanni Minnucci, "Alberico Gentili: Un protestante alle prese con il Corpus Iuris Canonici," *Ius Ecclesiae* 19 (2007): 347–68.

33 See, for instance, Cicero, *De re publica* 3.33 and *De officiis* 3.17.69. For Latin sources, I use *The Latin Library*, http://www.thelatinlibrary.com.

34 Gaius spoke of *ius gentium* at the beginning of his *Institutes* (1.1.1) and contrasted it, as did Cicero, with *ius civile*. Gaius said that civilized peoples—that is, those organized according to law and custom—govern themselves partly by their own law and partly by the law common to all people. The law proper to the city is civil law; the one established by natural reason among all people is called the law of nations because of its universal observance. Natural reason determines, in the abstract, what the law of nations is or could be, and its enforced general application among nations makes it so concretely.

35 Ulpian, in *Digest* 1.1.6, differentiated the civil law, which he considered *proprium* or local (*ius proprium, id est civile*), from a common law comprising both the law of nations and natural law. For Ulpian, however, Cicero's and Gaius's bipartite division becomes tripartite (civil law, law of nature, law of nations). According to Ulpian (*Digest* 1.1.1.3), the reason for this is that the law of nations would be common only to people, whereas the natural law would in general encompass animals as well. For the whole *Corpus iuris*, I use the edition of Theodor Mommsen et al., eds., *Corpus Iuris Civilis*, 3 vols. (Hildesheim: Weidmann, 1989–93).

36 Emperor Justinian adopted Gaius's definition of *ius gentium* and its later three-way division by Ulpian in the sixth century in his *Institutes* (1.2.1) and *Digest* (1.1.1.2).

work solidly on Western legal tradition, Gentili began with the premise that the law of nations belongs to the law of nature. Since the law of nations is a juridical embodiment of nature, jurists are responsible for resolving questions of the law of nations.

> Abundant light is afforded us by the definitions which the authors and founders of our laws are unanimous in giving to this law of nations which we are investigating. For they say that the law of nations is that which is in use among all nations, which native reason has established among all human beings, and which is equally observed by all humankind. Such a law is natural law. The agreement of all nations about a matter must be regarded as a law of nature.[37]

Gentili adopted the expression *societas gentium*, inspired by Cicero and Augustine,[38] to speak of a society of all the nations of the earth. This society of nations is based on the idea that "the human being was born for fellowship, and has a duty to aid others, not to live for self alone."[39] Human beings are "bound by natural law (so say the interpreters of the law) to aid one another."[40] For Gentili, the law of nations is the natural law of that society of nations. It is not comparable to a sovereign city, since rights and obligations in the society of nations cannot be determined by reference to civil law or national law. Sovereign states—as supreme, indivisible, and absolute power of the ruler over the citizens (here the influence of Jean Bodin is total)—are not subservient to any external legal authority. They are independent and submit only to natural law (which is divine law) and to the law of nations (which is a determination of natural law to govern the society of nations).

For Gentili, the *Corpus iuris* was a source of universal and unchanging secular law and, therefore, of the law of nations and natural law: "the law which is written in those books of Justinian," he pointed out, "is not merely that of the state, but also that of the nations and of nature."[41] The *Corpus iuris* of Justinian "holds for sovereigns also, although it was established by

---

37   Gentili, *De iure belli*, 1.1.10. The statement comes from Cicero, *Tusculanae Disputationes* 1.13.30.
38   Gentili, *De iure belli*, 1.15.109.
39   Gentili, *De iure belli*, 1.15.109.
40   Gentili, *De iure belli*, 1.15.110.
41   Gentili, *De iure belli*, 1.3.26.

Justinian for private individuals."⁴² The reason for this extension of the *Corpus iuris* to sovereigns is that it contains natural law, and natural law is universally valid. Not all of Roman law is natural law, but Roman law is not completely different from the law of nations.⁴³ For instance, according to Gentili, Roman law does not recognize every agreement as enforceable (for example, a bare agreement, or *pactum nudum*), and those unenforceable agreements do not belong to natural law; that is why the law of nations admits no difference in agreement. In this sense, Roman law is not entirely and permanently universal, unlike the law of nature. Gentili asked rhetorically, however,

> Are not the following principles for the books of Justinian applicable to sovereigns: to live honorably, not to wrong another, to give every man his due; to protect one's children; to defend oneself against injury; to recognize kinship with all people; and to maintain commercial relations, along with other similar and cognate matters which make up almost the whole of the books? These belong to the law of nations and to the laws of war. Justinian, not only adapted his laws to simplicity of nature, but also restored the old laws to harmony with nature,⁴⁴

for instance, giving equal rights to blood relations on the mother's side.⁴⁵

In sum, then, Gentili tried to reconcile the new Bodinian idea of sovereignty as an absolute and independent power with the notion of natural law and the validity of Roman law as a true law among nations.⁴⁶ His thought, though not wholly explicit, is as follows: (a) the society of nations is a society of fully independent sovereign states; (b) sovereign nations are not subject to any external common authority except God and natural law, which is divine law; (c) the law of nations is not civil law but natural law, and therefore the law

42 Gentili, *De iure belli*, 1.1.26.
43 Gentili, *De iure belli*, 1.1.27.
44 Gentili, *De iure belli*, 1.3.28.
45 Gentili, *De iure belli*, 1.3.27. On this topic, see Rafael Domingo, *Roman Law: An Introduction* (London: Routledge, 2018), 169.
46 On the value of *Corpus iuris* as a legal source among sovereign powers, see Benjamin Straumann, "The *Corpus Iuris* as a Source of Law between Sovereigns in Alberico Gentili's Thought," in *The Roman Foundations of the Law of Nations: Alberico Gentili and the Justice of the Empire*, ed. Benedict Kingsbury and Benjamin Straumann (Oxford: Oxford University Press, 2010), 102–23.

of nations can be applied in the society of nations without depletion of sovereignty; (d) the *Corpus iuris*, although it is a compilation of civil law, contains natural law and the law of nations (not, however, concerning war), and therefore, the *Corpus iuris* can be applied between and among sovereigns, too.

Antony Pagden is correct in pointing out that Gentili, "by making the law of nations into the content of the natural law, ... dispensed with any need for moral discernment. By making that content in all significant respects identical with Roman law, he also eliminated any need of further development."[47] Nevertheless, we will add the following, paraphrasing Pagden: by making the law of nations into the content of the natural law, Gentili protected the independent power of sovereign nations. By stipulating that content in all significant respects identical with Roman law, Gentili protected the province of jurisprudence against the theologians.

The Secularization of the Law of Nations

The word "secularization" is used here in the sense that Gentili advocated for the disentanglement of the law of nations from theology, and for the separation of religion, which is also a part of the law of nature,[48] from the province of the law of nations (*libertas religionis*). His concept of secularization does not question, as often happens in our day,[49] either the supremacy of the laws of God over human law, or the understanding of natural law as divine law, or, as a result, the supremacy of natural law over civil law. Gentili's secularization is theistic and firmly based on Christian principles and ideals.

Keep Silence, Theologians, in Other People's Business!
(Silete Theologi in Munere Alieno!)

This famous apostrophe appears in chapter 12 of the first book of *De iure belli*, after a series of chapters dedicated explicitly to the legitimacy of war.[50] With this apostrophe, Gentili underscored the necessary separation between law and theology, thus contributing to the presupposition of the creation of the European modern state as a way to neutralize religious conflicts.

47 Antony Pagden, *The Burdens of Empire: 1539 to the Present* (Cambridge: Cambridge University Press, 2015), 92.
48 Gentili, *De iure belli*, 1.9.65: "Religion is a part of the law of nature and therefore that law will not protect those who have no share in it."
49 See Rafael Domingo, *God and the Secular Legal System* (New York: Cambridge University Press, 2016).
50 Gentili, *De iure belli*, 1.12.92.

In his practical framework for the law of nations, Gentili granted no vital role to theological constructions, metaphysical assumptions, and philosophical abstractions but rather prioritized legal principles, rules, and arguments. As a Bartolist jurist, Gentili confined himself to the subject of jurisprudence and adopted an autonomous attitude about the law of nations.[51] He believed that questions related to the law of nations and, therefore, to natural law should be dealt with and resolved by legal scholars. The jurist, not the theologian, is the true interpreter of the law.

In 1601, in his work on marriage (*Disputationum de nuptiis libri septem*),[52] Alberico Gentili said his last word on the topic.[53] The Gentilian notion of jurist formulated in *De nuptiis*, and firmly rooted in Roman law,[54] unlike the concept he expressed in *De iuris interpretibus dialogi sex* (1582), is no longer that of a pure and simple exegete of a legal normative body, the *Corpus iuris*, but that of an authentic priest of justice (*sacerdos iustitiae*),[55] who deals with the "art of goodness and fairness."[56] "Our art is not to repeat what has been established in the books of Justinian," he argued, "but to define and explain what the law is in each particular case."[57] To explain what the law is, to build the edifice of justice, true jurists should understand the principles of human action, and to do this they might use not only the Justinian compilation but also other legal sources and even sources from other disciplines. The task of distinguishing the just from the unjust cannot be entrusted only to canonists or civil lawyers (a subdivision no longer acceptable in an era characterized by political and religious divisions) but to the jurist (*iurisperitum*).[58]

In the first book of *De nuptiis*, Gentili presents himself as the heir of the universalist tradition of the *ius commune* and, at the same time, as a reformer

---

51 In this sense, see Coleman Phillipson, introduction, in Alberico Gentili, *De iure belli libri tres* (New York: Oceana Publications, 1964), 9–51, at 20.

52 Alberico Gentili, *Disputationes de nuptiis libri septem* (Hanau: Apud Guilielmum Antonium 1601); hereafter *De nuptiis*.

53 On the importance of this work to understanding Gentili's thought, see Minnucci, *Silete theologi in munere alieno*, 190–96. See also Giovanni Minnucci, *Alberico Gentili iuris interpres della prima Età moderna* (Bologna: Monduzzi Editoriale, 2011), 19–60, with bibliography.

54 See Ulpian, *Digest* 1.1.1.

55 Gentili, *De nuptiis*, 57.

56 See Celsus, *Digest* 1.1.1pr.

57 See Gentili, *De nuptiis*, 57. On this topic, see Minnucci, *Silete theologi in munere alieno*, 213–14.

58 See Gentili, *De nuptiis*, 93.

of legal science that faces the new century. According to Gentili, the search for justice is not exclusively the result of an evolutionary interpretation of Justinian legislation but derives from a hermeneutic effort by the jurist who, with encyclopedic knowledge, can effectively act as the only intellectual capable of formulating valid principles of justice. Justice, like sovereignty, is indivisible; it cannot be fragmented. Therefore, the interpretation of the law should also be indivisible and unfragmented.

Freedom of Religion (Libertas Religionis)

According to Gentili, religion must be free. It can be recommended but never imposed, because it is "a kind of marriage between God and humanity."[59] "Force in connection with religion is unjust."[60] To deprive religion of its freedom will be a "justification of irreligion," and "to attempt by force what cannot be done by force is madness."[61]

Gentili accepts the argument of Bodin that "violence should not be employed against subjects who have embraced another religion than that of their ruler," but always with the reservation: "unless the state suffers harm in consequence."[62] For instance, "illicit gatherings under the guise of religion might be forbidden by rulers."[63] On the other hand, Gentili points out that private citizens cannot take arms against their sovereign for religious reasons—for instance, when the sovereign decides to change the religion of his subjects. In this case, the religious private citizen has to follow the order of Christ (one ought to obey God rather than men) and flee.[64] With the wisdom of his own experience, Gentili concludes: "It is hard to be despoiled of one's goods and fatherland; but this is the order of Christ."[65] For Gentili, the external forum and the forum of conscience must be kept clearly distinct, nor can it be ruled out that they may offer conflicting directives: it is not the

59   Gentili, *De nuptiis*, 1.9.61.
60   Gentili, *De nuptiis*, 1.9.59. These ideas are firmly rooted in early Christian thought (Tertullian and Lactantius, among others). See Robert Louis Wilken, *Liberty in the Things of God: The Christian Origins of Religious Freedom* (New Haven, Conn.: Yale University Press, 2019).
61   Gentili, *De nuptiis*, 1.9.60.
62   Gentili, *De nuptiis*, 1.10.71.
63   Gentili, *De nuptiis*, 1.10.71.
64   Gentili, *De nuptiis*, 1.11.79–84.
65   Gentili, *De nuptiis*, 1.11.84.

task of the civil law to declare an immunity from the sin of a person who is guilty of murder.[66]

Gentili affirmed that it is unlawful to make war for religious reasons: "since the laws of religion do not properly exist between persons, no one's rights are violated by a difference in religion, nor is it lawful to make war because of religion. Religion is a relationship with God. Its laws are divine, that is, between God and humanity. Therefore, one cannot complain of being wronged because others differ from him in religion."[67] Since war against other religious people will always be either vindictive or punitive, it cannot be just.[68] Gentili excludes the case against people "living rather like beasts than like human beings," without any kind of religious beliefs, since religion is part of the law of nature, and the law of nature should not protect those who do not share in it.[69]

Conclusion

Alberico Gentili was a transitional, erudite, legal thinker and practicing lawyer fully involved in the events of his lifetime and attentive to continuous and profound political and social changes. Educated in the Bartolist method, he gradually evolved to a more integrated jurisprudence following the humanist approach. He elaborated a new framework for the law of nations as a part of the law of nature to be applied between and among sovereign states and governed by Justinian Roman law. He also offered a systematic account of two of the most relevant institutions of international relations: diplomacy and war.

Gentili's severe critique of religious intolerance; his drawing of demarcation between the spiritual and the temporal, the internal and the external forum of conscience; his separation of functions between theologians and jurists; his continuous interpretative effort to find principles of natural law—all of these ideas and attitudes, among others, contributed to the establishment of the theoretical basis of the modern European state and to the building up of an international society of sovereign nations. Gentili probably could not match Vitoria's philosophical foundations of the law of nations, but

---

66 Gentili, *De nuptiis*, 1.11.84.
67 Gentili, *De iure belli*, 1.9.64.
68 Gentili, *De iure belli*, 1.9.66.
69 Gentili, *De iure belli*, 1.9.65.

he created a practical private framework for international relations in which sovereigns were linked by the natural law and the Justinian *Corpus iuris*.

Gentili's theory raises the same problems as the idea of sovereignty itself. An indivisible and absolute power, such as any sovereign nation, requires a fragmented international community of sovereign nations, united only by links that do not limit sovereign power (according to Gentili, links of natural law and consent). Inside this weak international framework, war is necessary, at least as the last legal resort to achieve peace. A legal framework that considers war a necessary legal tool is still rudimentary, and that necessity is an expression of the framework's own incompleteness.

Gentili enjoys an extraordinary topicality among scholars and practitioners of international law because the questions of the limits of sovereignty and the legitimization of war continue to be at the core of any serious debate on international law and relations.

CHAPTER 10

ROBERT SCHUMAN AND THE PROCESS OF EUROPEAN INTEGRATION

A CONVINCED CHRISTIAN DEMOCRAT of German education and French heart, and a profoundly committed Roman Catholic, Robert Schuman embodied the most genuine spirit of European reconciliation. He was raised in the contested border area of Alsace-Lorraine and thus experienced, from his youth, the desire for a Europe free from artificial boundaries and joined in mutual cooperation and solidarity. Schuman's life coincided with one of European history's most extensive periods of crisis. He was deeply marked by the consequences of the Franco-Prussian war, the two devastating World Wars, and the Cold War. Early in life, Schuman was introduced to a trilingual culture, and in time, he would hold two different citizenships—German and, later, French. He could defend without conflict of interest the particularities of Lorraine, the singularity of France, the special role of Germany in the construction of Europe, and the uniqueness of Europe as a supranational entity.

* This essay originally appeared as Rafael Domingo, "Robert Schuman and the Process of European Integration," in *Christianity and Global Law*, ed. Rafael Domingo and John Witte, Jr. (London: Routledge, 2020), 176–93.

Visionary and realist, he brought a new aim, dynamism, and aspiration to French diplomacy. Working in collaboration with West Germany, especially with its postwar chancellor Konrad Adenauer (1876–1967), and drawing on the creative work of French political economist Jean Monnet (1888–1979), Schuman was the leading advocate for and public author of the plan for the European Coal and Steel Community, which pooled French and German coal and steel industries and anticipated the European Union.

Illuminated by the Gospel, educated in Thomism, and fiercely influenced by Pope Leo XIII, Jacques Maritain, and Maurice Blondel, among others, Schuman tried to defend his political ideas from Christian humanism. He felt he was an instrument in the hands of divine providence to undertake a mission for his country rather than the designer of that mission.[1] Although much appreciated by his colleagues, he was neither a popular man nor a brilliant speaker. He was a hard worker with a pragmatic mind who exhibited legendary modesty, generosity, a great capacity for listening, and a deep sense of humor.[2] He was an atypical French politician because of his double culture, "monkish asceticism,"[3] and lack of personal ambition. Perhaps that is why he spent so little time in the political arena. He dignified the governmental debate of his time. A man of great originality and imagination, he was able to take a simple approach to big ideas. He was a lover of dialogue and persuasion, a passionate reader, an admirer of Shakespeare, a great student of history, and a devout collector of autographs of great men.

---

1 See Robert Schuman, *French Foreign Policy towards Germany since the War*, Stevenson Memorial Lecture, October 29, 1953 (London: Geoffrey Cumberlege; Oxford: Oxford University Press, 1954), 5. In a letter of 1942 to Robert Rochefort, Schuman wrote (in French): "We are the very imperfect instruments of a Providence which makes use of them in the accomplishment of great designs which go beyond us. This certainty demands a lot of modesty but gives us a serenity that would not always be justified by our personal experiences considered from a merely human point of view." See François Roth, *Robert Schuman: Du Lorrain des frontières au père de l'Europe* (Paris: Fayard, 2008), 562.

2 See some examples in Margriet Krijtenburg, *Schuman's Europe: His Frame of Reference* (Leiden: Leiden University, 2012), 52–53, https://openaccess.leidenuniv.nl/bitstream/handle/1887/19767/fulltext.pdf?sequence=17.

3 Dean Acheson, "Robert Schuman," in Dean Acheson, *Sketches from Life of Men I Have Known* (New York: Harper, 1961), 31–59, at 32.

No full biography of Robert Schuman has been written in English. So far, the best accounts are provided by Alan Paul Fimister[4] and Margriet Krijtenburg.[5] In French, the leading biography is by Raymond Poidevin, published in 1986.[6] Also useful is Christian Pennera's volume on Schuman's youth and early political years. Schuman's colleagues and friends—especially Robert Rochefort, René Lejeune, and Jean-Marie Pelt—have left very useful information, as have the hagiographers Francois Roth and Hans August Lücker.[7] Rudolf Mittendorfer's biography of Schuman, written in German, offers an especially good treatment of his European role.[8]

His Biographical Information

Jean-Baptiste Nicolas Robert Schuman was born on June 29, 1886, in Clausen, one of the oldest neighborhoods in Luxembourg City.[9] His father, Jean Pierre Schuman (1838–1900), was a French farmer born in Évrange, in the Moselle region of Lorraine, on the French border with Luxembourg. The father had fought with the French army for Napoleon III in the Franco-Prussian War of 1870, in which Prussia and its German allies overwhelmingly outnumbered the French.[10] After the war, due to the Treaty of Frankfurt of May 10, 1871,

---

4   Alan Paul Fimister, *Robert Schuman: Neo-Scholastic Humanism and the Reunification of Europe* (Frankfurt am Main: Peter Lang, 2011).
5   Krijtenburg, *Schuman's Europe*.
6   Raymond Poidevin, *Robert Schuman, homme d'État (1886–1963)* (Paris: Imprimerie nationale, 1986); Christian Pennera, *La jeunesse et les débuts politiques d'un grand européen de 1886 à 1924* (Sarreguemines: Editions Pierron, 1985).
7   Robert Rochefort, *Robert Schuman* (Paris: Cerf, 1968); René Lejeune, *Robert Schuman, père de l'Europe (1886–1963)* (Paris: Fayard, 2000); François Roth, *Robert Schuman* (Paris: Fayard, 2008); Hans August Lücker and Jean Seitlinger, *Robert Schuman und die Einigung Europas* (Bonn: Bouvier Verlag, 2000); and Jean-Marie Pelt, *Robert Schuman, Père de l'Europe—Father of Europe* (English version) (Thionville: General Council of Moselle, Serge Domini Publisher, 2001).
8   Rudolf Mittendorfer, *Robert Schuman. Architekt des neuen Europa* (Hildesheim: Georg Olms, 1983).
9   See the biographies listed in footnotes 2–7.
10 On the Franco-Prussian War, see Geoffrey Wawro, *The Franco-Prussian War: The German Conquest of France in 1870–1871* (Cambridge: Cambridge University Press, 2003); Michael Howard, *The Franco-Prussian War: The German Invasion of France 1870–1871*, 2nd ed. (London: Routledge, 2001).

some parts of Alsace-Lorraine, including Jean Pierre Schuman's birth village, were annexed to the German Empire.[11] Jean Pierre decided not to exercise the option of retaining his French nationality, which would have required him to leave the annexed area and immigrate to the trimmed and humiliated France, thereby losing his small farm. Thus, he became a German citizen automatically by misfortune. To escape the German annexation, however, and to make up for the scanty yields of the farm, Schuman decided to settle in Luxembourg in 1873 and live off his rents. In 1884, he married a Luxembourger, Eugénie Duren (1864–1911), who also became German by the marriage and therefore lost her Luxembourgish citizenship. This explains why Robert Schuman, although born in Luxembourg from a Luxembourger mother, was born with German citizenship. Like every child born in Luxembourg to foreign parents, Robert was eligible for Luxembourgish citizenship when he reached the age of majority, but he never chose that possibility.

Young Robert learned Luxembourgish at home because it was his mother's tongue.[12] He attended first the public school of Clausen-Luxembourg, where he mainly learned German, and at the age of ten, he was admitted to the Luxembourg Athenaeum, where courses were taught in both German and, in the upper classes, French. Trilingual from his youth, Robert also learned Latin, Greek, and English at school (although his English never was fluent). His Catholic education in Luxembourg schools and, especially, at home from his beloved mother influenced his life. From a very young age, he also developed a great love for his father's homeland, the Lorraine, where he spent seasons working on the family farm. All through his life, Schuman considered himself a Lorrainer like his father.

In 1900, when Robert was only fourteen, his father died, and his mother died eleven years later as result of an accident with a horse cart. These losses deeply affected Schuman all his life. The preserved correspondence between

---

11   The territory was made up of 93 percent of Alsace and 26 percent of Lorraine; the remaining portions of these regions continued to be part of France. Since its complete reversion to France following World War I, the territory has been referred to administratively as Alsace-Moselle. Since 2016, Alsace and Lorraine are a part of the new French administrative region in northeastern France called Great East. For an overview of the history of Alsace-Lorraine, see François Roth, *Alsace-Lorraine, de 1870 à nos jours: Histoire d'un pays perdu* (Nancy: Place Stanislas, 2010).

12   It is a west-Germanic language, very close to German and Dutch, with borrowed words from French. In Luxembourg, children study in Luxembourgish at kindergarten level and in German and French at primary level.

mother and child—often weekly and in French rather than Luxembourgish—testifies to the deep spiritual relationship between Schuman and his mother.[13] With her, Robert had traveled to Rome in 1909 to attend the beatification of Joan of Arc.

After finishing high school in Luxembourg, where there was no university, Robert moved to Lorraine. In 1903, he was admitted to the Kaiserliches Lyceum in the French city of Metz, just south of where France, Germany, and Luxembourg meet. One year later, he passed the German university-preparatory school exam (Abitur), which opened the door to German universities. As was customary at the time, Schuman attended different law schools to benefit from the scholarship of the most distinguished jurists: Josef Kohler, Otto von Gierke, Paul Laband, Lujo Brentano, Franz von Liszt, and Gustav von Schmoller, among others. He spent one semester in Bonn, two in Munich, and two in Berlin, and he finally graduated from the University of Strasbourg (then under the German rule) in 1908, after passing the first state examination. In 1912, Schuman received his law doctorate with a thesis on civil litigation under the supervision of the young professor Wilhelm Kisch, and he also passed the second state examination, which allowed him to practice law in the German empire. Then, Schuman decided to open a law firm in Metz.

Schuman also became actively involved in Catholic charities at this time. In 1912, the young lawyer of twenty-six met for the first time Bishop Willibrord Benzler. The prelate integrated Schuman into a group of lay diocesan leaders and put him at the head of an organization created specifically for him: the Diocesan Federation of Youth Groups. Benzler urged Schuman to deepen his Thomist thinking, and this period in Metz convinced Schuman that he must consecrate not only his activity but his whole person to God and to the service of others. He considered the possibility of becoming a priest but finally decided to live as a celibate lay apostle in the midst of the world. Increasing the frequency of his receiving the sacraments, he also devoted time to meditation on the Bible, as well as concentrated study of the magisterium

---

13 The letters received by Schuman from his mother (1906–1909) are deposited in the Schuman Papers (34 J 1) at the Departmental Archives in the Moselle. See Charles Hiegel and Marion Duvigneau, *Papiers de Robert Schuman. Répertoire numérique détaillé des fonds déposés sous les cotes 34 et 36 J* (Saint-Julien-lès-Metz: Archives départamentales de la Moselle, 2002), 10. For a commentary about these letters, see Poidevin, *Robert Schuman, homme d'État*, 17–19.

of the church. He especially studied the teachings of the pope of his youth, Leo XIII, author of the first encyclical letter on social issues, *Rerum Novarum* (1891), and father of the social teaching of the Catholic Church.

In 1914, when the First World War broke out, Schuman was not drafted into the German army because of weak health. Instead, he was assigned to administrative tasks in Boulay-Moselle and never wore a German military uniform. In 1919, just after the entrance of French troops under Marshal Pétain into Metz, and once the imperial territory of Alsace-Lorraine had reverted to France, Schuman became a French citizen and was elected to the French National Assembly from the Department of Moselle. During his years as a deputy (1919–1940), he worked to preserve the social legislation that had been applied in Moselle during the German annexation, because it was much more advanced and beneficial than the French policies: bilingualism in school and courts, special status of the railways, and moderate application of French secularism.[14] In 1924, Schuman purchased a piece of

---

14 In Alsace and Moselle, a local law is still in force. Established in 1919 after the end of the First World War, it is applied in the French departments of Bas-Rhin, Haut-Rhin, and Moselle, grouped under the generic name of Alsace-Moselle, which is now in the region Grand East. This local law retains the provisions set up by German authorities between 1871 and 1918, when those provisions were considered more favorable to the inhabitants of Alsace and Moselle. The local law also includes the pre-1870 French laws maintained by the German administration but abrogated by the French authorities before their return in 1918. Finally, the local law includes specific French laws after 1918 applicable only to theses territories. The local law mainly affects professional regulations, credit institutions, statutory holidays, legislation on the reimbursement of health expenses, social assistance for the poorest persons, the organization of justice and the courts, civil procedures, bankruptcy, the land register, the law of hunting, and the law of association. The French law on separation of the churches and the state of December 9, 1905, is not applied in Alsace and Moselle. Instead, the 1801 Concordat with the Holy See and the special laws of 1802 are still in force. As result, religious education is compulsory in primary and secondary schools (with permission of the parents); the University of Strasbourg and the University of Metz are the only French public universities to teach theology; and the remuneration of the ministers of the four recognized cults (Catholic priests, Lutheran and Reformed pastors, and Jewish rabbis) is taken over by the state. The appointments of the archbishop of Strasbourg and the bishop of Metz are made by the president of the French Republic, the last head of state in the world to appoint Catholic bishops. For an overview of the local law in Alsace and Moselle, see Institut Du Droit Local Alsacien-Mosellan, ed., *Le guide du droit local: Le droit applicable en Alsace et en Moselle de A à Z*, 4th ed. (Strasbourg: Institut Du Droit Local Alsacien-Mosellan, 2015).

land in Scy-Chazelles, a Lorraine village in the Moselle Valley, where today his house has been transformed into a museum and inspirational European convention center.

In March 1940, with World War II already begun, Schuman became a member of Paul Reynaud's government as undersecretary of state for refugees. Just months later, on June 14, Paris fell to Nazi Germany. On June 22, Marshal Pétain signed the armistice with the Germans, and the French government moved to Vichy, 220 miles south of Paris.[15] Schuman was confirmed in his position by Pétain. On July 10, 1940, Schuman voted with the majority of the National Assembly to grant extraordinary powers to Marshal Pétain to reform the constitution of France, but, unhappy with the attitude and guidance of the Petain government, Schuman resigned his ministry and returned to Metz at the end of August.

On September 14, 1940, Schuman was arrested by the Gestapo, the Nazi secret police, and on April 13, 1941, after the Nazis considered sending him to a concentration camp, he was finally placed under house arrest in Neustadt an der Weinstrasse, a German town in the Rhineland-Palatinate. This benevolent measure by gauleiter Joseph Burckel, the German party leader and governor of the annexed department of Moselle, may have been an attempt to persuade Schuman of the advisability of supporting the Nazi regime.[16] In Neustadt, Schuman enjoyed some degree of freedom, especially after gaining the confidence of the police. On August 1, 1941, helped by friends in Lorraine, he escaped to unoccupied France. Until the liberation at the hands of the Americans in August 1944, he lived secretly in twelve different hiding places, most of them religious houses, and worked for the French resistance. He also spent time improving his English and reading Shakespeare, Thomas Aquinas, and Saint John of the Cross. At that time, he experienced the need to make the best effort to engage France and Germany in a common project of unifying Europe.

After the war, Schuman was officially declared a collaborator of the Vichy regime and therefore disqualified from public office. General Charles de Gaulle, the undisputed leader of the French resistance, personally resolved the problem, however, and secured Schuman's rehabilitation, opening the door for Schuman to again enter French political life. He made his enormous

---

15 On the so-called Vichy regime, see Philippe Burrin, *France under the Germans: Collaboration and Compromise*, trans. Janet Lloyd (New York: New Press, 1996).

16 See Poidevin, *Robert Schuman, homme d'État*, 137.

political contribution over the next eight years of the so-called French Fourth Republic (1948–1956), which was marked by governmental instability and social insurrection.

Schuman was almost sixty years old when he began his national and international career. He served as minister of Finance (1946) under the governments of Georges Bidault, leader of a Christian democratic party called the Popular Republican Movement (MRP), and Paul Ramadier. In November 1947, the National Assembly elected Schuman himself as prime minister (only the Communists voted against him). Less than a year later, however, on July 27, 1948, Schuman stepped down as prime minister, unable to hold his political coalition together.[17] The new prime minister, André Marie, appointed Schuman as minister of foreign affairs, a post that Schuman retained through eight governments, until January 1953. Later, Schuman was appointed minister of justice (1955) for less than a year.

As prime minister and, especially, as foreign minister, Schuman was instrumental in negotiating major treaties and international initiatives such as the Marshall Plan (1948–52), the Council of Europe (founded on May 5, 1949), and the North Atlantic Treaty Organization (NATO), founded on April 4, 1949. Schuman believed that the North Atlantic Treaty, the European Convention on Human Rights (drafted in 1950 by the newly formed Council of Europe), and the European integration process itself would constitute the foundations of a new Western order.[18]

Schuman became internationally renowned for what is now called the Schuman Declaration,[19] which he issued on May 9, 1950, in Paris, at the Salon de l'Horloge (the Clock Room) in the Quai d'Orsay, headquarters of the French Ministry of Foreign Affairs. This declaration changed the history of Europe and is now considered the founding document of the European project that comprises the European aspirations of peace, solidarity, and cooperation.[20] There, just five years after the end of World War II, Schuman

17   Later, Schuman was prime minister again for one week, September 5–11, 1948.
18   See Lejeune, *Robert Schuman, père de l'Europe,* 153.
19   See the whole text, available at https://europa.eu/european-union/about-eu/symbols/europe-day/schuman-declaration_en.
20   On the spirituality of the declaration, see Gary Wilton, "Christianity and the Founding: The Legacy of Robert Schuman," in *God and the EU: Faith in the European Project*, ed. Jonathan Chaplin and Gary Wilton (London: Routledge, 2016), 13–32. As Fimister well pointed out, the 1950 declaration resulted from the "self-conscious application" by Schuman of the Catholic social thought and neo-Thomistic political philosophy

launched his proposal for France and West Germany to work together on the production of coal and steel, "under a common high authority in an organization open to the other countries of Europe"—and in the process making "any war between France and Germany not merely unthinkable but materially impossible." The common high authority would have decision-making power in accordance with the statutes, and was in reality an authority protected by a supranational jurisdiction.[21] This plan ended the means and incentives for new wars and laid the foundation for a potential supranational Europe. The Schuman Declaration marked the beginning of post–World War II Franco-German cooperation and the reintegration of West Germany into Western Europe. Schuman was always aware of the event's relevance: "In 1950," he wrote, "France was the forerunner of a new ideal. It was revolutionary in terms of design and range, but it was peaceful in how it was undertaken."[22]

The leading architect of the plan was Jean Monnet, the general planning commissioner.[23] With great humility, Schuman recognized the "exceptional merits of an exceptional man": Jean Monnet, who Schuman did not hesitate to call his friend.[24] Like all great men, Schuman discounted the significance

---

to international relations. See Fimister, *Robert Schuman: Neo-Scholastic Humanism and the Reunification of Europe*, 17.

21 See Robert Schuman, *For Europe* (Paris: Foundation Robert Schuman; Chêne-Bourg: Nagel, 2010), 110.

22 Schuman, *For Europe*, 20.

23 Schuman, *For Europe*, 119: "In a small hotel on Rue Martignac, it was Jean Monnet who, together with his collaborators, sketched out within a few months, discretely and in the utmost secrecy—not even the government knew—the idea of the coal and steel community." See also Jean Monnet, *Memoirs* (London: Third Millennium, 2015), 318–35. The first draft was prepared by Paul Reuter, Schuman's colleague and the lawyer at the Foreign Ministry, and it was edited mainly by Jean Monnet, Étienne Hirsch, Pierre Uri, and Bernard Clappier. In her doctoral thesis, Margriet Krijtenburg tries to recover Schuman's leadership in the project. See Margriet Krijtenburg, *Schuman's Europe: His Frame of Reference*. In the same vein, see also David Heilbron Price, *Robert Schuman, Jalonneur de la paix mondiale* (Berlin: Brons Communications, 2014), 61–62. On the role of Paul Reuter, see Antonin Cohen, "Le plan Schuman de Paul Reuter. Entre communauté nationale et fédération européenne," *Revue française de science politique* 48 (1998): 645–63. For a general overview, see Paul Reuter, *La Communauté européenne du charbon et de l'acier* (Paris: Librairie Geénérale de Droit et Jurisprudence, 1953), foreword by Robert Schuman.

24 Schuman, *For Europe*, 119. On this relationship, see Éric Roussel, "Les

of his own work: "It was the foreign minister's responsibility to provide his patronage and his backing, and to assume the political risks of the initiative."[25] Italy, Belgium, the Netherlands, and Luxembourg responded positively to the proposal and joined France and West Germany in creating the European Coal and Steel Community (ECSC) on April 18, 1951. The ECSC is considered the precursor to the European Economic Community established in 1957 and the beginning of what is now the European Union. Since 1985, May 9 is celebrated annually as Europe Day, and it is commonly recognized as one of the great "European constitutional moments."[26] In some sense, it can be said that the Schuman Declaration is of similar importance to the Declaration of Independence of the United States. Both are at the heart of the birth of two important political and social projects: the United States of America and the European Union. Both documents were produced by great men in difficult circumstances. Both were firmly based on religious principles. Both constitute a call to the common sense of the people: the one to justify the independence of a new nation, the other to seek the union of a devastated continent. Similarities abound.

After May 9, 1950, Schuman, the statesman, became identified with the cause of European integration. With the fall of Antoine Pinay's administration in December 1952, Schuman's ministry of foreign affairs ended. The German novelist Thomas Mann wrote to Schuman: "I cannot imagine that the country wants to or can give up your services."[27] Schuman returned to government in 1955 for a short term as a minister of justice in the Edgar Faure government, but in 1958, the return of General de Gaulle to power ended Schuman's political career in the French government. De Gaulle had never had great esteem for Schuman, let alone for his particular European project.[28]

---

paradoxes de la relation Jean Monnet–Robert Schuman," in *Robert Schuman et les Pères de l'Europe* (Brussels: Peter Lang, 2008), 87–92.

25 Schuman, *For Europe*, 119. An example of risk is, for instance, that two days before the declaration, on May 7, 1950, Schuman, without the consent of the French Council of Ministers, assured Chancellor Konrad Adenauer in a letter that the proposal of declaration would be approved a few days later by the French government. The letter is available at http://www.cvce.eu/content/publication/1999/2/10/5b2f4ed8-b98c-4dc3-b7de-0f53bf11ff55/publishable_en.pdf.

26 On constitutional European moments, see J. H. H. Weiler, *The Constitution of Europe* (Cambridge: Cambridge University Press, 1999), esp. 3–4.

27 See Rochefort, *Robert Schuman,* 317; Poidevin, *Robert Schuman, homme d'État,* 367.

28 The lack of understanding between De Gaulle and Schuman was profound.

Schuman then became the primary defender of the European cause, traveling throughout the continent (Rome, Vienna, London, Athens) and worldwide (Rio de Janeiro, Washington, Boston), promoting European reconciliation and unification. From 1955 to 1961, he was the president of the European Movement, and from 1958 to 1960, he was president of the European Parliamentary Assembly[29] (now the European Parliament) in Strasbourg.

Honored often, Schuman received honorary doctorates from the universities of Edinburgh, Birmingham, and Tilburg, the University of California, Los Angeles (UCLA), Fordham University, and the Catholic University of Leuven. In 1956, Pope Pius XII awarded him the Great Cross of the Order of Pius IX. In 1958, he received the Charlemagne Prize in Aix-la-Chapelle (Aachen), one of the most prestigious European prizes. In 1959, he received the Erasmus Prize along with the German-Swiss philosopher Karl Jaspers. The European Parliamentary Assembly awarded him the title of Father of Europe at the end of his term of office (1960).

At the end of 1959, Schuman's health declined, and in 1962, he announced his retirement from political life, devoting much of his time to meditating on sacred scripture. He decided not to write his memoirs to avoid personal judgments about other people and circumstances and because he did not want to feel like the center of attention in European political life. Instead, he wrote a short essay on Europe, consisting of a brief summary of the essential ideas and convictions that guided his political activity in favor of the European Union (see the next section).

Schuman died on September 4, 1963, at the age of seventy-six. His death went largely unnoticed because Gaullism then occupied the whole political

---

See Fimister, *Robert Schuman,* 170–71; Lejeune, *Robert Schuman, père de l'Europe,* 135–38. The divergences among the two politicians are explained by Hardev Singh Chopra, *De Gaulle and European Unity* (New Delhi: Abhinav Publications, 1974), 35–39.

29   After the establishment of the European Economic Community (ECC) and the European Atomic Energy Community (Euratom) in 1957, a single assembly was created with the powers and responsibilities assigned to it by the EEC and Euratom treaties. This assembly also replaced the Common Assembly of the European Coal and Steel Community. The single assembly held its first session on March 19, 1958. It was this new assembly that unanimously elected Schuman as president. The official and unified designation as European Parliament was made by Article 2 of the Single European Act of 1986. For an overview of the history of the European Parliament, see http://www.cvce.eu/en/obj/european_parliament-en-ad6a0d57-08ef-427d-a715-f6e3bfaf775a.html.

sphere. A few days before his death, the bishop of Metz, having administered the sacrament of the sick, read to him a telegram from Pope Paul VI. The old man was so much affected that he cried.[30] Schuman was buried in the twelfth-century fortified church of Saint-Quentin, adjacent to his house. His beatification process was officially opened in the diocese of Metz on June 9, 1990.[31] On June 19, 2021, Pope Francis authorized the Congregation (now Dicastery) for the Cause of Saints to publish the decree on heroic virtues, which granted Schuman the title of Venerable.[32]

The Robert Schuman Foundation was established in 1991 in Paris and Brussels to promote European research on the policies of the European Union, as well as to foster European values following the spirit and inspiration of the founding fathers of Europe. The European University Institute in Florence, Italy, is home to the Robert Schuman Centre for Advanced Studies (RSCAS), focusing on interdisciplinary, comparative, and policy research on the major issues of the European integration process.[33] In 2016, the University of Luxembourg inaugurated the Robert Schuman Institute of European Affairs, which focuses on the interdisciplinary study of European affairs and the European Union.[34] Schuman's papers are deposited at the departmental archive of the Moselle.[35] In addition, both the European Commission Library and the Robert Schuman Foundation hold abundant material. The archival collection of Hans August Lücker on the beatification process for Robert Schuman is now available for research at the Historical Archives of the European Union (HAEU).[36]

30 See Poidevin, *Robert Schuman, homme d'État*, 420.
31 On the cause of beatification, see Institut Saint-Benoît, *Actes des journées organisées à Metz du 4 au 8 septembre 2013* (Metz: Éditions des Paraiges, 2013), esp. 11–15.
32 Information available at https://www.vaticannews.va/en/pope/news/2021-06/robert-schuman-father-of-european-unity-on-path-to-sainthood.html.
33 Information available at http://www.eui.eu/DepartmentsAndCentres/RobertSchumanCentre/Index.aspx.
34 Information available at http://schuman-institute.eu/institute.
35 See Charles Hiegel and Marion Duvigneau, *Papiers de Robert Schuman*. http://www.archives57.com/phocadownload/6._FONDS_PRIVES/politique/frad57%20034-036j%20papiers%20schuman.pdf.
36 The inventory is available at http://archives.eui.eu/en/fonds/153157?item=HALK.

Schuman's European Vision

Schuman's vision of Europe has been reflected in the many speeches and lectures[37] he delivered throughout his life, but especially in what can be called his political testament—his essay *For Europe*.[38] Although written in the political context of the sixties, Schuman's essay on Europe continues to have great value for our time because of the powerful inspiration of its perennial principles. Schuman did not look for a provisional solution to resolve the problems of a devastated Europe after the Second World War but sought to develop a long-term common project based on legal solidarity and constructive endeavor. He was realistic, believing that partial agreements and success should be the starting point for more relevant and lasting achievements. Schuman saw the need to politically organize interdependence and diversity and maintain different levels of government, with different intensities, developing a healthy patriotism and solidarity among peoples.

The starting point for his project was the realization that the division of Europe had become anachronistic.[39] European borders had become an obstruction, a hindrance, or an impediment to the exchange of goods, the developing of ideas, and the mobility of people. More than a barrier, he thought, borders should constitute a venerable and respected meeting point of cultures and ideals. Union, cohesion, cooperation, and coordination between and among European nations was required. This new supranational level, illuminated by a universalist approach, should be founded on the principles of solidarity, international cooperation, majority rule freely accepted by the nation-states, and the principle of equality of rights among them. The aim would not be to join states to create a super-European state but to allow people to live in different countries that are part of a supranational structure. Key to understanding Schuman's approach to the organization of Europe is supranationality, which, Schuman explained, "is situated at the same distance between, on the one hand, international individualism that treats national sovereignty as intangible, and accepts no more limit of sovereignty

---

37 A list of Schuman's more than sixty minor writings, lectures, and speeches can be found in Poidevin, *Robert Schuman, homme d'État*, 481, 484–86. Most of them can be consulted in the Schuman Papers (34 J) at the Departmental Archives of Moselle. Some are available at www.schuman.info, led by David Heilbron Price.
38 Schuman, *For Europe*. The English translation of the essay must be improved.
39 Schuman, *For Europe*, 15.

than contractual obligation; and, on the other hand, a state federalism that is subordinated to a superstate endowed with its own territorial sovereignty."[40]

Behind this project lie no hidden imperialistic goals or any egoistic inclination, only the firm desire to achieve peace among nations and contribute to the development of humanity. The European project falls within a broader one, the "rational organization of the world,"[41] of which Europe will become an essential part. It is, therefore, a peaceful endeavor based on a matter of fact: countries need each other, regardless of the international power they might hold. Isolation of countries means decline. Patriotism is not opposed to Europeism, Schuman said, because "the national can flourish within the supranational."[42] Nations have a mission concerning their own peoples and vis-à-vis other nations. Nationalism itself, therefore, is a terrible refuge.

Europe was a "cultural community in the most elevated sense of the term"[43] before being a military alliance. It should be thought to have developed a soul in the diversity of its traditions and aspirations. Security is a necessary condition for peace and prosperity, and, like peace, has become indivisible. Thus, Schuman argued, Europe's legitimate and constructive goal is to guarantee collective defense. Merely defending Europe is not enough since the defense of Europe alone does not necessarily imply building Europe. "The present feeling of insecurity," Schuman affirms, "will be the direct cause of the European unification, but it will not be its raison d'être."[44] European countries are interdependent. For better or worse, all countries are united in a single destiny, and this unity demands solidarity between and among nations. According to Schuman, solidarity is based on "the conviction that the real interest of all lies in acknowledging and accepting the interdependency of all,"[45] a reality incompatible with claims to hegemony or egoistic superiority. Solidarity is also incompatible with any political nationalism, autarchic protectionism, or cultural isolationism. True political solidarity requires "democratic equality."[46] The European project is not imperialistic

---

[40] Robert Schuman, préface, in Paul Reuter, *La Communauté européenne du charbon et de l'acier*, 3–8, at 7. The legal approach to the idea of supranationality was deeply developed by Paul Reuter.

[41] Schuman, *For Europe*, 18.

[42] Schuman, *For Europe*, 22.

[43] Schuman, *For Europe*, 29.

[44] Schuman, *For Europe*, 134.

[45] Schuman, *For Europe*, 35.

[46] Schuman, *For Europe*, 36.

but supranational and therefore democratic in essence. It implies majority decisions (avoiding any dictatorial superiority), organized cooperation, and a free market, which in turn means competition and confidence.[47] Finally, the European project demands the cultural development of a real community of ideas, values, and aspirations.

Christian democracy constitutes the framework of Schuman's European ideal. He believed democracy and Christianity are strongly linked because "democracy owes its existence to Christianity."[48] "Like Bergson," he pointed out, "I have come to the conclusion that democracy is essentially evangelic, since love is its mainspring."[49] As a doctrine, democracy is linked to human dignity, individual rights and freedoms, and brotherly love toward others. Democracy is an expression of civilized maturity, and it took Europe over a thousand years to achieve it. "Christianity taught us that all men are equal by nature, children of the same God, redeemed by Christ regardless of race, color, social status, or profession.... The universal law of love and charity made every man our neighbor." All of these teachings, with crucial practical consequences, "have changed the world forever."[50]

But Christianity should not be a part of the structure of a political system, nor should it be identified with any form of government. Rather, it is necessary to distinguish what belongs to Caesar and what belongs to God. The administration of changing situations belongs to Caesar; the immutable principles of natural law belong to God.[51] On one hand, theocracy minimizes the necessary separation between the two domains. On the other hand, the nation-state, which seeks to separate the domains, cannot undermine religious inspiration's extraordinary value and moral authority in public life and in protecting people against social disintegration. For this reason, democracy must define a positive approach to religion.

The last chapters of Schuman's essay on Europe are more circumstantial, but they also contain relevant statements that later history has confirmed. First, Schuman states that without Germany, just as without France, building Europe would be impossible.[52] More than any other country, perhaps,

47 Schuman, *For Europe*, 37.
48 Schuman, *For Europe*, 43.
49 Schuman, *For Europe*, 51.
50 Schuman, *For Europe*, 44.
51 Schuman, *For Europe*, 46.
52 Schuman, *For Europe*, 61.

Germany has a deep sense of community that will make it a full player in a united Europe. Schuman firmly opposed the division of Germany into West and East for one convenient reason: "The policy of constraint, applied by the victors, only brings flimsy and deceptive solutions; and it generates new conflicts. On the other hand, as long as there is room for revenge, the risk of war can arise again."[53] According to Schuman, neutralizing or even nullifying Germany is contrary to the European project. He anticipated a unified Germany fully integrated into European institutions.[54]

Second, Schuman foresaw that the United Kingdom would agree to join an integrated Europe only when forced by events. Schuman did not consider the United Kingdom as particularly identified with the new European spirit. The issues for this were psychological, cultural, and political. According to Schuman, "it was inconceivable for the British government to grant a European body more authority than the Commonwealth."[55] The withdrawal of the United Kingdom from the European Union in 2020 harks back to the words of Schuman.

Third, Schuman believed economic integration was inconceivable in the long term without its logical complement, political integration.[56] Political integration for Europe means federation in the noblest sense of the idea. European countries should be partner states working together through collective diplomacy and supranational institutions led by a parliamentary assembly elected by universal suffrage,[57] with the capacity of imposing its will over national parliaments in serious decisions on war and peace, nations' independence, and integrity of territory.[58] This federation of states should avoid the mistakes of nation-states, particularly bureaucracy and technocracy[59]:

---

53 Schuman, *For Europe*, 79.
54 Schuman, *For Europe*, 139.
55 Schuman, *For Europe*, 86.
56 Schuman, *For Europe*, 93.
57 The decision and the act on European elections by direct universal suffrage were signed in Brussels on September 20, 1976. The act entered into force in July 1978, following ratification by all member states. The first elections took place on June 7 and 10, 1979. See http://www.europarl.europa.eu/ftu/pdf/en/FTU_1.3.1.pdf.
58 Schuman, *For Europe*, 108.
59 About thirty-three thousand people are employed by the European Commission. In the European Parliament, about six thousand people work in the general secretariat and in the political groups. In the Council of the European Union, approximately 3,500

"administrative paralysis," Schuman says, "is the basic danger that threatens any supranational organization."[60] Unfortunately, the European Union has disregarded the voice of one of its founders on a point as important as this.

Schuman's Contribution to the Idea of Global Law

Schuman did not develop the idea of global law. Moreover, he probably never used the expression "global law." However, some principles applied by Schuman to build up the European integration project are also useful for a general theory of global law. The principle of the centrality of the person, the need to eliminate wars through peaceful means rooted in the law, the importance of limiting the sovereignty of states without abolishing national communities, and the relevant role of solidarity and subsidiarity in the building up of supranational structures, are some of Schuman's intuitions that might also be applied in the development of global law.

The European and global human communities are different by nature since the former is particular and the latter universal, but both communities share one element. They are both incomplete and, therefore, complementary communities. That is why, in my opinion, the analogy between the two communities is possible and helpful. Incomplete communities are those that strive to satisfy only certain specific human needs, not as many as possible, in the way of complete communities (for example, the nation-state). All incomplete communities are complementary in nature, and this degree of complementarity might ultimately be determined through political decision-making according to the principles of solidarity and subsidiarity.[61]

A reading of Schuman's essay *For Europe* from this perspective, based on analogy, offers us some lessons, because he understood the European project as a complementary project to develop solidarity between and among European citizens and European countries. Paraphrasing *For Europe*, we can say: (1) the new global community should refer to a community of human beings and not just a community of nation-states (10); (2) the idea of global law is not to merge nation-states to create a super world nation-state (16);

---

people work in the general secretariat. See more basic information at https://europa.eu/european-union/about-eu/figures/administration_en.

60 Schuman, *For Europe*, 106.

61 For further development, see Rafael Domingo, "The New Global Human Community," *Chicago Journal of International Law* 12, no. 2 (2012): 563–87.

(3) no global law is possible without the union, cohesion, and coordination between and among nation-states (17); (4) democratic majority rule should be implemented at the global institutional level (17); (5) the end of global institutions is not to absorb the nation but to endow it with a broader and higher sphere of activity (21); (6) global security and peace have become indivisible (24); (6) the law of solidarity between peoples is a must for the modern global conscience (31); (7) global law is the implementation of widespread democracy in the Christian sense of the term (41); (8) each country should be aware of its interdependence with others (103); (9) administrative paralysis is the basic danger of supranational institutions; and (10) serving humanity is a duty similar to loyalty to the country (131).

Conclusion

Robert Schuman's life is closely linked to an international mission: bringing France and Germany together to lead the European unification process. He believed in an organized and united Europe based on the leadership of Germany and France, acting as two powerful lungs under equal rights with other nations. The heart of Europe should be, however, Christian in character, because Christianity is, according to Schuman, the trustworthy inspirational source of forgiveness and love. He embodied and anticipated the values Europe should develop politically: diversity, solidarity, forgiveness, magnanimity, and generosity. In this sense, Robert Schuman was the first citizen, the first founding father, of the European Union. He was a visionary but at the same time a very realistic politician. His proposals were courageous but accessible, without being lost in pure aspiration or abstraction. In all his political ideas and actions, he was guided and determined by his religious attitude. Out of his Christian outlook, he understood politics as a service to humanity, oriented to the common good, and in harmony between individuals and peoples. Since both the European and global communities are incomplete and complementary, some analogies based on Schuman's approach to Europe can be established in developing a theory of global law.

CHAPTER 11

ÓSCAR ROMERO, A MARTYR FOR SOCIAL JUSTICE

A CHRISTIAN MARTYR FOR THE gospel of social justice and a man of deep spirituality and great ethical stature, Óscar Romero, archbishop of San Salvador during years of brutal government and paramilitary repression, is a towering figure in the recent history of El Salvador and Latin America. Since his murder on March 24, 1980, while he was celebrating the Eucharist, his legacy and cultural influence have only grown. For decades, in life and after it, he was controversial and often manipulated, branded as both a communist and a conservative, as a provocateur of the Salvadoran civil war (1980–1992), and as a leader of people's liberation and human rights. Many political, military, and ecclesiastical authorities in and outside his country harshly criticized Romero's attitude and behavior. Salvadoran oligarchs denounced him repeatedly, but not so the hundreds of thousands of peasants who confirmed as true what Romero wrote about his own mission: "The ministry that God has given me is, like the one given to Moses, to lead our people to the Promised Land."[1]

---

* See the original version in Rafael Domingo, "Óscar Arnulfo Romero y Galdámez (El Salvador, 1919–1980)," in *Law and Christianity in Latin America: The Work of Great Jurists*, ed. M. C. Mirow and Rafael Domingo (London: Routledge, 2021), 498–510.

1 Letter to Ernestina R., November 26, 1979, in Óscar Romero, *The Church Cannot Remain Silent* (Maryknoll, N.Y.: Orbis Books, 2016), 15.

It is now widely accepted that Romero was the "voice of the voiceless," an advocate of the "violence of love," and a champion of human rights in the struggle for social justice. He devoted himself entirely to preventing the tragic civil war in his long-suffering country and to defending and protecting the poor. Not a politician, Romero became the cornerstone of Salvadoran political life. Not a professional theologian, he marked Latin American theology of the twenty-first century. Not a lawyer, he was an indefatigable defender of social justice. A martyr and a patriot, he preferred to die for God and his country rather than condone a repressive government that abused the poor's most basic human rights.

In 1998, life-size statutes of Archbishop Óscar Arnulfo Romero and other twentieth-century figures who died for their faith—including Martin Luther King, Jr., Maximilian Kolbe, and Dietrich Bonhoeffer—were unveiled in Westminster Abbey's main entrance in London. Years later, Romero's statue was included in the Human Rights Porch of the National Cathedral in Washington, D.C. In 2010, the United Nations General Assembly proclaimed March 24 as the International Day for the Right to the Truth Concerning Gross Human Rights Violations and for the Dignity of Victims, in recognition of Romero's role in defending the human rights of the most vulnerable populations.[2] In 2015, after Romero's cause had languished for years in the Vatican bureaucracy, the Catholic Church beatified Romero during a multitudinous Eucharistic celebration in San Salvador that brought together more than a quarter million people.[3] Three years later, in October 2018, Pope Francis canonized Romero along with Pope Paul VI in Saint Peter's Square. This coincidence was not accidental. Paul VI was, for Romero, a good shepherd, a teacher, and an inspirer.[4]

---

2 Further information is available at http://www.un.org/en/events/right-totruthday.

3 See BBC News, http://www.bbc.com/news/world-latin-america-32859627. See the ceremony at https://www.youtube.com/watch?v=Hssxhk4Izeo.

4 On January 28, 1980, Romero wrote in his diary: "I felt a special emotion on praying at the tomb of Paul VI. I remembered so many things from his conversations with me, in the visits in which I had the honor and the blessing to be admitted to a private audience." See entry for January 28, 1980, in Óscar Romero, *A Shepherd's Diary* (Cincinnati, Ohio: St. Anthony Press, 1993), 464. See also Romero, "The Church and the Popular Organizations: Third Pastoral Letter," in Romero, *Voice of the Voiceless* (Maryknoll, N.Y.: Orbis Books, 1988), 99.

Many books have been written about Romero, and many remain to be written. So far, three biographies stand out: the pioneering and well-documented biography in English written by James R. Brockman;[5] the first-hand account written in Spanish by Jesús Delgado, Romero's private secretary;[6] and the recent biography written in Italian by Roberto Morozzo della Rocca, based on the archive of the Archdiocese of San Salvador and on Romero's personal papers.[7] A revised short version (without footnotes) of Morozzo's biography was published in English in 2015.[8] For the last two years of his life, Romero's diary constitutes a beautiful account and source of inspiration.[9] Michael Lee and Matthew Phillip Whelan have recently offered two engaging and knowledgeable approaches to Romero's theological legacy. Lee highlights Romero's relevance for understanding the church's mission in today's world, and Whelan focuses on Romero's Catholic social teaching in the area of land reform.[10]

Biographical Information

Óscar Arnulfo Romero y Galdámez was born on August 15, 1917, in Ciudad Barrios, a municipality in the department of San Miguel in El Salvador, near the Honduran border. He was the second of the eight children (one of whom died at birth) of Santos Romero, the local telegraph operator, and Guadalupe

---

5   James R. Brockman, *Romero: A Life* (Maryknoll, N.Y.: Orbis Books, 2005).
6   Jesús Delgado, *Óscar A. Romero* (El Salvador: UCA, 2001).
7   Roberto Morozzo della Rocca, *Primero Dios. Vita di Óscar Romero* (Milan: Mondodori, 2005).
8   Roberto Morozzo della Rocca, *Óscar Romero: Prophet of Hope* (Boston: Pauline Books & Media, 2015). See also Scott Wright, *Óscar Romero and the Communion of the Saints* (Maryknoll, N.Y.: Orbis Books, 2016); Kevin Michael Clarke, *Óscar Romero: Love Must Win Out* (Collegeville, Minn.: Liturgical Press, 2014). Important information about Romero's life and bibliography is also available at the website of the Archbishop Romero Trust, http://www.romerotrust.org.uk. See also the website of the Kellogg Institute of the University of Notre Dame, https://kellogg.nd.edu/archbishop-Óscar-romero#tab-297.
9   See Romero, *A Shepherd's Diary*, hereafter *Diary*.
10 Michael Edward Lee, *Revolutionary Saint: The Theological Legacy of Óscar Romero* (Maryknoll, N.Y.: Orbis Books, 2018); Matthew Phillip Whelan, *Blood in the Fields: Óscar Romero, Catholic Social Teaching, and Land Reform* (Washington, D.C.: The Catholic University of America Press, 2020).

de Jesús Goldámez. Like their neighbors in the town, the family had neither electricity nor running water in their home. At the age of four, Óscar was struck with polio, affecting his ability to move and speak for months. He received his elementary education both in public school (the first three grades) and with a private teacher and was then was apprenticed to a carpenter. In 1930, he entered the minor seminary in San Miguel, run by the Claretians. To pay part of the expenses of the seminary, he spent one summer working in the Potosí gold mine, located a few miles from Ciudad Barrios.

In 1937, when his father died, Romero went to the national seminary run by the Jesuits in El Salvador, but at midyear, his bishop sent him to Rome. In the Eternal City, he lived at the Latin American College and studied at the Gregorian University, where he received a licentiate in theology in 1941 and started a doctorate on the ascetic theology of the Spanish Jesuit Luis de la Puente (1554–1624). On April 4, 1942, he was ordained as a priest in the college chapel. The words he wrote in his diary in February 1943 are a good summary of his high spiritual aspirations at that time: "In recent days after reading some of Father La Puente at the curia, principally his *Life of Father Álvarez*,[11] the Lord has inspired in me a great desire for holiness. I have been thinking of how far a soul can ascend if it lets itself be possessed entirely by God. It is a shame to waste such precious time and such valuable gifts."[12]

During World War II, in August 1943, Romero left the bombed city of Rome without completing his doctorate, summoned home by his bishop. However, Romero was unable to arrive in El Salvador until December 1943. As passengers coming from Italy to Cuba, Romero and his colleague and friend Rafael Valladares were suspected of being enemy aliens and sent to a prison camp. After being recognized as clerics by a Cuban priest and spending time in a hospital to recover, they were freed.

Romero's first assignment as a priest was in Anamorós, a small village in the La Unión department of El Salvador. In 1947, he moved to San Miguel to be the secretary of the bishop and pastor of the city-parish of Santo Domingo. He also was the rector of the minor seminary, the editor of the diocesan newspaper, the promoter of an Alcoholics Anonymous group, and

11   Luis de la Puente, *Vida del P. Baltasar Álvarez* (Barcelona: Editorial Linkgua, 2011).
12   Romero, *Diary*, February 4, 1943, quoted by Brockman, *Romero*, 38–39. The diary was discovered by Romero's biographer and friend Jesús Delgado. See Delgado, "Romero: Un joven aspirante a la santidad," *Orientación* 55, no 5462, March 25, 2007.

the committee leader for the completion of the construction of San Miguel's Cathedral Basilica of the Queen of Peace. On June 8, 1967, he was appointed secretary of the Bishops Conference of El Salvador and moved to San Salvador. One year later, in May 1968, he also became the secretary of the Central American Bishops' Secretariat (Secretariado Episcopal de América Central or SEDAC). Working unceasingly, Romero sometimes weakened his health, occasionally resulting in natural exhaustion.

On June 21, 1970, Romero was ordained bishop and became auxiliary bishop of El Salvador. His episcopal motto, "Think with the Church," drawn from the spiritual exercises of Saint Ignatius, reflected Romero's sentiments of moral and doctrinal union with Rome. During these complicated years for the Catholic Church in the aftermath of the Second Vatican Council, Romero sought a more cautious interpretation of the pronouncements of the Council and the Conference of Medellín.[13] He had complex relations with the diocesan clergy and with a group of young Salvadoran Jesuits who actively defended a controversial political theology of liberation. In 1972, he was named rector of the interdiocesan seminary, which was closed by the Bishops' Conference a year later owing to financial problems.

In 1974, the Holy See appointed Romero bishop of the diocese of Santiago de María, covering the territory of the department of Usulután, in the southeast of the country, and a small part of the department of San Miguel, including his hometown, Ciudad Barrios. Before being installed as a bishop by the papal nuncio on December 14, 1974, Romero went to Rome to thank Pope Paul VI for his appointment.

As a diocesan pastor, Romero developed a very intense activity of visiting the poor, preaching in the most remote corners of the dioceses, and spending time with and promoting the unity of the clergy. He opened some church buildings for use by hundreds of laborers as shelters during the fall harvest and ordered the churches to provide the workers with hot meals at night. He saw firsthand the suffering of the poor *campesinos* and how they were often

---

13   The Medellín Conference was the second meeting of Latin American bishops held in Medellín, Colombia, in 1968. The conference marked a change in the Latin American church, denouncing unjust social structures and embracing the concept of the "preferential option for the poor." See the English version of the conclusive document of the conference at http://www.povertystudies.org/TeachingPages/EDS_PDFs4WEB/Medellín%20Document-%20Poverty%20of%20the%20Church.pdf.

paid below the officially required minimum. He reported in a pastoral letter the treatment of the laborers who harvested coffee in the area.[14] On May 18, 1975, the Vatican named Romero consultor of the Pontifical Commission for Latin America, under the auspices of the Congregation for Bishops, and this allowed Romero to experience the Catholic Church's government at the Roman Curia's highest level.

The massacre of Tres Calles, in the city of San Agustín, Usulután, deeply impacted Romero. On Saturday, June 21, 1975, at 1:00 a.m., National Guard officers entered Tres Calles and cold-bloodedly murdered four members of the Ostorga family (José Alberto, José Alfredo, Hector David, and Jorge Alberto) and their neighbor Santos Morales, all alleged to be part of a subversive organization.[15] Romero visited and consoled the victims' relatives, celebrated the Eucharist for them, and protested in person before the local commander of the National Guard. The officer, however, attempted to intimidate Romero, telling him: "Cassocks are not bulletproof."[16] Some days later, Romero wrote a private letter to the president of El Salvador, Colonel Arturo Armando Molina, in the name of the voiceless poor, requesting a full investigation and indemnification of the victims' families. The government, however, did not investigate the incident.

Archbishop of San Salvador

On February 3, 1977, the Holy See appointed Romero as the new archbishop of San Salvador to replace Bishop Luis Chávez y González. Romero had been the favorite of the apostolic nuncio to El Salvador, Emanuele Gerada, but not of Chávez himself, nor of many Salvadoran diocesan priests. They preferred the longtime auxiliary bishop, Monsignor Arturo Rivera y Damas, whom they considered to be closer to the poor and to the spirit of Medellín. The government and the wealthiest families in the country respected Romero and supported his candidacy—as did the Vatican, although things would change.[17]

14   See Brockman, *Romero*, 55; Wright, *Óscar Romero and the Communion of the Saints*, 34.
15   Shortly after the massacre, a boy of Tres Calles was tortured, executed, and later found near the unpaved road leading away from Tres Calles. See Clarke, *Óscar Romero: Love Must Win Out*, 64.
16   Clarke, *Love Must Win Out*, 65.
17   On the difficulties with the Vatican, see Martin Maier, "Erzbishof Óscar Romeros Kirchenkonflikte," *Stimmen der Zeit* 130 (2005): 198–210.

Romero was installed on February 22 in a modest ceremony in the church attached to the seminary of San José de la Montaña, amid strong political and social tensions. He chose to live with great austerity at the Divine Providence Hospital, known as El Hospitalito (the little hospital), run by Carmelite sisters.

Two days before Romero's installation, General Carlos Humberto Romero (1924–2017), won the presidential election, which was marred by accusations of voting fraud. Popular protests against electoral fraud followed, and the government responded with violence. On February 28, the security forces opened fire against the crowd in the Plaza de La Libertad, killing dozens of civilians. Two months later, on May 1, security forces fired again at protesters in a public demonstration at the Metropolitan Cathedral (*la matanza de la Catedral*—the slaughter at the cathedral).

In the months around Romero's installation, the government started an intimidation campaign and persecution against the Catholic Church. The oligarchy and the military forces saw a potential threat in some priests who had become leaders among the landless laborers and were trying to organize them to confront Salvadoran social injustice. The oligarchs and the military accused the Catholic Church of meddling in political affairs and inciting peasants against the government. Some priests were arrested, and some foreign priests were deported or denied entry into the country, but up to that point, no priest had been killed. On March 12, 1977, however, the Salvadoran Jesuit Rutilio Grande, Romero's good friend and confidant, was murdered along with an old man, Manuel Solórzano, and a boy, Nelson Lemus, while traveling in a jeep toward El Paisnal.[18] A passionate preacher, Fr. Rutilio Grande worked hard with peasants and helped them organize to advocate for human rights. Right-wing extremists branded him a communist and, consequently, a target for shooting. The beatification of Fr. Grande and his two lay companions, approved by Pope Francis on February 21, 2020, took place in San Salvador on January 22, 2022.

The assassination of Rutilio Grande shocked Archbishop Romero. It was not only the slaying of a beloved priest and friend, a leader of Christian work with the poor, but also the confirmation that the killers served the interests of the Salvadoran oligarchy. Advised by his priests, Romero adopted two controversial, momentous decisions. First, he suspended the Sunday Masses on March 20 throughout the archdiocese and celebrated only one Mass in the

---

18 On the relationship between Romero and Rutilio, see Dean Brackley, *Rutilio and Romero: Martyrs for Our Time* (Notre Dame, Ind.: Kellogg Institute, 1997).

Cathedral as a sign of unity, grief, and protest for Fr. Rutilio Grande's assassination and the persecution of the church. The decision drew criticism from some ecclesiastical authorities, especially the apostolic nuncio. However, more than 150 priests joined the Mass as celebrants, and more than one hundred thousand people attended the liturgical celebration.[19] Second, Romero decided not to participate in any governmental official ceremony until the government led a serious investigation of the murders. In fact, Archbishop Romero did not attend General Romero's inauguration on July 1, 1977.

The two measures were taken as a challenge to the government. On May 11, 1977, death squads killed another priest, Alfonso Navarro, along with a young parishioner, Luis Torres, at the rectory. This assassination took place in revenge for the kidnapping and murder of the foreign minister, Mauricio Borgonovo Pohl, by the left-wing paramilitary organization Liberation People's Forces, an organization the oligarchy believed some revolutionary priests supported. Some days later, on May 17, two thousand soldiers occupied Aguilares to intimidate the population. Many civilians were tortured and killed, and the military desecrated the Blessed Sacrament at the parish church, which was used as a barracks. In 1978 and 1979, repression intensified with the murders of thousands of people, including four more priests. "Be a patriot: kill a priest!" was the statement that appeared in many advertisements, posters, and billboards.

Romero spoke forcefully: "The church is not involved in politics, but when politics touches the altar, the church defends the altar."[20] He denounced the disappearances, tortures, killings, and crimes from his cathedral pulpit during his Sunday homilies that were always transmitted over the radio and heard by thousands of Salvadorans. His sermons became the best and most popular report on human rights abuses in his country. Romero demanded justice and recompense for atrocities committed by security forces or paramilitary organizations. As a result, Romero's reputation grew considerably among the people, especially the priests, who initially had opposed him. He established a legal-aid office (Socorro Jurídico) that documented hundreds of kidnappings, tortures, and murders carried out by the armed forces and paramilitary groups. He also condemned the atrocities of partisan warfare.

---

19   See Romero's homily and justification of the single mass at http://www.romerotrust.org.uk/homilies-and-writings.

20   See Romero, Homily, May 8, 1977, available at http://www.romerotrust.org.uk/homilies-and-writings/homilies/1977.

Personally, he was convinced that the guerrillas would disappear once the repression ended.[21]

In the hopes of preventing a civil war, on October 15, 1979, young officers led a bloodless military coup and deposed General Romero. Some well-intentioned and reform-minded civilians were involved in the new government, called the Revolutionary Government Junta. Archbishop Romero understood the coup as a peaceful and necessary governmental change to stop corruption, violence, and social injustice, and he harbored some hope that the new government would contribute to the resolution of the deep conflict that polarized the Salvadoran society.[22] The opposite happened. Although the junta denounced the killing of campesinos, the National Guard, the police, and the death squads continued committing thousands of brutal criminal atrocities. The junta was weak, and while it made some efforts to improve the situation—for example, by land reform—it could not control the military and the oligarchy.

Government repression grew partly through help from the United States, which considered the Salvadoran government a U.S. ally in the context of the Cold War.[23] On February 17, 1980, Romero wrote, and read publicly during his Sunday homily,[24] a letter to U.S. President Jimmy Carter to try to avoid "greater bloodshed." He appealed to Carter's Christian convictions and asked him (1) to "forbid that military aid be given to the Salvadoran government," and (2) to guarantee that the U.S. government "will not intervene directly or indirectly, with military, economic, diplomatic, or other pressures, in determining the destiny of the Salvadoran people."[25] The letter had a tremendous global media impact, but it was not well received by the White House,[26] which started diplomatic conversations with the Vatican, or, of course, by

---

21 See Morozzo della Rocca, *Óscar Romero: Prophet of Hope,* 205.

22 On the relation between Romero and the Junta, see Delgado, *Óscar A. Romero,* 163–69.

23 See William M. LeoGrande, *Our Own Backyard: The United States in Central America, 1977–1992* (London: Eurospan, 1998); Russell Crandall, *The Salvador Option: The United States in El Salvador, 1977–1992* (Cambridge: Cambridge University Press, 2016); and Brian D'Haeseleer, *The Salvadoran Crucible: The Tragedy of U.S. Counterinsurgency in El Salvador, 1979–1992* (Lawrence: University Press of Kansas, 2017).

24 See Romero, Homily, February 17, 1980, http://www.romerotrust.org.uk/homilies-and-writings/homilies/poverty-beatitudes-force-true-liberation-people.

25 See the letter reproduced in Romero, *Voice of the Voiceless,* 188–90.

26 See further information in Lee, *Revolutionary Saint,* 139.

the Salvadoran oligarchy, which again responded violently. One day later, the archdiocesan radio transmitter that Romero used to broadcast his homilies was blown up, and two days later, a bomb exploded at the Central American University, run by the Jesuits.

Romero's Last Days

Romero was very conscious that his life was in constant danger. He received death threats from the right and the left and abundant slanders.[27] The Vatican suggested that he leave the country, but he rejected the offer. He had already accepted martyrdom as a spiritual option to express his faith in God and his love of his country. As he wrote in his diary during a trip to Rome: "I also visited Saint Peter's Basilica again, and ... I asked for great faithfulness to my Christian faith and the courage, should it be necessary, to die as those martyrs died, or to live a consecrated life as those modern successors to Peter did."[28] A personal testimony written during a spiritual retreat he made with some priests in February 1980 confirmed how close he felt to death during his last weeks: "I find it hard to accept a violent death that, in these circumstances, is very possible."[29] In addition, he added a personal consecration to the Heart of Jesus: "So, too, I place under His loving providence all my life and accept with faith in Him my death, however difficult it may be."[30]

Emotional fear of death and desire to live in no way diminished his confidence in the nonviolent struggle against repression. Instead, the opposite happened—the strength in his condemnation of repression grew. On March 23, 1980, his Sunday homily lasted almost two hours, and he was probably bolder than ever before. At the end of his sermon, he made his famous appeal to the National Guard and the police, which for many meant Romero's death sentence:

> Brothers: you are part of our own people. You kill your own campesino brothers and sisters. Before an order to kill that a man may

27 See Romero, *Diary*, January 4, 1979; June 1, 1979; September 7, 1979; November 5, 1979; February 23, 1980; and March 10, 1980.
28 Romero, *Diary*, May 3, 1979.
29 See Delgado, *Óscar A. Romero*, 190: "Me cuesta aceptar una muerte violenta que en estas circunstancias es muy posible."
30 Delgado, *Óscar A. Romero*, 191: "Así también pongo bajo su providencia amorosa toda mi vida y acepto con fe en Él mi muerte, por más difícil que sea."

give, God's law must prevail: Thou shalt not kill! No soldier is obliged to obey an order against the law of God. No one has to fulfill an immoral law. It is time to take back your consciences and to obey your consciences rather than the orders of sin. The church, defender of God's rights, the law of God, human dignity, and the person, cannot remain silent before such abominations. We want the government to understand seriously that reforms are worth nothing if they are stained with so much blood. In the name of God, and in the name of these suffering people, whose laments rise to heaven each day more tumultuous, I beg you; I beseech you, I order you in the name of God: Stop the repression!"[31]

The high military command considered the appeal subversive and incendiary, and Romero's death sentence was imminent. The next day, Monday, March 24, 1980, while celebrating the funeral mass on the first anniversary of the death of Sara Meardi de Pino, in the modest chapel of the Hospitalito, Romero was struck by a single gunshot and died within minutes.[32] Romero was standing behind the altar about to start the offertory. He had just ended the homily with these prophetic words: "May this body immolated and this blood sacrificed for humans nourish us also, so that we may give our body and our blood to suffering and to pain—like Christ, not for self, but to bring about justice and peace for our people."[33]

If blood bathed Romero's death, so, too, it bathed his funeral. The funeral Mass took place in front of the Metropolitan Cathedral on March 30, 1980. Television images of the immense crowd that filled the square are preserved.[34] In the middle of the ceremony, several bombs exploded, and

[31] The homily is available at http://www.romerotrust.org.uk/homilies-and-writings/homilies/church-serves-personal-communal-and-transcendent-liberation.

[32] To date, no one in El Salvador has been prosecuted for Romero's assassination. The assassins were members of the death squad led by the soldier and politician Roberto D'Aubuisson (1943–1992). For further information about the assassination, see Matt Eisenbrandt, *Assassination of a Saint: The Plot to Murder Óscar Romero and the Quest to Brings His Killers to Justice* (Oakland: University of California Press, 2017).

[33] Last homily of Archbishop Romero on March 24, 1980, http://www.romerotrust.org.uk/homilies-and-writings/homilies/final-homily-archbishop-romero.

[34] See images at https://www.youtube.com/watch?v=EN6LWdqcyuc&has_verified=1.

snipers opened fire, killing dozens of persons amid terror, confusion, and blood. The funeral was interrupted, and Romero was hurriedly buried in the cathedral's crypt.

Romero's death and funeral marked a turning point in the recent history of El Salvador. In 1980, more than twelve thousand people were killed. The escalating violence soon turned into a civil war in the international framework of the Cold War. More than seventy-five thousand Salvadorans died in the fighting, most of them victims of the military and its death squads. However, the war could not kill Romero's legacy.

Romero's Legacy on Social Justice

Romero did not develop an original theological thought of his own. He was not a professional theologian, but he tried to live following the Gospel during the dramatic situation of El Salvador in his time. His thinking was, therefore, predominantly practical and experiential, manifested as it was in his pastoral letters, homilies, and speeches. Romero's Christian convictions, doctrine, and ideals remained firmly rooted in the Catholic tradition, interpreted in the light of the Second Vatican Council and the most recent magisterium of the Catholic Church.[35] In particular, Pope Paul VI's teaching clarified Romero's own reflections, as he himself recognized.[36]

Some scholars say that there are two different Romeros: one conservative, before the death of Fr. Rutilio, and a new one, much more progressive, after Rutilio's murder.[37] Martín Baró probably exaggerated when he affirmed that the road from Aguilares (where Fr. Rutilio was assassinated) was to be Romero's "road to Damascus."[38] Jon Sobrino, although more cautious, has also overemphasized Romero's conversion.[39] More recently, Michael Lee has understood Romero's conversion or

---

35 See, in the same vain, Morozzo della Rocca, *Óscar Romero*, 221.

36 Romero, "Third Pastoral Letter," in *Voice of the Voiceless*, 99.

37 See María López Vigil, *Monseñor Romero: Memories in Mosaic* (Maryknoll, N.Y.: Orbis Books, 2013), xiii. On Romero and conversion, see Lee, *Revolutionary Saint*, 44–85.

38 Ignacio Martín Baró, "Óscar Romero: Voice of the Downtrodden," in Romero, *Voice of the Voiceless*, 6.

39 See Jon Sobrino, *Archbishop Romero: Memories and Reflections* (Maryknoll, N.Y.: Orbis Books, 2016), 9: "I believe that the murder of Rutilio Grande was the occasion of the conversion of Archbishop Romero—as well as being a source of light and courage to follow his new path."

"radical transformation"[40] as a "seeing anew"[41] and a "coming home"[42] in the sense of a profound understanding of "the gravity of social sin and the response that it demanded from him."[43]

Romero himself denied any tumbling conversion: "I would not speak of conversion, as many call it ... because I have always been devoted to the people and the poor."[44] My own view is that Romero's life was gradually evolving without any break or rupture with the past. His understanding and experience of his own mission as a pastor, and his constant updating of his moral judgment on the Salvadoran situation in light of new events and circumstances, marked the rhythm of Romero's continuous spiritual growth, without a disruptive conversion. Of course, the assassination of Rutilio Grande played a decisive role in that spiritual process and was relevant to his changing moral judgment about the Salvadorian situation.

Romero understood his pastoral mission as deeply religious and not political: "This is my greatest concern, namely, to build with Christ, to build a church according to the Heart of Jesus."[45] And a church, according to the Heart of Jesus, is in character with a church absolutely involved in the cause of the poor and social justice in action. On the other hand, Romero changed his moral judgment and, as a result, his behavior toward the government as long as he was convinced that the persecution of the church and the repression of the peasants was supported by the Salvadoran authorities. He concluded that the Catholic Church, and he as the highest authority of the church in El Salvador, could not remain silent and could not abstain from condemning the brutal atrocities committed by a repressive government, including the slaying of priests. Neutrality was not a moral option in that situation because it implied a way of collaborating with a repressive government and, therefore, unacceptable complicity with the crime. For Romero, raising his voice was not a political decision but a moral and deeply evangelical one: "Our voice as pastor of the archdiocese seeks only to be an

40   Lee, *Revolutionary Saint*, 69.
41   Lee, *Revolutionary Saint*, 195.
42   Lee, *Revolutionary Saint*, 195.
43   Lee, *Revolutionary Saint*, 195.
44   See the interview in March 1979 by Juan Rodríguez, quoted by Morozzo della Roca, *Primero Dios*, 152, 392. See Angelo Amato's introduction to Romero, *The Church Cannot Remain Silent*, xxiii.
45   Romero, Homily, September 3, 1978, http://www.romerotrust.org.uk/homilies-and-writings/homilies/cross-life.

instrument in the hands of Christ so that he can speak to his people today. We want to be faithful to the gospel, and we are aware of the consequences which that can bring."[46]

According to Romero, the triumph of Christianity in El Salvador, not the political fight, would bring peace to his beloved country. And to talk about Christianity was to talk about a person, Christ, who is the incarnated Truth. For Romero, the truth was the driving power of peace because only truth can unite people among themselves and with God. Four main ideas support Romero's theology of social justice.

The Political Dimension of the Faith

For Romero, faith and politics are united but should not be identified with each other.[47] When faith identifies with politics, faith is tainted, and freedom is enslaved. On the other hand, faith isolated from life in the world is not true faith. According to Romero, faith should inspire and illuminate politics, but Christian faith and political activity must not become confused and entangled with each other. When that happens, it is easy to "substitute for the demands of the faith and Christian justice the demands of a particular political organization."[48] In a practical way, Romero defends the notion that political organizations can expect the church to advocate for civil rights. No organization, even if Christian in inspiration or name, can require that the church become the direct means of propaganda for political purposes.

Integral Liberation

Romero believed that Christian liberation is more complete and deeper than any political, social, or economic liberation because it involves the person as a whole and, therefore, implies a genuinely spiritual and salvific dimension.[49] For this reason, simple structural changes cannot provide complete Christian liberation. Human beings cannot produce their own liberation. It

---

46 Letter to Roberto M. C., November 14, 1977, published in Romero, *The Church Cannot Remain Silent*, 15.

47 See, Romero, "Lovain Address: The Political Dimension of the Faith from the Perspective of the Option of the Poor," in Romero, *Voice of the Voiceless*, esp. at 182.

48 Romero, "Third Pastoral Letter," 100.

49 See Romero, *Diary*, April 9, 1978, 32.

comes from Christ, the Redeemer.[50] The fact that Christ says that his reign does not belong to this world (John 18:36) does not mean that "Christ is isolated from the power of the earth. It means that he will use a different basis, a religious basis, to judge the consciences of political leaders and of the rich (and of the poor also), judging them from the eschatological and transcendent perspective of God's reign."[51] Christian liberation, centered on the Kingdom of God established by Jesus Christ, fosters a deep desire for justice in love and demands a conversion of heart and mind.

The Violence of Love

Romero defended a constructive dynamism of nonviolence and excluded violence (except in the case of self-defense), considering it unchristian and unscriptural, ineffective, and out of keeping with the dignity of the people.[52] Romero did not believe in violent solutions, except what he called "the vioence of love."[53] He believed "in only one violence, that of Christ, who was nailed to the cross."[54] The revolution of Christ is a revolution of love. It is the revolution to establish a civilization of love but one "that did not demand justice of people would not be a true civilization. True love begins by demanding what is just in the relations of those who love."[55] It gives plenitude to all human duties. With love, justice becomes a brother's embrace. Without love, laws become inhuman, repressive, and cruel.[56]

---

50 Romero, Homily, December 1, 1977, http://www.romerotrust.org.uk/homilies-and-writings/homilies/mothers-disappeared-children.
51 Romero, Homily, January 14, 1979, http://www.romerotrust.org.uk/homilies-and-writings/homilies/baptism-epiphany-messianic-reality.
52 See Romero, "The Church and Popular Political Organizations," Third Pastoral Letter of Archbishop Romero, coauthored by Bishop Arturo Rivera y Damas, Bishop of Santiago de María, Feast of the Transfiguration, August 6, 1978; Romero, "The Church's Mission amid the National Crisis," Fourth Pastoral Letter of Archbishop Romero, Feast of the Transfiguration, August 6, 1979, nos. 68–83.
53 See Romero, *The Violence of Love*.
54 Romero, Homily, November 20, 1977, http://www.romerotrust.org.uk/homilies-and-writings/homilies/christ-prophet-priest-and-king.
55 Romero, Homily, April 12, 1979, http://www.romerotrust.org.uk/homilies-and-writings/homilies/holy-spirit-soul-new-covenant.
56 Romero, Homily, September 10, 1978, http://www.romerotrust.org.uk/homilies-and-writings/homilies/church-prophetic-sacramental-community-love.

Christian Preferential Option for the Poor

Like Jesus, the church was sent to bring good news to the poor. It has been incarnated in the world of the poor, giving them hope. Therefore, the church is firmly committed to the evangelization of the poor and to their defense and protection. This preferential option for the poor is not an expression of particularism or sectarianism but rather a manifestation of the church's evangelical mission, which is universal in character.[57] This option is not discriminatory at all since it does not exclude anyone. Even the rich must become spiritually poor to share with the poor the benefits and graces of God's kingdom. The poor "are the ones who make up in their own bodies that which is lacking in the passion of Christ. And for that reason, when the church has organized and united herself around the hopes and anxieties of the poor, she has incurred the same fate as that of Jesus and the poor: persecution."[58] This preferential option for the poor cannot be reduced to ideological categories nor become a source of sociological conflict. It is spiritual and evangelical, but with important social and political implications.

Conclusion

A patriotic Salvadoran of strong fortitude and high Christian ethical values and ideals, Archbishop Romero advocated for a form of Christian humanism based on the Gospel and the magisterium of the Catholic Church, especially the Second Vatican Council. Following the tradition of the prophets, he denounced extortion, injustice, and corruption, defending human rights and social justice in a country wounded by political, military, and paramilitary crime. Romero understood that the denunciation of brutal governmental atrocities was not a political issue but a necessary requirement to establish the Kingdom of God on earth. He advocated the nonviolent defense of justice inspired by love, forgiveness, and social participation. The preferential option for the poor was at the heart of his pastoral mission and action.

Romero spoke with profound moral authority, absolutely deprived of all political power, and detached from self-interest. His primary weapon was his own moral authenticity. His message was as resounding and accurate as

---

57   See Romero, "Lovain Address," 177–87. See also Óscar Romero, Homily, February 17, 1980, http://www.romerotrust.org.uk/homilies-and-writings/homilies/poverty-beatitudes-force-true-liberation-people.

58   See Romero, "Lovain Address," 182.

it was annoying to the political parties and factions of the left and right. Romero felt the loneliness of the leader and was often misunderstood and misinterpreted by political, military, and ecclesiastical authorities. As repression became firmly fixed in El Salvador, Romero was ever more resolute in denouncing the government's cruel attitude and demanding the urgent need for nonviolent social change. His moral judgment on the Salvadoran situation was clear and forceful: the desirable church-state cooperation in developing the common good in society must never lead to any complicity with crime and repression. Only the truth liberates.

Romero's theological reflection on social justice, sealed with his own martyrdom and based on his preferential option for the poor, constitutes an outstanding contribution to the ideal of Christian justice and the international implementation of human rights in our globalized world. The figure of Romero, martyred for his commitment to social justice and the poor, deserves universal respect.

CHAPTER 12

JOHN PAUL II'S CONTRIBUTION TO LAW

CONSIDERED ONE OF THE GREAT protagonists of world history in the twentieth century, Pope John Paul II, born Karol Józef Wojtyła in Wadowice on May 18, 1920, died at the Vatican on April 2, 2005, and since then has risen to even greater stature and esteem over time.[1] An intellectual and mystic with a Polish heart and a cosmopolitan soul, a playwright and a ruler, a bishop and a professor, a sportsman and a pope, a witness to faith and a herald of reason, John Paul II rightly deserves to be called a Christian jurist

---

*   See the original version in Rafael Domingo, "Karol Józef Wojtyła, Pope John Paul II (1920–2005)," in *Law and Christianity in Poland: The Legacy of the Great Jurists*, ed. Franciszek Longchamps de Bérier and Rafael Domingo (London: Routledge, 2022), 247–62.

1   George Weigel is an internationally recognized biographer of John Paul II. See George Weigel, *Witness to Hope: The Biography of Pope John Paul II*, 3rd ed. (New York: Harper Perennial, 1999, 2020); George Weigel, *The End, and the Beginning: Pope John Paul II: The Victory of Freedom, the Last Years, the Legacy* (New York: Doubleday, 2010). Interesting autobiographical reflections are in the following books: John Paul II, *Crossing the Threshold of Hope* (New York: Alfred A. Knopf, 1994); John Paul II, *Rise, Let Us Be on Our Way* (New York: Warner Books, 2004); John Paul II, *Memory and Identity: Personal Reflections* (London: Weidenfeld & Nicolson, 2006); and John Paul II, *In God's Hands: The Spiritual Diaries of John Paul II (1962–2003)*, trans. Joanna Zepa (London: Harpers Collins, 2007).

as well, given his monumental contributions to the law and legal theory. It is no surprise that La Sapienza University of Rome, in recognition of his significant contributions, awarded him an honorary doctorate in law on May 17, 2003, to mark the seventh centenary of the founding of this prestigious academic center.[2]

John Paul II did not approach law tangentially but rather went through it like an arrow through a target. For him, this target was the human person, who, beginning in his youth, took the place of honor in his thought, as it should in any system worthy of the name of law. The word "law" appears profusely in the Polish pope's encyclicals: ninety-nine times in the *Centesimus annus*, eighty-five times in *Evangelium vitae*, forty-three in *Sollicitudo rei socialis*, and twenty-five times in *Veritatis Splendor*, to consider a few examples. His thoughts about law are also found in famous speeches, such as the addresses he gave to the United Nations General Assembly (1979 and 1995), to UNESCO (1980), to the Polish Parliament (1999), and to the world in his twenty messages for World Day of Peace (1986–2005). Fundamental legal ideas and proposals for legal reform also mark his less well-known speeches, such as the traditional ones to the legendary Tribunal of the Rota or his many speeches or addresses on the occasion of various legal congresses.

John Paul II built his legal thought on the profound conviction that the justice to which the law aspires, the dignity that justifies the law, the freedom that protects the law, the truth that sustains the law, and the good that the law procures constitute the same reality and are therefore entirely interdependent. He reached this profound conviction from his Christocentric vision, which enabled him to distinguish between, yet at the same time integrate, divine law and human law, natural law and positive law, justice and love, private good and public good, patriotism and cosmopolitanism, family and community, freedom and order, individual conscience and objective truth, and private property and universal charity and destination of goods.

From his Christian humanism, John Paul II understood the law as a necessary ethical component in his project to revitalize and renew the world

---

2 John Paul II, "Address for the 7th Centenary of the Founding of La Sapienza University of Rome," May 17, 2003, no. 2. Most of Pope John Paul II's writings to which I refer can be found on the Vatican website, http://www.vatican.va/content/john-paul-ii/en.html. Whenever this is not so, I expressly quote the source. When it was required, I made some improvements in the official English translation.

of culture and social justice in Christ, placing faith at the service of reason and reason at the service of faith. He saw the law as an indispensable social instrument for achieving peace and harmony among peoples. With his Christian humanism, Wojtyła shook the foundations of the oppressive communist system in his beloved Poland and in Eastern Europe, which collapsed during the first half of his pontificate. Today, all experts acknowledge the vital role that John Paul II played in the fall of the Berlin Wall and the Iron Curtain.

The Human Person and Human Dignity at the Center of Legal Systems

Influenced by Saint Thomas Aquinas, Max Scheler, Gabriel Marcel, Edith Stein, and Jacques Maritain, among others, John Paul II developed a personalist anthropology and ethics, which, together with Christian humanism, acted as a framework for his legal thinking.[3] He understood that no legal theory explained the law entirely, just as no mathematical theory gives perfect meaning to mathematics, and nothing within physics can thoroughly explain the physical dimension. Therefore, the starting point of Wojtyła's legal thinking is not strictly legal but spiritual, namely, that it is human persons, not states or social classes, who love and are loved by God as God's favorite children. Therefore, people, not states or social classes, are the main targets of the civilization of love and must be placed at the center of all legal systems.

John Paul II's conception of the human person is profoundly Christian. In no way does he consider that this conception should be secularized. Nor should it be overpositivized—if I may put it that way—when applied to the law, as most of the positivists in the world have done, beginning with Hans Kelsen, who was influential in Poland as Karol Wojtyła started his ministry. John Paul II was clear that the person is not a creation of the law but exists before it. The law follows the human person—it protects, respects, accompanies, and facilitates the life and work of each person. The pope explained this to those attending the symposium on *Evangelium vitae* and law in 1996: "The classical aphorism effectively expresses the centrality of the human person in law: *hominum causa omne ius constitutum est* [every law has been created for the

---

3   In this regard, see Karol Wojtyła, *The Acting Person*, trans. Andrzej Potocki (Dordrecht: D. Reider Publishing, 1979). About Pope John Paul II's personalism, see John Crosby, *The Personalism of John Paul II* (Steubenville, Ohio: Hildebrand Press, 2019).

sake of men].[4] This means that law is such if and to the extent it is based on a man in his truth."[5]

For John Paul II, what defined a person is not just being the subject of rights and duties but being "the visible image of the invisible God."[6] The fact is that a subject of rights and duties does not necessarily love, as does a human person. By contrast, a visible image of God does love because God—love itself—cannot stop loving. In addition to the capacity to love, this divine image is shown in the human ability to know the truth objectively and in the human capacity to adhere freely to it.

The status to which every person is entitled by being created in the image of God is called dignity, which "[is] revealed in all its fullness in the mystery of the Incarnate Word."[7] Dignity is, therefore, the most radical and inherent quality of the human being. It is more than a right, a primary good, a moral value, or a philosophical principle. It is the transcendent premise of human equality, individual and collective freedom and responsibility, and human rights and duties. The status conferred by dignity is neither temporary nor territorial. It is central to any human being, since the image of God follows every human being regardless of who or where they are. In this sense, each person is unique and occupies an unrepeatable position in the legal system. Dignity gives the human being preeminence over the rest of creation, from which ensues an unalienable responsibility and obligation of collaboration and service with the created work.

For John Paul II, dignity is a metalegal reality, not a legal concept based on a contract or a crime. Dignity calls for the protection of law but not the control of law—not the manipulation of law but its recognition and defense. The human person's transcendent nature goes beyond the realm of what is changeable, what is material, temporal, and fleeting—even beyond the realm of law.

For the Polish pope, dignity and the soul are interchangeable concepts, since human beings receive dignity from God through spiritual human nature. Therefore, denying God, in any form of theoretical or practical

---

4 On this Roman law aphorism coming from Hermogenian, *Digest* 1.5.2, see Rafael Domingo et al., ed., *Principios de Derecho Global. 1000 reglas jurídicas y aforismos comentados*, 2nd ed. (Cizur Menor: Thomson Aranzadi, 2006), 402.

5 John Paul II, "Speech to Participants in the Symposium on *Evangelium vitae* and Law," May 24, 1996, no. 4.

6 John Paul II, Encyclical Letter *Centesimus annus* (May 1, 1991), 44.

7 John Paul II, *Centesimus annus*, 47.

atheism, deprives the person's dignity of its foundation and consequently induces humanity to organize the social order in a way that dispenses with the person's authentic freedom and responsibility: "At the heart of every culture lies the attitude man takes to the greatest mystery: the mystery of God. Different cultures have different ways of facing the question of the meaning of personal existence. When this question is eliminated, nations' culture and moral life are corrupted."[8] The pope's emphatic statement also remains valid in legal culture.

This theistic vision of dignity provides an objective validity (*imago Dei*) to the idea of dignity that is beyond the reach of any agnostic or atheistic approach. Without this theistic perspective, dignity can easily be reduced to a substantial subjective self, to a pure capacity for rational autonomy, to mere self-respect as a prerequisite for living well and taking moral responsibilities seriously, or to a simple right to be recognized as a person in law. In the worst case, dignity absent the image of God can become a formal, empty concept without a specific function in the legal sphere because of its dangerous ambiguity. When the idea of human dignity weakens, legal systems teeter. When dignity ceases to have its origin in God, it becomes the rationale for a falsely divinized humanity, no longer a child of God but master and ruler of itself, ethically sovereign, with no other limit than its own will and its responsibility for the rights of others.

Natural Law Protecting the Person's Dignity

In his encyclical letter *Veritatis splendor* (August 6, 1993), John Paul II extensively broaches the issue of natural law in a way very similar to the thinking of Saint Thomas Aquinas. For John Paul II, the ultimate foundation of the human person's dignity does not lie in its being granted by positive law, that is, in the consent of human society. Instead, dignity is external to every human being; it comes from without. Something similar occurs with life itself. If dignity is received, given by God, so is the law that governs it: the so-called natural law. This law acts as a moral guide and limit to the legal system and to positive law as a whole, because when a person strays from natural law, their divine image is tarnished and disfigured and their conscience is troubled.

For John Paul II, this natural law is a "light of understanding infused in us by God, whereby we understand what must be done and what must

---

8   John Paul II, *Centesimus annus*, 24.

be avoided";[9] it gives us "an objective criterion of good and evil, beyond the will of those in power."[10] In other words, the human person, owing to the dignity of intelligence, is equipped to know the truth, seek the absolute, and do so freely. Freedom and truth are the two wings that allow human dignity to fly high, to expand, and to facilitate the development of each human person and all human peoples. John Paul II's exploration of this relationship between truth and freedom, in the light of the Second Vatican Council, is at the heart of his book *The Acting Person*—namely, that the human person is capable of achieving with free actions something objectively good, because it is true.[11]

The human being's capacity for freedom unfolds entirely only through the quest for and acceptance of truth: "Affirming the right of the person to freedom while depriving the objective truth of that person, makes it impossible to construct an intrinsically just legal system."[12] In a world without truth, freedom is emptied of its content, and the human person falls prey to utilitarianism, relativism, and totalitarianism. Therefore, the genuine moral autonomy of the human being entails accepting moral law.

This inseparable relationship between truth and freedom is manifest in the essential link between divine wisdom and human will and justifies the universal character of natural moral law. This universality, in turn, John Paul II explains, "does not ignore the individuality of human beings, nor is it opposed to the absolute uniqueness of each person. On the contrary, it embraces at its root each of the person's free acts, which are meant to bear witness to the universality of the true good."[13] The encounter between human freedom and natural law takes place in the conscience of each person who, after assimilating the truth contained in the law, can pass judgment on the right conduct to be chosen at that precise moment of today and now. The stance that brings together truth and law in the temple of consciousness is the total opposite of the dominant individualistic ethics, which promotes a kind of *right to ethical independence*.[14]

---

9   John Paul II, Encyclical Letter *Veritatis splendor* (August 6, 1993), 12.
10 John Paul II, *Centesimus annus*, 45.
11 Wojtyła, *The Acting Person*.
12 John Paul II, "Speech on *Evangelium vitae and Law*," no. 3.
13 John Paul II, *Veritatis splendor*, 51.
14 Ronald Dworkin, *Justice for Hedgehogs* (Cambridge, Mass.: Harvard University Press, 2013), 368–69.

Human Rights, Common Human Patrimony

John Paul II earned the apt nickname of the "human-rights pope" because he put human rights at the center of his papal message. He explained this in his address at La Sapienza University, when he received his honorary doctorate:

> In my years of pastoral service to the church, I have considered it part of my ministry to give ample space to the affirmation of human rights because of their close connection with two fundamental features of Christian morality: the dignity of the person and peace.... Awareness of this has motivated me to do my utmost to serve these values; but I could not carry out the mission required of me by my apostolic office without having recourse to the categories of law.[15]

His life experiences supported the decision to put human rights at the heart of his message. He suffered under both the Nazi and communist totalitarian regimes in his native Poland and survived the assassination attempts in both St. Peter's Square (1981) and, less known, in Fatima (1982). These serious assaults on his own flesh contributed decisively to shaping John Paul II's thinking and to establishing his priorities. When Wojtyła spoke of human rights, he knew from experience what he was talking about. That gave his words an even more potent effect.

For John Paul II, a society that does not take human rights seriously—however democratic it may be—cannot live in peace or develop in harmony, because it ends up falling into political totalitarianism, moral relativism, and sometimes religious fundamentalism. In his two addresses to the United Nations General Assembly, John Paul II accepted and backed the international system of human rights that emerged from the ashes of the Second World War:

> The Universal Declaration of Human Rights—with its train of many declarations and conventions on highly important aspects of human rights, in favour of children, of women, of equality between races, and especially the two international covenants on economic, social and cultural rights and on civil and political rights—must remain

---

15 John Paul II, "Address for the 7th Centenary of La Sapienza University," no. 2.

the basic value in the United Nations Organization with which the consciences of its members must be confronted and from which they must draw continual inspiration.[16]

Entirely in line with the declaration's preamble, John Paul II saw the ultimate foundation of human rights in the dignity to which the human person is entitled by nature. These rights, which constitute a "common human patrimony,"[17] are not vague, abstract points but rather specific, objective, and inviolable demands ensuing from natural moral law. They remind us that "there is a moral logic which is built into human life and which makes possible dialogue between individuals and peoples."[18]

In his first address to the UN, in 1979, John Paul II proposed a distinction between the human rights that protect material goods (e.g., property and a minimum wage) and those that protect spiritual goods (e.g., cultural and religious freedom). He praised different states' efforts to develop rights regarding material goods, but, echoing Vatican II's *Dignitatis Humanae,* he insisted on the primacy of spiritual goods, since they, by their very nature, have an indestructible and immortal value and can be enjoyed and shared in solidarity by all people.

To achieve peace in the world, John Paul II proposed that nations place greater emphasis on developing the intangible dimension of human rights, since this would generate stronger bonds than those created by tangible goods: "For centuries, the thrust of civilization has been in one direction: that of giving the life of individual political societies a form in which there can be fully safeguarded the objective rights of the spirit, of human conscience and of human creativity, including man's relationship with God."[19]

In his countless speeches and incessant cosmopolitan activity, John Paul II defended human rights in their specific manifestations. Among the main ones, he mentioned:

> the right to live in a united family and in a moral environment conducive to the growth of the child's personality; the right to develop one's intelligence and freedom in seeking and knowing the truth; the

---

16   John Paul II, "Address to the General Assembly of the United Nations, New York, October 2, 1979, no. 9.
17   John Paul II, "Address to the United Nations, New York," October 5, 1995.
18   John Paul II, "Address to the United Nations," October 5, 1995.
19   John Paul II, "Address to the United Nations," October 2, 1979, no. 19.

right to share in the work which makes wise use of the earth's material resources, and to derive from that work the means to support oneself and one's dependents; and the right freely to establish a family, to have and to rear children through the responsible exercise of one's sexuality.[20]

Yet, without a doubt, John Paul II always showed a special predilection for two human rights: the right to life and the right to religious freedom. This predilection was in no way arbitrary, since both rights, to a certain extent, underpin all the others.

The Right to Life

John Paul II dedicated one of the most emblematic encyclicals of his pontificate, *Evangelium vitae* (March 25, 1995), to the issue of life. It is a highly significant document, which describes life as God's greatest gift to humanity. He declared that this divine gift deserves the utmost social and scientific respect and the most outstanding legal protection. In this encyclical, the Polish pope clearly and forcefully denounced the great threats to human life in the so-called era of human rights.

According to John Paul II, society risks severe moral deterioration and a kind of cultural contradiction in trying to make the brilliant international human-rights declarations and the entire institutional system surrounding them compatible with the scandal of laws that permit or command aberrant attacks on human life: "How can we reconcile these declarations with the refusal to accept those who are weak and needy, or elderly, or those who have just been conceived? These attacks go directly against respect for life and they represent a direct threat to the entire culture of human rights."[21] For John Paul II, to advocate or legalize the right to abortion, infanticide, or euthanasia implies attributing to human freedom an annihilating power over and against others. It is precisely therein that lies "the death of true freedom."[22] Choosing life means that law must have a higher moral and spiritual vision, and it implies an unwavering rejection of any form of physical or moral violence: the violence of material poverty, arms and armed conflict, racism, drug trafficking, or environmental violence.

20   John Paul II, *Centesimus annus*, 47.
21   John Paul II, Encyclical Letter *Evangelium vitae* (March 25, 1995), 18.
22   John Paul II, *Evangelium vitae*, 20.

John Paul II also spoke out against the death penalty, which he saw as cruel and unnecessary: "Today, however, as a result of steady improvements in the organization of the penal system, such cases are very rare, if not practically nonexistent."[23] (The practice remains common in fifty-four countries, including, notoriously, the United States, which witnessed eighteen executions in 2020.) Pope Francis, in full accord with Pope John Paul II's doctrine, has taken a further step forward and has settled the question of capital punishment with a reform of the *Catechism of the Catholic Church* that absolutizes the principle: "The death penalty is inadmissible because it is an attack on the inviolability and dignity of the person."[24]

The source and sanctuary of life is the family, the teacher of love, compassion, happiness, and forgiveness. The Polish pope dedicated his encyclical *Familiaris consortio* to this on November 22, 1981. This document and *Evangelium vitae* form a whole, and the two must be read and interpreted together.

Religious Freedom

First as capitular vicar (1962–1964), and then as archbishop of Krakow (1964–1978), Wojtyła had to defend the exercise of his own faith, the religious freedom of his faithful parishioners, and negotiate hard with the Communist regime for the necessary permits to build new parishes and pastoral centers and to restore religious processions and pilgrimages. Famous cases included the creation of the parishes of Nowa Huta, a town specifically designed to have no church, and of Miestrzejowice. Wojtyła's remarkable strategic ability and invincible courage did not go unnoticed by the Communist authorities, who subjected him to oppressive surveillance.[25]

With these and other experiences of religious freedom violations, Wojtyła's opinion was given the highest *auctoritas* in the debates at the Second Vatican Council concerning the drafting of the declaration on religious freedom, *Dignitatis humanae*, of December 7, 1965. Together with other council fathers, Wojtyła proposed additions to the final document that were considered and included.[26] He was always proud of this council's declaration, which he considered revolutionary: "The Council's Declaration on

23 John Paul II, *Evangelium vitae*, 56.
24 *Catechism of the Catholic Church*, no. 2267. See also Pope Francis, Encyclical Letter *Fratelli tutti* (October 3, 2020), 263–70.
25 Weigel, *Witness to Hope*, 189.
26 On this intervention and its context, see Weigel, *Witness to Hope*, 158–66.

Religious Freedom resulted in the release of enormous moral and religious energies, which have had a real bearing on the social and political transformations of recent years, and indeed on the whole structure of international relations," he affirmed in his address of December 7, 1995, marking the thirtieth anniversary of *Dignitatis humanae*. John Paul II regarded the right to religious freedom as the foundation of the person's rights, and he often said that no social progress is possible without respect for the truth and the right to know the truth, including, notably, divine truth. He explained this himself in one his addresses on the World Day of Peace: "The civil and social right to religious freedom, inasmuch as it touches the most intimate sphere of the spirit, is a point of reference of the other fundamental rights."[27] So for John Paul II, protecting religious freedom was not just a strategy of *aggiornamento* adopted by the church to bring its dialogue up to date with contemporary culture, even if it naturally facilitated such a modernization. Nor was the protection of religious freedom a mere instrument to achieve peace in the world, however much it contributed to it. Instead, religious freedom was the source and foundation of other human rights—"the first right." Precisely this freedom, he said, is understood "as the right to live in the truth of one's faith and in conformity with one's transcendent dignity as a person."[28]

This firm internal conviction of the good of religious freedom led John Paul II, as pontiff, to substantially improve the Catholic Church's relations with Jewish and Islamic communities, and to promote a fresh and dynamic ecumenism with Rome's Protestant and Orthodox Christian brothers and sisters. The fruit of his passionate love for religious freedom and interreligious dialogue was the creation of the Pontifical Council for Interreligious Dialogue in 1988. John Paul II also became the first pope to visit a synagogue—the Grand Synagogue in Rome—and the first to pray inside a mosque, in Damascus. In 1986, he convened the World Day of Prayer for Peace, a tradition that has continued to this day.

The Rights of Nations and Eradication of War

John Paul II went even further in his defense of human rights than the Universal Declaration of Human Rights. On October 5, 1995, addressing the Fiftieth General Assembly of the United Nations, he proposed a Universal

---

27 John Paul II, "Message for the Celebration of the World Day of Peace," January 1, 1988.
28 John Paul II, *Centesimus annus*, 47.

Declaration on the Rights of Nations. These were his words: "The Universal Declaration of Human Rights, adopted in 1948, spoke eloquently of the rights of persons; but no similar international agreement has yet adequately addressed the rights of nations. This situation must be carefully pondered, for it raises urgent questions about justice and freedom in the world today."[29] There is little doubt that he was thinking about the tragic history of his own nation, Poland, which had been literally wiped off the European map for over a century. Divided among Russia, Prussia, and Austria in 1795, Poland did not regain its independence until the end of the First World War, and in 1939, it was invaded by Nazi Germany and the Soviet Union. Yet he was also thinking about the fall of the Berlin Wall and the Iron Curtain, which occurred peacefully as a nonviolent revolution.

The rights of nations that he proposed are the same human rights enumerated in the Universal Declaration, but seen from the perspective of community life. These rights therefore have nothing to do with breaking up the international community through exclusive nationalism, as they are oriented toward the common good of humanity. The Polish pope argued that nations and peoples have the right to existence, freedom, autonomy, cultural identity, self-government, handling of their own affairs without outside interference, and so much more. John Paul II insisted on this idea in his message on the fiftieth anniversary of the start of the Second World War: "There is no peace if the rights of all peoples—particularly the most vulnerable—are not respected! The whole edifice of international law is based on the principle of equal respect, by the States, of the right to self-determination of each people and their free cooperation in view of the higher common good of mankind."[30]

He intended his proposed Universal Declaration of the Rights of Nations to become the right legal framework for settling international conflicts, without the need to resort to war or violent encounters. For John Paul II, war had ceased to be the last suitable legal instrument for settling conflicts between peoples when diplomacy had been exhausted. War is monstrously cruel and must simply be eradicated, he argued, even as a possibility or threat. In this regard, John Paul II can be considered a forerunner of what we now call global law, which, unlike international law, does not

---

29   John Paul II, "Address to the United Nations," October 5, 1995, no. 6.
30   John Paul II, "Message on the Occasion of the 50th Anniversary of the Beginning of the Second World War," August 27, 1989, no. 8.

contemplate war as a possibility. Without speaking expressly about a global right, John Paul II sensed it when he said that humanity "(today) needs a *greater degree of international ordering*, at the service of the societies, economies and cultures of the whole world."³¹ These were his words in his first address to the United Nations:

> It is therefore necessary to make a continuing and even more energetic effort to do away with the very possibility of provoking war, and to make such catastrophes impossible by influencing the attitudes and convictions, the very intentions and aspirations of governments and peoples. This duty, kept constantly in mind by the United Nations Organization and each of its institutions, must also be a duty for every society, every regime, every government.³²

Twelve years after giving this address, John Paul II complained about the inefficiency of the United Nations in this regard: "The United Nations, moreover, has not yet succeeded in establishing, as alternatives to war, effective means for the resolution of international conflicts. This seems to be the most urgent problem which the international community has yet to resolve."³³

Firmly convinced of the effectiveness of diplomacy and peaceful means of struggle, which had brought such good results in Eastern Europe during the "velvet revolution" that he helped to lead in Poland, John Paul II devoted all of his energy to preventing any declaration of war on the planet. He made tireless, even if futile, diplomatic efforts to prevent, at any cost, the Falklands War (1982), the Gulf War (1990–1991), and the Iraq War (2003–2011). He described these wars as a failure of humanity.³⁴ Thanks to his mediation, the so-called Beagle conflict between Argentina and Chile was resolved with a peace treaty (1984). Yet above all, his mediation enabled Poland to undergo a peaceful transition from a totalitarian communist regime in the orbit of the USSR to a democratic state governed by the rule of law and part of the

---

31   John Paul II, Encyclical Letter *Sollicitudo rei socialis* (December 30, 1987), 43.
32   John Paul II, "Address to the United Nations," October 2, 1979, no. 11.
33   John Paul II, *Centesimus annus*, 21.
34   Paul Kengor, *A Pope and a President: John Paul II, Ronald Reagan, and the Extraordinary Untold Story of the 20th Century* (Wilmington, Del.: ISI Books, 2017); Weigel, *Witness to Hope*, 272–73, 434–36, and 619–23.

European Union. He recounted this with joy in his famous address to the Polish Parliament on June 11, 1999, probably one of the happiest and most historic moments in his life. All of his efforts as a great promoter of justice had borne fruit in his beloved homeland.

Solidarity as the Inspiring Principle of Social Justice

Solidarity takes center stage in two of John Paul II's encyclicals: *Sollicitudo rei socialis* (December 30, 1987) and *Centesimus annus* (May 1, 1991). Human persons not only have dignity because they are created in the image of God, they also have solidarity. For John Paul II, dignity and solidarity go hand in hand. It is characteristic of dignified persons to act in solidarity with their neighbors and with their surroundings in general.

Insofar as it affects all human action, solidarity touches the very essence of law. John Paul II's thought clearly shows that the quality of a legal system can be measured by the degree to which people's dignity is protected through the defense of their fundamental rights and the degree to which citizens are required to act in solidarity with each other, their environment, their religion and culture, and the institutions of modern society. Just as dignity, for the Polish pope, is a profoundly Christian principle, so too is solidarity:

> In the light of faith, solidarity seeks to go beyond itself, to take on the specifically Christian dimension of total gratuity, forgiveness and reconciliation. One's neighbor is then not only a human being with his or her own rights and a fundamental equality with everyone else, but becomes the *living image* of God the Father, redeemed by the blood of Jesus Christ and placed under the permanent action of the Holy Spirit. One's neighbor must therefore be loved, even if an enemy, with the same love with which the Lord loves him or her; and for that person's sake one must be ready for sacrifice, even the ultimate one.[35]

According to John Paul II, the principle of solidarity manifests itself in many different ways in the field of social and economic justice, whether at the local, regional, national, or global level. I refer briefly to five of the ways that solidarity affects legal systems very directly.

35   John Paul II, *Evangelium vitae*, 40.

a. *Universal destination of goods and respect for private property.* Creation is originally meant for all persons. Therefore, the necessary right to private property is not absolute but has an intrinsically social function and is under a kind of social mortgage. At the heart of this social mortgage lies the preference for the poor.[36] That is why no legal system is completely fair, unless it exemplifies solidarity and guarantees the complete disappearance of poverty at all levels.

b. *Ecological solidarity.* The principle of solidarity requires us to look after the planet as a treasure to be enjoyed without damaging it, in order to preserve it for future generations. Legal systems play an outstanding supportive function by regulating the ecological question from the perspectives of administrative law, health law, and criminal law, among others.[37]

c. *Principle of subsidiarity.* The principle of subsidiarity is a practical expression of the principle of solidarity, which applies when subsidiarity acts vertically. A social structure of a higher order, if it is truly supportive, should not interfere in the internal life of a community of a lower order, limiting its competencies and preventing its development. The higher structure should support the lower structure, not stifle it, and should work with it to achieve the common good. Subsidiarity gives people enough freedom to act freely and develop, while preventing them from being subjected to suffocating structures.[38]

d. *Solidarity of democracy.* John Paul II valued the democratic system "inasmuch as it ensures the participation of citizens in making political choices, guarantees to the governed the possibility both of electing and holding accountable those who govern them, and of replacing them through peaceful means when appropriate."[39] For a democracy to be truly supportive, John Paul II demanded that it be sustained by a state of law and based on a correct conception of the human person.

e. *Solidarity of the economic model.* John Paul II called for a model of economic organization—at the regional, national, and international levels—that supports and respects the person's dignity. For the Polish pope, neither the socialist model nor the capitalist model meets the necessary requirements of dignity and solidarity. As an alternative, and without in any way claiming to define the model, he proposed "a society of free work, of enterprise and of

---

36 John Paul II, *Evangelium vitae*, 42, and *Centesimus annus*, 30.
37 John Paul II, *Centesimus annus*, 37–39.
38 John Paul II, *Centesimus annus*, 48.
39 John Paul II, *Centesimus annus*, 46.

participation. Such a society is not directed against the market, but demands that the market be appropriately controlled by the forces of society and by the State, so as to guarantee that the basic needs of the whole of society are satisfied."[40]

The Great Reformer of the Catholic Church's Canon Law

To bring the law of the Catholic Church into line with the prescriptions of the Second Vatican Council, John Paul II carried out a profound legislative reform of canon law, thus completing the work begun by his predecessors Pope John XXIII and Pope Paul VI. This reform rested mainly on three main pillars: the 1983 Code of Canon Law (*Codex Iuris Canonici*), the 1990 Code of the Canons of Eastern Churches (*Codex Canonum Ecclesiarum Orientalium*), and the 1988 apostolic constitution *Pastor bonus* on the reform of the organization and government of the Roman Curia.

The new Code of Canon Law, applicable to the (Western) Church of the Latin rite, replaced that of 1917. It was promulgated on January 25, 1983, by the apostolic constitution *Sacrae disciplinae leges*, which John Paul II drafted personally.[41] He reviewed the code of 1983 in detail before its approval. It is structured differently from the European codes of Roman tradition, which the 1917 code had followed, and its organizational structure is clearly ecclesiological. More doctrinal and theological than the 1917 code, the 1983 code represents an effort to translate the ecclesiology of the Second Vatican Council into legal language.

The renewed ecclesiology of the Second Vatican Council revolves around the notion of communion as a hermeneutic key to the mystery of the church. Communion gives one a better understanding of the meaning of the church as the people of God, collegiality, hierarchical authority as a service, the relations between the universal church and the particular church, the importance of ecumenism, and the central role that laypeople play in the church's life, since all of God's people participate in the priestly, prophetic, and royal functions of Christ.[42]

40 John Paul II, *Centesimus annus*, 35.
41 Weigel, *Witness to Hope*, 445.
42 See John Paul II, Apostolic Constitution *Sacrae disciplinae leges* (January 25, 1983).

The 1983 code has been reformed many times by John Paul II himself, by Pope Benedict XVI, and, above all, by Pope Francis. The crisis that the Catholic Church went through after clerical sexual abuses came to light underscored the code's shortcomings in criminal and procedural matters and the need to strengthen the code with subsequent complementary legislation. John Paul II himself began this reform on his own initiative with the apostolic letter *Sacramentorum sanctitatis tutela* in 2001, in which, among many other measures, John Paul II reserved judgment on any sexual offense committed by a cleric with a minor to the competence of the Sacred Congregation for the Doctrine of the Faith. The pope's desire to eradicate sexual abuse in the church was profoundly sincere, and when he shouted at the cardinals to meet the challenge with "uncompromising courage," the cry came straight from his heart, aching at the damage caused to the victims and to the whole church.[43] This does not mean that John Paul II did not make mistakes, as any human being would—sometimes with serious consequences, for not correctly interpreting the facts and circumstances with the information available to him, for not having sufficient proof, or for being cynically deceived by someone in whom he placed his trust. This seems to be clear from the Holy See's extensive report on the case of former Cardinal Theodore Edgar McCarrick, who has been defrocked, or the case of Marcial Maciel and the Legionaries of Christ.[44]

What is more, the fact that John Paul II suffered the slander orchestrated by the secret services for so many years—and was even accused in 1983 of having sexual relations with an acquaintance who had died, on the basis of a forged diary purported to belong to her—could no doubt have influenced his excessive prudence before condemning anyone for sexual abuse unless the evidence was guaranteed to be fully reliable.[45] Attempting to damage the memory and annihilate the legacy of Pope John Paul II for these regrettable events during his pontificate is clearly meaningless. As he himself said,

---

43 John Paul II, "Address to the Cardinals of the United States," April 23, 2002.

44 "Report on the Holy See's Institutional Knowledge and Decision-Making Related to Former Cardinal Theodore Edgar McCarrick," November 10, 2020, https://www.vatican.va/resources/resources_rapporto-card-mccarrick_20201110_en.pdf. On the Maciel case, see Weigel, *The End and the Beginning*, 512–15.

45 About these false accusations, see Weigel, *The End and the Beginning*, 132, and José María Zavala, *El enigma Wojtyla. Un retrato desconocido de Juan Pablo II* (Madrid: Ediciones Martínez Roca, 2020), 182–84.

referring to the work of the Catholic Church: "A great work of art may be blemished, but its beauty remains; and this is a truth which any intellectually honest critic will recognize."[46]

On October 18, 1990, by means of the apostolic constitution *Sacri canones*, John Paul II promulgated the Code of Canons of the Eastern Churches, which contains the norms of canon law applicable to the twenty-three Eastern Catholic Churches *sui iuris* (Armenian, Chaldean, Maronite, and Coptic, among others). This is a complete code, common to all the Eastern churches, which aims to reinforce and protect the richness of the diversity of rites in the Catholic Church. Each rite is considered "the liturgical, theological, spiritual, and disciplinary patrimony, culture, and circumstances of history of a distinct people, by which its own manner of living the faith is manifested in each autonomous *[sui iuris]* Church."[47] The underlying idea behind the whole legal text is that the full union of the Eastern Catholic Churches with the Church of Rome must in no way entail their losing sight of their own traditions and authenticity, since each rite embellishes the universal church itself. John Paul II referred to the two codes as the two lungs—of the East and of the West—through which the Catholic Church breathed.[48]

With *Pastor bonus*, John Paul II adapted the Roman Curia to the inspiring principles of the Second Vatican Council. He designed ecclesiastical power as a service and made canon law even more dependent on ecclesiology. The new constitution expressly states that "The Curia is the complex of dicasteries and institutes which help the Roman pontiff in the exercise of his supreme pastoral office for the good and service of the whole Church and of the particular Churches," to strengthen "the unity of the faith and the communion of the people of God" and to promote "the mission proper to the church in the world."[49] After more than thirty years of applying the apostolic constitution, and owing to the economic scandals generated within the Vatican, Pope Francis is carrying out, little by little, a profound reform of the curia.

Along with these three important reforms, John Paul II made other important contributions to canon law, such as the establishment of the first personal prelature, Opus Dei (1982), thus challenging the fundamental

---

46   John Paul II, "Address to the Cardinals of the United States."
47   Canon 28 § 1 of the *Code of Canons of the Eastern Churches* (Washington, D.C.: Canon Law Society of America, 2001).
48   John Paul II, Apostolic Constitution *Sacri canones* (October 18, 1990).
49   See Apostolic Constitution *Pastor bonus* (June 28, 1988), art. 1.

principle of territoriality, and the establishment of the Pontifical Council for the Interpretation of Legislative Texts (1986), the organization of spiritual assistance to the military (1986), the reform of the universities and ecclesiastical faculties (1979), the reform for the election of the supreme pontiff (1996), and the publication of the *Catechism of the Catholic Church* (official Latin text of 1997), which condenses and updates all the magisterium of the Second Vatican Council.

Conclusion

Pope John Paul II's contribution to the realm of law remains relevant to the church and the broader world, and the Polish pope well deserves the name of lawyer. He approached law from the perspective of philosophy, ethics, and theology, but also as a statesman, world leader, and pastor of the Catholic Church. Not only was he a theoretician of law, but he also created and applied it, as a pastor of the Catholic Church and head of the Vatican state. Through his public action, he contributed to the substantial transformation of the legal systems in Eastern Europe and especially in his beloved Poland.

John Paul II grasped the importance of law for the establishment of a culture of love, which represented the purpose of his pontificate. Without law there is no justice, and without justice there is no love. At the heart of the legal system, John Paul II placed the human person, whose dignity stems from being created in the image of God. Dignity, therefore, is a metalegal and transcendent idea that needs to be protected by the law, yet which in turn transcends the legal system. When dignity ceases to stem from God, it is easy for systems to focus attention on a falsely divinized human being, no longer a child of God but master and lord of self, ethically independent of any divine command. That is when dignity becomes trapped by the arbitrariness of one's own behavior. By acknowledging the gift of dignity, one can find full harmony between moral law and conscience, nature and freedom, justice and truth.

From the dignity of human nature spring human rights, which are objectively true, so that their existence does not depend on the will of public authorities. Human rights are not granted but rather acknowledged. Among these rights, the right to life and the right to religious freedom shine in Karol Wojtyła's mind. For John Paul II, solidarity is the principle that shows how people act and confirms their dignity. Any fair system must be essentially supportive. This solidarity is shown in the universal destination of all goods, in the responsibility to care for the planet, in the preferential option for the poor, in the principle of subsidiarity, in the political participation of citizens, and in an economic organization of solidarity that goes beyond the socialist and capitalist models.

Last of all, Pope John Paul II was a great reformer of canon law. To him we owe, among other legal texts, the promulgation of the 1983 Code of Canon Law, the 1990 Code of Canons of the Eastern Churches, and the 1988 apostolic constitution *Pastor bonus* (in force until June 2022) on the reform of the organization and government of the Roman Curia.

CHAPTER 13

ÁLVARO D'ORS AS A CHRISTIAN JURIST AND LEGAL SCHOLAR

Biographical Introduction

ÁLVARO D'ORS PÉREZ-PEIX WAS a great polymath of Spanish education in the twentieth century and a central figure in the development of the University of Navarra in northern Spain.[1] A distinguished scholar of antiquity, d'Ors devoted himself to the advance of scholarship, wisdom, and knowledge from a Christian perspective. While he is best known for his work on Roman law, he also made significant contributions to political theology, political philosophy, legal theory, and legal history, mentoring scholars from Spain, Portugal, Chile, Mexico, Colombia, Peru, Argentina, and Japan. D'Ors emulated Immanuel Kant's quiet and productive life, Theodore Mommsen's deep and fruitful scholarship, and Max Weber's imagination and originality. As a fervent Catholic, d'Ors followed Josemaría Escrivá's spirituality, looking

---

[*] The original version of this essay appears in Rafael Domingo, "Álvaro d'Ors (1915–2004)," in *Great Christian Jurists in Spanish History*, ed. Rafael Domingo and Javier Martínez-Torrón (Cambridge: Cambridge University Press, 2018), 344–60.

[1] See the excellent biography written in Spanish by Gabriel Pérez, *Álvaro d'Ors. Sinfonía de una vida* (Madrid: Rialp, 2020).

for God in ordinary life, and as a loyal husband, he loved his wife, Palmira Lois, who gave birth to eleven children.

Although d'Ors was fluent in English, French, Catalan, Italian, German, and Latin, he wrote mainly in Spanish to promote his native language in European academia. This decision greatly limited his influence outside the Spanish-speaking world and partially explains why his works have not attracted the attention of philosophers and political theorists in the United States. An exception was Frederick Wilhelmsen, who considered d'Ors among the best twentieth-century political philosophers.[2] "His speculations," Wilhelmsen pointed out, "are as original as are those of Leo Strauss and Eric Voegelin, to mention the two contemporary political philosophers best known in this country."[3]

Álvaro d'Ors Pérez-Peix was born at the Casa de les Punxes in Barcelona,[4] on April 14, 1915.[5] His father, Eugenio d'Ors Rovira (1881–1954), was a distinguished philosopher, gifted essayist, and remarkable art critic who led the Catalan cultural renaissance of the early twentieth century (*Noucentisme*).[6] Xénius, as he was often called, is considered one of the more influential thinkers of Spanish culture of the first half of the twentieth century. Álvaro's mother, María Pérez-Peix (1879–1972), was a sculptor of great artistic sensitivity and manual ability. Álvaro's own birth was soon known to the cultural elite of that time through a letter that Eugenio d'Ors addressed to his dear friend and poet Juan Ramón Jiménez[7]: "Know and tell my friends that my

---

2   See Frederick D. Wilhelmsen, "The Political Philosophy of Álvaro d'Ors," *The Political Science Reviewer* 20 (1991): 145–87, at 145: "I am personally convinced that Álvaro d'Ors is among the half dozen or so first political philosophers of this century."

3   Wilhelmsen, "The Political Philosophy of Álvaro d'Ors," 145.

4   It is a renowned building located in the Diagonal Avenue 420 and designed by the modernist architect Josep Puig i Cadalfach. See https://www.barcelona.de/en/barcelona-casa-de-les-punxes.html.

5   For a familiar biographical approach and characterization of d'Ors, see Miguel d'Ors, "Mi padre," in *Álvaro d'Ors (1915–2004), in memoriam*, ed. Rafael Domingo (Pamplona: Universidad de Navarra, 2004), 33–43.

6   The term *noucentisme* was coined by Eugenio d'Ors in 1916 as a label for the cultural movement. It was a reaction against *modernisme*, both in art and in political ideology. On *noucentisme*, see Aleix Catasús and Bernat Puigdollers, *El Noucentisme a Barcelona* (Barcelona: Barcelona Libres, 2016).

7   Juan Ramón Jiménez (1881–1958) was a Spanish poet who received the 1956 Nobel Prize for Literature for his lyrical poetry. His prose poem about a writer and his

third offspring has been born this day, a male like the other two, and that he will be baptized tomorrow with the name of Álvaro. Take note of him as a future resident.[8] You see, I am already made a young patriarch, while, apparently, you keep in 'Zenobite.'"[9]

Álvaro d'Ors received an atypical and uneven education because of his stubborn resistance to schooling. He often recalled the fine day when he was six and his beloved mother taught him to read in only one afternoon session. This new ability to read allowed the young Álvaro to immerse himself in his father's voluminous library, where Álvaro spent hundreds of hours, especially during his father's frequent trips. In this family environment, d'Ors strengthened and developed his aesthetic temperament, which was always present in his work. At the end of his life, he claimed that the use of the maternal potter's wheel to collect and classify insects, to draw maps, and produce translations (as a child, he had learned Spanish, Catalan, French, and English) shaped his early formation.[10]

At the beginning of the twentieth century, the family moved to Madrid, and d'Ors was admitted to the Instituto-Escuela, a secular institution founded in 1918 following the leading European pedagogical trends. There he met and was educated with the children of influential Spanish intellectuals. His attraction to the beauty of classical antiquity marked his formation in adolescence. In 1931, he spent the summer in London, where his daily visits to the department of Greece and Rome at the British Museum helped him to mature his decision to devote his life to the classical world. By that time, he was already familiar with Latin and Greek. He also developed a fascination for the English Romantic poets, particularly for the end of the

---

donkey, *Platero y yo* (1914), was celebrated. This letter from Eugenio d'Ors was partially reproduced, among others, by Álvaro d'Ors in *La violencia y el orden* (Madrid: Dyrsa, 1987), 7.

8 He refers to the Residencia de Estudiantes (student residence) in Madrid: "The Residencia de Estudiantes became the first cultural center of Spain. Until the Spanish Civil War the Residencia remained a vibrant focal point for scientific and artistic work and exchange in Europe."

9 The last phrase ironically alluded to the lack of descendants of the poet, making a joke with the name of his wife, Zenobia, and the near homonym "cenobite," or member of a monastic community.

10 See Rafael Domingo, "Álvaro d'Ors," in Domingo, ed., *Juristas Universales IV* (Madrid: Marcial Pons, 2004), 662–66, at 662.

famous "Ode on a Grecian Urn," by John Keats: "Beauty is truth, truth beauty—that is all / Ye know on earth, and all ye need to know."[11] In 1932, d'Ors started attending the law school at the Central University in Madrid (now Complutense University).

Álvaro d'Ors's idyllic life soon met with two important events: the divorce of his parents at his father's initiative in 1932 and the outbreak of the Spanish Civil War in 1936. In July 1936, d'Ors enlisted as a Carlist volunteer[12] of the Nationalist faction in the Spanish Civil War (1936–1939). His experience in the war left an indelible mark on his personal life and deeply influenced his political thought.[13] He was not resentful, however. He understood the Spanish Civil War as a national religious war (a true crusade) against international communism and progressive democratic secularization. To be a soldier under these concrete circumstances of political chaos and religious persecution was a way for him to serve his beloved country and the Catholic Church. When the war ended in 1939, d'Ors returned to university life.

After graduating in 1939, d'Ors spent a year in Rome working on his doctoral thesis under Emilio Albertario, who was a defender of radical interpolation research in Roman law, which was based on the false premise that the compilers of Justinian's *Corpus Iuris Civilis* (530 CE) had modified, revised, and dramatically changed the earlier works of the classical Roman jurists. Therefore, defenders of radical interpolationism established sophisticated criteria to detect the alterations. The turn away from this false premise came in the mid-twentieth century led by Franz Wieacker and Max Kaser. D'Ors accommodated and even advocated for this new scientific methodology.

In 1941, d'Ors defended his doctoral dissertation at the Central University of Madrid, where Ursicino Álvarez Suárez had mentored him, and two years later, he became a tenured professor of Roman law at the University of Granada. In 1944, he moved to the University of Santiago of Compostela,

---

11   The poem is available at https://www.poetryfoundation.org/poems-and-poets/poems/detail/44477.

12   The Carlist militia (called *Requetés*) were monarchists and ardent traditional Catholics. They considered the Spanish Civil War as a crusade and were enlisted on religious grounds. See Julio Aróstegui, *Combatientes requetés en la Guerra Civil española 1936–1939* (Madrid: La Esfera de los Libros, 2013).

13   See, for instance, d'Ors, *La violencia y el orden*.

where he spent seventeen prolific years. In Santiago, d'Ors married Palmira Lois in 1945, and their first children were born. He developed a deep friendship with Carl Schmitt (1888–1985), whom he first met in Granada. He also started teaching at the University of Coimbra in 1948 and joined the Catholic institution Opus Dei in 1949. In 1953, d'Ors was appointed director of the Spanish Law Institute (Istituto Giuridico Spagnolo) in Rome and regularly travelled to Rome for twenty years to mentor young Spanish law scholars. His stays in Rome allowed him to keep permanent contact with the Italian Romanists (e.g., Vincenzo Arangio Ruiz, Giuseppe Grosso, Emilio Betti, Antonio Guarino, and Gabrio Lombardi) and to engage them in intellectual debate and historical research.

In 1961, d'Ors moved to the University of Navarra, a Catholic university founded by Saint Josemaria Escrivá in 1952 in northern Spain. Escrivá tried to build a politically independent and Christian-oriented university following the Anglo-American standards of academic excellence. At the University of Navarra, d'Ors remained a full professor in the Law School and the School of Canon Law (1961–1985), an emeritus professor (1985–1989), and ultimately an honorary professor (1989–2004). In recognition of his academic excellence, he received honorary doctorates from the University of Toulouse, the University of Coimbra, and La Sapienza University in Rome.

The promulgation of the new Code of Canon Law of 1983 stimulated d'Ors to study the law of the Catholic Church. He was interested mainly in the legal terminology used by the code and the critical exegesis of the canons in their Latin versions. He revised the Spanish translation of the code edited by the Martín Azpilcueta Institute of the University of Navarra.[14] In 1990, d'Ors was awarded the University of Navarra's Gold Medal by grand chancellor Álvaro del Portillo in recognition of his efforts to build up the university library structure and expand and strengthen the law school. Álvaro d'Ors died at the University of Navarra Hospital in Pamplona on February 1, 2004, at the age of eighty-eight. Ten years later, in 2014, a bust of Álvaro d'Ors was erected on the university campus at the University of Navarra Library entrance.

---

14   Álvaro d'Ors, Código de Derecho Canónico, 6th ed., ed. Instituto Martín Azpilcueta (Pamplona: Eunsa, 2001).

His Works

Álvaro d'Ors wrote more than eight hundred academic publications from 1939 to 2004,[15] thousands of op-eds and notes to newspapers and magazines, and several thousand letters with intellectual reflections.[16] In familiar conversations, with the irony that characterized him, he used to say that writing was like a tic. And he was right. This ability to turn ideas into writing with admirable ease was so embedded in his own life that he could never abandon it, even in times of illness. The first drafts of his *Cartas a un joven estudiante* (*Letters to a Young Student*, 1991), the entirely rewritten version of his *Elementos de Derecho romano* (*Elements of Roman Law*, 1992), his lectures on *Derecho y sentido común* (*Law and Common Sense*, 1995), and his essay *La posesión del espacio* (*The Possession of Space*, 1998) were written as if in one breath.

Álvaro d'Ors's prose is elegant, clear, and concise. Unlike his father, who wrote in a Socratic style addressed to an imagined interlocutor, Álvaro d'Ors frequently sought and found real-life interlocutors (alive or deceased) for his writing. In the field of Roman law, they mainly were Theodor Mommsen (1817–1903) and Otto Lenel (1849–1935), as well as his teachers, Leopold Wenger (1874–1953) and Emilio Albertario (1885–1948). Special note should be made of the aforementioned two leading figures of Roman law in the second half of the twentieth century, Max Kaser (1906–1997) and Franz Wieacker (1908–1994). D'Ors's main interlocutors in political theory were, in order of importance, Carl Schmitt (1888–1985), Michel Villey (1914–1987), and Max Weber (1864–1920). D'Ors did not have American interlocutors. In fact, he was not familiar with American legal theory. Some of his intuitions, however—especially his definition of law as "what the judges say it is"[17]—have parallels with the doctrinal approach of American legal realism, which reduced law to the activity of courts.[18]

---

15 For a summary of all of them, see Rafael Domingo, *Álvaro d'Ors. Una introduction a su obra* (Cizur Menor: Thomson Aranzadi, 2005).

16 His son, Xavier d'Ors, professor of law at the University of Santiago de Compostela, is devoted to the difficult task of cataloguing these letters.

17 See Álvaro d'Ors, "Derecho es lo que aprueban los jueces" (1970), in *Escritos varios sobre el Derecho en crisis* (Rome: Consejo Superior de Investigaciones Científicas, 1973), 45–54.

18 See Oliver Wendell Holmes, Jr., "The Path of the Law," *Harvard Law Review* 10 (1897): 457–78, at 457: "The prophecies of what the courts will do in fact, and nothing more pretentious, are what I mean by the law."

D'Ors committed himself to resolve complex legal science questions rather than writing general considerations and approaches. This passion for concrete issues explains his decision to be a jurist, although he was temperamentally closer to other disciplines. However, toward the end of his life, he chose to write a few books and papers summarizing his original thinking, such as his *Claves conceptuales* (*Conceptual Keys*, 1996) and his *Nueva introducción al estudio del derecho* (*New Introduction to Law*, 1999).

D'Orsian scientific work is of considerable thematic variety. Roman law is undoubtedly its main thread, but his intellectual interests ranged much more broadly, including papyrology, epigraphy, ancient history, civil law, legal theory, politics, canon law, Catholic theology, Navarra regional law, social philosophy, and university education. His most beautiful prose dates to the 1940s, and it is probably best represented by his prologue to the Spanish edition of Romano Guardini's book *Der Heilbringer in Mythos, Offenbarung und Politik* (*The Miraculous in Myth, Revelation, and Politics*), drafted in the Abbey of Samos (Lugo) in July 1947.[19] His most erudite paper is his contribution to the *Studies in Honor of Camilo Barcia Trelles* on the "transmarini negotiatores" in Visigothic legislation (1958).[20] His book *De la Guerra y de la paz* (*On War and Peace*, 1954) was awarded the 1954 Spanish National Prize in Literature.

The following sections focus on the two disciplines in which I believe d'Ors made his most important contributions: Roman law and political theory.

His Contributions to Roman Law

D'Ors was, above all, a scholar of Roman law, not only because he devoted most of his research and teaching to this field but also because his legal (and even political) thinking was framed by his studies of Roman law. Indeed, some conceptual keys of his *Weltanschauung* are inspired by Roman law.

From the beginning of his academic career, d'Ors grasped that papyrology, particularly epigraphy, represented one of the better sources of knowledge of Roman law and, therefore, an appropriate means to develop

---

19 See Romano Guardini, *El mesianismo en el mito, la revelación y la política*, trans. Valentín García Yebra, foreword by Álvaro d'Ors (Madrid: Rialp, 1948).

20 Álvaro d'Ors, "Los 'transmarini negotiatores' en la legislación visigótica," in *Estudios de Derecho Internacional en homenaje al Profesor Camilo Barcia Trelles* (Santiago de Compostela: Universidad de Santiago de Compostela, 1958), 467–83, reproduced in Álvaro d'Ors, *Parerga histórica* (Pamplona: Eunsa, 1997), 213–38.

his own scholarship. D'Ors started with the *Constitutio Antoniniana*, which became the topic of his 1941 doctoral thesis. *Constitutio Antoniniana* is the popular name of an imperial edict issued by Emperor Caracalla in 212 CE commanding inhabitants of the Roman Empire to become citizens. Although both Cassius Dio (77.9.5) and Ulpian (Digest 1.5.17) state that the citizenship order was universal, the publication of papyrus Giessen 40 from Egypt, which contains the text of the edict in a Greek translation, states that a group called the *dediticii* was excluded from it. Both the nature of this group and the reason for the exclusion remain an open academic discussion in which d'Ors was immersed.[21] Two years later, in 1943, he published his *Presupuestos críticos para el estudio del Derecho romano* (*Critical Assumptions for the Study of Roman Law*), in which he adopts a critical attitude toward the Roman legal sources, advocating rigorous historical-critical methods. This book constitutes the guiding thread of all d'Orsian research on the subject of Roman law.

However, his most important book on Roman law came out ten years later. In 1953, d'Ors published his *Epigrafía Jurídica de la España Romana* (*Legal Epigraphy of Roman Spain*),[22] a volume in which he collected and commented extensively on all the known epigraphic fragments relating to the juridical-administrative organization of Roman Spain. D'Ors would continue working on new inscriptions for the rest of his life, but he did so again most passionately following the discovery of the *lex Irnitana* in the village of El Saucejo (Seville) in 1981. The *lex Irnitana* was the municipal statute of a hitherto unknown town, Irni. D'Ors quickly realized it contained the most complete copy yet discovered of the Flavian municipal law, previously known only in fragmentary form from municipal statutes from Salpensa and Malaca.[23]

21 See, for instance, Álvaro d'Ors, "Estudios sobre la 'Constitutio Antoniniana' I. Estado de la cuestión," *Emerita* 11 (1943): 297–337; "Estudios sobre la 'Constitutio Antoniniana' II. Los dediticios y el Edicto de Caracala," *Anuario de Historia del Derecho Español* 15 (1944): 162–204; "Estudios sobre la 'Constitutio Antoniniana' III. Los 'peregrini' después del Edicto de Caracala," *Anuario de Historia del Derecho Español* 17 (1946): 586–604; "Estudios sobre la 'Constitutio Antoniniana' V. Caracala y la unificación del Imperio," *Emerita* 24 (1956): 1–26; and "Nuevos estudios sobre la 'Constitutio Antoniniana,'" *Atti dell'XI Congresso Internazionale di Papirologia de 1965* (Milan: Istituto Lombardo di Scienze e Lettere, 1966), 408–32.

22 Álvaro d'Ors, *Epigrafía Jurídica de la España Romana* (Madrid: Instituto Nacional de Estudios Jurídicos, 1953).

23 Álvaro d'Ors, *La ley Flavia municipal (Texto y comentario)* (Rome: Pontifical Lateran University, 1986); Álvaro d'Ors and Xavier d'Ors, *Lex Irnitana. Texto bilingüe* (Santiago de Compostela: Universidad de Santiago de Compostela, 1988).

After the publication of his *Legal Epigraphy*, d'Ors focused on revising the reconstruction of the edict of the praetor (*edictum perpetuum*). The praetorian edict represented the driving principle behind the development of classical Roman law until the middle of the second century CE. The edict consisted of individual announcements (technically called edicts) establishing both the circumstances under which the praetor would grant new remedies (*actiones*) and guidelines for these remedies. By order of Emperor Hadrian, in about 130 CE, jurist Salvius Julianus, one of the greatest Roman jurists, definitively revised the praetorian edict. Based on the commentaries on the praetorian edict by some classical Roman jurists, Otto Lenel published a notable reconstruction of it.[24] Lenel's work is crucial for any research on classical Roman law. It enables modern scholars to take into consideration the original context of the legal source as well as to understand the technicalities of the Roman legal system. D'Ors realized that the final reconstruction offered by Lenel, although exceptional, remained technically insufficient. More than thirty years of work in this field and tens of relevant monographs and papers published by d'Ors or his students confirmed his intuition.[25]

The separate location for contracts from credit operations in the praetor's edict led d'Ors to conclude that the classical division of the obligations proposed by the jurist Gaius did not enter classical Roman legal understanding.[26] Gaius (*Institutes* 3.89) offers a fourfold classification of contracts, which Emperor Justinian followed (Inst. 13.3.2). According to Gaius, contracts were concluded by the delivery of a thing (*re*), by the uttering of formal words (*verbis*), by a documentary form (*litteris*), or by formless consent (*consensu*). Thus, contracts could be real contracts (e.g., loans for consumption), verbal contracts (e.g., stipulations), literal contracts (e.g., ledger entries), or consensual contracts (e.g., sales). D'Ors defended Labeo's attempt to restrict the concept of contract to bilateral contracts as one not to be underestimated (Ulpian-Labeo, D. 50.16.19). Labeo associated the Latin word *contractus* with

---

24   Otto Lenel, *Das Edictum Perpetuum. Ein Versuch Seiner Wiederherstellung,* 3rd ed. (Leipzig: Tauchnitz, 1927; reprint, Aalen, 1956).

25   Extensive bibliography is offered by Rafael Domingo, "Sobre las supuestas rúbricas del Edicto pretor," *Zeitschrift der Savigny-Stiftung für Rechtsgeschichte (Romanistische Abteilung)* 108 (1991): 290–303, at 290, and Rafael Domingo, "Un siglo de Derecho romano en España," in *Iuris vincula. Studi in onore di Mario Talamanca* I (Naples: Jovene, 2001), 487–509.

26   Álvaro d'Ors, "Observaciones sobre el 'edictum de rebus creditis,'" *Studia et Documenta Historiae et Iuris* 19 (1953): 134–201.

the Greek *synallagma* and therefore considered contractual only those obligations in which the parties were mutually obliged (*ultro citroque obligatio*).[27] Nevertheless, d'Ors's attempt to reduce the concept of a Roman contract to bilateral relations protected by specific remedies was not generally accepted by Roman scholars.[28]

Still at the University of Santiago de Compostela, d'Ors paid special attention to the Code of Euric,[29] a codification for use in the Visigothic kingdom of Toulouse attributed to King Euric (466–484). Fragments of the text survived in the palimpsest manuscript discovered in the mid-seventeenth century and preserved at the National Library in Paris (Paris Lat. 12161). D'Ors prepared an edition of the manuscript and an erudite introduction in which he defended the Code of Euric as a kind of vulgarized Roman law, influenced by Gallia's jurists and with a territorial character, more than proper Germanic law as some scholars argued. D'Ors's efforts to decipher the palimpsest caused him visual fatigue, and he began to wear glasses for reading. He would continue using the same glasses for the rest of his life, demonstrating his academic commitment to Roman legal history.

In 1960, he also published his *Elementos de Derecho romano* (*Elements of Roman Law*), which would develop into his challenging textbook, *Derecho privado romano* (*Private Roman Law*, 1968; 10th ed. 2004). In it, d'Ors depicted a lucid picture of the structure of the Roman legal system together with the collected results of his research and that of his students. This book has shaped scholarly thinking on Roman law and often constitutes the starting point of contemporary Roman law research.

D'Ors admired classical Roman jurists for their legal imagination and intellectual achievements. His five readings of Justinian's Digests to translate them into Spanish[30] gave him a unique insight into the Roman jurists. For four decades, he focused mainly on one of them: Sextus Caecilius Africanus,[31]

---

27 Álvaro d'Ors, "Creditum und Contratus," *Zeitschrift der Savigny-Stiftung für Rechtsgeschichte (Romanistische Abteilung)* 74 (1957): 73–99.

28 See Max Kaser, *Das römische Privatrecht*, vol. 1, *Das altrömische, das vorklassische und klassische Recht*, 2nd ed. (Munich: Beck Verlag, 1971), 523.

29 Álvaro d'Ors, *El Código de Eurico. Edición, Palingenesia, Índices* (Rome: Instituto Jurídico Español, 1960).

30 See Álvaro d'Ors, ed., *El Digesto de Justiniano*, 3 vols. (Pamplona: Aranzadi, 1968–75).

31 Álvaro d'Ors, *Las Quaestiones de Africano* (Rome: Pontifical Lateran University, 1997).

a jurist of the mid-second century CE and a pupil of the great Julianus. D'Ors wrote an extensive commentary of Africanus's nine books of difficult cases (*Quaestiones*), in which Africanus stated Julianus's views together with comments of his own. The monograph exemplifies d'Ors's high level of scholarship and excellence. In it, he achieved what he called historical meaning, that is, the reconstruction of the classic jurists' casuistic method.

His Contributions to Political Theory

Álvaro d'Ors never attempted to elaborate a political theory as such and would write on political theory only when he perceived the need to rationalize his personal experience of the war, when he considered that Roman law could illuminate political debate, or when there were political implications in his approach to significant legal questions. Like Carl Schmitt and Hans Kelsen, d'Ors was a legal thinker who offered a juridical perspective in the interpretation of political issues. Unlike Kelsen and Schmitt, however, d'Ors answered any political question by starting with private law, not constitutional law. For this reason, it is sometimes not easy to distinguish d'Ors's political theory from his legal theory. His reflections on political theory are contained mainly in the following books: *De la guerra y de la paz* (*On War and Peace*, 1954); *Ensayos de teoría política* (*Essays on Political Theory*, 1979); *La violencia y el orden* (*On Violence and Order*, 1987); *La posesión del espacio* (*The Possession of Space*, 1998); *Nueva introducción al estudio del derecho* (*New Introduction to the Study of Law*, 1999), and *Bien común y enemigo público* (*Common Good and Public Enemy*, 2001).

D'Orsian political theory begins as a critique against modernity and specifically against the modern idea of the nation-state and its constituent institutions and principles. Rooted in the sixteenth-century concept of sovereignty to overcome the tensions derived from religious wars, the nation-state was a product of the Protestant Reformation. Nation-states are a "form of artificial organization of national groups" and not "an expression of the natural development of essential human sociability."[32] The concept of sovereignty definitively closed the door to a harmoniously ordered international order.

D'Ors claimed that modernity rejected relevant Christian ideas and Roman categories. The idea of sovereignty, as Jean Bodin conceptualized it in *The Six Books of the Commonwealth* (1576), excluded the dogma of the kingship of Christ. The idea of separation of powers rejected the (natural)

---

32   Álvaro d'Ors, *Nueva introducción al estudio del derecho* (Madrid: Civitas, 1999), § 103.

Roman distinction between authority (*auctoritas*) and power (*potestas*). The idea of secular democracy exalted legality (*lex*) and obliterated legitimacy (*ius*). Finally, d'Ors believed that modern legal and political thinkers erroneously applied the idea of ownership instead of the idea of possession to the distribution of the territory of the earth, developing thus an artificial international community of fabricated nation-states.

According to d'Ors, the doctrine of the kingship of Christ has important implications for the political and social order. With Christ as the supreme ruler of the universe, no other absolute and exclusive political power (i.e., sovereignty) is possible. Political power is, therefore, inherently limited, both from within and without, making political dualism a categorical requirement. At this point in his discourse, d'Ors takes advantage of his expertise in Roman law to introduce three crucial Roman distinctions ignored in the current political discourse. Let me summarize them.

Auctoritas and *Potestas*

The distinction between moral authority (*auctoritas*) and constituted power (*potestas*) is critical to understanding Orsian political and legal theory.[33] *Auctoritas* comes from *augere*, which means "to increase, to grow, to fulfill." *Auctoritas* is the influence that derives from personal respect, wisdom, and virtue without having legal power. *Potestas*, on the other hand, comes from the Indo-European lexeme *pot-*, which refers to the established power. The division of roles between the *auctoritas* of augurs, jurists, judges, and senators, on the one hand, and the *potestas* of magistrates and family fathers, on the other hand, served to establish not only a wise and healthy political, social, and legal balance in society but also an ontological equilibrium. Because power was considered indivisible by nature (Cicero, *De re publica* 1.38.60), it must respond to something or someone beyond itself and be limited by an external agent (i.e., by moral authority). Moral authority was, therefore, an effective check on the power of Rome.

The most primitive distinction between moral authority and power lay in the role of the college of augurs, who could recognize the will of the gods in the behavior of birds and thus divine approval or disapproval of a proposed

---

[33] On this distinction, see Álvaro d'Ors, *Escritos varios sobre el Derecho en crisis* (Rome: Instituto Jurídico Español, 1973). For a revised and developed synthesis, see Rafael Domingo, *Auctoritas* (Barcelona: Ariel, 1999).

action. Before making critical decisions, Roman kings would often ask the augural college for advice, mixing the sacral authority of the augural college with the political power of the kings into a propitious unity. The gradual replacement of the augurs by the haruspices during the republican period represents a blurring of the distinction between authority and power. The haruspices predicted the future and read the omens of the gods, but only at the command of the magistrates. The haruspex was a civil servant to the political powers and not an autonomous adviser or consultant, as the college of augurs had been.

The republican Senate expanded the role of the earlier college of augurs. At the heart of the Roman republican constitution, enshrined in the famous acronym SPQR (*Senatus Populusque Romanus*: The Senate and People of Rome), the relationship between authority and power can be found again. During the Roman republic, the moral authority of the Senate (*auctoritas Senatus*) limited the power of the magistrates (*potestas* or *imperium*), which was but a determination of the popular majesty (*maiestas populi*). It was the *auctoritas* of the Senate that morally and effectively held the executive power of the magistrates in check. As a result, as Cicero pointed out, "a compromise takes place whereby the power is vested in the people, but authority in the hands of the Senate" (*De legibus* 2.30). With the start of the principate, this well-balanced order was substantially altered. Augustus's decision to rule the republican institutions with his personal superior moral authority (*auctoritas principis*) eventually led to the full identification of the authority and power in the person of the emperor.

The distinction between power and authority was in some sense reborn in the Middle Ages, when royal power was counterpointed by papal authority. The modern nation-state, on the other hand, fully identified authority with political power. This is one of the reasons why the distinction between authority and power is confusing in modern languages, including English. The modern political concept of separation of powers is, according to d'Ors, just a way to resolve the current confusion between authority and power.

Legitimacy vs. Legality

Based on the Roman distinction between *ius* (law) and *lex* (statute), and influenced by Max Weber's typology of domination, d'Ors argued that legality and legitimacy are foundational principles potentially at odds with any political constitution.³⁴ The Roman jurist Celsus (D. 1.1.1pr) defined *ius* as "the art of goodness and fairness" (*ius est ars boni et aequi*). The idea of *lex* is different from *ius*, but complementary to it. *Lex* comes from *legere*, which means the act of establishing a new ritually binding formula, whether private or public. In the public realm, the primary meaning of *lex* is a statute.

The legitimacy of *ius* lies in the tradition of the political community recognized by the citizens. Norms, rules, and standards are not properly a new creation of the legal order but an expression of the vitality of that tradition of ideas, usages, and customs. As *ius* constitutes a limit on *lex*, and tradition constitutes a limit on the current will of a people, legitimacy acts as the limit on positive laws (legality). Natural law is the primary source of legitimacy, since it emanates from human nature, which is common to all men, recognized by common sense and unalterable.³⁵

D'Ors replaced the French revolutionary triad of "liberty, equality, fraternity" with that of "responsibility, legitimacy, paternity," in accordance with natural law. Freedom is the essential presupposition of responsibility and not a consequence of it. Hence, the starting point of any well-founded political theory is responsibility and not freedom, and the starting point of any theory of law is the idea of "service"³⁶ and not the idea of "right" in the liberal sense of the word. The horizontal principle of equality opposes the vertical principle of legitimacy, which comes from the faithful observance of natural law and tradition. Finally, fraternity can be adequately understood only from the idea of paternity and family, which constitutes the source of legitimacy.

Dominium vs. Possessio

D'Ors believed that land should be distributed not in accordance with the principle of territorial sovereignty, based on the Roman idea of ownership, but with personal and social preferences, based on the Roman idea of possession.³⁷ The distinction between ownership (*dominium*) and possession (*possessio*) is the most important in Roman property law. While ownership represents

---

34   See Álvaro d'Ors, *Ensayos de teoría política* (Pamplona: Eunsa, 1979), 135–52.
35   See Álvaro d'Ors, *Derecho y sentido común. Siete lecciones de derecho natural como límite del derecho positivo*, 3rd ed. (Madrid: Civitas, 2001).
36   D'Ors, *Nueva introducción al estudio del Derecho*, § 62.
37   See Álvaro d'Ors, *La posesión del espacio* (Madrid: Civitas, 1998).

the supreme right over a thing (*res*), possession is the actual holding of and therefore effective control over it. Ownership is a matter of entitlement, while possession is a matter of fact and preferences.

The Roman doctrine of *dominium* became key for international law theorists, because the primary subject of international law, the nation-state, could not exist without a territory. The Bodinian theory of sovereignty was strongly associated with Roman law, especially by Alberico Gentili.[38] Under this doctrine, just as the Roman owner (*dominus*) had the right to use, enjoy, possess and dispose of things in the most absolute way, so also does each sovereign state have an absolute and exclusive right over its own territory, which would include a definite portion of land, territorial waters, and the atmosphere above.

One consequence of applying this Roman doctrine of *dominium* to the territory of the sovereign state was that the land of the earth, along with its territorial waters, was partitioned with the capacity to belong to different absolute owners (the nation-states) as independent entities. These nation-states, as absolute and total owners of their respective territories, would have the power to decide how they would be disposed of. D'Ors, however, argued that the space—conceived as the totality of the perceptible environment—and thus any specific portion of it, could not be owned, only possessed, owing to its inherent indivisibility and inability to be fully controlled. He proposed a new science, *geodieretics*,[39] to study the fair and rational sharing (not division) of space in accordance with individual and social preferences. The most crucial difference between geodieretics and geopolitics is that the latter presupposes the idea of the nation-state.

Conclusion

Álvaro d'Ors was a scholar of antiquity and an original legal and political thinker devoted to university life. He made relevant contributions to Roman law and developed an original political and legal theory based on Roman ideas and Catholic principles. He approached political theory from a legal perspective. He was a conservative on some political issues (e.g., political

---

38 On Gentili, see Benedict Kingsbury and Benjamin Straumann, eds., *The Roman Foundations of the Law of Nations: Alberico Gentili and the Justice of Empire* (Oxford: Oxford University Press, 2011). See also chapter 9 in this volume.

39 D'Ors, *La posesión del espacio*, 18–19.

consequences of the doctrine of the reign of God) and a reformist on others (e.g., the distribution of the land of the earth). His critique of the modern idea of the nation-state and his defense of natural law and common sense opened the doors to the concept of global law. D'Ors especially advocated for: (a) the recovery of the Roman distinction between moral authority (*auctoritas*) and constituted power (*potestas*); (b) the primacy of legitimacy over legality; and (c) building an international community of peoples based on individual and social preferences instead of territorial sovereign states. Although most of his writings remain unknown in the English-speaking world, he was a central figure in the development of the University of Navarra and mentored relevant scholars, especially in the Spanish-speaking world.

CHAPTER 14

JOHN WITTE, JR., ON CHRISTIANITY AND LAW

Introduction: John Witte as a Christian Jurist

John Witte's entire life and vast intellectual output have been marked by one fundamental fact: he is, first and foremost, profoundly Christian. Witte's Christianity determines his being, character, status as a leading scholar, and academic work. As a Christian, Witte knows and feels himself to be a child of God, made in God's image, regenerated by the waters of baptism and called upon to participate in this world in the royal, prophetic, and priestly mission of Christ through his work as a historian and jurist, his dedication to his family and friends, and his commitment to liberty and the communities in which he lives. This vocational, radical, and transformative Christian identity suffuses Witte's person and his work, which forms an unbreakable unity. Witte cannot be understood apart from his academic work, nor can the work be understood apart from the man, just as a self-portrait cannot be understood without the artist.[1]

---

1   See the two extensive interviews conducted with Witte on "Freedom and Order: Christianity, Human Rights, and Culture" (August 2019) and "Christianity and Law (May 2015)," in John Witte, Jr., *Faith, Freedom, Family: New Essays in Law and Religion*, ed. Norman Doe and Gary S. Hauk (Tübingen: Mohr Siebeck, 2021), 691–732. See also the introduction to that volume written by Norman Doe, pages 1–7, also published in Norman Doe, "Faith, Freedom, and Family: An Introduction to the Work of John Witte, Jr," *Ecclesiastical Law Journal* 24, no. 2 (2022): 175–91.

To speak of Christianity and law in John Witte—or of law and Christianity; the words can be reversed because their influence is reciprocal—is to speak of every one of the thousands of pages that Witte has written on the history of law, marriage, family, children, the relationship between law and religion, human rights, religious freedom, and political and social philosophy.[2] That is why this chapter, to a certain extent, is all-encompassing, because even when Witte approaches other topics and religions, he does so from the analogies and perspectives of Christianity. It is also his own Christianity that has prompted Witte's interest in and love for other religions, which he in no way sees as competitors but rather as sister faiths (especially Judaism and Islam) or as admirable treasures full of human and divine wisdom (Greco-Roman thought, Buddhism, Confucianism, Hinduism, and Indigenous traditions).[3] The fact is that every Christian is a *homo religiosus*, a being open to transcendence and in a permanent quest for truth, before being properly a *homo Christianus* by baptismal grace.

Witte's Christianity is anchored in the Protestant Reformed tradition and heavily influenced by the well-known Dutch pastor, theologian, and politician Abraham Kuyper (1837–1920),[4] who, within Calvinism, emphasized the sovereignty of Christ over salvation, the world, and indeed all of creation. Thus, words such as "creation," "sovereignty," and "covenant" echo with a special musicality in Witte's writings.[5] As Witte himself states:

---

2   See "Bibliography of John Witte, Jr., 1981–2021," in Witte, *Family Faith and Freedom*, 733–62.

3   See, for example, Don Browning, M. Christian Green, and John Witte, Jr., eds., *Sex, Marriage, and Family in World Religions* (New York: Columbia University Press, 2006); John Witte, Jr., and Johan D. van der Vyver, eds., *Religious Human Rights in Global Perspective*, 2 vols. (The Hague: Martinus Nijhoff, 1996); and John Witte, Jr., and M. Christian Green, eds., *Religion and Human Rights: An Introduction* (New York: Oxford University Press, 2012).

4   See John Witte, Jr., introduction, in Abraham Kuyper, *On Charity & Justice*, ed. Matthew J. Tuininga (Bellingham, Wash.: Lexham Press, 2022). See also Witte, "Abraham Kuyper on Family, Freedom and Fortune," in *Faith, Freedom, and Family*, 199–214.

5   See, especially, John Witte, Jr., *The Reformation of Rights: Law, Religion and Human Rights in Early Modern Calvinism* (Cambridge: Cambridge University Press, 2007); John Witte, Jr., *The Blessings of Liberty: Human Rights and Religious Freedom in the Western Legal Tradition* (Cambridge: Cambridge University Press, 2021); John Witte, Jr., *Church, State, and Family: Reconciling Traditional Teachings and Modern Liberties* (Cambridge:

Kuyperian thinking remains an important orientation for me. It provides a set of intellectual habits and methodological instincts—particularly the basic respect for scripture, tradition, reason, and experience; the emphasis on social pluralism and sphere sovereignty and the wariness of political, ecclesiastical, or any other kind of monism or monopoly in social organization and authority structuring; the appetite for covenant thinking; and the insistence that everyone operates with a basic worldview, a basic set of founding beliefs, values, or metaphors, even if they remain mostly implicit.[6]

Over time, Witte, without abandoning his roots, has opened up toward a more interdenominational and ecumenical Christianity and has broadened his capacity to admire and embrace not only the best of all the families of Protestantism but also many other aspects of Roman Catholicism and Orthodox Christianity.[7] This explains why both ecumenical and interreligious dialogues flow so naturally with him, because of his understanding of Christian unity. Witte feels a deep attraction for everything that is good within Christianity, as well as beyond it, and he bases this on a healthy regard for the creation order, common grace or general revelation, and natural law. This attraction to all denominations and traditions is not in any way a matter of eclecticism, nor of doctrinal relativism. His work exudes conviction and love of tradition but also openness to the future. He is also aware of the sins of the Christian tradition inside and outside the church.

Although Witte's Christianity is a precondition for understanding his intellectual production, it is not a sufficient condition. Witte's Christianity must be considered along with what we could call his "fundamental intuition." Behind all great scholars usually lie one or a few major intuitions that mark their intellectual trajectory. Intuitions in the strictest sense of the term are lights in our understanding acquired without recourse to conscious reasoning.[8]

Cambridge University Press, 2019); and John Witte, Jr., and Eliza Ellison, eds., *Covenant Marriage in Comparative Perspective* (Grand Rapids, Mich.: Eerdmans, 2005).

6   Witte, *Faith, Freedom, and Family*, 694.

7   See, for example, John Witte, Jr., and Frank S. Alexander, eds., *The Teachings of Modern Christianity on Law, Politics, and Human Nature,* 3 vols. (New York: Columbia University Press, 2005) (with separate Catholic, Protestant, and Orthodox volumes); John Witte, Jr., and Michael Bourdeaux, eds., *Proselytism and Orthodoxy in Russia: The New War for Souls* (Maryknoll, N.Y.: Orbis Books, 1999; reprint, 2013).

8   On intuition, see Jacques Maritain, *The Degrees of Knowledge*, trans. Gerald B.

Intuitions are sources of inspiration with which we fully identify because they show us an attractive path to follow. That is why sometimes intuitions are not expressed in literal words but in metaphors, which Witte is so fond of.[9] When these intuitions mature in the soul, they end up turning into intentions, and these, in turn, evolve into major research projects.

Intuitions are the point of departure and driving force of all serious academic research. We come back to them repeatedly throughout our academic lives, just as we return to our birthplace and family home. These intuitions may be original or shared, often reach beyond our own area of knowledge and, every now and then, shed new light on an old idea, opening up a new horizon for knowledge. The intuition of Friedrich Carl von Savigny (1779–1861) and his historical school of jurisprudence, for instance, was to underscore the connection between history and law and to understand the latter as a product of "the spirit of the people" (the *Volksgeist*).[10] Hans Kelsen (1881–1973) had the intuition to purify law of all extraneous political elements to develop a true science of law based on a fundamental norm (*Grundnorm*).[11] John Rawls (1921–2002), for his part, understood "justice as fairness," within the framework of a society of free citizens holding equal basic rights. Therein lay his fundamental intuition.[12]

The intuition that has marked Witte's academic life, which he shared with his mentor Harold J. Berman (1918–2007),[13] is that law and religion have more in common than it seems at first sight: that law has a religious dimension

---

Phelan, reprint ed. (Notre Dame, Ind.: University of Notre Dame Press, 2011 [1995]), esp. 263–70.

   9   See John Witte, Jr., "Law, Religion, and Metaphor," in *Faith, Family and Freedom*, 37–55, esp. 39.

   10   Friedrich Carl von Savigny, *Vom Beruf unserer Zeit für Gesetzgebung und Rechtswissenschaft* (Heidelberg: Mohr und Zimmer, 1814); in English, *Of the Vocation of Our Age for Legislation and Jurisprudence* (Kitchener, Ont.: Batoche, 1999); and Friedrich Carl von Savigny, *System des heutigen römischen Rechts*, 3rd ed. (Berlin: De Gruyter, 2019).

   11   Hans Kelsen, *Reine Rechtslehre. Einleitung in die rechtswissenschaftliche Problematik* (Leipzig: F. Deuticke, 1934; 2nd ed., 1960). The second edition was translated into English by Max Knight: Hans Kelsen, *Pure Theory of Law* (Berkeley: University of California Press, 1967).

   12   John Rawls, *A Theory of Justice*, rev. ed. (Cambridge, Mass.: The Belknap Press of Harvard University Press, 1999); John Rawls, *Justice as Fairness: A Restatement*, ed. Erin Kelly (Cambridge, Mass.: Harvard University Press, 2001).

   13   Harold J. Berman, *The Interaction of Law and Religion* (Nashville, Tenn.: Abingdon Press, 1974).

and religion a juridical one.¹⁴ Religion and law share origins, principles, values, rites, customs, rituals, formalities, methods, concepts, and hierarchies, and they depend on each other. When this interaction is culturally hidden or even manipulated, religion is diluted into ethereal spiritualism, and law is reduced to coercive regulatory imposition. But when law and religion are held in a healthy dialectical relation, each side is improved by the other, and society and its core institutions are best positioned to achieve justice, peace, order, and freedom.¹⁵

This fundamental intuition that Witte shares with Berman is very old, even pre-Christian, as Witte recognized already in his earliest published work, in 1981.¹⁶ His work has consisted, in part, in excavating this enduring intuition and applying it with new insights and overtones in a pluralistic and secularized society. To highlight this intuition's long lifespan, one only needs to point out that the Latin word for law (*ius*) is derived from the god Jupiter, or that the ancient Romans used the word *sacramentum* to refer to judicial processes¹⁷ many centuries before Christianity began using the same expression to refer to the signs instituted by Christ by which divine grace is dispensed to humans. During the Middle Ages, divine law was both religious

---

14   John Witte, Jr., ed., "A Conference on the Work of Harold J. Berman," *Emory Law Journal* 42, no. 2 (1993): 419–589.

15   See, especially, John Witte, Jr., and Christopher Manzer, introduction, in Harold J. Berman, *Law and Language: Effective Symbols of Community*, ed. John Witte, Jr. (Cambridge: Cambridge University Press, 2013), 1–35; John Witte, Jr., "Harold J. Berman," in *Great Christian Jurists in American History*, ed. Daniel L. Dreisbach and Mark A. Hall (Cambridge: Cambridge University Press, 2019), 230–44.

16   See Witte's very first publication reflecting this: "Hellenic Philosophy of Law: Essential Terms," in *The Association for the Advancement of Christian Scholarship: Academic Paper Series*, no. 1 (November 1981): 1–34. He has returned to Greco-Roman sources often in his work on the history of the family, human rights, and religious freedom. See, for example, John Witte, Jr., *From Sacrament to Contract: Religion, Marriage, and Law in the Western Tradition*, 2nd ed. (Louisville, Ky.: Westminster John Knox Press, 2012), 17–30; John Witte, Jr., *The Sins of the Fathers: The Law and Theology of Illegitimacy Reconsidered* (Cambridge: Cambridge University Press, 2009), 49–72; John Witte, Jr., *The Western Case for Monogamy over Polygamy* (Cambridge: Cambridge University Press, 2015), 101–43; and Witte, *The Blessings of Liberty*, 23–27.

17   See Franz Wieacker, *Römische Rechtsgeschichte*, vol. 1 (Munich: Beck, 1988), no. 15, 310–40, with bibliography. See also Olga Tellegen-Couperus, *Law and Religion in the Roman Republic* (Leiden: Brill, 2012); Rafael Domingo, *Roman Law: An Introduction* (London: Routledge, 2018).

and juridical, as Thomas Aquinas and the great glossators and commentators on canon, civil, and feudal law all confirmed.[18] In the modern age, Gottfried Wilhelm Leibniz (1646–1716) insisted on this connection because he saw law and religion as having a common structure, a common vocabulary, a common formalism, and a shared interest.[19] Yet it is true that this idea has been lost in our secular age and has needed to be relaunched in a different context.[20] Witte has devoted all his efforts to this endeavor since beginning his career at the Center for the Study of Law and Religion at Emory University after completing his legal studies at Harvard Law School with Berman, before both of them moved to Emory in 1985.

For forty years, Witte has been applying and developing this fundamental intuition about law and religion in various fields of legal history, in line with his personal convictions and abilities but above all with his deepest experiences: his attachment to Protestantism, his love for his family and friends, and his respect for human rights. Witte substantiates all of these commitments with the triad *faith, freedom, and family*.[21] By way of example, the happy yet sad experience of the life and death of his brother Ponkie (1964–1980), who was born out of a nonmarital relationship and adopted by Witte's parents, was the force that drove Witte to write one of his more beautiful and essential books in defense of children's rights: *The Sins of the Fathers*.[22] This is probably Witte's freshest and most creative book, or at least the one that reflects his innermost personality. It has so far been translated into Chinese (2011) and Korean (2022).

In this chapter, I focus on the relationship between Christianity and law as such, as part of a specific project that integrates and transcends these other, specific fields in which Witte has stood out as an author. Out of necessity, because Witte's work must be taken as a whole, I will refer to these other topics, adding cross references.[23]

---

[18] See John Witte, Jr., and Rafael Domingo, eds., *The Oxford Handbook of Christianity and Law* (Oxford: Oxford University Press, 2023), esp. chaps. 6–8.

[19] See Gottfried Wilhelm Leibniz, *The New Method of Learning and Teaching Jurisprudence*, trans. Carmelo Massimo de Iuliis (Clark, N.J.: Talbot Publishers, 2017), pt. 2, para. 4, p. 33.

[20] Charles Taylor, *A Secular Age* (Cambridge, Mass.: The Belknap Press of Harvard University Press, 2007).

[21] See Witte, *Faith, Freedom, and Family*.

[22] Witte, *The Sins of the Fathers*, xi–xiv.

[23] For a general view of Witte's contribution, see Doe, "Faith, Freedom, and Family: An Introduction to the Work of John Witte, Jr."

Relations between Christianity and Law as an International Project

Witte has become one of the most outstanding global scholars in studying the relationship between Christianity and law as a significant branch of the massive three-millennium-old tree of law and religion. This project is "interdisciplinary, interdenominational, and international," as Witte usually categorizes it,[24] and right now, more than five hundred Protestant, Roman Catholic, and Orthodox scholars (jurists, theologians, philosophers, historians, and sociologists) are contributing to it. Underlying this project is the idea that the relationship between Christianity and law is not merely accidental but inherent, with metahistorical significance and permanent value for the development of humanity.

A great lover of triads, Witte turns to them to explain the project. "I try to study this history with three "r's" in mind—retrieval of the religious sources and dimensions of law in the Western tradition, reconstruction of the most enduring teachings of the tradition for our day, and reengagement of a historically informed religious viewpoint with the hard legal issues that now confront church, state, and society."[25] Witte believes that Christians must regain a leading role in public life, not dogmatically or nostalgically but "fully equipped with the revitalized resources of the Bible and the Christian tradition in all their complexity and diversity."[26]

Just as you have to excavate before building a house, Witte has embarked on his project by initiating a deep international and interdisciplinary conversation on the mission of Christianity in the secular era, especially in the field of law, to ensure that the project is underpinned by solid foundations. At a time when many intellectuals advocate a public space free from religion, Witte argues that Christian values and principles should be democratically restored to public life. This is how he puts it:

> The easy notions of a public reason that brackets all comprehensive doctrines and that brackets especially religious discourse about fundamental matters of the state is giving way to a more realistic and

---

[24] John Witte, Jr., *God's Joust, God's Justice: Law and Religion in the Western Tradition* (Grand Rapids, Mich.: Eerdmans, 2006), x–xi, 4–9; unpublished lecture on receiving an honorary doctorate in theology at the University of Heidelberg, February 8, 2017.
[25] Witte, *God's Joust, God's Justice*, x.
[26] Witte, *God's Joust, God's Justice*, 464.

inclusive epistemology. Even early architects of religion-free public reason, like John Rawls and Jürgen Habermas, began to realize that a de-theologized discourse, a bleached and bland public reason, could not work in debates about such fundamental institutions as marriage and family life. Christians and persons of other faiths, as a consequence, are invited back into the conversation.[27]

To channel the project, Witte founded and began directing the Cambridge Studies in Law and Christianity Series in 2015, and to date, it includes more than thirty published books.[28] Witte is also a frequent contributor to other collections, such as the Routledge Series on Law and Religion, edited by Norman Doe,[29] and works from other important presses, including Oxford University Press and Mohr Siebeck, which have taken on individual titles. Some of this project's results and reviews have been published in the *Journal of Law and Religion*, published by Cambridge University Press for the Center for the Study of Law and Religion at Emory. Last but not least, a major instrument for disseminating this great project has been *The Canopy Forum*, an online publication published by the center. The McDonald Agape Foundation has been instrumental in launching this project, especially by funding scholarships for research fellowships and projects among bright young scholars who have been working with Witte and his fellow colleagues at the center.

Witte uses a broad definition of Christianity that encompasses the three major Catholic, Protestant, and Orthodox branches, as well as various denominations within them. To date, the Orthodox world is the most underrepresented in the law-and-religion field, thus fulfilling the old Latin adage that law indeed comes from the West, just as light comes from the East: *ex Oriente, lux; ex Occidente, ius*.[30] Witte has worked hard to include Orthodox voices alongside other Christian views in his projects.

---

27 John Witte, Jr., "Christianity and Law: Interview, May 2015," in *Faith, Freedom, and Family*, 726.

28 Information available at https://www.cambridge.org/core/series/law-and-christianity/6D77992447E6BD14E748AE05E137D92B. https://www.cambridge.org/core/series/law-and-christianity/6D77992447E6BD14E748AE05E137D92B

29 Information available at https://www.routledge.com/Law-and-Religion/book-series/LAWRELIG. Of the twenty-two volumes in this series, nine have been directed or commissioned by Witte.

30 See Rafael Domingo, *Ex Roma ius* (Cizur Menor: Thomson Reuters Aranzadi, 2005).

As could not be otherwise in a project of this quality and ambition, Witte refers to law in its broadest sense, which is also the one that best captures its meaning. Law is a regulatory social order of justice, powers, rights, and freedoms, exercised and maintained by institutions that exercise authority individually or collectively, and that affect local, national, international, and global private and public human relations.

The key to understanding the relationship between Christianity and law is that law precedes Christianity in time, but Christianity elevates the very idea of law to a new dimension, which is love. Christianity assumed and adopted Jewish and Roman law but effected a profound spiritualization of law: *ius Evangelio praecedit, Evangelium autem ius elevat* (law precedes the Gospel, but the Gospel elevates law). In the same way that light blinds and harms us when we look too closely, however, so too the relationship between law and Christianity can be blinding when religion comes too close to law, or when law tries to conquer the religious space illegitimately, contravening Christ's own mandate: "Give therefore to Caesar the things that are Caesar's and to God the things that are God's" (Matt 22:21; Mark 12:17; Luke 20:24).[31]

Witte has approached this massive project in law and Christianity from three different perspectives: one that we could call merely relational, another biographical, and a third jurisprudential.[32] Though operating in different stages of his work, these different perspectives coincide in time and are cumulative and mutually supportive. They are not closed but rather interdependent perspectives, as exemplified by the works coedited by Witte—*Christianity and Family Law* (2017), which takes a biographical approach, and *Christianity and Global Law* (2020), which addresses both the relational and biographical perspectives.[33]

The Relational Perspective

From the relational perspective, Witte has sought to map the historical, conceptual, categorical, and dogmatic ties between Christianity and law, both as ideas and in their most varied institutional forms and ramifications. That is

---

31   See Rafael Domingo, *God and the Secular Legal System* (Cambridge: Cambridge University Press, 2016).

32   John Witte, Jr., "What Christianity Offers to the World of Law," in *Faith, Freedom, and Family*, 57–66.

33   John Witte, Jr., and Gary S. Hauk, eds., *Christianity and Family Law: An Introduction* (Cambridge: Cambridge University Press, 2017); Rafael Domingo and John Witte, Jr., eds., *Christianity and Global Law* (London: Routledge, 2020).

why the titles of books written from this relational perspective usually include the word "Christianity" (or some denominational version of it) followed by the conjunction "and."

This relational perspective was firmly consolidated with the publication of his early book on *Christianity and Democracy in Global Context* (1993), a collection of speeches given by renowned speakers (Desmond M. Tutu, Harold Berman, Richard John Neuhaus, Bryan Hehir, and Jean Bethke Elshtain, among others) at a four-day international conference convened by the Emory center in 1991.[34] With a foreword by former U.S. president Jimmy Carter, who has maintained academic solid ties with Emory University for four decades, the book examines Christianity's positive and negative influences in shaping and consolidating democracies. The conclusion one draws from reading it, in line with Jacques Maritain's stance, is that democracy was morally and legally enhanced when it became symbiotically related to Christianity.[35]

Early modern Protestantism first embraced the democratic ideal; centuries later, modern Roman Catholicism followed suit, especially with the Second Vatican Council, but above all, with John Paul II, who applauded the idea of civic participation and collaboration and peaceful succession among rulers.[36] On the other hand, the embrace of democratic ideals in Orthodox Christianity seems to be less widespread, and in general, Orthodox-majority countries have lagged behind in the process of democratic transformation, although the direction of causality between teaching and political circumstances is difficult to establish.

Witte's analysis of the relational perspective of law and Christianity matured and gained new momentum with the publication of his monographs on *Law and Protestantism: The Legal Teachings of the Lutheran Reformation* (2002), *Sex, Marriage, and Family in John Calvin's Geneva* (2006), and *The Reformation of Rights: Law, Religion, and Human Rights in Early Modern Calvinism* (2007). These volumes zeroed in on how classic Protestantism related to law and what contributions the Reformation movements made to transforming public, private, penal, and procedural law and legal theory in European lands and their colonies.

---

34 John Witte, Jr., ed., *Christianity and Democracy in Global Context* (Boulder, Colo.: Westview Press, 1993; London: Routledge, 2018).

35 See Jacques Maritain, *Christianity and Democracy* (San Francisco: Ignatius Press, 2012); Jacques Maritain, *The Rights of Man and the Natural Law* (San Francisco: Ignatius Press, 1986; reprint, 2011).

36 See John Paul II, Encyclical Letter *Centesimus annus* (May 1, 1991), no. 46.

While the relationship between Protestantism and law has continued to occupy him as a scholar,[37] Witte took a much broader, pan-Christian, and interdisciplinary view in *Christianity and Law: An Introduction* (2008), a volume coedited with his colleague and friend Frank Alexander. This marked the start of what we could call his expansion phase. In this volume, prestigious scholars from the fields of law, history, philosophy, and theology—including Luke Timothy Johnson, Brian Tierny, R. H. Helmholz, Don S. Browing, Michael J. Perry, David Novak, David Little, and Norman Doe, among others—analyzed the connections between law and Christianity in the different branches of legal knowledge, ranging from canon and natural law to contract, criminal, and procedural law. This volume constituted Witte's roadmap for the coming years, as he eventually turned each chapter of the book into a new volume that further studied the relationship between Christianity and law in each specific area of law. Witte personally oversaw his areas of expertise and commissioned other experts to edit the remaining volumes.[38]

First, Witte edited a volume on *Christianity and Human Rights* (2010), again with Frank Alexander. South African Archbishop Desmond Tutu, whose opposition to apartheid in his country resulted in his receiving the Nobel Peace Prize in 1984, wrote the preface. "I can testify that our own struggle for justice, peace, and equity would have floundered badly had we not been inspired by our Christian faith and assured of the ultimate victory of goodness and truth, compassion and love against their ghastly counterparts," Tutu declared.[39] Human rights are not a Christian invention nor a creation of the Enlightenment. Instead, they derive from a combination of Jewish, Greek,

---

37   See, for example, John Witte, Jr., and Amy Wheeler, eds., *The Reformation of the Church and the World* (Louisville, Ky.: Westminster John Knox Press, 2017); forthcoming volumes, *Sex, Marriage, and Family in John Calvin's Geneva 2: The Christian Household* and *A New Reformation of Rights: Calvinist Contributions to Modern Human Rights*.

38   See, for example, Norman Doe, ed., *Christianity and Natural Law: An Introduction* (Cambridge: Cambridge University Press, 2017); Daniel Crane and Samuel Gregg, eds., *Christianity and Market Regulation: An Introduction* (Cambridge: Cambridge University Press, 2021); Jeffrey B. Hammond and Helen M. Alvaré, eds., *Christianity and the Laws of Conscience: An Introduction* (Cambridge: Cambridge University Press, 2021); and Pamela Slotte and John D. Haskell, eds., *Christianity and International Law: An Introduction* (Cambridge: Cambridge University Press, 2021).

39   Desmond M. Tutu, "The First Word: To Be Human Is to Be Free," in *Christianity and Human Rights: An Introduction*, ed. John Witte, Jr., and Frank S. Alexander (Cambridge: Cambridge University Press), 1–7, at 6.

and Roman teachings with the new and radical teachings of Christ based on the love of every human being with the same love of God. Christianity has illuminated the concepts of dignity, equality, freedom, compassion, and democracy that underlie the modern human rights paradigm and has deepened them with its insights into sanctity and grace.

In 2017, Witte and his friend and colleague Gary Hauk coedited the study on *Christianity and Family Law*,[40] which biographically analyzes the contribution of Christian thinkers from Saint Paul to John Paul II in shaping the doctrine and law of marriage and the family. It is undoubtedly one of the volumes where the inseparable unity between law and Christianity in the West is most evident, as Witte has shown in several other monographs, not least his *Sins of the Fathers* (2009), *From Sacrament to Contract* (1999; 2nd. ed. 2012), and *Church, State, and Family* (2019). Three years later, in 2020, Witte published two more coedited volumes—one with Mark Hill, Norman Doe, and Dick Helmholz on the relationship between Christianity and criminal law,[41] and the other with me on Christianity and global law, understood as a law beyond international law, where state interest and cooperation between states give way to a deeper, fuller human solidarity.[42] Several other volumes in this series of introductions to Christianity and law are in print, most of them with forewords or chapters by Witte, engaging Christianity and freedom, natural law, justice and agape, private law, church law, international law, the laws of conscience, market regulation, migration, and taxation.[43] Forthcoming in this series are new studies on Christianity and the law of alternative dispute resolution, animal law, capital punishment, child law, constitutional law, disability law, education law, evidence law, environmental law, health law, intellectual property law, labor and employment law, legal ethics, poor law, and social-welfare law.

Once the project had expanded and been applied to various fields of law, Witte decided to embark on a major review, recapping the best of Christianity's influence on law in a new, more comprehensive global work, *The*

---

[40] Witte and Hauk, *Christianity and Family Law*.

[41] Mark Hill, Norman Doe, R. H. Helmholz, and John Witte, Jr., eds., *Christianity and Criminal Law* (London: Routledge, 2020).

[42] See Domingo and Witte, *Christianity and Global Law*. On the idea of global law, see Rafael Domingo, *The New Global Law* (Cambridge: Cambridge University Press, 2010).

[43] See list of introductions in print and production in Witte, "What Christianity Offers to the World of Law," in Witte, *Faith, Freedom, and Family*, 57–66.

Oxford Handbook of Christianity and Law (2023).⁴⁴ In this collection, which he and I coedited, more than sixty experts from five continents address the relationship between Christianity and law from a historical, theological, juridical, and philosophical perspective. The handbook sums up Witte's four decades of work on this subject and, at the same time, is a new roadmap for studying this fertile relationship of Christianity of law historically and in our current age of secularization and globalization. Witte has come back to the ground he excavated more than thirty years ago and started work on a great building with solid foundations. There is still a long way to go, however.

Witte is also working on a multiyear project with his German colleague, the theologian Michael Welker, on the roles of religion, the market, family, health care, the military, and other institutions in character building—a project featuring, among other things, the civic and educational function of law.⁴⁵ Law under justice distills moral values, thus contributing to the moralization of modern liberal societies. Hence the need to draw up a basic civil morality for modern liberal societies and to analyze the appropriate instruments, mechanisms, and procedures for cultivating and enforcing morality.

The Biographical Perspective: The Idea of the Christian Jurist

The second perspective from which Witte analyzes the relationship between Christianity and law is biographical. This is no longer just a matter of putting together two ideas and analyzing similarities, differences, and reciprocal influences and connections throughout history but also of ascertaining how Christianity and law are forged and intertwined in the minds and hearts of specific Christian jurists, philosophers, and theologians who, with their writings and actions, have guided law along the paths of justice. In essence, this biographical perspective is a projection of Witte's own experience as a Christian jurist. Christianity is not a passing fashion but instead touches upon an essential part of every person's being. *Ius ex persona oritur*, we could say in the manner of the classics: "law comes from the person."⁴⁶

---

44   Witte and Domingo, *The Oxford Handbook of Christianity and Law*.
45   See, for example, John Witte, Jr., and Michael Welker, eds., *The Impact of the Law on Character Formation, Ethical Education, and the Communication of Values in Late Modern Pluralistic Societies* (Leipzig: Evangelische Verlagsanstalt, 2021).
46   See Domingo, *The New Global Law*, xvi.

Witte knows better than anyone that Martin Luther had condemned jurists as "bad Christians" (*Juristen böse Christen!*[47]), yet Witte's own experience as a Christian jurist is much more decisive than the impulsive reformer's whimsical cry. On this question, Witte prefers to side with Jimmy Carter, who, when asked about this question, answered, "It is a matter of what we Christians are going to do about democracy" and its law.[48] Indeed, the relationship between Christianity and law has a strong biographical content that cannot be ignored.

The category of Christian jurist encompasses any Christians who have devoted themselves to the cause of justice in its broadest sense and have had a significant impact on law and the legal system. Being a Christian jurist does not necessarily entail having a law degree or having practiced law; instead, it involves making an essential contribution to law that has enlightened legal systems and political communities with Christian values. John Paul II, for example, never studied law. Even so, during his lifetime, he was called "the Pope of human rights" and was awarded an honorary doctorate in law by the University of La Sapienza.[49] Something similar can be said of the philosopher Jacques Maritain, whose contribution to the Universal Declaration of Human Rights makes him worthy of the title of Christian jurist.[50] One could cite many more such examples: Isidore of Seville, Thomas Aquinas, Catherine of Siena, John Calvin, Martin Luther King, Jr., Óscar Romero, and many others.

This biographical approach is based on the empirical fact that specific human beings, flesh and blood, are behind the significant developments and reforms of law, as is also the case in empirical science. Just as the history of the theory of relativity would not have begun in 1905 without the Swiss patent-office clerk Albert Einstein, so the concept of constitutional courts would not have taken hold in Western Europe in the 1920s without the Austrian-American jurist Hans Kelsen.

---

[47] The phrase was popularized before Luther, though it is attributed to him. See Michael Stolleis, *Juristenbeschimpfung, oder, "Juristen—böse Christen,"* in *Politik—Bildung—Religion. Hans Maier zum 65. Geburtstag*, ed. Theo Stammen et al. (Paderborn: Schöningh, 1996), 163–70.

[48] Jimmy Carter, foreword, in Witte, *Christianity and Democracy,* xv.

[49] See chapter 12 in this volume and Rafael Domingo, "Karol Józef Wojtyła, Pope John Paul II (1920–2005)," in *Law and Christianity in Poland: The Work of Great Jurists,* ed. Franciszek Longchamps de Bérier and Rafael Domingo (London: Routledge, 2022), 247–62.

[50] William Sweet, "Jacques Maritain," in *Great Christian Jurists in French History*, ed. Olivier Descamps and Rafael Domingo (Cambridge: Cambridge University Press, 2019), 387–403.

The biographical approach has great potential for studying law and legal history because it shows both the complexity and ambiguity and even the accidental nature of historical and modern legal systems. What lies behind legal documents and rules are facts and, beyond them, people. The who of the person always prevails over the what and the how. To the extent that critical legal actors are Christians, the law and legal systems that they shape are, of necessity, imbued and permeated with their Christian values and beliefs. The reason is that legal systems are simultaneously a whole in themselves and thus, to a degree, self-sufficient, but they also a part of and thus interdependent with other parts of society. Christian jurists participate not only in legal institutions and the church but also in many other institutions in their societies, thus carrying their faith into those other systems.

John Witte has used this biographical approach to the study of law and Christianity throughout his many monographs on the history of family law, religious freedom, and human rights. He has returned again and again to retrieve and reconstruct the work of many of the "legal titans" of the Christian tradition, as he calls them—especially Lactantius, Augustine, and Chrysostom among the church fathers; Gratian, Lombard, and Aquinas in the Middle Ages; Luther, Melanchthon, Calvin, Beza, Althusius, Cranmer, Hooker, and Vitoria in the Reformation era; Grotius, Coke, Selden, Blackstone, Adams, Madison, Jefferson, and Story among the early moderns; and Kuyper, Dooyeweerd, Maritain, Brunner, King, Niebuhr, and their modern progeny. One of Witte's strengths has been to read these historical figures in and on their own terms and in their own contexts, but then to extract enduring lessons from their writings for the ongoing legal challenges of the tradition and of our day.

In 2005, Witte began to extend this biographical approach with an eye to eventually create a multivolume and multiauthored series on *Great Christian Jurists in World History*. He began with the publication of *The Teachings of Modern Christianity on Law, Politics, and Human Nature*, in which—again in collaboration with Frank Alexander—he brought together a series of outstanding essays on central modern Roman Catholic, Protestant, and Orthodox Christian figures in the world of the relationship between Christianity and law.[51] But it was really in 2015, with the appearance of the *Cambridge Studies in Law and Christianity Series*, that Witte expanded this project, commissioning

---

51   Witte and Alexander, eds., *The Teachings of Modern Christianity on Law, Politics, and Human Nature*, 3 vols.

volumes from legal historians around the world, which he has published in this Cambridge series (on the first millennium, England, Spain, France, the Netherlands, and the United States), in Norman Doe's Law and Religion Series with Routledge (on Italy, the Nordic countries, Russia, Latin America, and Poland), and with Mohr Siebeck (on Germany) and Federation Press (on Australia).[52] In this biographical project, Witte has written specific chapters on jurists (Johann Oldendorp, John Calvin, Johannnes Althusius, John Selden, Abraham Kuyper, and Harold Berman)[53] and coedited the book on German jurists in collaboration with Matthias Schmoeckel,[54] but above all, he set up editorial teams, collected financial support, coordinated with publishing houses, and written forewords (for the Polish, Russian, Latin American, and Italian volumes).

Such an extensive project, in which the methodology has been steadily polished with experience and experimentation and which involves so many different people, has inevitably produced mixed results. In each volume, one can criticize whether a particular jurist deserves the status of Christian in the strict sense, even whether the person chosen deserves the status of jurist. There are also notable absences; for example, the English jurists should have included Thomas More. However, with ever more tremendous success, most legal historians have risen and responded to this idea of reappraising the biographical perspective to legal history and appreciating the expansive category of a "Christian jurist."

The fact that the project is divided into geographical areas and nations, rather than chronologically, apart from the volume on the first millennium, is also open to criticism. But Witte has mapped the path as he has gone along. Instead of outlining in advance a perfect methodology, which does not exist, and then applying it, what he has done is to explore the issues, analyze them, and gradually polish the methodology over time. Law, like cooking, entails a lot of artistry, which can only be learned by practicing. The highly visible result is manifest and has served to let outsiders know what is happening with law and Christianity in each country studied. The substantial language barriers and the local nature of law are two further real obstacles that only a global project like this one can overcome. While the project has prompted strong

---

52   See list in Witte, *Faith, Freedom and Family*, 62–64.
53   See reprinted collection in Witte, *Faith, Family, and Freedom*, 119–228.
54   Mathias Schmoeckel and John Witte, Jr., eds., *Great Christian Jurists in German History* (Tübingen: Mohr Siebeck, 2020).

criticism from conventional legal historians, this is outweighed by the amount of support it enjoys and the promise it holds as it opens ever more expansive frontiers of law and Christianity.[55]

The Jurisprudential Perspective: Toward a Christian Jurisprudence

The third perspective from which Witte addresses the relationship between Christianity and law endeavors to build a general jurisprudential framework, based on Christian values, for a pluralistic society. Following in the footsteps of his mentor, Harold Berman, who at the end of his academic career devised an "integrative jurisprudence," Witte is seeking theoretically to integrate and harmonize the Christianity-law relationship by creating a narrative suitable for a pluralistic, post-Christian society.[56] No modern jurist has trodden this path yet, but, if I may say so, Witte's subconscious has already prompted him to work on it. One only has to read the reflective conclusions of his latest historical books—reflections that are ever more extensive, ever more theoretical, and transcending the main historical topic of the book.[57] One glimpses a change of focus in Witte's intellectual project—from "retrieval" of the relationships of Christianity and law and the teachings of great Christian jurists to "reconstruction" of a Christian jurisprudence for our modern day.

Witte is a man of synthesis, an intellectual cartographer, adept at generating new understandable paradigms. He knows how to create narratives and convincingly explain religious and, in particular, Christian phenomena to anyone familiar with the world of the transcendent. He demonstrated this with his studies on Protestantism and law, as well as his histories of marriage, family, children, religion, human rights, and religious freedom. He is now on

---

55   See, for example, Christoph J. H. Meyer, "Was von christlichem Recht und Juristenleben übrigblieb," review of Orazio Condoerlli and Rafael Domingo, eds., *Law and the Christian Tradition in Italy* (2020), in *Rechtsgeschichte—Legal History. Zeitschrift des Max-Planck-Instituts für Rechtsgeschichte und Rechtstheorie* 29 (2021): 302–6. For a very positive approach, however, see Kyle C. Lincoln, review of Rafael Domingo and Javier Martínez-Torrón, eds., *Great Christian Jurists in Spanish History* (2018), in *Bulletin of Medieval Canon Law* 38 (2021): 452–57.

56   John Witte, Jr., "Law and Religion: The Challenges of Christian Jurisprudence," *St. Thomas Law Journal* 2 (2005): 439–52; "The Integrative Christian Jurisprudence of Harold Berman," in Witte, *Faith, Freedom, and Family*, 215–28.

57   See, for example, Witte, *The Blessings of Liberty*, 290–303.

a relentless quest for a new paradigm between faith and law, between Gospel and culture in the context of a pluralistic and highly secularized society. After reflecting and heading such a large group of people for so many years, Witte now intends to offer the world a more personal and all-encompassing theoretical reflection on the relationship between law and Christianity. He does not aspire to be a theologian or a philosopher, which he is not, but rather a legal theorist of the relationship between Christianity and law in its broadest sense within the framework of the relationship between religions and law.

Witte judges that the necessary protection of nonbelievers and secular thought is not a sufficient reason to erect a Berlin Wall between law and religion, particularly between Christianity and law, as if their relationship were a taboo subject. Any exclusion of religion from the public sphere will always be artificial, because law has an unavoidable religious dimension. In the West, this religious dimension is mainly Judeo-Christian. It is not surprising that, in his acceptance speech upon receiving an honorary doctorate in theology from the University of Heidelberg, Witte used the metaphor of the cathedral to refer to law: "The law is like a massive medieval cathedral, always under construction, always in need of new construction. It stands at the center of the city, at the center of matters spiritual and temporal, at the center of everyone's life."[58] If, up to now, Witte has been occupied, as a historian of law, with telling us the story of how this cathedral was built, it now seems that he wants to participate in its design and construction, putting his best talents at its service.

As Witte is so fond of triads,[59] some of which I have already mentioned, I will turn to them in this initial phase of this new, more theoretical perspective to encourage Witte to continue along this path. In addition to the triads he has already generated, I offer four more that I think capture Witte's thinking, which I gladly submit for consideration and critique.

Christianity, Community, Culture

Christianity provides a unique metadimensional Trinitarian paradigm for the law that illuminates all the legal aspects from within and without. If the revelation of God as Father, Son, and Holy Spirit (Matthew 28:19) is the central

---

58 Witte, lecture on receipt of honorary doctorate; "Afterword: The Cathedral of the Law," in *God's Joust, God's Justice*, 466–67.
59 On Witte's triads, see Gary S. Hauk, foreword, in Witte, *Faith, Freedom, and Family*, xix.

mystery of Christian faith and the center of the whole of reality, this mystery must enlighten all human existence and dimensions, including the legal realm.

The doctrine of the Trinity understands God relationally. The Triune God is certainly a unique and absolute unity, the Absolute One, whose three divine persons manifest the pure communication of love, the most profound depths of free self-giving. Each divine person freely gives the plenitude of love to others, glorifying them.[60] This revealed truth serves to illuminate a united and diverse political community; the greater the diversity, the greater the unity, and the greater the unity, the greater the diversity. This sense of communal inclusion, which does not exclude other communities but rather affirms that all are part of a global community, calls for cultural change. Our Western secularized culture has often promoted fragmentation, territorialization, and exclusionary nationalism.

Creation, Covenant, Conscience

Creation occupies a central place in Witte's thought. It is a manifestation of God's infinite love, which permeates the entire universe, most particularly the human being, explicitly made in God's image and likeness (Gen 1:27). Creation establishes a covenant between God and humankind over the created order. A covenant institutes a more solid and permanent framework than a contract, because the covenant includes the natural order of creation and assumes a conceptual framework of truths that cannot be altered by mere human consent. God does not enter into contracts, but God does enter into covenants. Moreover, every human contract that respects the natural order and puts God as a witness becomes a covenant (e.g., marriage). Conscience is a divine light within human beings that helps them to interpret God's will in every covenant.[61] This creation-covenant-conscience triad clashes with a world vision based on mere chance without creation, where human liberty is reduced to simple freedom of choice without respecting the natural order, and the conscience is mistaken for personal conviction without recognition of prior truths.

---

60   See John Witte, Jr., "Law, Religion, and Metaphor," in *Faith, Freedom, and Family*, 37–55, esp. 53–55.

61   John Witte, Jr., "Covenant Liberty in Puritan New England," in *Jurisprudenz, Politische Theorie und Politische Theologie*, ed. Frederick S. Carney, Heinz Schilling, and Dieter Wyduckel (Berlin: Duncker & Humblot, 2004), 169–89.

Law, Liberty, Love

Christianity has elevated law, liberty, and love to a new divine order. Law cannot be reduced to pure legalism because justice reaches all dimensions of reality and participates in the same created order (*ius divinum*). Liberty is a gift of God to fulfill our obligations to God, to ourselves, to others, and to the universe as such. It is the necessary, though not sufficient, condition for fully loving God and, in God, all creatures and the created universe. Law's mission is to protect this liberty as one of the most precious divine gifts,[62] as it is to protect and impart justice: without justice there is no love, and love perfects justice by imbuing it with charity. This triad of love, liberty, and law directly opposes the triad that reduces law to legalism, freedom to arbitrariness, and love to personal satisfaction.

Sovereignty, Society, Solidarity

Witte employs a broad concept of sovereignty, inherited from Kuyper, that can be applied to God, to the nation-state, to the smaller political community, and to all institutions (family, church, school, business) and power structures that order society according to the principles of liberty and justice. Witte conceives society as a network of relationships and institutions united by the bonds of cooperation and solidarity, a solidarity born of the sharing of all human beings in the one and only image of a Triune God. This law of human solidarity, without excluding the rich variety of persons, cultures, and peoples, assures us that all men and women are truly brothers and sisters.

Evaluation and Impact

As I have indicated, Witte's work on Christianity and law reflects his own life—a deeply Christian man, educated in the Protestant Reformed tradition, in love with history and law and committed to the challenges of his time. Following the example of his mentor, Harold Berman, Witte has placed his faith at the service of the ideals of justice and law. Witte is a Christian jurist who has devoted himself primarily to studying the relationship between law and religion from a historical perspective. He has done so primarily in the area of the influence of Protestantism, especially in the early stages of its

---

62   Witte, *The Blessings of Liberty*, 290–303.

first reformers—and, by extension, in the areas of human rights, religious freedom, and marriage and the family, which he has traced from classical and biblical sources to the latest legal developments.

Over time, Witte has spearheaded a bold and far-reaching project that aims to encompass the relationship between law and Christianity as such, in which more than five hundred scholars from six continents are collaborating, making him one of the leading scholars in the field. He is working on this contribution from three perspectives: a relational one, a biographical one, and a jurisprudential one. Despite having already borne much fruit, the project still requires greater methodological clarity and maturity. Witte is an instinctual and experimental thinker; he maps the scholarly and methodological path as he goes along, letting his sources and intuitions guide and inspire him. He still needs to produce an extensive programmatic series of publications that create a paradigm for the study of the relationship between Christianity and law in modern pluralistic societies. His article titled "What Christianity Offers to the World of Law" is only a first draft of that more enormous effort.[63] Witte knows this and is working on it. The theoretical and jurisprudential part is fundamental to consolidating and completing his life-long project. This theoretical part could be based on the four alliterative triads that I now suggest, inspired by Witte's works: (a) Christianity, community, culture; (b) creation, covenant, conscience; (c) law, liberty, love; and (d) sovereignty, society, solidarity.

---

63 Witte, *Faith, Freedom, and Family*, 57–66.

CONCLUSION

I summarize below some of the conclusions I have reached in this volume.

1. Profound Connectivity between Law and Spirituality

The connection between spirituality and law is real because of the holistic character of spirituality, which provides secular legal systems a broader paradigm and a deeper purpose, preventing immoderate legalism. The legal triad of *justice, agreement, and right* is connected to the spiritual triad of *love, communion, and gift*. Justice is a manifestation of love, an agreement is an expression of communion, and a right is a gift. The more intense the relationship between the two triads, the more influential the spiritualization of law.

Law and, indirectly, legal systems evolve through spiritualization by prioritizing the human person, supporting dematerialization, inspiring the reduction of coercion, stimulating democracy and participation, encouraging solidarity and cohesion, and fostering respect for ethics and human rights. These expressions are just examples, since spiritualization affects law as a whole, and therefore its influence encompasses all legal activities and development. This spiritual influence on law can be only partially measured scientifically because love (and spirituality is a question of love) overcomes the scientific method and the very idea of social sciences.

2. Restoring the Dialogue between Theology and Jurisprudence

Legal scholars and theologians should discover the fittingness of restoring the dialogue between theology and jurisprudence in the era of secularization. From a secular point of view, it is suitable for legal thinkers and philosophers to be familiar with theology, just as an architect should be familiar with the type of soil on which to build a structure. From a theological point of view, it is also appropriate for theologians to be familiar with the secular-legal, just as it is suitable for an environmental soil scientist to know the type of structures built on a landscape. Interactions, synergies, and communication between sciences are essential in developing a scientist's knowledge.

Modern secular systems have been shaped and structured to be profoundly theological because jurisprudence, in some ways, is a distillation of religion. Taking advantage of the connections and analogies between theology and jurisprudence is consistent with the principles of secular legal systems, but a legal theology, in the sense of a legal doctrine that emanates directly from theology as a legal dogma, would contravene the essence of the secular legal system and should not be recognized by secular legal systems.

3. Foundational Significance of the Idea of God

A legal system enlightened by God is more understandable and human than a legal system that does not consider God, because God illuminates secular legal systems by strengthening the commitment to respecting the universe and enhancing and embellishing the ideas of the human person, dignity, equality, moral freedom and responsibility, solidarity, and human rights. All of these ideas are at the heart of secular legal systems. All of them can be defended and protected without any reference to God, but the existence of a personal God bolsters these crucial ideas.

For instance, the theistic approach to dignity provides an objective validity to the general idea of dignity that no agnostic or atheistic approach can match. Without a theistic approach, dignity can be reduced to a substantial subjective self, a pure capacity for rational autonomy, mere self-respect as a necessary condition for living well and taking seriously moral responsibilities, or a simple right to be recognized as a legal person. In the worst case, it can be transformed into a formal and empty concept.

4. Spirit of God and Spirit of the Law

The triad of body, soul, and spirit is instrumental to understanding the deepest internal and external connections of legal systems. Like the human being, the law is not only corporeal but also spiritual in character, and the spirit of the law is essentially communicative and solidary, like the Spirit of God. The spirit of the law might influence legal systems by illumination, attraction, and other modalities of causality or by moral authority, but not by coercive power. The spirit of the law operates within the secular legal system as a value, a source of transcendent wisdom and knowledge. It is an expression of the priority of the spirit over the body, and the communion of the human spirit with the Spirit of God. By transcending legality (the body of laws), spiritualized law protects secular legal systems from the virus of legalism.

The body-soul-spirit metaphor encourages us to see constitutions as living documents and legal systems as living entities—to recognize the goodness of an emerging global law founded on solidarity and not the self-interest of nation-states, and to seek reconciliation between law and love, and a reasonable interaction between human and divine law. In short, the body-soul-spirit metaphor offers a powerful antidote to legal reductionism.

5. The Image of God and the Law

The doctrine of the image of God privileges the centrality of the human person in secular legal systems. It is fundamentally personal, not only in the sense that each human being, male or female, is made in the image of God (Genesis 1:27) but also in the sense that the image is of an incarnated divine person, Christ, and ultimately the image of a personal triune and loving God. The plural pronoun used in the Genesis narrative ("Let us make humankind in our image after our likeness") emphasizes this Trinitarian context. Each person is substantially a mirror of God, reflecting their personal relationship with God. In other words, the relationship of representation and the resemblance to God are constitutive of, and inseparable from, the human being.

6. Legal Protection of Religion

The ultimate justification for legally protecting religion lies in the protection of suprarationality. Suprarationality cannot be expressed according to the requirements of legal discourse, since the language of suprarationality is fully understood only within the life of a religious community. It can, however, be protected by the law. Suprarationality constitutes an extrinsic constitutional limit of the secular legal system and has at least three important legal consequences: (a) suprarational acts in the strictest sense (pursuits of the suprarational) should not be validated as legal acts; (b) suprarational argumentation should not be used in legal discourse; and (c) the secular legal system cannot regulate the essentials of any religious community.

7. The Right to Religious Freedom Is a First-Class Right

The right to religious freedom operates in the three dimensions of the human person. In the individual dimension (along with freedom of conscience), it protects the human person in their personal search for God, the divine, and the truth against any constraint by political authorities. In the social dimension, the right to religious freedom allows individual persons to live their faith in a community and protects political communities against religious and secularist fundamentalisms as rejections of legitimate pluralism. Finally, in the transcendent dimension, the right to religious freedom operates by protecting religion as such as a basic good and by opening the door to transcendent truths.

Because freedom of religion is the inclusive patrimony of both religious believers and nonbelievers, it fully protects from religion those who choose to have nothing to do with it, just as it protects the religious from those who wish to use constructions of secularism that unduly restrict religious people and their communities from appropriate public involvements.

8. Transcendent Global Law

Sacred natural law theories are strongly oriented to the individual because every person has been created in the image of God. Consequently, they support the priority of the person in the international legal realm. As sacred natural law theories are not mandatory but optional, respect individual moral conscience, and acknowledge the obligatory force of positive law, they are valid for developing a universal (not compulsory), international, metalegal framework that illuminates positive law (transcendent global law).

Transcendent global law might transform a self-interest-oriented international community of nation-states into a value-oriented global human community of image-of-God bearers. In this process, not only jurists but also philosophers and, especially, the theologians condemned to silence have something to say.

9. Toward a Global Canon Law

The Catholic Church should develop a truly global canon law based on the centrality of all persons as created in the image of God, and pertaining not only to baptized persons. This new law in no way undervalues baptism but emphasizes the universal human condition. If every human being can be baptized, it is precisely because he or she is a repository of the *imago Dei*. This transition from modern to global canon law calls for the spiritualization of canon law and greater legal harmony with the Catholic Church's intrinsic evangelizing mission.

10. Biographical Approach to Legal Science

Behind many legal and social achievements, such as the integration of Europe after World War II and the fall of communism after the Cold War, one finds Christian values and ideals. And behind those ideals, one often finds a particular Christian figure who left an indelible mark on our legal culture. The biographical approach to law has excellent potential in legal science because it shows both the complexity, ambiguity, and even the accidental nature of secular legal systems. Lying behind rules and legal documents are facts and, beyond them, people. The *who* of the person always prevails over the *what* and the *how*. The members of the School of Salamanca, Alberico Gentili, Robert Schuman, Óscar Romero, and John Paul II, among others, are some examples of how Christianity affects the law through the life and work of Christian jurists.

BIBLIOGRAPHY

Acheson, Dean. *Sketches from Life of Men I Have Known.* New York: Harper, 1961.

Alexy, Robert. *The Argument from Injustice: A Reply to Legal Positivism.* Translated by Stanley Paulson and Bonnie Litschewski Paulson. Oxford: Oxford University Press, 2002.

———. *Begriff und Geltung des Rechts.* Freiburg im Breisgau: Verlag Karl Alber, 1992.

———. "Some Reflections on the Ideal Dimension of Law and on the Legal Philosophy of John Finnis." *American Journal of Jurisprudence* 58, no. 2 (2013): 97–110.

———. *A Theory of Constitutional Rights.* Translated by Julian Rivers. Oxford: Oxford University Press, 2002.

Allen, Amy, and Eduardo Mendieta, eds. *The Cambridge Habermas Lexicon.* Cambridge: Cambridge University Press, 2019.

Angier, Tom, Iain T. Benson, and Mark D. Retter, eds. *The Cambridge Handbook on Natural Law and Human Rights.* Cambridge: Cambridge University Press, 2022.

Anscombe, G. E. M. *Intention.* Cambridge, Mass.: Harvard University Press, 1957.

Ashworth, Andrew, and Jeremy Horder. *Principles of Criminal Law*, 7th ed. Oxford: Oxford University Press, 2013.

Aquinas, Thomas. *Corpus Thomisticum. S. Thomae de Aquino Opera Omnia.* Edited by Enrique Alarcón. Pamplona: Universitatis Studiorum Navarrensis 2000. http://www.corpusthomisticum.org/iopera.html.

Arendt, Hannah. *The Human Condition*, 2nd ed. Chicago: University of Chicago Press, 1971.

Aróstegui, Julio. *Combatientes requetés en la Guerra Civil española 1936–1939.* Madrid: La Esfera de los Libros, 2013.

Audi, Robert. *Democratic Authority and the Separation of Church and State.* Oxford: Oxford University Press, 2011.

———. *Rationality and Religious Commitment.* Oxford: Clarendon Press, 2011.

Audier, Serge. *La pensé solidariste.* Paris: Presses Universitaires de France, 2010.

Augustine, Saint. *De libero arbitrio.* Edited by and translated by Francs E. Touscher. Philadelphia: Peter Reilly, 1937.

———. *The Trinity (De Trinitate)*, 2nd. ed. Translated by Edmund Hill, edited by John E. Rotelle. Hyde Park, N.Y.: New City Press, 2012.

Azo of Bologna. *Brocardica aurea D. Azonis Bononiensis antiquorum iuris consultorum facile principis. In quibus omnes fere iuris antinomiae conciliantur, atque concordantes leges suis locis collocantur.* Naples, 1568; reprint, Turin: Ex officina Erasmiana, 1967.

Balboni, Michael J., and Tracy A. Balboni. *Hostility to Hospitality: Spirituality and Professional Socialization within Medicine.* Oxford: Oxford University Press, 2018.

Baldwin, Richard. *The Great Convergence: Information Technology and the New Globalization.* Cambridge, Mass.: Harvard University Press, 2016.

Balkin, Jack M. *Living Originalism.* Cambridge, Mass.: The Belknap Press of Harvard University Press, 2011.

Barshack, Lior. "Constituent Power as Body: Outline of a Constitutional Theology." *University of Toronto Law Journal* 56 (2006): 185–222.

Bartolini, Giulio, ed. *A History of International Law in Italy.* Oxford: Oxford University Press, 2020.

Bayertz, Kurt, ed. *Solidarity.* Dordrecht: Kluwer, 1999.

Benedict XVI, Pope. *Caritas in veritate.* Encyclical Letter. June 29, 2009.

———. *Christianity and the Crisis of Cultures.* San Francisco: Ignatius Press, 2006.

———. *Deus caritas est.* Encyclical Letter. December 25, 2005.

———. "Eucharist, Communion, and Solidarity." In *The Essential Pope Benedict XVI*, edited by John F. Thornton and Susan B. Varenne, 69–84. New York: Harper Collins, 2007.

———. "Faith, Reason and the University: Memories and Reflections." University of Regensburg, September 12, 2006.

———. *The Garden of God: Toward a Human Ecology.* Edited by Maria Milvia Morciano. Washington, D.C.: The Catholic University of America Press, 2014.

———. "Speech to the German Parliament." Berlin, September 22, 2011.

Benedictis, Angela de. "Gentili, Alberico." In *Dizionario Biografico degli Italiani*, vol. 53, 245–51. Rome: Istituto della Enciclopedia Italiana, 2000.

Benson, Iain T. *Civic Virtues and the Politics of Full-Drift Ahead.* Sydney: Center for Independent Studies, 2017.

———. "Considering Secularism." In *Recognizing Religion in a Secular Society*, edited by Douglas Farrow, 83–88. Montreal: McGill-Queens, 2004.

Bentham, Jeremy. *An Introduction to the Principles of Morals and Legislation*, 2nd ed. Edited by James H. Burns and Herbert L. A. Hart. Oxford: Oxford University Press, 1996.

———. *The Works of Jeremy Bentham*, vol. 2. Edited by John Bowring. Edinburgh: William Tait, 1843.

Berlin, Isaiah. *Four Essays on Liberty.* Oxford: Oxford University Press, 1969.

Berman, Harold J. *Faith and Order: The Reconciliation of Law and Religion.* Grand Rapids, Mich.: Eerdmans, 1993; reprint, 2000.

———. *The Interaction of Law and Religion.* Nashville, Tenn.: Abingdon Press, 1974.

———. *Law and Language: Effective Symbols of Community*. Edited by John Witte, Jr. Cambridge: Cambridge University Press, 2013.

———. *Law and Revolution I: The Formation of the Western Legal Tradition*. Cambridge, Mass.: Harvard University Press, 1983.

Biggar, Nigel, ed. *The Revival of Natural Law: Philosophical, Theological, and Ethical Responses to the Finnis-Grisez School*. London: Routledge, 2016.

Birocchi, Italo. "Persona giuridica nel diritto medievale e moderno." In *Digesto. Sezione Civile*, vol. 13, 407–20. Turin: UTET, 1995.

Blais, Marie-Claude. *La solidarité. Histoire d'une idée*. Paris: Éditions Gallimard, 2007.

Blomquist, Robert F. "Law and Spirituality: Some First Thoughts of an Emerging Relation." *UMKC Law Review* 71 (2003): 583–622.

Böckenförde, Ernst-Wolfgang. *Religion, Law, and Democracy: Selected Writings*. Edited by Mirjam Künkler and Tine Stein. Translated by Thomas Dunlap. Oxford: Oxford University Press, 2020.

Bodin, Jean. *On Sovereignty*. Edited by Julian H. Franklin. Cambridge: Cambridge University Press, 1992.

———. *Les six livres de la République*. Myriel: Le Plessis Trévise, 2017.

Bonaventure. *The Works of Bonaventure*. Translated by Jose de Vinck. Mansfield Centre, Conn.: Martino Publishing, 2016.

Bouckaert, Luk, and Laszlo Zsolnai, eds. *The Palgrave Handbook of Spirituality and Business*. London: Palgrave Macmillan, 2011.

Brady, Kathleen A. *The Distinctiveness of Religion in American Law: Rethinking Religion Clause Jurisprudence*. Cambridge: Cambridge University Press, 2015.

Brague, Rémi. *The Law of God: The Philosophical History of an Idea*. Translated by Lydia G. Cochrane. Chicago: University of Chicago Press, 2007.

Brockman, James R. *Romero: A Life*. Maryknoll, N.Y.: Orbis Books, 2005.

Browning, Don, M. Christian Green, and John Witte, Jr., eds. *Sex, Marriage, and Family in World Religions*. New York: Columbia University Press, 2006.

Brunkhorst, Hauke. *Solidarity: From Civic Friendship to a Global Legal Community*. Cambridge, Mass.: MIT Press, 2005.

Burrin, Philippe. *France under the Germans: Collaboration and Compromise*. Translated by Janet Lloyd. New York: New Press, 1996.

Cahill, Maria Catherine. "Subsidiarity." In *Catholic Social Teaching: A Volume of Scholarly Essays*, edited by Gerard V. Bradley and E. Christian Brugger, 414–32. Cambridge: Cambridge University Press, 2019.

Calabresi, Steve G., ed. *Originalism: A Quarter Century of Debate*. Washington, D.C.: Regnery Publishing, 2007.

Cane, Peter, ed. *The Hart-Fuller Debate in the Twenty-First Century*. Oxford: Hart Publishing, 2010.

Carozza, Paolo. "Human Dignity." In *International Human Rights Law*, edited by Dina Shelton, 345–60. Oxford: Oxford University Press, 2013.

———. "Subsidiarity as a Structural Principle of International Human Rights Law." *American Journal of International Law* 97 (2003): 38–79.

Casanova, José. "The Secular, Secularizations, Secularism." In *Rethinking Secularism*, edited by Craig Calhoun, Mark Juergensmeyer, and Jonathan Van Antwerpen, 54–74. Oxford: Oxford University Press, 2011.

Catasús, Aleix, and Bernat Puigdollers. *El Noucentisme a Barcelona*. Barcelona: Barcelona Libres, 2016.

Catechism of the Catholic Church, 2nd ed. Vatican City: Libreria Editrice Vaticana, 1997.

Celsus and Ulpian. *Libro primo institutionum*. In *The Digest of Justinian*. Edited by Alan Watson, vol. 1. Philadelphia: University of Pennsylvania Press, 1985.

Cerami, Pietro. "La concezione celsina del ius." *Annali del Seminario Giuridico dell'Università di Palermo* 38 (1985): 5–249.

Charles, Patrick J. *Historicism, Originalism, and the Constitution: The Use and Abuse of the Past in American Jurisprudence*. Oxford: Oxford University Press, 2014.

Chopra, Hardev Singh. *De Gaulle and European Unity*. New Delhi: Abhinav Publications, 1974.

Cicero. *On the Orator*. Edited by E. W. Sutton and H. Rackham. Cambridge, Mass.: Harvard University Press, 1948.

Clarke, Kevin Michael. *Óscar Romero: Love Must Win Out*. Collegeville, Minn.: Liturgical Press, 2014.

Cobb, Mark, Christina M. Puchalski, and Bruce Rumbold. *Oxford Textbook of Spirituality in Healthcare*. Oxford: Oxford University Press, 2012.

Cochran, Robert F., Jr., ed. *Agape, Justice, and Law: How Might Christian Love Shape Law?* Cambridge: Cambridge University Press, 2017.

Code of Canons of the Eastern Churches. Washington, D.C.: Canon Law Society of America, 2001.

Cohen, Antonin. "Le plan Schuman de Paul Reuter. Entre communauté nationale et fédération européenne." *Revue française de science politique* 48 (1998): 645–63.

Cohen, I. Bernard. *Science and the Founding Fathers*. New York: W. W. Norton, 1995.

Coke, Edward. *The First Part of the Institutes of the Laws of England; or A Commentary Upon Littleton*. Edited by Francis Hargrave and Charles Butler. Dublin: Brooke, Clarke and Sons, 1809.

Congar, Yves. *I Believe in the Holy Spirit*. Translated by David Smith. New York: Crossroad, 1997; reprint 2000.

Conrad, Stephen A. "Metaphor and Imagination in James Wilson's Theory of Federal Union." *Law and Social Inquiry* 13 (1988): 1–70.

Cover, Robert. *Narrative, Violence, and the Law: The Essays of Robert Cover*. Edited by Martha Minow, Michael Ryan, and Austin Sarat. Ann Arbor: University of Michigan Press, 1992.

Crandall, Russell. *The Salvador Option: The United States in El Salvador, 1977–1992*. Cambridge: Cambridge University Press, 2016.

Crane, Daniel, and Samuel Gregg, eds. *Christianity and Market Regulation: An Introduction.* Cambridge: Cambridge University Press, 2021.

Crawford, James. *Brownlie's Principles of Public International Law.* Oxford: Oxford University Press, 2019.

Crosby, John. *The Personalism of John Paul II.* Steubenville, Ohio: Hildebrand Press, 2019.

Cross, Frank. *The Failed Promise of Originalism.* Stanford, Calif.: Stanford University Press, 2013.

Cushing, Kathleen G. "Sinibaldo Fieschi (Pope Innocent IV) (1180/90–1254)." In *Law and the Christian Tradition in Italy: The Legacy of the Great Jurists,* edited by Orazio Condorelli and Rafael Domingo, 70–81. London: Routledge, 2021.

Davis, Derek H. "The Continental Congress and Emerging Ideas of Church-State Separation." In *No Establishment of Religion: America's Original Contribution to Religious Liberty,* edited by T. Jeremy Gunn and John Witte, Jr., 180–207. Oxford: Oxford University Press, 2012.

Davis, Donald R., Jr. *The Spirit of Hindu Law.* New York: Cambridge University Press, 2013.

de la Puente, Luis. *Vida del P. Baltasar Álvarez.* Barcelona: Editorial Linkgua, 2011.

Delgado, Jesús. *Óscar A. Romero.* El Salvador: UCA, 2001.

———. "Romero: Un joven aspirante a la santidad." *Orientación* 55, no. 5462 (March 25, 2007).

D'Haeseleer, Brian. *The Salvadoran Crucible: The Tragedy of U.S. Counterinsurgency in El Salvador, 1979–1992.* Lawrence: University Press of Kansas, 2017.

Dicey, Albert Venn. *Introduction to the Study of the Law of the Constitution,* 8th ed. Indianapolis, Ind.: Liberty Classics, 1982.

Dinan, Desmond. *Origins and Evolution of the European Union,* 2nd ed. Oxford: Oxford University Press, 2014.

Doe, Norman, ed. *Christianity and Natural Law: An Introduction.* Cambridge: Cambridge University Press, 2017.

———. "Faith, Freedom, and Family: An Introduction to the Work of John Witte, Jr." *Ecclesiastical Law Journal* 24, no. 2 (2022): 175–91.

———. *Law and Religion in Europe: A Comparative Introduction.* Oxford: Oxford University Press, 2011.

Domingo, Rafael. "Álvaro d'Ors." In *Great Christian Jurists in Spanish History,* edited by Rafael Domingo and Javier Martínez-Torrón, 344–60. Cambridge: Cambridge University Press, 2018.

———. "Álvaro d'Ors." In *Juristas Universales IV,* edited by Domingo, 662–66. Madrid: Marcial Pons, 2004.

———. "Álvaro d'Ors. Derecho y sentido común: Siete lecciones de Derecho natural como límite del Derecho positivo." *Persona y Derecho* 35 (1996): 293–98.

———. *Álvaro d'Ors. Una introduction a su obra.* Cizur Menor: Thomson Aranzadi, 2005.

———. *Auctoritas*. Barcelona: Ariel, 1999.

———. "Body, Soul, and Spirit of the Law: Towards a Holistic Legal Paradigm." *Oxford Journal of Law and Religion* 7, no. 2 (2018): 230–49.

———. "Christianity, Solidarity, and Law." In *The Oxford Handbook of Christianity and Law*, edited by John Witte, Jr., and Rafael Domingo, 832–39. Oxford: Oxford University Press, 2023.

———. "The Constitutional Justification of Religion." *Ecclesiastical Law Journal* 18 (2016): 14–35.

———. "Derecho global y comunidad humana global." In *Las transformaciones del derecho en la globalización*, edited by Jorge Fabra Zamora, 45–58. Mexico City: Universidad Autónoma de México, 2020.

———. "El derecho y la moral: Cien años de soledad." *Scripta Theologica* 52, no. 3 (2020): 763–92.

———. "The Dworkinian Religion of Value." *Journal of Law and Religion* 29, no. 3 (2014): 526–34.

———. *Ex Roma ius*. Cizur Menor: Thomson Reuters Aranzadi, 2005.

———. "Gaius, Vattel, and the New Global Law Paradigm." *European Journal of International Law* 22, no. 3 (2011): 627–47.

———. "Global Law and the New Global Human Community." *Revista Brasileira di Direito* 13, no. 3 (2017): 27–39.

———. *God and the Secular Legal System*. Cambridge: Cambridge University Press, 2016.

———. "The Individual in International Law from the Contemporary Sacred Natural Law Perspective." In *The Individual in International Law: History and Theory*, edited by Anne Peters and Tom Sparks, chapter 9. Oxford: Oxford University Press, 2024.

———. *Iuris vincula. Studi in onore di Mario Talamanca* I. Naples: Jovene, 2001.

———. "*Ius, ius suum, res iusta:* Una crítica a la *Introducción crítica* de Hervada." *Persona y Derecho* 86 (2022): 249–66.

———. "Karol Józef Wojtyła, Pope John Paul II (1920–2005)." In *Law and Christianity in Poland: The Legacy of the Great Jurists*, edited by Franciszek Longchamps de Bérier and Rafael Domingo, 247–62. London: Routledge, 2022.

———. "The Metalegal God." *Ecclesiastical Law Journal* 16, no. 1 (2014): 147–67.

———. "The New Global Human Community." *Chicago Journal of International Law* 12, no. 1 (2012): 563–87.

———. *The New Global Law*. Cambridge: Cambridge University Press, 2010.

———. "A New Global Paradigm for Religious Freedom." *Journal of Church and State* 56, no. 3 (2014): 427–53.

———. "Óscar Arnulfo Romero y Galdámez (El Salvador, 1919–1980)." In *Law and Christianity in Latin America: The Work of Great Jurists*, edited by M. C. Mirow and Rafael Domingo, 498–510. London: Routledge, 2021.

———. "Religion for Hedgehogs? A Critique against the Dworkinian Approach to Religious Freedom." *Oxford Journal of Law and Religion* 2, no. 2 (2013): 371–92.

———. "Restoring Freedom of Conscience." *Journal of Law and Religion* 30, no. 2 (2015): 176–93.

———. "A Right to Religious and Moral Freedom? A Response to Michael Perry." *International Journal of Constitutional Law* 12, no. 1 (2014): 226–47.

———. *Roman Law: An Introduction*. London: Routledge, 2018.

———. "Ronald Dworkin's Religion without God and the Challenges of Theistic Epistemology." *Journal of Law and Religion* 29 (2014): 510–47.

———. "Sobre las supuestas rúbricas del Edicto pretor." *Zeitschrift der Savigny-Stiftung für Rechtsgeschichte (Romanistische Abteilung)* 108 (1991): 290–303.

———, ed. *Textos de Derecho Romano*. Pamplona: Aranzadi, 2000.

———. "Theology and Jurisprudence: A Good Partnership?" *Journal of Law and Religion* 32, no. 1 (2017): 79–85.

———. "Thomas Sanchez." In *Christianity and Family Law: An Introduction*, edited by John Witte, Jr., and Gary S. Hauk, 245–58. Cambridge: Cambridge University Press, 2017.

———. "Toward a Global Canon Law Centered on the Human Person." *Ius Canonicum* 62 (2022): 1–22.

———. "Why Spirituality Matters for Law: An Explanation." *Oxford Journal of Law and Religion* 8, no. 2 (2019): 326–34.

Domingo, Rafael, and Gonzalo Rodriguez-Fraile. *Spiritualizing Humanity*. Miami: self-published, 2021.

Domingo, Rafael, and John Witte, Jr., eds. *Christianity and Global Law*. London: Routledge, 2020.

Domingo, Rafael et al., ed. *Principios de Derecho Global. 1000 reglas jurídicas y aforismos comentados*, 2nd ed. Cizur Menor: Thomson Aranzadi, 2006.

Domingo-Osle, Marta, and Rafael Domingo. "Nursing and Spirituality: A Discussion Paper on Intertwining Metaparadigms." *Journal of Nursing Management* 28, no. 6 (2020): 1268–74.

d'Ors, Álvaro. *Código de Derecho Canónico*, 6th ed. Edited by Instituto Martín Azpilcueta. Pamplona: Eunsa, 2001.

———. *El Código de Eurico. Edición, Palingenesia*, Índices. Rome: Instituto Jurídico Español, 1960.

———. "Creditum und Contratus." *Zeitschrift der Savigny-Stiftung für Rechtsgeschichte (Romanistische Abteilung)* 74 (1957): 73–99.

———. *Derecho privado romano*, 10th ed. Pamplona: Eunsa, 2004.

———. *Derecho y sentido común*. Madrid: Thomson Civitas, 1995.

———. *Derecho y sentido común. Siete lecciones de derecho natural como límite del derecho positivo*, 3rd ed. Madrid: Civitas, 2001.

———, ed. *El Digesto de Justiniano*, 3 vols. Pamplona: Aranzadi, 1968–75.

———. *Ensayos de teoría política*. Pamplona: Eunsa, 1979.

———. *Epigrafía Jurídica de la España Romana*. Madrid: Instituto Nacional de Estudios Jurídicos, 1953.

———. *Escritos varios sobre el Derecho en crisis*. Rome: Instituto Jurídico Español, 1973.

———. "Estudios sobre la 'Constitutio Antoniniana' I. Estado de la cuestión." *Emerita* 11 (1943): 297–337.

———. "Estudios sobre la 'Constitutio Antoniniana' II. Los dediticios y el Edicto de Caracala." *Anuario de Historia del Derecho Español* 15 (1944): 162–204.

———. "Estudios sobre la 'Constitutio Antoniniana' III. Los 'peregrini' después del Edicto de Caracala." *Anuario de Historia del Derecho Español* 17 (1946): 586–604.

———. "Estudios sobre la 'Constitutio Antoniniana' V. Caracala y la unificación del Imperio." *Emerita* 24 (1956): 1–26.

———. *La ley Flavia municipal (Texto y comentario)*. Rome: Pontifical Lateran University, 1986.

———. *Nueva introducción al estudio del derecho*. Madrid: Civitas, 1999.

———. "Nuevos estudios sobre la 'Constitutio Antoniniana,'" *Atti dell'XI Congresso Internazionale di Papirologia de 1965*, 408–32. Milan: Istituto Lombardo di Scienze e Lettere, 1966.

———. "Observaciones sobre el 'edictum de rebus creditis,'" *Studia et Documenta Historiae et Iuris* 19 (1953): 134–201.

———. *Parerga historica*. Pamplona: Eunsa, 1997.

———. *La posesión del espacio*. Madrid: Civitas, 1998.

———. *Las Quaestiones de Africano*. Rome: Pontifical Lateran University, 1997.

———. *Estudios de Derecho Internacional en homenaje al Profesor Camilo Barcia Trelles*. Santiago de Compostela: Universidad de Santiago de Compostela, 1958.

———. *La violencia y el orden*. Madrid: Dyrsa, 1987.

——— and Xavier d'Ors. *Lex Irnitana. Texto bilingüe*. Santiago de Compostela: Universidad de Santiago de Compostela, 1988.

d'Ors, Miguel. "Mi padre." In *Álvaro d'Ors (1915–2004), in memoriam*, edited by Rafael Domingo, 33–43. Pamplona: Universidad de Navarra, 2004.

Durham, W. Cole, Jr. "Patterns of Religion State Relations." In *Religion and Human Rights: An Introduction*, edited by John Witte, Jr., and M. Christian Green, 360–78. Oxford: Oxford University Press, 2012.

Durkheim, Émile. *The Elementary Forms of Religious Life*. Oxford: Oxford University Press, 2001.

Dworkin, Ronald. *Is Democracy Possible Here? Principles for a New Political Debate*. Princeton, N.J.: Princeton University Press, 2006.

———. *Justice for Hedgehogs*. Cambridge, Mass.: The Belknap Press of Harvard University Press, 2011.

———. *Law's Empire*. Cambridge, Mass.: Belknap Press of Harvard University Press, 1986; reprint, 2006.

———. *Life's Dominion: An Argument about Abortion, Euthanasia, and Individual Freedom*. New York: Vintage, 1994.
———. *A Matter of Principle*. Cambridge, Mass.: Harvard University Press, 1985, 2000.
———. "The Model of Rules." *University of Chicago Law Review* 35 (1967–1968): 14–46.
———. *Religion without God*. Cambridge, Mass.: Harvard University Press, 2013.
———. *Taking Rights Seriously*. Cambridge, Mass.: Harvard University Press, 1977.
———. *Taking Rights Seriously: New Impression with a Reply to Critics*. London: Duckworth, 2005.
Dybowski, Maciej, and Rafael García Pérez, eds. *Globalization of Law: The Role of Human Dignity*. Cizur Menor: Thomson, Reuters Aranzadi, 2018.
Eberle, Christopher J. *Religious Conviction in Liberal Politics*. Cambridge: Cambridge University Press, 2002.
Einstein, Albert. *Einstein on Cosmic Religion and Other Opinions and Aphorisms*. Mineola, N.Y.: Dover Publication, 2012.
———. *The World as I See It*. Translated by Alan Harris. New York: Philosophical Library, 1949.
Eisenbrandt, Matt. *Assassination of a Saint: The Plot to Murder Óscar Romero and the Quest to Brings His Killers to Justice*. Oakland: University of California Press, 2017.
Eisgruber, Christopher L., and Lawrence G. Sager. *Religious Freedom and the Constitution*. Cambridge, Mass.: Harvard University Press, 2010.
Emon, Anver M. *Islamic Natural Law Theories*. Oxford: Oxford University Press, 2010.
Emon, Anver M., Matthew Levering, and David Novak, eds. *Natural Law: A Jewish, Christian, and Islamic Trialogue*. Oxford: Oxford University Press, 2014.
Epstein, Steven B. "Rethinking the Constitutionality of Ceremonial Deism." *Columbia Law Review* 96 (1996): 2083–174.
Errázuriz, Carlos José. "La persona nell'ordinamento canonico: Il rapporto tra persona e diritto nella Chiesa." *Ius Ecclesiae* 10 (1998): 3–36.
Fassbender, Bardo, and Anne Peters, eds. *The Oxford Handbook of the History of International Law*. Oxford: Oxford University Press, 2014.
Feingold, Mordechai. "What's in a Date? Alberico Gentili and the Genesis of *De legationibus libri tres*." *Notes & Queries* 64 (2017): 312–17.
Fercia, Riccardo. "'Aliud petere' e la metafora dell'ὸδοί." *Rivista di Diritto Romano* 4 (2004): 1–16, http://www.ledonline.it/rivistadirittoromano/allegati/dirittoromano04fercia.pdf.
Fimister, Alan Paul. *Robert Schuman: Neo-Scholastic Humanism and the Reunification of Europe*. Frankfurt am Main: Peter Lang, 2011.
Finkelman, Paul. *Slavery and the Founders: Race and Liberty in the Age of Jefferson*, 3rd ed. London: Routledge, 2014.
Finnis, John. *Aquinas: Moral, Political, and Legal Theory*. Oxford: Oxford University Press, 1998.
———. "Law as Fact and as Reason for Action: A Response to Robert Alexy on Law's Ideal Dimension." *American Journal of Jurisprudence* 59, no.1 (2014): 85–109.

———. "Natural Law and the Ethics of Discourse." *Ratio Iuris* 12 (1999): 354–73.
———. *Natural Law and Natural Rights*. Oxford: Oxford University Press, 1980; 2nd ed., 2011.
Fleming, James E., and Jacob T. Levy, eds. *Federalism and Subsidiarity*. New York: NYU Press, 2014.
Ford, Kenneth W., and Diane Goldstein. *The Quantum World: Quantum Physics for Everyone*. Cambridge, Mass.: Harvard University Press, 2005.
Forst, Rainer. *Toleration in Conflict: Past and Present*. Translated by Ciaran Cronin. Cambridge: Cambridge University Press, 2013.
Francis, Pope. "Address to the Participants in the Plenary Session of the Pontifical Council for Culture." November 18, 2017
———. *Fratelli tutti*. Encyclical Letter. October 3, 2020.
———. *Laudato si'*. Encyclical Letter. May 24, 2015.
———. *Lumen fidei*. Encyclical Letter. June 29, 2013.
Frisch, David. "Rational Retroactivity in a Commercial Context." *Alabama Law Review* 58 (2007): 765–809.
Fuller, Lon L. *Anatomy of the Law*. New York: Frederick A. Praeger, 1968.
———. *The Morality of Law*. New Haven, Conn.: Yale University Press, 1964; 2nd ed., 1969.
———. "Positivism and Fidelity to Law: A Reply to Professor Hart." *Harvard Law Review* 71 (1958): 630–72.
Galgano, Francesco. *Le insidie del linguaggio giuridico: Saggio sulle metafore nel diritto*. Bologna: Il Mulino, 2010.
García Márquez, Gabriel. *One Hundred Years of Solitude*. New York: Vintage Español, 1967.
Gardner, John. *Law as a Leap of Faith: Essays on Law in General*. Oxford: Oxford University Press, 2012.
———. "Legal Positivism: 5½ Myths." *The American Journal of Jurisprudence* 46, no. 1 (2001): 199–227.
Gaius. *The Institutes of Gaius*. Edited by Francis De Zulueta. Oxford: Clarendon Press, 1953.
———. *Institutes*. Edited by W. M. Gordon and O. Robinson. London: Duckworth, 1988.
Gaudemet, Jean. *La doctrine canonique médiévale*. London: Routledge, 1994.
———. "Persona." *Christianesimo nell storia* 9 (1988): 465–92.
Gensler, Harry J. *Ethics and Religion*. Cambridge: Cambridge University Press, 2016.
Gentili, Alberico. *De iure belli libri tres*. In *Classics of International Law*. Translated by John C. Rolfe, vol. 2. New York: Oceana Publications, 1964.
———. *De legationibus libri tres*. Translated by Gordon J. Laing. New York: Oceana Publications, 1964.
———. *De Papatu Romano Antichristo*. Edited by Giovanni Minnucci. Milan: Monduzzi Editoriale, 2018.

———. *Disputationes tres:* I. *De libris Iuris Canonici.* Hanau: Apud Guilielmum Antonium, 1605.

———. *Disputationes de nuptiis libri septem.* Hanau: Apud Guilielmum Antonium, 1601.

———. *Hispanicae Advocationis libri duo.* Translated by Frank Frost Abbott. New York: Oceana Publications, 1968.

———. *The Wars of Romans: A Critical Edition and Translation of De Armis Romanis* (1599). Edited by Benedict Kingsbury and Benjamin Straumann. Translated by David Lupher. Oxford: Oxford University Press, 2010.

George, Robert P. "The Achievement of Finnis." In *Reason, Morality, and Law*, edited by John Kewon and Robert P. George, 1–9. Oxford: Oxford University Press, 2013.

———. *Conscience and Its Enemies.* Wilmington, Del.: ISI Books, 2013.

———. *In Defense of Natural Law.* Oxford: Oxford University Press, 1999; rev. ed. 2001.

———. *Entre el derecho y la moral.* Translated by Pedro José Izquierdo. Cizur: Thomson Aranzadi, 2009.

———, ed. *Natural Law Theory: Contemporary Essays.* Oxford: Clarendon Press 1992.

Gierke, Otto. *Natural Law and the Theory of Society* (1883). Translated by Ernest Barker, vol. 1, 2nd ed. Cambridge: Cambridge University Press, 1934.

Giorgetti, Chiara. "Rethinking the Individual in International Law." *Lewis & Clark Law Review* 22 (2019): 1085–149.

Glendon, Mary Ann. "Is Religious Freedom an Orphan Right?" In *The Changing Nature of Religious Rights Under International Law*, edited by Malcolm Evans et al., 1–8. Oxford: Oxford University Press, 2015.

———. "Making the Case for Religious Freedom in Secular Societies." *Journal of Law and Religion* 33, no. 3 (2018): 329–39.

———. "Religious Freedom: A Second-Class Right?" *Emory Law Journal* 61 (2012): 971–90.

Glenn, H. Patrick. "A Concept of Legal Tradition." *Queen's Law Journal* 34 (2008): 427–45.

Goethe, Johann Wolfgang von. *Werke*, vol. 6, *Vermischte Schriften.* Frankfurt: Insel, 1981.

Goris, Wouter, and Jan Aertsen. "Medieval Theories of Transcendentals." In *The Stanford Encyclopedia of Philosophy, edited by* Edward N. Zalta. Winter 2016, https://plato.stanford.edu/archives/win2016/entries/transcendentals-medieval.

Grabill, Stephen J. *Rediscovering the Natural Law in Reformed Theological Ethics.* Grand Rapids, Mich.: Eerdmans, 2006.

Green, Joel B. *Body, Soul, and Human Life: The Nature of Humanity in the Bible.* Grand Rapids, Mich.: Baker Academic, 2008.

Greenawalt, Kent. *Religion and the Constitution*, vol. 1, *Free Exercise and Fairness.* Princeton, N.J.: Princeton University Press, 2006.

———. *Religion and the Constitution*, vol. 2, *Establishment and Fairness*. Princeton, N.J.: Princeton University Press, 2008.

Greene, Brian. *The Fabric of the Cosmos: Space, Time, and the Texture of Reality*, 2nd. ed. New York: W. W. Norton, 2011.

Grotius, Hugo. *De Iure Belli ac Pacis Libri Tres*. Edited by James Scott. Translated by Francis Kelsey. Oxford: Clarendon Press, 1925. Reprint, New York: Oceana Publications, 1964.

———. *The Truth of the Christian Religion*. Edited by Maria Rosa Antognazza. Indianapolis, Ind.: Liberty Fund, 2012.

Guardini, Romano. *El mesianismo en el mito, la revelación y la política*. Translated by Valentin García Yebra, foreword by Álvaro d'Ors. Madrid: Rialp, 1948.

———. *The Lord*. Translated by Elynor Castendyk. Washington, D.C.: Regnery, 1996.

Guest, Stephen. *Ronald Dworkin*, 3rd ed. Stanford, Calif.: Stanford University Press, 2013.

Gunn, T. Jeremy. "Religion and Law in France: Secularism, Separation, and State Intervention." *Drake Law Review* 57 (2008–2009): 949–84.

———. "The Separation of Church and State versus Religion in Public Square: The Contested History of the Establishment Clause." In *No Establishment of Religion: America's Original Contribution to Religious Liberty*, edited by T. Jeremy Gunn and John Witte, Jr., 15–44. Oxford: Oxford University Press, 2012.

Gurnham, David. "Law's Metaphor: Introduction." *Journal of Law and Society* 43 (2016): 1–7.

Haarscher, Guy. *La Laïcité*, 5th ed. Paris: PUF, 2011.

Habermas, Jürgen. *Between Facts and Norms: Contributions to a Discourse Theory of Law and Democracy*. Translated by William Rehg. Cambridge, Mass.: MIT Press, 1996.

———. *Faktizität und Geltung. Beiträge zur Diskurstheorie des Rechts und des demokratischen Rechtsstaats*. Frankfurt am Main: Suhrkamp, 1992.

———. *Justification and Application*. Translated by Ciaran Cronin. Cambridge, Mass.: MIT Press, 1996.

———. *Law and Morality*. The Tanner Lectures on Human Values, delivered at Harvard University, October 1–2, 1986, https://tannerlectures.utah.edu/_documents/a-to-z/h/habermas88.pdf.

———. "Reply to Symposium Participants." *Cardozo Law Review* 17 (1996): 1477–557.

Haight, Roger. *Spiritual and Religious: Explorations for Seekers*. New York: Orbis Books, 2016.

Hamburger, Philip. *Separation of Church and State*. Cambridge, Mass.: Harvard University Press, 2002.

Harris, Sam. *Waking Up: A Guide to Spirituality without Religion*. New York: Simon and Schuster, 2014.

Hart, H. L. A. *The Concept of Law*, 3rd ed. Oxford: Oxford University Press, 2012.

———. *Essays in Jurisprudence and Philosophy*. Oxford: Oxford University Press, 1983.

———. "Positivism and the Separation of Law and Morals." *Harvard Law Review* 71 (1958): 593–629.

———. Review of Lon L. Fuller, *The Morality of Law*, in *Harvard Law Review* 78 (1964–65): 1281–95.

Hart, H. L. A., and Tony Honoré. *Causation in the Law*, 2nd ed. Oxford: Clarendon Press, 1985.

Hammond, Jeffrey B., and Helen M. Alvaré, eds. *Christianity and the Laws of Conscience: An Introduction*. Cambridge: Cambridge University Press, 2021.

Hanvey, James. "Dignity, Person, and Imago Trinitatis." In *Understanding Human Dignity*, edited by Christopher McCrudden, 209–28. Oxford: Oxford University Press, 2013.

Harakas, Stanley S. "Eastern Orthodox Perspectives on Natural Law." *The American Journal of Jurisprudence* 24, no.1 (1979): 86–113.

Hawthorne, Gerald F., Ralph P. Martin, and Daniel G. Reid. *Dictionary of Paul and His Letters*. Downers Grove, Ill.: InterVarsity, 1992.

Hedrick, Todd. *Rawls and Habermas: Reason, Pluralism, and the Claims of Political Philosophy*. Stanford, Calif.: Stanford University Press, 2010.

Heffter, August Wilhelm. *Das europäische Völkerrecht der Gegenwart, auf den bisherigen Grundlagen*, 8th ed. Berlin: H. W. Müller, 1888.

Heller, Hermann. *Die Souveranität. Ein Beitrag zur Theorie des Staats- und Völkerrechts*. Berlin: Walter de Gruyter, 1927.

Hervada, Javier. *El ordenamiento canónico, I. Aspectos centrales de la construcción del concepto*. Pamplona: Universidad de Navarra, 1966.

———. *Introducción crítica al derecho natural*. Pamplona: Ediciones Universidad de Navarra, 1981; 11th ed., 2011.

———. *Lecciones propedéuticas de filosofía del derecho*. Pamplona: Ediciones Universidad de Navarra, 1992.

Heschel, Abraham Joshua. *Heavenly Torah as Refracted through the Generations*. New York: Continuum, 2006.

Hesselink, Martijn W. "A Toolbox for European Judges." *European Law Journal* 17 (2011): 441–69.

Hessler, Kathy et al. *Animal Law: New Perspectives on Teaching Traditional Law*. Durham, N.C.: Carolina Academic Press, 2017.

Hermogenian. *Digesta. Corpus Iuris Civilis*, vol. 1. Edited by Theodor Mommsen and Paul Krüger, 16th ed. Berlin: Weidmann, 1954.

Hiegel, Charles, and Marion Duvigneau. *Papiers de Robert Schuman. Répertoire numérique détaillé des fonds déposés sous les cotes 34 et 36 J*. Saint-Julien-lès-Metz: Archives départamentales de la Moselle, 2002.

Hill, Mark, Norman Doe, R. H. Helmholz, and John Witte, Jr., eds. *Christianity and Criminal Law*. London: Routledge, 2020.

Hirschl, Ran. *Constitutional Theocracy*. Cambridge, Mass.: Harvard University Press, 2010.

Hittinger, Russell. *A Critique of the New Natural Law Theory*. Notre Dame, Ind.: University of Notre Dame Press, 1988.
Hobbes, Thomas. *Leviathan*. Edited by J. C. A. Gaskin. Oxford: Oxford University Press, 1996.
Hoeflich, H. "Law and Geometry: Legal Science from Leibniz to Langdell." *American Journal of Legal History* 30, no. 2 (1986): 95–121.
Holland, Thomas Erskine. *An Inaugural Lecture on Albericus Gentilis Delivered at All Souls College, November 7, 1874*. London: Macmillan, 1874.
Holmes, Oliver Wendell, Jr. *The Occasional Speeches of Oliver Wendell Holmes*. Edited by Mark DeWolfe. Cambridge, Mass.: Harvard University Press, 1962.
———. "The Path of Law." *Harvard Law Review* 10 (1897): 457–78.
Honoré, Tony. *Making Law Bind*. Oxford: Clarendon Press, 1987.
Howard, Michael. *The Franco-Prussian War: The German Invasion of France 1870–1871*, 2nd ed. London: Routledge, 2001.
Index librorum prohibitorum SS. Domini nostri Gregorii XVI Pontificis Maximi. Rome: Monteregali, 1841.
Ihering, Rudolph von. *Geist des römischen Rechts auf den verschiedenen Stufen seiner Entwicklung*, 2 vols. Leipzig: Breitkopf und Härtel, 1866.
Institut Du Droit Local Alsacien-Mosellan, ed. *Le guide du droit local: Le droit applicable en Alsace et en Moselle de A à Z*, 4th ed. Strasbourg: Institut Du Droit Local Alsacien-Mosellan, 2015.
Institut Saint-Benoît, *Actes des journées organisées à Metz du 4 au 8 septembre 2013*. Metz: Éditions des Paraiges, 2013.
John Paul II, Pope. "Address for the 7th Centenary of the Founding of La Sapienza University of Rome." May 17, 2003.
———. "Address to the Cardinals of the United States." April 23, 2002.
———. "Address to the General Assembly of the United Nations, New York." October 2, 1979.
———. "Address to the United Nations." October 5, 1995.
———. *Centesimus annus*. Encyclical Letter. May 1, 1991.
———. *Crossing the Threshold of Hope*. New York: Alfred A. Knopf, 1994.
———. *Ecclesia de Eucharistia*. Encyclical Letter. April 17, 2003.
———. *Evangelium vitae*. Encyclical Letter. March 25, 1995.
———. *Fides et ratio*. Encyclical Letter. September 14, 1998.
———. *In God's Hands: The Spiritual Diaries of John Paul II (1962–2003)*. Translated by Joanna Zepa. London: Harpers Collins, 2007.
———. *Memory and Identity: Personal Reflections*. London: Weidenfeld & Nicolson, 2006.
———. "Message for the Celebration of the World Day of Peace." January 1, 1988.
———. "Message on the Occasion of the 50th Anniversary of the Beginning of the Second World War." August 27, 1989.
———. *Pastor bonus*. Apostolic Constitution. June 28, 1988.

———. *Ordinatio Sacerdotalis*. Apostolic Letter. May 22, 1994.
———. *Redemptor hominis*. Encyclical Letter. March 4, 1979.
———. *Rise, Let Us Be on Our Way*. New York: Warner Books, 2004.
———. *Sacrae disciplinae leges*. Apostolic Constitution. January 25, 1983.
———. *Sacri canones*. Apostolic Constitution. October 18, 1990.
———. *Sollicitudo rei socialis*. Encyclical Letter. December 30, 1987.
———. "Speech to Participants in the Symposium on *Evangelium vitae and Law*." May 24, 1996.
———. *Veritatis splendor*. Encyclical Letter. August 6, 1993.
John XXIII, Pope. *Pacem in terris*. Encyclical Letter. April 11, 1963.
Jackson, Timothy P. *Political Agape: Christian Love and Liberal Democracy*. Grand Rapids, Mich.: Eerdmans, 2015.
———. *The Priority of Love: Christian Charity and Social Justice*. Princeton, N.J.: Princeton University Press, 2003.
Kantorovicz, Ernst. *The King's Two Bodies: A Study in Mediaeval Political Theology*. Princeton, N.J.: Princeton University Press, 1957.
Kaser, Max. *Das römische Privatrecht*, vol. 1, *Das altrömische, das vorklassische und klassische Recht*, 2nd ed. Munich: Beck Verlag, 1971.
Kaufmann, Arthur. *Rechtsphilosophie*. Munich: Beck Verlag, 1994; 2nd ed., 1997.
Kelch, Thomas G. *Globalization and Animal Law*. Alphen aan den Rijn: Kluwer, 2011.
Kelly, John Maurice. *A Short History of Western Legal Theory*. Oxford: Clarendon Press, 1999.
Kelsen, Hans. *General Theory of Law and State*. Translated by Andres Wedberg. Cambridge, Mass.: Harvard University Press, 1945.
———. *General Theory of Norms*. Translated by Michael Hartney. Oxford: Clarendon Press, 1991.
———. *Principles of International Law*. Clark, N.J.: The Lawbook Exchange, 2009.
———. *Pure Theory of Law*. Translated by Max Knight. Berkeley: University of California Press, 1967.
———. *Reine Rechtslehre. Einleitung in die rechtswissenschaftliche Problematik*. Leipzig: F. Deuticke, 1934; 2nd ed., 1960. English: *Pure Theory of Law*.
———. *Veröffentlichte Schriften 1905–1910 und Selbstzeugnisse*, vol. 1 of *Hans Kelsen, Werke*. Edited by Matthias Jestaedt. Tübingen: Mohr Siebeck, 2007.
———. *What Is Justice? Justice, Law, and Politics in the Mirror of Science*. Clark, N.J.: The Lawbook Exchange, 2013.
Kengor, Paul. *A Pope and a President: John Paul II, Ronald Reagan, and the Extraordinary Untold Story of the 20th Century*. Wilmington, Del.: ISI Books, 2017.
King, Stephen D. *Grave New World: The End of Globalization, the Return of History*. New Haven, Conn.: Yale University Press, 2017.
Kingsbury, Benedict, and Benjamin Straumann, eds. *The Roman Foundations of the Law of Nations: Alberico Gentili and the Justice of Empire*. Oxford: Oxford University Press, 2011.

Klauck, Hans-Josef et al. *The Encyclopedia of the Bible and Its Reception*. Berlin: DeGruyter, 2022.

Koestler, Arthur. *The Ghost in the Machine*. London: Hutchinson, 1967.

Koh, Harold Hongju. "International Law as Part of Our Law." *American Journal of International Law* 43 (2004): 43–57.

Koppelman, Andrew. *Defending American Religious Neutrality*. Cambridge, Mass.: Harvard University Press, 2013.

Krijtenburg, Margriet. *Schuman's Europe: His Frame of Reference*. Leiden: Leiden University, 2012.

Kuby, Gabriele. *Abuse of Sexuality in the Catholic Church*. Menomonee Falls, Wisc.: Divine Providence Press, 2019.

Kurki, Visa A. J., and Tomasz Pietrzykowski, eds. *Legal Personhood: Animals, Artificial Intelligence and the Unborn*. Cham: Springer, 2017.

Kuyper, Abraham. *On Charity & Justice*. Edited by Matthew J. Tuininga with introduction by John Witte, Jr. Bellingham, Wash.: Lexham Press, 2022.

Lee, Michael Edward. *Revolutionary Saint: The Theological Legacy of Óscar Romero*. Maryknoll, N.Y.: Orbis Books, 2018.

Leibniz, Gottfried Wilhelm. *The New Method of Learning and Teaching Jurisprudence*. Translated by Carmelo Massimo de Iuliis. Clark, N.J.: Talbot Lawbook Exchange, 2017.

Lejeune, René. *Robert Schuman, père de l'Europe (1886–1963)*. Paris: Fayard, 2000.

Lenel, Otto. *Das Edictum Perpetuum. Ein Versuch Seiner Wiederherstellung*, 3rd ed. Leipzig: Tauchnitz, 1927; reprint, Aalen, 1956.

LeoGrande, William M. *Our Own Backyard: The United States in Central America, 1977–1992*. London: Eurospan, 1998.

Leiter, Brian. *Why Tolerate Religion?* Princeton, N.J.: Princeton University Press, 2013.

Lewis, C. S. *The Four Loves*. Fort Washington, Pa.: Harvest Book Company, 1971.

Lincoln, Kyle C. Review of Rafael Domingo and Javier Martínez-Torrón, eds. *Great Christian Jurists in Spanish History* (2018), in *Bulletin of Medieval Canon Law* 38 (2021): 452–57.

Lindkvist, Linde. *Religious Freedom and the Universal Declaration of Human Rights*. Cambridge: Cambridge University Press, 2017.

Locke, John. *The Selected Political Writings of John Locke*. Edited by Paul E. Sigmund. New York: W. W. Norton, 2005.

Lombardía, Pedro. "Contribución a la teoría de la persona física en el ordenamiento canónico." *Ius Canonicum* 57 (1989): 11–106.

López Vigil, María. *Monseñor Romero: Memories in Mosaic*. Maryknoll, N.Y.: Orbis Books, 2013.

Lücker, Hans August, and Jean Seitlinger. *Robert Schuman und die Einigung Europas*. Bonn: Bouvier Verlag, 2000.

Maceratini, Ruggero, ed., *La persona nella Chiesa. Diritti e doveri dell'uomo e del fedele Atti del Convegno, Trento, 6–7 giugno 2002*. Padua: CEDAM, 2003.

MacIntyre, Alasdair. *After Virtue: A Study in Moral Theory*. Notre Dame, Ind.: University of Notre Dame Press, 1984.

Macklem, Timothy. *Independence of Mind*. Oxford: Oxford University Press, 2006.

Maclean, I. W. F. *Learning and the Market Place: Essays in the History of the Early Modern Book*. Leiden: Brill, 2009.

Madunic, Jelena, and John J. Kirton, eds. *Global Law*. New York: Routledge, 2009.

Maier, Martin. "Erzbishof Óscar Romeros Kirchenkonflikte." *Stimmen der Zeit* 130 (2005): 198–210.

Maitland, Frederick. "The Corporation Sole." *Law Quarterly Review* 16 (1900): 335–54.

March, Andrew F. "Rethinking Religious Reason in Public Justification." *American Political Science Review* 107 (2013): 523–39.

Maritain, Jacques. *Christianity and Democracy*. San Francisco: Ignatius Press, 2012.

———. *The Degrees of Knowledge*. Translated by Gerald B. Phelan, reprint ed. Notre Dame, Ind.: University of Notre Dame Press, 2011 [1995].

———. *Man and State*. Washington, D.C.: The Catholic University of America Press, 1984, 1998.

———. *Natural Law: Reflections on Theory and Practice*. Edited by William Sweet. South Bend, Ind.: St. Augustine's Press, 2001.

———. *The Rights of Man and the Natural Law*. San Francisco: Ignatius Press, 1986; reprint, 2011.

Maskulak, Marian. *Edith Stein and the Body-Soul-Spirit at the Center of Holistic Formation*. New York: Peter Lang, 2007.

McConnell, Michael W. "Secular Reason and the Misguided Attempt to Exclude Religious Argument from Democratic Deliberation." *Journal of Law, Philosophy and Culture* 1 (2007): 162–64.

———. "Why Protect Religious Freedom?" *Yale Law Journal* 123 (2013): 772–810.

McGinnis, John O., and Michael B. Rappaport. *Originalism and the Good Constitution*. Cambridge, Mass.: Harvard University Press, 2013.

Meiser, Martin. "Some Facets of Pauline Anthropology—How Would a Greco-Roman Reader Understand It?" In *Anthropology in the New Testament and Its Ancient Context*, edited by Michael Labahn and Outi Lehtipuu, 55–85. Leuven: Peeters, 2010.

Meyer, Christoph J. H. "Was von christlichem Recht und Juristenleben übrigblieb." Review of Orazio Condoerlli and Rafael Domingo, eds. *Law and the Christian Tradition in Italy* (2020), in *Rechtsgeschichte—Legal History. Zeitschrift des Max-Planck-Instituts für Rechtsgeschichte und Rechtstheorie* 29 (2021): 302–6.

Micklethwait, John, and Adrian Wooldridge. *God Is Back: How the Global Revival of Faith Is Changing the World*. New York: Penguin Books, 2009.

Mill, John Stuart. *On Liberty and Other Essays*. Edited by John Gray. Oxford: Oxford University Press, 2008.

Miller, Lisa J., ed. *The Oxford Handbook of Psychology and Spirituality*. Oxford: Oxford University Press, 2012.

Minow, Martha. "Forgiveness, Law, and Justice." *California Law Review* 103 (2015): 1615–45.
Minnucci, Giovanni. "Alberico Gentili: Un protestante alle prese con il Corpus Iuris Canonici." *Ius Ecclesiae* 19 (2007): 347–68.
———. "Alberico Gentili (1552–1608)." In *Law and the Christian Tradition in Italy. The Legacy of the Great Jurists*, edited by Orazio Condorelli and Rafael Domingo, 281–96. London: Routledge, 2021.
———. *Alberico Gentili iuris interpres della prima Età moderna*. Bologna: Monduzzi Editoriale, 2011.
———. "Gentili, Alberico." In *Dizionario Biografico dei giuristi italiani*, XII-XX sec., edited by Italo Birocchi et al.:967–69. Bologna: Il Mulino, 2013.
———. *Silete theologi in munere alieno. Alberico Gentili tra diritto, teologia e religione*. Milan: Monduzzi Edizione, 2016.
Mittendorfer, Rudolf. *Robert Schuman. Architekt des neuen Europa*. Hildesheim: Georg Olms, 1983.
Moatti, Claudia. *The Birth of Critical Thinking in Republican Rome*. Cambridge: Cambridge University Press, 2015.
Mommsen, Theodor, and Paul Krüger, eds. *Digesta. Corpus Iuris Civilis*, vol. 1, 16th ed. Berlin: Weidmann, 1954.
Mommsen, Theodor et al., eds. *Corpus Iuris Civilis*, 3 vols. Hildesheim: Weidmann, 1989–93.
Monnet, Jean. *Memoirs*. London: Third Millennium, 2015.
Montesquieu. *The Spirit of the Laws*. Translated by Thomas Nugent. New York: D. Appleton, 1900.
Morgan, Lewis H. *Ancient Society or Researches in the Lines of Human Progress from Savagery through Barbarism to Civilization*. New York: Henry Holt, 1878.
Morozzo della Rocca, Roberto. *Primero Dios. Vita di Óscar Romero*. Milan: Mondodori, 2005.
———. *Óscar Romero: Prophet of Hope*. Boston: Pauline Books & Media, 2015.
Moyn, Samuel. *Christian Human Rights*. Philadelphia: University of Pennsylvania Press, 2005.
Mullhall, Stephen, and Adam Switt. *Liberals and Communitarians*, 2nd ed. Malden, Mass.: Blackwell Publishing, 2007.
Nagel, Thomas. *Secular Philosophy and the Religious Temperament*. Oxford: Oxford University Press, 2010.
Navarro, Luis. *Persone e soggetti nel diritto della Chiesa. Temi di diritto della persona*, 2nd ed. Rome: Edusc, 2017.
Neuman, Gerald L. "Subsidiarity." In *International Human Rights Law*, edited by Dina Shelton, 360–78. Oxford: Oxford University Press, 2013.
Neumann, Ulfrid. "Arthur Kaufmann (1923–2001)." In *Juristas universals*, edited by Rafael Domingo, vol. 4, 692–98. Madrid: Marcial Pons, 2004.
Nicholas of Cusa, *Selected Spiritual Writings*. Translated by H. Lawrence Bond. Mahwah, N.J.: Paulist Press, 1997.

Nijman, Janne E. "Grotius' *Imago Dei* Anthropology: Grounding *Ius Naturae et Gentium*." In *International Law and Religion: Historical and Contemporary Perspectives*, edited by Martii Koskenniemi, Mónica García-Salmones Rovira, and Paolo Amorosa, 87–110. Oxford: Oxford University Press, 2017.

Norris, Pippa, and Ronald Inglehart. *Sacred and Secular: Religion and Politics Worldwide*, 2nd ed. Cambridge: Cambridge University Press, 2012.

Novak, David. *Covenantal Rights: A Study in Jewish Political Theory*. Princeton, N.J.: Princeton University Press, 2000.

———. *Natural Law in Judaism*. Cambridge: Cambridge University Press, 2008.

Nussbaum, Martha. *Liberty of Conscience: In Defense of America's Tradition of Religious Equality*. New York: Basic Books, 2008.

Oberdorfer, Bernd. "Human Dignity and Image of God." *Scriptura* 204 (2010): 231–39.

Oppenheim, Lassa. *International Law: A Treatise*, vol. 1, *Peace*, 2nd ed. London: Longmans Green, 1912.

Orrego, Cristóbal. "Iusnaturalismo contemporáneo." In *Enciclopedia de teoría y filosofía del derecho*, vol I, edited by Jorge Luis Zabra Zamora and Álvaro Núñez Vaquero, 37–59. Mexico City: Instituto de Investigaciones Jurídicas, 2015.

———. "Persona física." In *Diccionario de Derecho Canónico* 6, 172–79. Cizur Menor: Universidad de Navarra, Aranzadi, 2012.

Otaduy, Javier. "Quién es persona en Derecho canónico." *Fidelium Iura* 11 (2011): 65–87.

Pagden, Antony. *The Burdens of Empire: 1539 to the Present*. Cambridge: Cambridge University Press, 2015.

Panikkar, Raimon. *The Cosmotheandric Experience: Emerging Religious Consciousness*. New York: Orbis Books, 1993.

———. *Opera Omnia*, vol. 2, *Religion and Religions*. Edited by Milena Carrara Pavan. Maryknoll, N.Y.: Orbis Books, 2015.

Panizo Orallo, Santiago. *Persona jurídica y ficción: Estudio de la obra de Sinibaldo de Fieschi (Inocencio IV)*. Pamplona: Eunsa, 1975.

Parenti, Lucio. *In solidum obligari. Contributo allo studio della solidarietà da atto lecito*. Naples: Edizioni Scientifiche Italiane, 2012.

Parry, Richard. "*Episteme* and *Techne*." In Zalta, *The Stanford Encyclopedia of Philosophy*, Fall 2014, https://plato.stanford.edu/archives/fall2014/entries/episteme-techne.

Paul VI, Pope. *Discorso al Sacro Collegio*, June 22, 1973, https://www.vatican.va/content/paul-vi/it/speeches/1973/june/documents/hf_p-vi_spe_19730622_sacro-collegio.htm.

Pelt, Jean-Marie. *Robert Schuman, Père de l'Europe—Father of Europe* (English version). Thionville: General Council of Moselle, Serge Domini Publisher, 2001.

Pennera, Christian. *La jeunesse et les débuts politiques d'un grand européen de 1886 à 1924*. Sarreguemines: Editions Pierron, 1985.

Perelman, Jeremy, and Katharine G. Young. "Rights as Footprints: A New Metaphor for Contemporary Human Rights Practice." *Northwestern Journal of International Human Rights* 9 (2010–2011): 27–58.

Pérez, Gabriel. *Álvaro d'Ors. Sinfonía de una vida*. Madrid: Rialp, 2020.

Perry, Michael J. *Human Rights in the Constitutional Law of the United States*. Cambridge: Cambridge University Press, 2013.

———. "A Right to Religious and Moral Freedom? A Reply to Rafael Domingo." *International Journal of Constitutional Law* 12, no. 1 (2014): 248–55.

Peters, Anne. *Beyond Human Rights: The Legal Status of Individuals in International Law*. Cambridge: Cambridge University Press, 2016.

Peters, Anne et al., eds. *Non-State Actors as Standard Setters*. New York: Cambridge University Press, 2009.

Petroncelli, Mario. "I soggetti dell'ordinamento canonico." *Il diritto ecclesiastico* 53 (1942): 276–82.

Pius XI, Pope. *Quadragesimo Anno*. Encyclical Letter. May 15, 1931.

Max Planck Encyclopedia of Public International Law. Oxford: Oxford University Press, 2007. Online.

Plotinus. *The Essential Plotinus*. Translated by Elmer O'Brien. Indianapolis, Ind.: Hackett Publishing Company, 1964.

Poidevin, Raymond. *Robert Schuman, homme d'État (1886–1963)*. Paris: Imprimerie nationale, 1986.

Polkinghorne, John. *Quantum Physics and Theology: An Unexpected Kinship*. New Haven, Conn.: Yale University Press, 2008.

Poulat, Émile. *Notre Laïcité Publique*. Paris: Berg International, 2003.

Pound, Roscoe. *The Spirit of Common Law*. Boston: Marshall Jones, 1921.

Prest, Wilfrid. "Blackstone as Architect: Constructing the Commentaries." *Yale Journal of Law and Humanities* 15 (2003): 103–33.

Price, David Heilbron. *Robert Schuman, Jalonneur de la paix mondiale*. Berlin: Brons Communications, 2014.

Pseudo-Dionysius, *The Complete Works*. Translated by Col Luibheid and Paul Rorem. Mahwah, N.J.: Paulist Press, 1987.

Radbruch, Gustav. *Gesamtausgabe*, vol. 3. Edited by Arthur Kaufmann. Heidelberg: C. E. Müller, 1990.

Rasilla, Ignacio de la. *International Law and History: Modern Interfaces*. Cambridge: Cambridge University Press, 2021.

Ratzinger, Joseph. "The Holy Spirit as *Communio*: Concerning the Relationship of Pneumatology and Spirituality in Augustine." *Communio: International Catholic Review* 25 (1998): 324–37.

———. *Introduction to Christianity*. San Francisco: Ignatius Press, 2000.

———. *Truth and Tolerance*. Translated by Henry Taylor. San Francisco: Ignatius Press, 2003.

Raucher, Alan. "Sunday Business and the Decline of Sunday Closing Laws." *Journal of Church and State* 36 (1994): 13–33.

Rawls, John. *Justice as Fairness: A Restatement*. Edited by Erin Kelly. Cambridge, Mass.: Harvard University Press, 2001.
———. *The Law of Peoples*. Cambridge, Mass.: Harvard University Press, 1999; 2nd ed., 2001.
———. *Political Liberalism*. New York: Columbia University Press, 1993; 2nd ed., 2005.
———. *A Theory of Justice*. Cambridge, Mass.: Harvard University Press, 1971; rev. ed. Cambridge, Mass.: The Belknap Press of Harvard University Press, 1999.
Raz, Joseph. *Ethics in Public Domain: Essays in the Morality of Law and Politics*. Oxford: Oxford University Press, 1994.
———. *The Morality of Freedom*. Oxford: Clarendon Press, 1986.
Reuter, Paul. *La Communauté européenne du charbon et de l'acier*. Paris: Librairie Geénérale de Droit et Jurisprudence, 1953.
Ricoeur, Paul. *The Rule of Metaphor: The Creation of Meaning in Language*. Translated by Robert Czerny. London: Routledge, 1977, 2003.
Robbers, Gerhard, ed. *Church Autonomy: A Comparative Survey*. Frankfurt am Main: Peter Lang, 2001.
Robinson, John A. T. *The Body: A Study in Pauline Theology*. London: SCM, 1952.
Robinson, O. F., T. D. Fergus, and W. M. Gordon. *European Legal History*, 3rd ed. Oxford: Oxford University Press, 2000.
Rochefort, Robert. *Robert Schuman*. Paris: Cerf, 1968.
Rockefeller, Steven C. "Global Interdependence, the Earth Charter, and Christian Faith." In *Earth Habitat: Eco-Injustice and the Church's Response*, edited by Dieter T. Hessel and Larry Rasmussen, 101–21. Minneapolis, Minn.: Fortress Press, 2001.
Roldan-Figueroa, Rady. "Spiritualité, Spirituality, and Espiritualidad: A Lexicographical Approach to the Conceptual History of the Modern Notion of Spirituality." *Church History and Religious Culture* 101, no. 4 (2021): 496–525.
Romero, Óscar. *The Church Cannot Remain Silent*. Maryknoll, N.Y.: Orbis Books, 2016.
———. *A Shepherd's Diary*. Cincinnati, Ohio: St. Anthony Press, 1993.
———. *Voice of the Voiceless*. Maryknoll, N.Y.: Orbis Books, 1988.
Rosen, Michael. *Dignity: Its History and Meaning*. Cambridge, Mass.: Harvard University Press, 2018.
Rosenblum, Bruce, and Fred Kuttner, *Quantum Enigma: Physics Encounters Consciousness*, 2nd ed. New York: Oxford University Press, 2011.
Roth, François. *Alsace-Lorraine, de 1870 à nos jours: Histoire d'un pays perdu*. Nancy: Place Stanislas, 2010.
———. *Robert Schuman. Du Lorrain des frontières au père de l'Europe*. Paris: Fayard, 2008.
Roussel, Éric. *Robert Schuman et les Pères de l'Europe*. Brussels: Peter Lang, 2008.
Sager, Lawrence G. "In the Name of God: Structural Injustice and Religious Faith." *Saint Louis University Law Journal* 60, no. 4 (2016): 585–600.

Sandel, Michael. *Liberalism and the Limits of Justice*. Cambridge: Cambridge University Press, 1981.
Sarra, Claudio. *Lo scudo di Dionisio. Contributo allo studio della metafora giuridica*. Milan: Franco Angeli Edizioni, 2010.
Savigny, Friedrich Carl von. *Of the Vocation of Our Age for Legislation and Jurisprudence*. Kitchener, Ont.: Batoche, 1999.
———. *System des heutigen römischen Rechts*, 3rd ed. Berlin: De Gruyter, 2019.
———. *Vom Beruf unserer Zeit für Gesetzgebung und Rechtswissenschaft*. Heidelberg: Mohr und Zimmer, 1814. English: *Of the Vocation of Our Age for Legislation and Jurisprudence*.
Scalia, Antonin. "God's Justice and Ours." *Law and Justice: Christian Law Review* 156 (2006): 3–10.
Schmidt, Jan. *Religion, Gott, Verfassung. Der Religions- und Gottesbezug in der Verfassung pluralistischer Gesellschaften*. Frankfurt: Peter Lang, 2010.
Schmitt, Carl. *The Nomos of the Earth in the International Law of the Ius Publicum Europeaum*. Translated by G. L. Ulmen. Candor, N.Y.: Tellos Press, 2006.
———. *Political Theology: Four Chapters on the Concept of Sovereignty*. Translated by George Schwab. Chicago: University of Chicago Press, 2005.
Schmoeckel, Mathias, and John Witte, Jr., eds. *Great Christian Jurists in German History*. Tubingen: Mohr Siebeck, 2020.
Schragger, Richard, and Micah Schwartzman. "Against Religious Institutionalism." *Virginia Law Review* 99, no. 5 (2013): 917–85.
Schuman, Robert. *For Europe*. Paris: Foundation Robert Schuman; Chêne-Bourg: Nagel, 2010.
———. *French Foreign Policy towards Germany since the War*, Stevenson Memorial Lecture, October 29, 1953. London: Geoffrey Cumberlege; Oxford: Oxford University Press, 1954.
Schomerus, Voler. *A Primer on String Theory*. Cambridge: Cambridge University Press, 2017.
Schwartzman, Micah. "What If Religion Is Not Special?" *University of Chicago Law Review* 79, no. 4 (2012): 1351–427.
Scolnicov, Anat. *The Right to Religious Freedom in International Law: Between Group Rights and Individual Rights*. London: Routledge, 2011.
Seewald, Peter. *Benedict XVI: A Life*, vol. 1, *Youth in Nazi Germany to the Second Vatican Council 1927–1965*. Translated by Linah Livingston. Oxford: Bloomsbury Continuum, 2020.
Shapiro, Scott. "The Hart-Dworkin Debate: Law, Morality, and the Guidance of Conduct." *Legal Theory* 6 (2000): 127–70.
Sitaraman, Ganesh. "The Use and Abuse of Foreign Law in Constitutional Interpretation." *Harvard Journal of Law and Public Policy* 32 (2009): 653–93.
Sitzia, Francesco. "L'azione nelle Novelle di Giustiniano." *Bullettino dell'Istituto di Diritto Romano* 37–38 (1995–96): 171–98.

Slotte, Pamela, and John D. Haskell, eds. *Christianity and International Law: An Introduction*. Cambridge: Cambridge University Press, 2021.

Smail, Thomas A. "In the Image of the Triune God." *International Journal of Systematic Theology* 5, no. 1 (2003): 22–32.

Sobrino, Jon. *Archbishop Romero: Memories and Reflections*. Maryknoll, N.Y.: Orbis Books,

Soskice, Janet. "Human Dignity and the Image of God." In *Understanding Human Dignity*, edited by Christopher McCrudden, 229–43. Oxford: Oxford University Press, 2013.

Spaemann, Robert. *Love and the Dignity of Human Life: On Nature and Natural Law*. Grand Rapids, Mich.: Eerdmans, 2011.

———. *Persons: The Difference between Someone and Something*. Translated by Oliver O'Donovan. Oxford: Oxford University Press, 2007.

Spitzer, Robert J. *New Proofs for the Existence of God: Contributions of Contemporary Physics and Philosophy*. Grand Rapids, Mich.: Eerdmans, 2010.

Stein, Edith. *Finite and Eternal Being*. Translated by Kurt F. Reinhardt. Washington, D.C.: ICS Publications, 2002.

———. *Philosophy of Psychology and the Humanities*, vol. 7 of *The Collected Works of Edith Stein*. Translated by Mary Catharine Baseheart and Marianne Sawicki. Washington, D.C.: ICS Publications, 2000.

Stein, Tine. "The Böckenförde Dictum—On the Topicality of a Liberal Formula." *Oxford Journal of Law and Religion* 7, no. 1 (2018): 97–108.

Stolleis, Michael. *Juristenbeschimpfung, oder, "Juristen—böse Christen."* In *Politik—Bildung—Religion. Hans Maier zum 65. Geburtstag*, edited by Theo Stammen et al., 163–70. Paderborn: Schöningh, 1996.

Straumann, Benjamin. "The *Corpus Iuris* as a Source of Law between Sovereigns in Alberico Gentili's Thought." In *The Roman Foundations of the Law of Nations: Alberico Gentili and the Justice of the Empire*, edited by Benedict Kingsbury and Benjamin Straumann, 102–23. Oxford: Oxford University Press, 2010.

Strauss, Leo. *Natural Right and History*. Chicago: University of Chicago Press, 1953; 2nd ed., 1971.

Sweet, William. "Jacques Maritain." In *Great Christian Jurists in French History*, edited by Olivier Descamps and Rafael Domingo, 387–403. Cambridge: Cambridge University Press, 2019.

Taylor, Bron, ed. *Encyclopedia of Religion and Nature*. Oxford: Oxford University Press, 2010. Online.

Taylor, Charles. *A Secular Age*. Cambridge, Mass.: The Belknap Press of Harvard University Press, 2007.

———. *Sources of the Self: The Making of the Modern Identity*. Cambridge, Mass.: Harvard University Press, 1989.

Teitel, Ruti. *Humanity's Law*. Oxford: Oxford University Press, 2011.

Tellegen-Couperus, Olga. *Law and Religion in the Roman Republic*. Leiden: Brill, 2012.

Thomas, Gabrielle. *The Image of God in the Theology of Gregory of Nazianzus.* Cambridge: Cambridge University Press, 2019.
Tibbitts, Bernard J. "Making Sense of Metaphors: Visuality, Aurality, and the Reconfiguration of American Legal Discourse." *Cardozo Law Review* 16 (1994–1995): 229–356.
Troper, Michel. "Sovereignty and Laïcité." *Cardozo Law Review* 30, no. 6 (2009): 2561–574.
Tuck, Richard. "The 'Modern' Theory of Natural Law." In *The Languages of Political Theory in Early-Modern Europe*, edited by Anthony Pagden, 99–119. New York: Cambridge University Press, 1987.
Tushnet, Mark. "When Is Knowing Less Better than Knowing More? Unpacking the Controversy over Supreme Court Reference to Non-US Law." *Minnesota Law Review* 90 (2006): 1275–1302.
Tutu, Desmond M. "The First Word: To Be Human Is to Be Free." In *Christianity and Human Rights: An Introduction*, edited by John Witte, Jr., and Frank S. Alexander, 1–7. Cambridge: Cambridge University Press, 2010.
Twining, William. *Globalization and Legal Theory.* Cambridge: Cambridge University Press, 2000.
Ulpian. *Libro primo institutionum.* In *Corpus Iuris Civilis*, vol. 1. Edited by Theodor Mommsen and Paul Krüger, 16th ed. Berlin: Weidmann, 1954.
Underhill, Evelyn. *Mysticism: A Study in the Nature and Development of Spiritual Consciousness.* Mineola, N.Y.: Dover Publications, 2002.
van der Molen, Gesina H. J. *Alberico Gentili and the Development of International Law: His Life, Work and Times*, 2nd ed. Leiden: A. W. Sijthoff, 1968.
VanDrunen, David. *Divine Covenants and Moral Order: A Biblical Theology of Natural Law.* Grand Rapids, Mich.: Eerdmans, 2014.
Van Kooten, George H. "The Anthropological Trichotomy of Spirit, Soul and Body in Philo of Alexandria and Paul of Tarsus." In *Anthropology in the New Testament and Its Ancient Context*, edited by Michael Labahn and Outi Lehtipuu, 87–119. Leuven: Peeters, 2010.
Vatican Council II. *Gaudium et spes.* Pastoral Constitution. December 7, 1965.
———. *Lumen gentium.* Dogmatic Constitution. November 21, 1964.
Vattel, Emmer de. *Le droit des gens, ou Principes de la loi naturelle, appliqués à la conduite et aux affaires des nations et des souverains*, 3 vols. Washington, D.C.: Carnegie Institution of Washington, 1916.
Vico, Giambattista. *New Science.* Translated by David Marsh. New York: Penguin Books; reprint, 2013.
Villey, Michel. *La formation de la pensée juridique moderne*, 2nd ed. París: PUF, 2003.
Waldron, Jeremy. *Dignity, Rank, and Rights.* Oxford: Oxford University Press, 2012, 2015.
———. "How Law Protects Dignity." *The Cambridge Law Journal* 71, no. 1 (2012): 200–22.

———. "The Image of God: Rights, Reason, and Order." In *Christianity and Human Rights: An Introduction*, edited by John Witte, Jr., and Frank S. Alexander, 216–35. Cambridge: Cambridge University Press, 2010.

———. *"Partly Laws Common to All Mankind": Foreign Laws in American Courts*. New Haven, Conn.: Yale University Press, 2012.

———. *Torture, Terror, and Trade-Offs: Philosophy for the White House*. Oxford: Oxford University Press, 2010.

———. "Two-Way Translation: The Ethics of Engaging with Religious Contributions in Public Deliberation." *Mercer Law Review* 63 (2012): 845–68.

———. "What Is Natural Law Like?" In *Reason, Morality, and Law: The Philosophy of John Finnis*, edited by John Keown and Robert P. George, 72–89. Oxford: Oxford University Press, 2013.

Walker, Neil. *Intimations of Global Law*. Cambridge: Cambridge University Press, 2015.

Waluchow, W. J. *Inclusive Legal Positivism*. Oxford: Oxford University Press, 1994.

Waluchow, Wilfrid J., and Stefan Sciaraffa, eds. *The Legacy of Ronald Dworkin*. Oxford: Oxford University Press, 2016.

Walzer, Michael. *Interpretation and Social Criticism*. Cambridge, Mass.: Harvard University Press, 1987.

———. *Spheres of Justice; A Defense of Pluralism and Equality*. Oxford: Basil Blackwell, 1983.

Wawro, Geoffrey. *The Franco-Prussian War: The German Conquest of France in 1870–1871*. Cambridge: Cambridge University Press, 2003.

Weber, Max. *Methodology of Social Sciences*. Translated by Edward A. Shils and Henry A. Finch. New Brunswick, N.J.: Transaction Publishers, 2011.

Weigel, George. *The End, and the Beginning: Pope John Paul II: The Victory of Freedom, the Last Years, the Legacy*. New York: Doubleday, 2010.

———. *Witness to Hope: The Biography of Pope John Paul II*, 3rd ed. New York: Harper Perennial, 1999, 2020.

Weiler, J. H. H. *The Constitution of Europe*. Cambridge: Cambridge University Press, 1999.

———. *Un'Europa cristiana. Un saggio esplorativo*. Milan: Rizzoli, 2003.

Weiss, Thomas G., and Sam Daws, eds. *The Oxford Handbook of the United Nations*. Oxford: Oxford University Press, 2009.

Welker, Michael, ed. *The Depth of the Human Person: A Multidisciplinary Approach*. Grand Rapids, Mich.: Eerdmans, 2014.

Whelan, Matthew Phillip. *Blood in the Fields: Óscar Romero, Catholic Social Teaching, and Land Reform*. Washington, D.C.: The Catholic University of America Press, 2020.

Whitman, James Q. "Separating Church and State: The Atlantic Divide." *Historical Reflections* 34, no. 3 (2008): 86–104.

Wieacker, Franz. *A History of Private Law in Europe*. Translated by Tony Weir. Oxford: Clarendon Press, 1995.

---. *Römische Rechtsgeschichte*, vol. 1. Munich: Beck, 1988.
Wilber, Ken. *Sex, Ecology, Spirituality: The Spirit of Evolution*, 2nd ed. Boston: Shambhala, 2000.
Wilhelmsen, Frederick D. "The Political Philosophy of Álvaro d'Ors." *The Political Science Reviewer* 20 (1991): 145–87.
Wilson, Edward Osborne. *Consilience: The Unity of Knowledge*. New York: Vintage, 1999.
Wilton, Gary. "Christianity and the Founding: The Legacy of Robert Schuman." In *God and the EU: Faith in the European Project*, edited by Jonathan Chaplin and Gary Wilton, 13–32. London: Routledge, 2016.
Wilken, Robert Louis. *Liberty in the Things of God: The Christian Origins of Religious Freedom*. New Haven, Conn.: Yale University Press, 2019.
Williams, Roger. *On Religious Liberty: Selections from the Works of Roger Williams*. Edited by James Calvin Davis. Cambridge, Mass.: The Belknap Press of Harvard University Press, 2008.
Wilson, James. *The Works of James Wilson*. Edited by Robert Green McCloskey. Cambridge, Mass.: Harvard University Press, 1967.
Winter, Steven L. *A Clearing in the Forest: Law, Life, and Mind*. Chicago: University of Chicago Press, 2001.
Witte, John, Jr. *The Blessings of Liberty: Human Rights and Religious Freedom in the Western Legal Tradition*. Cambridge: Cambridge University Press, 2021.
---, ed. *Christianity and Democracy in Global Context*. Boulder, Colo.: Westview Press, 1993; London: Routledge, 2018.
---. *Church, State, and Family: Reconciling Traditional Teachings and Modern Liberties*. Cambridge: Cambridge University Press, 2019.
---, ed. "A Conference on the Work of Harold J. Berman." *Emory Law Journal* 42, no. 2 (1993): 419–589.
---. "Covenant Liberty in Puritan New England." In *Jurisprudenz, Politische Theorie und Politische Theologie*, edited by Frederick S. Carney, Heinz Schilling, and Dieter Wyduckel, 169–89. Berlin: Duncker & Humblot, 2004.
---. *Faith, Freedom, Family: New Essays in Law and Religion*. Edited by Norman Doe and Gary S. Hauk. Tübingen: Mohr Siebeck, 2021.
---. *From Sacrament to Contract: Religion, Marriage, and Law in the Western Tradition*, 2nd ed. Louisville, Ky.: Westminster John Knox Press, 2012.
---. *God's Joust, God's Justice: Law and Religion in the Western Tradition*. Grand Rapids, Mich.: Eerdmans, 2006.
---. "Harold J. Berman." In *Great Christian Jurists in American History*, edited by Daniel L. Dreisbach and Mark A. Hall, 230–44. Cambridge: Cambridge University Press, 2019.
---. "Hellenic Philosophy of Law: Essential Terms." In *The Association for the Advancement of Christian Scholarship: Academic Paper Series*, no. 1 (November 1981): 1–34.

———. "Law and Religion: The Challenges of Christian Jurisprudence." *St. Thomas Law Journal* 2 (2005): 439–52.

———. "The Metaphorical Bridge between Law and Religion." *Pepperdine Law Review* 47, no. 2 (2020): 435–62.

———. *The Reformation of Rights: Law, Religion and Human Rights in Early Modern Calvinism*. Cambridge: Cambridge University Press, 2007.

———. "The Right of Freedom of Religion: An Historical Perspective from the West." In *Routledge Handbook on Freedom of Religion and Belief*, edited by Silvio Ferrari et al., 9–24. London: Routledge, 2020.

———. *The Sins of the Fathers: The Law and Theology of Illegitimacy Reconsidered*. Cambridge: Cambridge University Press, 2009.

———. *The Western Case for Monogamy over Polygamy*. New York: Cambridge University Press, 2015.

Witte, John, Jr., and Frank Alexander, eds. *Christianity and Human Rights*. Cambridge: Cambridge University Press, 2010.

———. *The Teachings of Modern Christianity on Law, Politics, and Human Nature*, 3 vols. New York: Columbia University Press, 2005–2006.

Witte, John, Jr., and Michael Bourdeaux, eds. *Proselytism and Orthodoxy in Russia: The New War for Souls*. Maryknoll, N.Y.: Orbis Books, 1999; reprint, 2013.

Witte, John, Jr., and Rafael Domingo, eds. *The Oxford Handbook of Christianity and Law*. Oxford: Oxford University Press, 2023.

Witte, John, Jr., and Eliza Ellison, eds. *Covenant Marriage in Comparative Perspective*. Grand Rapids, Mich.: Eerdmans, 2005.

Witte, John, Jr., and M. Christian Green, eds. *Religion and Human Rights: An Introduction*. New York: Oxford University Press, 2012.

Witte, John, Jr., and Gary S. Hauk, eds. *Christianity and Family Law: An Introduction*. Cambridge: Cambridge University Press, 2017.

Witte, John, Jr., and Richard C. Martin, eds. *Sharing the Book: Religious Perspectives on the Rights and Wrongs of Proselytism*. Maryknoll, N.Y.: Orbis Books, 1999.

Witte, John, Jr., Joel A. Nichols, and Richard W. Garnett. *Religion and the American Constitutional Experiment*, 5th ed. Oxford: Oxford University Press, 2022.

Witte, John, Jr., and Johan D. van der Vyver, eds. *Religious Human Rights in Global Perspective*, 2 vols. The Hague: Martinus Nijhoff, 1996.

Witte, John, Jr., and Michael Welker, eds. *The Impact of the Law on Character Formation, Ethical Education, and the Communication of Values in Late Modern Pluralistic Societies*. Leipzig: Evangelische Verlagsanstalt, 2021.

Witte, John, Jr., and Amy Wheeler, eds. *The Reformation of the Church and the World*. Louisville, Ky.: Westminster John Knox Press, 2017.

Wittgenstein, Ludwig. *Tractatus Logicus Philosophicus*. Translated by C. K. Ogden. Mineola, N.Y.: Dover Publications, 1999.

Wojtyła, Karol. *The Acting Person*. Translated by Andrzej Potocki. Dordrecht: D. Reider Publishing, 1979.

———. *Love and Responsibility*. Translated by H. T. Willetts. San Francisco: Ignatius Press, 1981.

Wolterstorff, Nicholas. *Justice in Love*. Grand Rapids, Mich.: Eerdmans, 2015.

Wright, Scott. *Óscar Romero and the Communion of the Saints*. Maryknoll, N.Y.: Orbis Books, 2016.

Zavala, José María. *El enigma Wojtyla. Un retrato desconocido de Juan Pablo II*. Madrid: Ediciones Martínez Roca, 2020.

Ziccardi Capaldo, Giuliana. *The Pillars of Global Law*, 2nd ed. London: Routledge, 2016.

Zimmermann, Reinhard. *The Law of Obligations: Roman Foundations of the Civilian Tradition*. Oxford: Oxford University Press, 1996.

Zsolnai, Laszlo, and Bernardette Flanagan. *The Routledge International Handbook of Spirituality in Society and the Professions*. London: Routledge, 2019.

Zucca, Lorenzo. *A Secular Europe: Law and Religion in the European Constitutional Landscape*. Oxford: Oxford University Press, 2013.

INDEX

abortion, 80, 125, 128, 131, 166n22, 236
accommodation, 103–5, 113
act of faith, 60–61, 63, 71, 76, 83, 87
Adenauer, Konrad, 26, 145, 194, 202n25
African Charter on Human and Peoples' Rights (1981), 163
Africanus, Sextus Caecilius, 257–58
agreement, 14–16, 17, 149, 187, 285
Albertario, Emilio, 251, 253
Alexy, Robert, 92n39, 93n43, 120, 135, 137
Alsace-Lorraine, 195–96, 198
ambassadors, 182
American Convention on Human Rights (1969), 163
animal law, 27, 167, 275
Aquinas: as Christian jurist, 277; on divine law, 268; on image of God, 146; influence on John Paul II, 230, 232; influence on Schuman, 194, 197, 199; on just war, 24; on love, 17n63; on natural law, 117, 132, 135, 136, 139; Witte's scholarship on, 278
Arendt, Hannah, 155
Aristotle/Aristotelianism, 117, 132, 133, 136, 178
atheism: Dworkin's "religious atheism," 59, 107, 109–10; interpretations of physics, 61; matter of toleration rather than recognition, 70–71
auctoritas and *potestas*, 46, 54, 259–60
Audi, Robert, 74n2, 80–81

augurs, 259–60
Augustine of Hippo: Gentili drew on, 178; on image of God, 145; on justice, 15; on just war, 24; and natural law theory, 132, 139; on society of nations, 186; on the Trinity, 13, 148; Witte's scholarship on, 278
Austin, John, 117, 118, 122, 124
autonomy of religious communities, 89–91, 93, 104
Azo of Bologna, 22

Bacon, Francis, 180
Baldus de Ubaldis, 179, 180
baptism, 159, 165–66, 169–73, 264, 265, 288
barbarism, 29–31
Bartolus de Saxoferrato, 179, 180, 189
Beccaria, Marchese de, 25
Bech, Joseph, 26, 145
Benedict XVI, Pope (Joseph Ratzinger): and Catholic social teaching, 153n54; on conscience, 67n25; on creative reason, 109n47; on ecology, 27n90; on love and communion, 13n42, 13n48, 14nn50–51, 17, 44n59, 152n52; on personhood, 171n27; on physics and existence of God, 61nn12–13; reforms of canon law, 244; on relation of law and morality, 116–17; on transcendent truth, 74n3

Bentham, Jeremy, 38–39, 117, 118, 122, 160–61
Benzler, Willibrord, 197
Berlin Wall, 116, 230, 239
Berman, Harold, 7n20, 8n21, 16n58, 53, 54n90, 69n34, 267–69, 273, 279, 280, 283
Bill of Rights (England), 23
Bill of Rights (US), 38. *See also* U.S. Constitution
Blackstone, William, 36, 278
blue laws, 79
Böckenförde, Ernst-Wolfgang, 140, 141
Böckenförde dictum, 140
Bodin, Jean, 177, 179, 186–87, 190, 258, 262
body-soul-spirit metaphor: antidote to legal reductionism, 53, 55, 287; classical applications to law, 39–41; new applications to law, 45–55, 286–87; and tradition of legal metaphors, 35–39; in writings of St. Paul and St. Edith Stein, 41–44
Bonaventure, 10
Boyle, Joseph M., 134
Britain. *See* United Kingdom
Bruno, Giordano, 180
Buddhism, 5, 265

Calvin, John, 277, 278, 279
Calvinism, 79, 265
canon law: argument for global canon law focused on the human person, 170–73, 288–89; body metaphor for, 39; canonical personality limited to baptized Christians, 165–66, 169–72; compared with international law, 158–59; drafting of 1917 Code, 162; Gentili's attitude toward, 178, 184–85; on ordination of women, 91n36; reformed by Pope Francis, 91n36, 244, 245; reformed by Pope John Paul II, 243–46; relation to theology, 168; status of human person in, 155–56, 167–70, 172; studied by d'Ors, 252
capital punishment. *See* death penalty
Carlists, 249
Carter, Jimmy, 219, 273, 277
Cassius Dio, 255
catechumens, 166, 169
Catholicism: attitude toward natural law, 134, 140; Catholic social teaching, 153, 98, 222–26, 241–43; and church-state relations in Alsace and Moselle, 198n14; Eastern rites, 245; and ecumenism, 238, 266; embrace of democracy, 273; independence from legal power, 90–91; Roman Curia, 216, 245; sainthood causes of Christian jurists, 204, 212, 217; sexual abuse crisis, 168, 244–45; and Spanish Civil War, 249; universal sacramentality of the Church, 171–72. *See also* canon law; John Paul II, Pope; Romero, Óscar; Schuman, Robert; Second Vatican Council
causa Curiana, 22, 48n70
Celsus, Publius Iuventius, 8, 9n24, 15n53, 133n68, 189n56, 261
ceremonial deism, 57
children, rights of, 164, 269
Christ. *See* Jesus Christ
Christianity: God as a matter of both fact and value, 107–9; natural law tradition, 140–41; and revealed law, 54; in Romero's theology of social justice, 224–26; in Schuman's European vision, 207, 210; and unity of reality, 6; Witte as Christian jurist, 264–69; in Witte's intellectual project, 270–83. *See also* canon law; Catholicism; Orthodox Christianity; Protestantism

church-state relations. *See* structural dualism
Cicero, 22n72, 35, 48n70, 178, 185, 186, 259, 260
Cino da Pistoia, 180
circumcision, 94
civil rights movement, 80
Code of Euric, 257
coercion: by civil authorities during Catholic Church sexual abuse crisis, 168; incompatible with suprarationality, 75–76, 78–79, 82–83, 105; necessary aspect of law, 16; and spiritualization of legal systems, 25–26. *See also* domination
Coke, Edward, 36, 278
Cold War, 116, 219, 222
Coleman, Jules, 126
collaborationism, 85, 87–88
common good, 151–52, 239, 242
communion: and birth of European Union, 26–27, 145; relation to agreement, 15, 285; and spiritualization of legal systems, 23–24, 26–27, 29–33; as spiritual value, 20–21; in theology of Second Vatican Council, 243; triad of love, communion, gift, 12–14, 16–18, 19, 285; and the Trinity, 12–14, 281–82; and union with God, 171
communism, 200, 211, 217, 230, 234, 237, 240, 251, 289
conscience, freedom of: contrasted with freedom of religion, 92–93, 94; demands accommodation, not toleration, 103–5, 113; in early America, 98; and ethical autonomy, 114; Gentili on, 190; and natural law, 232; priority of, 67; religious freedom not reducible to, 100–105, 112–15; as suprarational law, 54; in Witte's intellectual project, 282
Constitutio Antoniniana, 255

constitutions: and body-soul-spirit metaphor, 47–48; of Ecuador, 167n23; and structural dualist models, 82–89; unwritten British constitution, 23. *See also* U.S.Constitution
contracts, 22, 39, 256–57
corporate social responsibility (CSR), 28
Corpus Iuris Civilis: body metaphor for, 39–40; Gentili's scholarship on, 179, 185–88, 189–90, 262; d'Ors's scholarship on, 255, 256, 257; radical interpolationism research on, 251
cosmotheandric experience, 4
Council of Europe, 163, 200
covenants, 282
Crassus, Lucius Licinius, 22, 48n70
creation, divine, 109, 282, 287. *See also* image of God
culture, 281–82

death penalty, 25–26, 80, 237, 275
Declaration of Independence (1776), 24, 202
De Gasperi, Alcide, 26, 145
De Gaulle, Charles, 199, 202, 203
dematerialization of law, 21–23
dharma, 41
dignity. *See* human dignity
diversity, 150
Doe, Norman: bibliographic mentions, 57n2, 76n7, 86n27, 90n35, 91n38, 138n2, 140n8, 145n31, 269n23; collaboration with Witte, 271, 274, 275, 279; natural law theory, 141
domination, 23–24, 28–29, 30–32, 261–62
dominium and *possessio*, 261–62
d'Ors, Álvaro: on *auctoritas* and *potestas*, 46n64, 259–60; biography, 248–52; contributions to political theory, 258–59; contributions to Roman law, 254–58, 259–62; on *dominium*

d'Ors, Álvaro *(continued)*
and *possessio*, 261–62; on legitimacy and legality, 260–61; on natural law, 133–34, 261; on right as service, 18n65, 148n43; works, 253–54
d'Ors Rovira, Eugenio, 249–50, 251, 253
Douglas, William O., 58
Dred Scott, 68
dualism. *See* structural dualism
Dudley, Robert, 180
Durkheim, Émile, 59
Dworkin, Ronald: account of religion as value, 105–12, 114–15, 126; bibliographic mentions, 11n29, 35n3, 48n69, 147n40; compared to Leiter, 100; considers God epistemologically irrelevant, 100, 106–8, 110, 115; critique of positivism, 52–53, 117, 123–27; engagement with other scholars, 127, 129, 131n58, 135, 136; on equal concern and respect, 125–26; on integrity of law, 52–53; objects to special protection of religious freedom, 96–97, 111–12; on "religious atheism," 59, 107, 109–10; on right of ethical independence, 97, 111–15, 125–26, 137, 233

Earth Charter (2000), 27
Eberle, Christopher, 79
ecology, 27, 242
Ecuador, 167n23
Einstein, Albert, 106, 277
Elizabeth I, Queen, 180, 182
El Salvador. *See* Romero, Óscar; Salvadoran civil war
England. *See* United Kingdom
epistemology, 5, 107–12
equal protection, 50, 98, 113
Erasmus, 184
Errázuriz, Carlos José, 172
Escrivá, Josemaría, 248, 252

establishment of religion: Leiter on, 104; model of church-state relations, 85–87; no establishment in U.S. Constitution, 38, 58, 61, 72, 79, 85–88, 91; not best way to protect religious freedom, 77
ethical autonomy, 114
ethical independence. *See* right of ethical independence
Eucharist, 14
European Civil Code, 39
European Coal and Steel Community, 195, 200–202
European Convention on Human Rights (1950), 200
European Court of Human Rights, 89n34, 163
European Economic Community (ECC), 202, 203n29
European Union: anticipated by European Coal and Steel Community, 195, 200–202; Charter of Fundamental Rights, 25; contract law, 39; excessive bureaucracy, 207–8; Poland's entry into, 241; and Schuman's European vision, 205–10; Treaty on European Union, 153; use of principle of subsidiarity, 153; values of communion, reconciliation, and forgiveness, 26–27, 79–80, 145
euthanasia, 125, 128, 131, 236

facticity, 130
Finnis, John, 116, 117, 118n3, 131, 132, 134–36, 137, 141
First World War, 198
foreign law, 49–50. *See also* international law
forgiveness: and birth of European Union, 26–27, 79–80, 145; and justice, 17, 155–56
Forst, Rainer, 69n35, 71

France: abolition of judicial torture, 25; during First and Second World Wars, 198–99; Franco-Prussian War, 195; French Civil Code, 22–23, 49–50, 166; French Revolution, 150, 261; laïcité model of church-state relations, 85–87; Schuman's political career in, 199–203

Francis, Pope: on death penalty, 25–26; on human brotherhood, 69n31; on personhood, 171n27; reforms of canon law, 91n36, 244, 245; sainthood causes of Christian jurists, 204, 212, 217; on solidarity, 153n54; on spirituality, 5

Franco-Prussian War, 195

freedom. *See* conscience, freedom of; human freedom; religious freedom

French Civil Code, 22–23, 49–50, 166

French Revolution, 150, 261

Fuller, Lon, 40, 122, 123, 125

Gaius, 151, 160, 185, 256

Gandhi, 26, 31

Gardner, John, 117, 136

Gaudemet, Jean, 165–66

Geneva Conventions (1949), 24

Gentili, Alberico: approach to law of nations, 141–42, 185–88; on freedom of religion (*libertas_religionis*), 188, 190–91; legacy and significance, 177–79, 191–92; life and works, 180–85; on natural law, 141–42, 185–88; on relationship of law and theology, 142, 157, 178, 182, 184, 188; on Roman law, 179, 185–88, 189–90, 262; *silete theologi in munere alieno,* 142, 178, 184, 188–90; on sovereignty, 177, 178, 183, 184, 185–88, 190, 192, 262; theistic approach to secularization of law, 141, 179, 182, 188–91; on war, 178, 183–84, 188, 191

Gentili, Scipione, 180, 184

George, Robert P., 67n24, 78n11, 117, 131, 134–35, 141, 144n27

German Civil Code, 49–50, 166

German Historical School, 36, 53

Germany: abolition of judicial torture, 25; collaborationist model of church-state relations, 85, 87–88; during First World War, 198; Franco-Prussian War, 195; modern civil law, 49–50, 166; Nazi regime, 9, 116, 119, 139, 199, 234, 239; and postwar European unification, 201–2, 207–8

Gierke, Otto, 156–57, 197

gift: and creation in the image of God, 148; triad of love, communion, gift, 12–14, 16–18, 19, 285; within the Trinity, 12–14, 282

Glendon, Mary Ann, 75n4, 97, 141

globalization and new technology, 28–29, 116, 136

global law: and body-soul-spirit metaphor, 50–51, 287; global canon law, 170–73, 288–89; and image of God, 154–55, 157; John Paul II as forerunner of, 239–40; Schuman's contribution to, 209–10; transcendent global law, xvi; transition of international law toward, 158, 164, 170, 172

God: and covenants, 282; creation by, 109, 282, 287; distinct from religion, 58–63, 105–6; Dworkin considers epistemologically irrelevant, 100, 106–8, 110, 115; existence/ nonexistence of, 58–63, 65–66, 100, 106–8, 115; freedom of, 147–48; in Gentili's theistic approach to secularization of law, 179, 182, 188–91; invocation of in public sphere, 57–58, 71; as love, 19, 155, 231, 282;

God *(continued)*
matter of both fact and value, 107–9; as metalegal concept, 63–69, 71–72, 144; object of suprarational acts, 76; and purpose of religious freedom, 97; role in sacred natural law, 139, 141, 142, 143, 232; secular legal systems should recognize, 69–71, 286; as source of morality, 64–65, 67–68, 108; union with, 19, 44, 171; and unity of reality, 6, 9–10; in Western legal tradition, 56–58. *See also* image of God; Trinity
Goethe, Johann Wolfgang von, 70
good/goodness, 7, 133, 188, 261
Gothofredus, Dionysius (Denis Godefroy), 40
Grande, Rutilio, 217–18, 222–23
Great Awakening, xi
Grisez, Germain, 134, 136
Grotius, Hugo, 24, 142, 145, 177, 179, 278
Grundnorm, 119, 267

Habermas, Jürgen, 20, 116, 117, 129–31, 137, 271
Hart, Herbert L. A.: critiques of, 117, 122, 123, 124, 125, 127, 135, 137; influence on subsequent scholars, 127, 135, 136; on legal causation, 144n25; positivist theory, 116, 121–23
Heffter, August Wilhem, 161–62
Hervada, Javier, 117, 132, 133–34, 141, 170
Hinduism, 5, 41, 265
Hittinger, Russell, 134n75, 141
Hobbes, Thomas, 23, 36, 117, 133
Holland, Sir Thomas Erskine, 179
Holmes, Oliver Wendell, Jr., 38n25, 121, 253n18
holon/holonic, 10–12, 20
Holy See, 163, 169

Holy Spirit, 12–14, 19, 43, 286–87. *See also* Trinity
Hosanna-Tabor, 91
Hotman, Jean, 182
human dignity: and death penalty, 25; and image of God, 146–48, 152, 231–32, 286; John Paul II on, 230–33, 234; as metalegal concept, 231; as "personal status," 66; premise of human rights, 146–47; proper to the individual, 83
human freedom: John Paul II on, 231, 232, 233, 235, 236, 239, 242; reflects divine freedom, 147–48; and spiritual intention, 19; as spiritual reality, 13, 14, 23–24; and subsidiarity, 152–53
human person: argument for global canon law focused on, 170–73, 288–89; central for John Paul II, 171n27, 229, 230–32; end of legal systems is to protect, 66–67; integrity/unity of, 137; multidimensionality of, 139, 143; status in canon law, 155–56, 167–70, 172; status in international law, 159–64, 167–70, 172. *See also* body-soul-spirit metaphor; image of God
human rights: human dignity as premise of, 146–47; John Paul II on, 234–38, 277; and natural law, 133; right to life, 236–37; and status of individuals in the international order, 163; in Western tradition, 274–75

Ibn al-Arabi, 6
Ihering, Rudolph von, 40
image of God: and body-soul-spirit metaphor, 42, 50; and connection between law and love, 155–56; global canon law centered on, 159, 171, 172, 288–89; and global law

community, 154–55, 157; as ground for protection of the person in international law, 145–46; in human body, 42–43; and human dignity, 146–48, 152, 231–32, 286, 287; and human equality, 68; and pluralism and diversity, 150; and solidarity, 150–52; and subsidiarity, 152–53; and universal moral principles, 149–50
incorporation doctrine, 48
independence of religious communities, 89–91
integral liberation, 224–25
integrative jurisprudence, 53, 280
integrity of law, 52–53
intellectual property, 23
intentions, 18–20, 22, 48n69
International Court of Justice, 162
International Covenant on Civil and Political Rights (1966), 163
international law: and agreements, 15; and body-soul-spirit metaphor, 50–51; compared with canon law, 158–59; and *dominium*, 262; Eurocentric until recently, 165; Grotius on, 142; implications of image-of-God doctrine for, 145–57; and levels of legal spiritualization, 30–32; and metalegal concepts, 143–44; status of human person in, 159–64, 167–70, 172; transition toward global law, 158, 164, 170, 172; and war, 239–40
intuition, 266–69
Iron Curtain, 230, 239
Islam, 6, 54, 84, 90, 107–9, 134, 140, 238, 265
ius cogens, 144, 149
ius commune, 182, 189

Japanese Civil Code, 49–50
Jefferson, Thomas, 24, 37–38, 278
Jesus Christ: and ecclesiology, 243; Eucharist, 14; and image of God, 43n48, 146, 231, 287; in John Paul II's thought, 229, 241; resurrection, 108; in Romero's thought, 220, 223–24, 225–26; sovereignty of, 258–59, 265; teachings on political authority, 190, 272
Jiménez, Juan Ramón, 249
John of the Cross, 44n53, 199
John Paul II, Pope: on centrality of human person, 171n27, 229, 230–32; as Christian jurist, 228–30, 246–47, 277; on democracy, 242, 273; on the Eucharist, 14; on human dignity, 230–33, 234; on human freedom, 231, 232, 233, 235, 236, 239, 242; on human rights, 234–38, 277; on natural law, 232–33; on ordination of women, 91n36; on rationality and suprarationality, 75n5; reform of canon law, 243–46; on rights of nations and eradication of war, 238–41; on self-gift, 18n64; on solidarity as the principle of social justice, 153n54, 241–43
John XXIII, Pope, 171n27, 243
Judaism, 6, 54, 83, 90, 94, 107–9, 134, 140, 238, 265, 274
Julianus, Salvius, 256, 258
justice: and critiques of positivism, 119–20; Gentili on, 189–90; in Rawls's public reason, 127–29; relation to love, 16–17, 155–56, 225, 246, 283, 285; role in natural law, 125, 131, 133; and spiritual and corporeal domains, 52; triad of justice, agreement, right, 14–16, 285. *See also* social justice
Justinian. See *Corpus Iuris Civilis*

Kant, Immanuel, 117, 118, 120n7, 127, 248

Kaser, Max, 251, 253, 257n28
Kaufmann, Arthur, 120
Kelsen, Hans: attempted to purify law of extraneous elements, 39, 267; compared to d'Ors, 258; critiques of, 117, 127, 137; decision to write in German, 121n12; influence on subsequent scholars, 117, 121, 122, 124, 135, 230, 277; on international agreements, 15; on legal dimension, 10n27; on norms, 45n61, 119, 124, 135, 267; positivist theory, 116–17, 118–20, 137; on right and interest, 16n57
King, Martin Luther, Jr., 26, 80, 277, 278
kirpan, 101, 103, 105, 112
Koestler, Arthur, 10–11
Kramer, Matthew, 126
Kuyper, Abraham, 265–66, 278, 279, 283
Kymlicka, Will, 129

Labeo, 256–57
laïcité, 85–87
law of nations: Gentili's approach to, 141–42, 185–88; Grotius on, 142; John Paul II on rights of nations, 238–41; in Roman law, 161; term replaced by "international law," 160. *See also* international law
Leibniz, Gottfried Wilhelm, 36, 269
Leiter, Brian, 70n37, 97, 100–105, 114–15
Lenel, Otto, 253, 256
Leo XIII, Pope, 194, 198
Levering, Matthew, 141
Lewis, C. S., 141, 155n63
lex Irnitana, 255
liability, 151
liberty, 283. *See also* human freedom; religious freedom
life, right to, 236–37
Locke, John, 66, 71n38, 98n11, 98n13, 117

Lorraine, 195–97, 199
love: God as love, 19, 155, 231, 282; relation to law and justice, 16–17, 155–56, 225, 246, 283, 285; and spiritualization of legal systems, 26–27, 272, 285; as spiritual value, 20–21; triad of love, communion, gift, 12–14, 16–18, 19, 285
Luther, Martin, 179, 184, 277, 278
Luxembourg, 196–97

Maciel, Marcial, 244
MacIntyre, Alasdair, 117, 129
Madison, James, 67, 98, 278
Mandela, Nelson, 26
Maritain, Jacques, 116–17, 132–33, 137, 139n3, 141, 194, 230, 266n8, 273, 277, 278
marriage, 63–64, 160, 166, 184, 189
Marshall Plan, 200
McCarrick, Cardinal Theodore, 244
McLean, John, 68
Medellín Conference, 215, 216
Mendoza, Bernardo de, 182
Merkl, Adolf Julius, 39n29
metalegal concepts: definition, 63–64, 143–44; and global human community, 154; God as, 63–69, 71–72, 144; human dignity, 231; marriage, 63–64; sacred natural law, 143–45; used in both international and canon law, 168
metaphor. *See* body-soul-spirit metaphor
Mommsen, Theodore, 248, 253
monarchy, 182. *See also* sovereignty
money, 30–32
Monnet, Jean, 26, 145, 194, 201
Montesquieu, Charles de, 40, 45n60
morality: distinct from spirituality, 7; distinction between the basic and the relevant, 136–37; in Dworkin's epistemological paradigm, 106, 108; Habermas's distinction between

ethics and morals, 129–31; and image of God, 149–50; interpretation of law relies on moral principles, 9, 52n78, 102–3, 113–14; modern natural law theorists on, 131–37; modern positivist theorists on, 118–31, 136–37; and multidimensionality of reality, 139–40; overview of modern debates on relation of law and morality, 116–18; presupposes reason, 109; and resolution of hard cases, 4, 53, 124–25; sources of, 64–65, 67–68, 108
More, Thomas, 279
Moselle, 198–99
multidimensionality of reality, xiii, 10–12, 139–40, 143–44

Nagel, Thomas, 106, 109
national soul (*Volksgeist*), 36, 53, 267
nations. *See* international law; law of nations; sovereignty
Native American religion, 94, 113n57
natural law: Aquinas's significance for, 117, 132, 135, 136; and body-soul-spirit metaphor, 53; in Gentili's law of nations, 141–42, 185–88; Gierke on, 156–57; John Paul II on, 232–33; and legitimacy, 261; and multidimensionality of reality, xii–xiii; predominantly Christian tradition, 140–41; Protestant and Catholic attitudes toward, 134; and Rawls's public reason, 128; role of justice in, 125, 131, 133. *See also* sacred natural law
Nazi Germany, 9, 116, 119, 139, 199, 234, 239
neutrality, 62–63, 85–88, 94–95
Nicholas of Cusa, 10
nonviolent resistance, 26, 225
norms: in Kelsen's legal theory, 45n61, 119, 124, 135, 267; peremptory, 144

North Atlantic Treaty Organization (NATO), 200

Oppenheim, Lassa, 162
Order of Malta, 163, 169
originalism, 47–48
Orthodox Christianity, 140, 238, 266, 271, 273

Pagden, Antony, 179n8, 188
Panikkar, Raimon, 4
Papinian, 22
parliaments, 23, 33
paterfamilias, 161, 259
Paul, Saint, 6, 41–44, 149
Paul VI, Pope, 153n54, 171, 212, 215, 222, 243
Peace of Westphalia (1648), 159, 162
peremptory norms, 144
Pérez-Peix, María, 249, 250, 251
Permanent Court of International Justice, 162
personality/personhood: corporate personhood, 23; fictitious personhood, 167–68, 172. *See also* human person
peyote, 94, 113n57
Plotinus, 5, 6
pluralism, 21, 150, 280, 281
Poland, 230, 234, 239, 240–41
polygamy, 81
pornography, 125
positivism: contrasted with natural law theory, 119, 137; Dworkin's critique of, 52–53, 117, 123–27; of Hart, 121–23; of Kelsen and his German critics, 118–20; and metaphor, 38–39, 52–53; of Raz, 126–27; soft positivism, 126
possessio, 261–62
potestas. See *auctoritas* and *potestas*
Pound, Roscoe, 40
praetorian edict, 256

preferential option for the poor, 215n13, 226, 247
proselytism, 77
Protestantism: attitude toward natural law, 134, 140; and John Paul II's ecumenism, 238; Protestant Reformation, 26, 96, 180, 182, 258, 273; relationship with law and democracy, 273–74; and Witte's Christianity, 265–66, 283. *See also* Gentili, Alberico; Witte, John, Jr.,
Prussia, 195
Pseudo-Dionysius, 6, 12
public reason, 78, 82n22, 105n30, 127–29, 270–71
pyramid metaphor, 39, 119, 124

quantum physics, 5n8, 8, 45, 61–62

Radbruch, Gustav, 116, 119–20, 123
Rainolds, John, 180, 182
Ratzinger, Joseph. *See* Benedict XVI, Pope (Joseph Ratzinger)
Rawls, John: compared to Habermas, 129, 131n58; critiques of, 135, 137; on justice, 15, 16n60, 127–28, 156n69, 267; on public reason, 78, 82n22, 105n30, 127–29, 271; on well-ordered societies, 15, 150n47
Raz, Joseph, 114, 116, 117, 126–27, 135, 136
reality. *See* multidimensionality of reality; unity of reality
reason: compatibility of creative and scientific reason, 109; public reason, 78, 82n22, 105n30, 127–29, 270–71; Rawls's critique of rationalist believers, 128. *See also* suprarationality
Red Cross, 163, 169
religion: definition, 59; distinct from God, 58–63, 105–6; distinct from spirituality, xii, 6–7; Dworkin's account of religion as value, 105–12, 114–15; extrinsic limit on the law, 75, 81, 82, 91, 102, 287; in Gentili's law of war, 178, 188, 191; Leiter reduces to "commands and consolation," 101–2, 114–15; object of toleration rather than recognition, 69–71; public dimension of, 75, 114; right to religion, 91–95; in Schuman's European vision, 207; suprarationality justification for protection of, xii, 73–74, 102, 287. *See also* suprarationality
religious education, 77, 88
religious exemptions, 105, 112–13
religious freedom: arguments against special protection of, 96–97, 100–115; autonomy and independence of religious communities, 89–91, 93, 104; demands toleration, not accommodation, 103–5; distinct from right to religion, 91–95; example of spiritualization of legal systems, 26; as first or first-class right, 97, 99, 115, 238, 288; "freedom from religion," 99, 270, 288; Gentili on, 188, 190–91; individual, social, and transcendent dimensions of, 114–15, 288; John Paul II on, 237–38; not reducible to freedom of conscience, 100–105, 112–15; protected by structural dualism, 77, 82–89; protects both religious and political communities, 102; and Protestant Reformation, 26, 96; and religious exemptions, 105, 112–13; in U.S.Constitution, 38, 58, 61, 72, 79, 91; in Western tradition, 97–99
revelation, divine, 107–8
Rhonheimer, Martin, 141
right of ethical independence, xii, 97, 111–15, 125–26, 137, 233

rights: as "enforceable services," 18, 31–32, 148; and levels of legal spiritualization, 30–32; relation between right and self-gift, 17–18; triad of justice, agreement, right, 14–16, 285. *See also* human rights
Roberts, John, 91
Roman law: *auctoritas* and *potestas*, 46, 54, 259–60; *causa Curiana*, 22, 48n70; contracts, 22, 256–57; degrees of domination, 24, 260; *dominium* and *possessio*, 261–62; d'Ors's contributions to, 254–58, 259–62; example of egoic law, 31; family law, 161, 164, 259; *hominum causa omne ius constitutum est*, 230–31; law of nations (*ius gentium*), 161; *lex* and *ius*, 260–61; radical interpolationism research on, 251; *sacramentum*, 268; on solidarity (*in solidum*), 151; Villey on, 133. *See also Corpus Iuris Civilis*
Roman Senate, 260
Romero, General Carlos Humberto, 217, 218, 219
Romero, Óscar: as archbishop of San Salvador, 216–20; as Christian jurist, 277; early life and career, 213–16; last days and death, 220–22; legacy and theology of social justice, 222–26; significance, 211–12, 226–27

sacramentum, 268
sacred natural law: as Christian and biblical tradition, 141; connection between theology and jurisprudence, 143, 157; implications of the image-of-God doctrine, 145–57, 288; as metalegal concept, 143–45; and multidimensionality of reality, 139–40; and rational natural law, 138, 143; role of God in, 139, 141, 142, 143, 232
Salvadoran civil war, 211–12, 219, 222

Sánchez, Tomás, 160
Sandel, Michael, 129
Savigny, Friedrich Carl von, 36, 267
Scaevola, Quintus Mucius, 22, 48n70
Scalia, Antonin, 47, 58, 61, 64n18, 113n57
Schmitt, Carl, 142n17, 143n22, 178n4, 252, 253, 258
scholasticism, 133, 135, 178, 182
Schuman, Robert: achievements, 193–94; biographical information, 195–204; contribution to the idea of global law, 209–10; European vision, 205–10; as founding father of European Union, 26
Schuman Declaration, 200–201
Second Vatican Council: embrace of democracy, 273; and reform of canon law, 166, 171, 243, 245; Romero's interpretation of, 215, 222; and thought of John Paul II, 233, 235, 237–38, 243, 245, 246
Second World War, 116, 162, 199, 205, 214, 234
secularization: central phenomenon of modern age, 96; Gentili's theistic approach to, 141, 179, 182, 188–91; and recognition of right to religion, 91–92; secularism vs. secularization, xi; and Witte's intellectual project, 281
secular legal systems: and God as a metalegal concept, 63–69, 71–72; importance of structural dualism, 82–85, 104–5; models of structural dualism, 85–89; relation to suprarationality, 73–76; and religious neutrality, 62–63; and role of God in American legal system, 57–58; and role of theology, 286; should distinguish between God and religion, 58–63; should not regulate essentials of religious communities, 89–91, 287;

secular legal systems *(continued)* should not require suprarational acts, 76–77, 87, 287; should not use suprarational arguments, 78–81, 87, 287; should protect right to religion, 91–95; should tolerate religion but recognize God, 69–71
separationism, 121–22
sharia, 90
Sidney, Sir Philip, 182
Sikh dagger case, 101, 103, 105, 112
slavery, 24, 68
social justice: John Paul II's theology of, 241–43; and Medellín Conference, 215n13; Romero's theology of, 213, 222–26
society of nations, 186, 187
solidarity: and accommodating individual conscience, 104; complements subsidiarity, 153; and global law, 51, 287; and human brotherhood, 68–69; and image of God, 150–52; John Paul II on, 153n54, 241–43; and levels of legal spiritualization, 30; and metalegal concept of God, 68–69; in Schuman's European vision, 205, 209, 210; and self-gift, 18; Witte on, 283
soul. *See* body-soul-spirit metaphor
sovereignty: Bodin's theory of, 177, 186–87, 258–59, 262; Gentili on, 177, 178, 183, 184, 185–88, 190, 192, 262; in Schuman's European vision, 205–6; in Witte's intellectual project, 283
Soviet Union, 239, 240
Spaemann, Robert, 15n56, 116, 117, 141, 146n36
Spain, 248–52, 255
Spanish Civil War, 251
spirit. *See* body-soul-spirit metaphor
spirituality: definition, 4–5; distinct from morality and religion, xii, 6–7; interacts with law through intentions and values, 18–21; metadimensional and holonic, 10–12; recent attention by various disciplines, 3–4; similarities to law, 8–10; triad of love, communion, gift, 12–14, 16–18, 19, 285. *See also* spiritualization of law
spiritualization of law: of canon law, 172–73, 289; by Christianity, 272; historical examples of, 21–28; levels of, 29–33; risks of new technologies and globalization, 28–29; and split between law and religion, 6
Spitzer, Robert, 61–62
Stein, Edith, 41–44, 145n32
Strauss, Leo, 120, 249
structural dualism: advantages of, xi, 82–85, 104–5; collaborationist model, 85, 87–88; establishment model, 85–87; laïcité model, 85–87; protects suprarationality, 82–89; state neutrality model, 85–88
subsidiarity, 152–53, 209, 242
supranationality, 205–6
suprarationality: extrinsic limit on the secular, 75, 81, 82, 91, 102, 287; incompatible with coercion, 75–76, 78–79, 82–83, 105; justification for protection of religion, xii, 73–74, 102, 287; protected by structural dualism, 82–89; rational and suprarational law, 54, 83–84, 90; secular legal systems should not regulate, 89–91, 287; secular legal systems should not require suprarational acts, 76–77, 87, 287; secular legal systems should not use suprarational arguments, 78–81, 87, 287; subjective and objective, 74–75

Taoism, 5
Taylor, Charles, 96n1, 116, 129, 269n20

technology. *See* globalization and new technology
Tertullian, 97, 178, 190n60
theocracy, 85, 207
theology: relation to canon law, 168; relation to jurisprudence, 285–86; relation to law in Gentili's thought, 142, 157, 178, 182, 184, 188; relation to morality, 117; relation to sacred natural law, 143, 157
Thirty Years' War, 159
toleration/tolerance, 103–5, 131
torture, 25, 68, 80, 216n15, 218
totalitarianism, 83–85
transcendence. *See* suprarationality
Tres Calles massacre, 216
Trinity: and communion, 12–14, 281–82; and creation in the image of God, 44, 146, 148, 150, 152, 241, 287; and solidarity, 241
Tutu, Desmond, 273, 274
two-bodies doctrine, 40

Ulpian, 8n23, 9n24, 15n53, 133n68, 178, 185, 189n54, 255, 256
United Kingdom: abolition of judicial torture, 25; establishment model of church-state relations, 85–86; Gentili's career in, 180–82, 184; in Schuman's European vision, 208; unwritten constitution, 23
United Nations: birth of, 116; example of spiritualization of law, 27; honored Óscar Romero, 212; individuals' access to, 163; John Paul II's addresses to, 229, 234–35, 238–40
United States: God in the American legal experience, 57–58; motto, 150n46; d'Ors's unfamiliarity with, 253; and Romero's political activity, 219; state neutrality model of church-state relations, 85–88. *See also* U.S.Constitution; U.S.Supreme Court
unity of reality, 6, 9–10, 20, 137
Universal Declaration of Human Rights (1948), 68–69, 116, 147, 163, 166, 234–35, 238–39, 277
universal destination of goods, 242
University of Navarra, 133, 252
US Constitution: church-state relations, 37–38, 58, 61, 72, 79–80, 91; free exercise of religion, 38, 79; incorporation doctrine, 48; influenced by but does not contain religious arguments, 79–80; no establishment of religion, 38, 58, 61, 72, 79, 91; resolution of hard cases, 124
US Supreme Court, 37n18, 49, 68, 91

validity, 118–19, 130, 149
value: Dworkin's account of religion as value, 105–12, 114–15; spirituality interacts with law through, 20–21; unity of, 20, 105, 111
VanDrunen, David, 117, 134, 138nn1–2, 141, 145n31
Vatican, 216, 219, 220. *See also* John Paul II, Pope
Vatican II. *See* Second Vatican Council
Vattel, Emmer de, 160–61, 162
Vienna Convention, 144
Villey, Michel, 116, 117, 132–34, 137, 141, 253
Vitoria, Francisco de, 98, 177, 178n2, 184, 191, 278
Vogelin, Eric, 249
Volksgeist, 36, 53, 267

Waldron, Jeremy, 25n83, 49n71, 50n73, 65n20, 66n23, 68, 80n18, 136, 144n27, 146n36
wall of separation, 37–38, 57
Walsingham, Sir Francis, 180

Waluchow, Will, 52n79, 126
Walzer, Michael, 129
war: and early modern international law, 161; Gentili's law of, 178, 183–84, 188, 191; John Paul II on, 238–41; just war, 24; and levels of legal spiritualization, 30–32; in Schuman's European vision, 208, 209
Watson, Alan, 41
Weber, Max, 21, 117, 248, 253, 260
Wenger, Leopold, 253
Wieacker, Franz, 36n12, 251, 253, 268n17
Wilhelmsen, Frederick, 249
Williams, Roger, 37, 59n8, 97
wills, 22, 48n70
Wilson, E. O., 5
Wilson, James, 37
Witte, John, Jr.,: bibliographic mentions, 7n20, 9n25, 26n85, 35n4, 54n90, 57n2, 69n32, 69n34, 73n1, 81n21, 86n27, 90n35, 93n41, 97n6, 98nn9–10, 100n16, 102n23, 141n13, 148n42; biographical perspective, 276–80; as Christian jurist, 264–69; intellectual project on Christianity and law, 270–83; jurisprudential perspective, 280–83; relational perspective, 272–76; significance, 283–84; use of triads, 269, 270, 281–84
Wittgenstein, Ludwig, 5
Wojtyla, Karol. *See* John Paul II, Pope
Wolff, Christian, 161
Wolterstorff, Nicholas, 16, 156
World War I. *See* First World War
World War II. *See* Second World War
worship, 74, 76